Safety in Numbers

NICHOLAS FAITH

Safety in Numbers

THE MYSTERIOUS WORLD
OF SWISS BANKING

THE VIKING PRESS   NEW YORK

Copyright © 1982 by Nicholas Faith
All rights reserved
Published in 1982 by The Viking Press
625 Madison Avenue, New York, N.Y. 10022

Published simultaneously in Canada by
Penguin Books Canada Limited

LIBRARY OF CONGRESS CATALOGING IN PUBLICATION DATA
Faith, Nicholas, 1933–
    Safety in numbers.
    Bibliography: p.
    Includes index.
    1. Banks and banking—Switzerland.   I. Title
HG3204.F33   332.1' 09494   82-70121
ISBN 0-670-61463-7   AACR2

Grateful acknowledgment is made to W. W. Norton & Company,
Inc., for permission to reprint a selection from *Present at the Creation*
by Dean Acheson. Copyright © 1969 by Dean Acheson.

Printed in the United States of America
Set in Baskerville

Contents

Acknowledgements

Writing this book would have been impossible without the helpfulness and understanding of a number of people. My research assistant, Kathleen Brown, explored the German sources for me thoroughly and imaginatively; in doing so she uncovered the first evidence as to the true origins of banking secrecy. Dr Max Homberger provided me with a unique insight on Swiss bankers' reaction to the Nazi menace. Padraic Fallon, the editor of *Euromoney* magazine, encouraged me in numerous ways; most notably he indulged with exemplary patience my continuing obsession with Swiss financial institutions. Hugh Stephenson, then the editor of *The Times Business News*, also encouraged me to write on the subject. In Geneva Alan Macgregor allowed me to explore his splendid collection of press cuttings.

In Washington my brother- and sister-in-law, Ab and Jen Hamilton, welcomed me more often and more enthusiastically than I had any right to expect. I was lucky in securing the whole-hearted help of John Taylor, the omniscient keeper of Modern American Military Archives, and of Bill Lewis at the Suitlands branch of the Federal Archives. Both of them uncovered many important documents whose existence I had never suspected. In Washington, too, I came across Marco Durrer, whose study of Swiss diplomacy during World War II will be a major contribution to the subject. He helped me greatly, both by guiding me to sources within Switzerland and by introducing me to his fellow-historians.

The staffs of the Bodleian Library (especially at Rhodes House and the Law Library), the London Library, Chatham House, the Public Records Office, the Centre Pompidou, the Library of Congress, the New York Public Library, the Bibliothèque Publique et Universitaire in Geneva, and the Bibliothèque Nationale in Berne were unfailingly helpful and courteous. Crown copyright material in the Public Record

Office is quoted by permission of the Comptroller of HMSO.

Jack Latimer, Jane Gordon-Cumming, and especially Lilette Burnard coped personfully with typing my tangled manuscript. This was then briskly trimmed by Christopher Sinclair-Stevenson at Hamish Hamilton. His colleague, Caroline Tonson-Rye, much improved it with many delicate touches. At Viking Press in New York Elisabeth Sifton forced me to clarify many convoluted and unclear passages and tried to impose some pattern on the idiosyncrasies of my grammar and punctuation.

PART ONE

_____

The Most Swiss Community

1 / Fascinating legends, elusive reality

Once in a while the legends surrounding the banks and bankers of Switzerland are confirmed by reality. More than two hundred years ago Voltaire, a major client of the bankers of Geneva, set the tone when he uttered the famous aphorism: 'If you see a Geneva banker jump out of the window, follow him, for there is sure to be money where he lands.' A century and a half later, among the passengers on the *Titanic* were two senior managers from the Swiss Bank Corporation. They survived.

More frequently, the truth as it appears to the Swiss themselves differs sharply from reality as perceived by outsiders. In April 1976 the distinguished American journalist C. L. Sulzberger provided readers of the *New York Times* with the received local wisdom transmitted direct from well placed Swiss sources. These, he assured his readers, 'make it clear that under freer interpretation of their amended banking secrecy laws the government is always quietly advised of suspected irregularities in the source of deposits. In such cases it is inclined to make records available to foreign inspection when there is reason to suspect irregularity in the origin of funds'. Less than a year later the Swiss National Bank and the Swiss Bankers Association signed an unprecedented convention, by which the bankers pledged themselves to ensure that they knew the ultimate owners of any funds deposited with them. Clearly the convention would not have been necessary had the official Swiss view reflected the real situation. The signature of the convention was a major step in the abandonment of the pretence that most of the foreign clients of Swiss banks had some open, legal reason for using these, rather than institutions of another nationality.

For it is one of the major paradoxes connected with Swiss banks that they are most competitive in precisely those fields

3

for which they are least renowned – in arranging the financial affairs of major companies, in the mechanical business of transferring funds. In the activities for which they are most renowned, the reception, safeguarding and management of the funds of wealthy foreigners, they do not have to compete. Foreign bankers, jealous of their rivals' success, often point to their generally poor record in forecasting the movements of stock markets. Cynical American stockbrokers boast of the fortunes they have made investing in precisely the opposite direction to that of their Swiss clients. The Swiss banks themselves always claim that the services they offer emphasise security rather than performance in portfolio management. For the fortune of Swiss banks depends, more than they would admit, on a steady flow of new clients who have liquid assets at their disposal and are also fearful of the future.

Run-of-the-mill foreigners free to shop around for the banking services they require may be deterred by the sheer expense of using Swiss banks. In the words of Ray Vicker of the *Wall Street Journal*, in general one of their supporters: 'Swiss banks charge for many of the services which might be free at an American bank. In Switzerland there will be a debiting fee, a crediting fee, a charge for this, a charge for that.' One British banker connected with a bank in Geneva quips, 'if you leave your money long enough with a Swiss bank, the charges will eat it up.' Swiss banks charge agreed – and by no means negligible – fees for such routine services as the safe keeping of securities and the collection of cheques and dividends. The appeal of Swiss banks lies elsewhere, in the mystery attached to them, in the clients, in their relationship with the world outside, in their efforts to defend themselves and their clients against external assaults – and in the basic service they are offering their clients, the ability to deposit money they can then pretend – to their local tax collectors, even to their own families – they do not possess.

Fascination leads inevitably to romantic exaggeration. Outsiders want to believe that these banks enshrine the secret of all wealth, all the world's ill-gotten gains, that in their vaults is guarded the *real* truth concerning innumerable crimes known (or merely suspected), the reality behind all the many versions of 'the greatest conspiracy the world has ever known'.

Outside Switzerland the mere possession of a Swiss bank account, if not actually illegal, is taken as proof of a sophistication bordering on decadence; the fact that a deal, or a payment, has been made through such an account is taken as a reliable indication that the transaction involved is, at best, dubious.

Indeed the customers, real and imagined, of Swiss bankers throughout the ages have been the stuff of which history – and thrillers – are made. From Voltaire to the Shah of Persia via King Farouk and the Mafia, they read like the cast of characters of a dream historical novel. And if some of the chapters of this book read like the raw material from which Eric Ambler constructs his incomparable tales of coolly amoral men in positions of power plotting intricate international conspiracies, then this is merely yet another case of reality imitating art.

If the popular image of the Swiss banks' clients resembles the reality, the same is not true of the institutions themselves. The Swiss are convinced that their banks are, generally, ancient, rooted establishments, not liable to the upsets that characterise lesser institutions in less serious countries, and that their banks are staffed by men sharing the qualities of the institutions for which they work and the society that produced them. They also want to believe that their very discretion, their defiance of interfering outsiders, was justified and legally reinforced when the Nazis came to look for funds which German Jews had deposited in Switzerland.

This latter, crucial myth is long overdue for exposure – the labyrinthine reality is explained in Chapter II – but none of the other ideas has much resemblance to reality either. Swiss banks are relatively new and even more liable to disaster than their counterparts elsewhere. More than half the 1200 or so banks founded in Switzerland since the eighteenth century have failed, and an additional 150 more have got into such trouble that they have been taken under the wing of more stable institutions. At the same time the term 'banker' has a wider and not necessarily more reputable meaning in Switzerland than elsewhere, and to an astonishing degree Switzerland is, financially, a 'permissive society'.

Swiss banks now control up to $400 billion of funds, from

many sources and many lands. Their size means that these bankers' financial (and indeed political) assumptions carry considerable economic weight. Their investment criteria are bound to affect the ways money can be raised internationally, the ebb and flow of international investment fashion. A sudden rush to gold, or away from the dollar, can often be traced to them. And the world recognises – and resents – their importance, and the secrecy and deviousness associated with their activities.

It took only a few months for the soubriquet 'Gnomes of Zurich' to sweep the world after it had first been employed by British journalists and politicians during sterling's agonies in the mid-1960s.

The way the label stuck so firmly, so promptly and so universally to the – generally upright and often rather portly – denizens of Zurich's Bahnhofstrasse is a tribute to the universal nature of their image (and how much more sinister it sounds in German: financial manipulators based in 'Station Road' Zurich do not sound menacing at all). Gnomes, like the Swiss bankers of popular myth, are secretive, clannish, happiest out of sight, disturbed by the light of day; their only positive qualities a sense of self-preservation and an indifference to external standards reinforced by considerable native shrewdness.

The coiners of the phrase may have hit on an important truth: but in the context they were mistaken. Most of the financial world thought at the time that sterling was at a level unjustified by the economic facts; moreover financiers agree that the Swiss were among the last players on the markets to sell sterling short, to assume that it must inevitably be devalued: the first were the Gnomes of Lombard Street, the notoriously unpatriotic bankers of the City of London.

Many of these English bankers – certainly but unprovably – had accounts in Swiss banks, which were then illegal under English foreign exchange controls. For the evasion of domestic laws and taxes forms probably the single most substantial feature common to Swiss banking clients. Only a minority of the banks' foreign clientele have legal or ethically acceptable reasons for their actions. They may, like so many dictators of Third World countries, simply be salting money away in anticipation of the next *coup d'état*, the inevitable successor to the one from which they themselves seized power. They may, like many of these dictators' better-off subjects, be hiding money away from the tax authorities, or the police. These sums are enormous – a cynical American expert calculated that his government's aid to Latin America in the 1950s was approximately matched by the deposits placed in Swiss banks from that continent. This tidy equilibrium has, not unnaturally, worried Swiss radicals recently, and is one of the elements in the increasing Swiss dissatisfaction with their banks.

The money flowing into Switzerland from European countries is also economically important. For nearly two hundred years it has been obligatory for well-off Frenchmen to maintain at least one account in Switzerland. They provided the base for the whole business (indeed there are still small banks whose sole purpose is the management of the funds of a few rich French families); and the fact that so great a proportion of French savings had been siphoned out of the country must have contributed greatly to the disproportionate extent to which in present-day France the state finances – and thus controls – industry. With Italians, the importance is purely fiscal. The Swiss marvel at the way Italians in their thousands arrange, sometimes at great trouble and expense, for their savings to be transported across the border, only to insist that the bulk of it be invested straight back into Italy. (The contrast with the British clients is striking. They invariably insist that their money should be placed anywhere except their home country.) As for the Americans – apart from a small minority of mafiosi and stock market manipulators – they are as likely to be escaping from their wives and their presumed future demands for alimony as they are from the Internal Revenue service. But, whatever their final destination, these foreign funds are at least put into useful circulation. The Swiss argue with some justice that the alternative is not the treasuries of the clients' home countries, but the mattresses under which the money would otherwise be kept to no one's particular benefit. Swiss bankers can be perceived as recipients of the world's ill-gotten gains or, with equal justification, as useful recirculators of the world's wealth.

All these customers have in common a desire for escapism. In political terms, this ability to evade fiscal reality is obviously going to sap the general willingness to pay taxes. As Robert Morgenthau, arguably the banks' most effective foe, told the House of Representatives' Banking Committee in the late 1960s: 'a substantial percentage of our citizens are evading the payment of taxes and violating other laws through the use of Swiss and other foreign banks. This is a serious problem in itself, and if it goes unchecked, more and more people are going to try to use this device. If a very small percentage are evading the law and reaping profits from that evasion, you are going to have first a basic unfairness, and second, you are going to have pressure put on the great majority of people to start trying to cut corners, also'.

The national fiscal demoralisation of which Morgenthau was afraid had already happened in France and Italy. It can be avoided: although some well-off Germans funnelled their money into Switzerland in the 1960s, the numbers were not large and the fuss within West Germany was sufficiently loud and effective to check any possible downhill slide. The practice represents a mass evasion of reality by the rich, combined with a resignation that they cannot alter their own government's policies to suit their convenience. This escape to a dream world is unrelated to the level of taxes being imposed at home. Rich Americans, for instance, have any number of tax shelters available to reduce or even eliminate their tax burdens, and the level of personal taxation in West Germany is low by international standards.

With these millions of Swiss accounts we return, in part, to the world of myth. These are an escape route from the complication and harassments of real life. The simplicity and attractiveness of Swiss bank accounts compare to the complexities of tax returns, mortgages, overdrafts, and insurance payments as, say, the contemplation of the centre-fold of *Playboy* contrasts with the realities of married life.

It is only to outsiders that Swiss banks, bankers and their clients have taken such mythical attributes over the past couple of hundred years. To the Swiss, by and large, the banks are something else, places to keep money, large and well-paying employers, a powerful magnet to attract a steady flow of well-heeled foreigners, providing increased business for the hoteliers and shopkeepers catering for them. Only recently has an alternative attitude emerged, that of the banks as the major symbols of a deep-seated Swiss disease.

This book is an attempt to try and reconcile the Swiss' own idea of their banks with that held outside their country, to cut through the thicket of myth which surrounds the subject, and to explain some of the more significant episodes that occurred when the customs and practices of Swiss bankers came into conflict with those of other countries – notably those of the United States. It is in no way a history of Swiss banking and its relation to economic and financial history in general – a subject of enormous importance which no historian has ever tackled.

The 1980s provide an excellent opportunity for such a study. An unparalleled series of scandals that erupted in the 1970s has produced far more information about the Swiss banking system than was previously available, from sources in the United States even more than in Switzerland itself. Bankers, officials, and their clients are now far more open than they were. In other ways, too, they have started to resemble their counterparts in other countries. Indeed the last part of this book is devoted to showing how the gulf that used to separate the subjects of this book from their counterparts elsewhere is now slowly, painfully, and gradually being bridged. It was a deep one.

The past was very different, and most of it remains obscure. No one can blame the historians for their avoidance of the subject. For one thing, the relevant archives are still securely preserved in the impenetrable fastnesses of the banks themselves. (Three major banks have, however, commissioned corporate histories using their own records. I have found these – especially the massive and handsome tome on the Swiss Banking Corporation by Hans Bauer – immensely useful). Nevertheless, any attempt to interpret often exceedingly emotive words and actions across the Swiss frontiers – which are linguistic, social and cultural as well as geographic – has considerable limitations. Because of the aura of secrecy and discretion which envelops the subject – and which has provided those involved with their *raison d'être* through the ages –

the only reliable information emerges during times of crisis. This bias inevitably gives the impression that the history of Swiss banks and their relations with the outside world have been even more endemically troubled and turbulent than they have been in reality.

To make matters worse, much of the so-called 'information' available is both anonymous and unreliable. Bankers, inside or outside Switzerland, are simply not prepared to be quoted. They tend to make empty gestures and remarks. 'I have it,' one will say, tapping the side of his nostril meaningfully with his forefinger, 'from an unimpeachable source not unconnected with one of the bigger institutions not unadjacent to the Paradeplatz' (the square in the middle of Bahnhofstrasse, the very epicentre of Zurich banking) 'and of course this is totally off the record – I know I can trust you – that the truth about those Hebraic gentlemen in Geneva has never been fully revealed and that more than one head of state including one who still retains her crown' (pause, nudge, nudge, wink, wink) 'was greatly discomfited by their downfall.'

My attempt to bring the subject down from the clouds, to confine myself to hard – or hardish – facts is, to employ these bankers' terminology, not greatly assisted by the near-universality of such convolutions.

The first question to be faced is: why have the banks and bankers of Switzerland, and not the financial institutions of any other country, attracted so much attention, so many clients, such importance in the world? The usual explanation is religious: the theories of Max Weber and Richard Tawney are trundled out to explain the alleged relationship between Protestantism and the rise of capitalism, the way in which Protestantism liberated the world of finance from any limitations imposed by individual guilt or ecclesiastical rules. The theocratic rule imposed on Geneva by that implacable French refugee Jean Calvin is perceived as crucial. And more sophisticated observers attach great importance to Zurich's own Protestant hero, the soldier-priest Ulrich Zwingli. To Janet Kramer in an article in the *New Yorker* in December 1980, the key historical moment was when Zwingli consigned all the statues in the city's biggest church, the Grossmünster, into the River Limmat: 'the saving grace, so to speak, about

Zwingli', she noted, 'being that he had already stripped those wicked Catholic objects of their gold and silver and their precious stones, turned the treasure over to the Zurich Town Council, and in the process started what has come to be called, reverently, Swiss banking.'* She goes on to note shrewdly that the Swiss bankers are offering absolution from the guilt associated elsewhere with the possession of considerable wealth. 'A dozen other small countries, from Lebanon to Costa Rica, have tried over the years to set themselves up as bankers to the world, with the assurances of discreet and oligarchic democracy, but the fact is that only the Swiss have been able to satisfy their clients with the right mixture of steel and guilelessness. What the Swiss offer, beyond the obvious pleasures of their country and the services of their banks and tax havens, is a kind of theatre of rectitude.'

This 'theatre' is perceived as irresistible because it is backed, not only by Swiss attitudes but by the long and internationally accepted tradition of Swiss neutrality and its consequent protection against foreign invaders or intruding foreign taxmen.

Unfortunately, these ideas, however elegantly expressed, provide only a partial explanation. The contrast between Protestant and Catholic attitudes to finance relates, essentially, to the sixteenth century; 'Swiss banking' dates back in some respects to earlier periods, but has a continuous history dating only from the end of the seventeenth century, so the 'religious' explanation is doubly anachronistic. Moreover, there are at least two other European countries with broadly the same background as the Swiss, Holland and Sweden. The Swedes have been exclusively Lutheran for four centuries, while the Dutch, like the Swiss, are divided between Calvinist and Catholic. Proponents of the Protestant theory of the origins of Swiss banking also ignore the number of Catholic Swiss banks and bankers. Sweden and Holland, like Switzerland, have been stable and soberly run societies for hundreds of years. Neither country would yield to the Swiss in their respect for financial rectitude – historically bankers in both

* Four hundred years later that great banker Dr Alfred Schaefer made amends by commissioning Marc Chagall to design stained-glass windows for another famous Zurich church, the Frauminster.

countries have proved more prudent in watching over funds placed in their charge than the Swiss. The Dutch have a long tradition of trading abroad and have thus enjoyed the same opportunity as the Swiss to shift from a trading to a financial role on the world commercial scene.

Even the supposed uniqueness of Swiss neutrality can be questioned. The Dutch, too, were at peace from 1815 to 1940 – escaping World War I entirely. Many German industrial groups – including the powerful empire of Alfred Krupp – chose Holland rather than Switzerland as the domicile for the holding companies through which they tried to shelter their foreign investments from sequestration in a future conflict. And even though the Netherlands was invaded by the Nazis, the Swedes contrived precisely the same sort of uneasy compromise with the Germans – and their own consciences – as did the Swiss between 1939 and 1945.

Once we filter out the simpler and incorrect explanations for the uniqueness and importance of Swiss banks we are left with a knotty, and itself misunderstood, residual factor, Swiss history and the peculiar 'Swissness' of the country's six million inhabitants. From this cultural soil sprang Swiss banks and bankers, and it is this we must first examine before the complexities of the country's banking scene make any kind of sense.

2 / Those different Swiss

The Swiss are a famously hard-working people, but even they stop work on August 1st every year to celebrate a national holiday. This commemorates an event of formidable antiquity: the meeting of the representatives of the three 'forest cantons', the pioneer members of the Swiss Confederation, at the 'Rütli meadow' on the shores of Lake Lucerne in 1291.

They pledged an alliance, and formed themselves into a 'league for the maintenance of the public peace.'

They were also, by no coincidence, protecting their valuable rights over access to the St. Gotthard Pass, which had become the major trade route between Italy and northern Europe in the previous few years.

The Rütli meadow has remained a sacred spot for the Swiss: and they are also naturally proud of the length and continuity of their existence as an independent people. But they do not mention that for five and a half centuries until the Federation was re-formed in 1848 there was virtually no constitutional progress. Other cantons joined the original three, but they all remained highly independent with literally no common bond except a willingness to hand over the right of making war and peace to the Confederation. Apart from that, nothing. The inhabitants were divided by race, religion and language: they did not even use the same systems of measurement or share a common currency system.

Under these circumstances, it is ridiculous to talk as if there were any such real entity as 'Switzerland' or any such people as 'the Swiss' before 1848. Most major towns, indeed, looked outward, rather than towards their own nominal 'country'. The outlook was often dictated by economics, for until 1848, when they were abolished, the customs barriers between the cantons were complex and formidable. No wonder cities like Basle and Geneva looked to France and Germany for their livelihood. Significantly Zurich, the most inward-looking of Swiss cities, rose to its present position as the country's unquestioned industrial and financial capital only in the half century after 1848.

Even in 1848 the new constitution emerged only after a civil war the previous year had frightened the cantons into tightening the links between them. Inevitably it reflected the differences among the new country's constitutent parts; an extreme sensitivity to local sovereignty; and a consequent and continuing need to compromise rather than any attempt to impose any uniformity on the cantons' laws and customs. The Swiss constitution is still based, as it has been since 1291, on the assumption that the Federal government possesses only those powers which have been positively given to it. It is no more than the sum of its constituent parts. And today, although the Federal government plays a far more important role in Swiss life than was foreseen by the founding fathers in 1848, the tendency to separatism still continues.

Switzerland today is still a melting-pot within which the temperature has never been raised sufficiently to force the ingredients to fuse. Legal and taxation systems differ, children enjoy completely different educational experiences (so that moving within Switzerland is often impossible, because children find it so difficult to adapt); and even the most basic of all attributes, citizenship, belongs, not to the country, but to the little place your parents came from, that most Swiss of all entities, the *gemeinde*, the gathering of all the (male) inhabitants of a commune which the Swiss still cherish – in theory anyway – as the embodiment of their ideals. This acceptance of diversity reinforces Swiss stubbornness, the characteristic that enabled them to survive in their early wars against their more powerful neighbours. The Swiss are also extremely conservative – famously the last people in Western Europe to allow women the vote. These qualities, combined with the need to arrive at a consensus among the country's many different peoples, make any course of action hesitant, slow and painfully prolonged. The Swiss usually have to submit any major change to popular vote by referendum. This is a genuinely democratic inheritance from their fabled past and even then, as they boast, 'we never accept anything unless it has been presented to us at least twice'.

The most deeply entrenched difference is, of course, in language. And even though German is theoretically dominant, as the first language of more than half the country's inhabitants, yet its domination is subject to two enormous qualifications: the French-speaking minority often steadfastly refuses to learn it, and there are profound differences in the language as spoken even in neighbouring German-speaking cantons.

For there are two languages in these cantons. Ordinary, 'high' German, *Hochdeutsch*, is learned at school and is used in official life. But at home, among friends, the local dialect, the particular variant of *Schwyzerdütsch* is equally universal – it is used even in the senior management meetings of major Swiss companies, which would never dream of issuing their annual reports in anything other than official, formal, German. Yet *Schwyzerdütsch* varies enormously from canton to canton. These linguistic divisions ensure that most Swiss accept that they will have to learn at least one 'foreign' language. This helps the banks, 'the only credit institutions in the world', claims Dr. Hans Mast of Crédit Suisse, 'which serve customers in all five major languages of the western world.'

As a result of their particular history the Swiss are separated from each other – and, to a far greater extent, from foreigners – by a whole series of barriers, which no Swiss would be so tactless as to try and penetrate. The whole country, after all, is built on mutual tolerance. Neither the Federal government nor even the most important canton or interest group can ever impose its views, however sensible these may seem. By contrast the delicate Swiss balancing mechanism provides individual interest groups – occupational, as much as geographic – with considerable negative power to block even the most elementary advances. In 1848, notes one historian: 'Switzerland was the only European country which still had no railways. For the carters, the coachmen, and the innkeepers opposed their development. As for the peasants, they were afraid that their precious holdings would be broken up.' (Much the same happened with the development of the country's motorway system a century later: for decades Switzerland was littered with fragments of half-completed new roads, their completion prevented for years by the inhabitants of the local commune.)

This undue respect for every established institution in communal life springs from a very Swiss duality of outlook. There is one clear set of standards operative within his community, his *gemeinde*, his profession or trade, in which each person has his place, which must be respected and mutually protected. Equally there is a considerable degree of trust within the group. In theory this excludes foreigners, but can benefit any stranger accepted by the community. Right through World War II even the highest Swiss government officials thought that the German minister in Berne, who, presided over all the Nazis' machinations against Switzerland's safety, was a true friend – because he could express himself in a Basle dialect.

This mentality also results in a severe limitation of the competitive element in Swiss industrial and, above all, commercial life. Until the rules were changed by the growth of the Migros co-operative retail chain, the number of shops, for instance, was carefully controlled – the famous saying that it was 'easier to open a bank than a grocery store in Geneva' even in the 1950s, was a tribute to the formal rules surrounding retail competition as well as to the laxity of Swiss banking regulation.

Within the *gemeinde* there are, as a rule, few policy differences between the various political parties competing for power. The consensus system has operated too well for too long for that. Politics, at every level, are simply an extension of a sort of spoils system. Until recently only 'extremists' thought it odd that almost every member of the two houses of the Swiss Parliament represents an interest group, or a company, or a bank, or all three, and has been enlisted as a director because of his supposed political influence. Indeed the country possesses its own variant of the 'military-industrial complex'. Military service – and thus the army – is taken extremely seriously by every Swiss. The officer corps, made up almost exclusively of volunteers, represents the whole spectrum of the Swiss establishment – it was said that promotion in the Union Bank of Switzerland, for instance, invariably went to the executive with the best military record. In any other society such a system would ensure that the rich and powerful monopolised political influence, but the Swiss version is cunningly designed to ensure that virtually every Swiss, of whatever degree, is properly represented. Even the poor Alpine peasants, theoretically at the bottom of the economic pecking order, in fact enjoy undue political influence. For the areas where they are concentrated, especially the Swiss heartland, the 'forest cantons', benefit from the Swiss constitution, which, modelled on the American, provides an upper legislative house – like the Senate – whose seats are allocated not by size of population but by cantons. The result is that Swiss agriculture enjoys an elaborate system of protectionist measures; even the wine-growers, not a numerous lobby, have ensured that the wine any individual Swiss can bring home is limited, and commercial imports are equally strictly regulated.

The system does not breed cynicism. On the contrary, the Swiss are profoundly attached to it and the benefits it brings them all. But such parochialism of outlook also involves an indifference to the outside world, its opinions, its values, and its people. The Swiss attitude towards the immigrant workers who have been absolutely essential elements in the country's growing prosperity since World War II has been disgraceful. Many of them have been treated as little better than peons, obliged to return home when no longer of economic benefit to Switzerland, whereas richer settlers profit from the considerable (though by no means uniform) fees levied by different cantons on anyone desiring to purchase citizenship: 'it is far from the most admirable of Swiss political customs,' notes the historian Jonathan Steinberg, 'since it offers sanctuary to the wealthy tax-dodger and excludes the sons of immigrants who may have been born in the community and speak its dialect.' Provided the newcomer is not going to compete for jobs – or ordinary housing – with the locals, then he is welcome. In this, as in so many other instances, Swiss life is dominated by an unbelievably insular moral and physical outlook, combined with an apparent absence of any abstract moral values which might conflict with the desire to maximise the financial gain accruing to a community – or its individual members.

This moral blind spot is itself based on Swiss history. For many centuries after the Confederation was formed, the major export of its constituent members was – men. The poor rural cantons invariably had more inhabitants than they could support, and for 500 years – until the rise of national armies at the time of the French Revolution – very few Continental armies were complete without their quota of Swiss mercenary soldiers – their only survivors today being the gorgeously apparelled members of the Vatican Guard.

The mercenary business was well organised. 'In each Swiss state', writes one historian, 'there were officials, notables and heads of ancient families at whose command or suggestion well-armed, orderly companies would go forth to serve others, and large rewards remained with those who sent them. It was thus possible to hire, buy or corrupt high and low; the wisdom or justice of the quarrel mattered little in comparison with its proceeds.'

The 'notables' had other sources of income. One of the major curiosities of the Swiss economy has always been that no canton could rely on any other for the bulk of its income. It had always to look outwards – generally outside the Confederation – since the chance of making a living out of its other small, jealously protectionist states or cities was always minimal.

There was one direction in which both the mercenary and the trading traditions pointed: finance. The traders became money-changers – as they had to be, with so many types of coinage, of local as well as foreign origin, circulating in their cantons; and, as guardians of the savings and pensions of the returning mercenaries, they became bankers, or rather, portfolio managers, to employ rather a grandiose term. From the outset they were middle-men, investing other people's money, not acting as deposit bankers and putting their own funds at risk. In a world full of emperors, kings, and lesser sovereigns everlastingly short of money, they found ready customers, as a surplus of money gradually replaced a surplus of men as the cantons' primary economic weapon.

More than fifty years ago a Swiss professor, Jules Landmann, summed up the extent to which his forebears had supplied capital to Europe. In a much-quoted article he wrote: 'From His Imperial Majesty in Vienna and the Kings of France and England, down to little German kinglets and to French municipalities, all the public authorities of the eighteenth century were in debt to the Swiss cantons. From the Bank of England to the East India Company, there was practically no instrument of collective capital investment in which the authorities of the Swiss Cantons were not involved.' Although most of the cantons took part in this early international financing, the prototype of modern Swiss banking was not at the time in Switzerland at all. It was the proud, independent city-state of Geneva.

3 / The Genevan model

In theory, a number of cities could serve as models for an examination of Swiss banking in the centuries before there was any such entity as Switzerland. In some respects Basle, historically the most important centre of trade among all the cantons, would be more suitable than Geneva, which, at the beginning of the eighteenth century, was not even a member of the Confederation; nor have any of Geneva's ancient financial institutions survived. Basle probably had more foreign exchange dealers than Geneva. Its merchants probably had a wider experience of international banking. But Geneva provides a microcosm of all the habits, assumptions and practices which have made Swiss banking famous and important, and it was at the end of the seventeenth century that all these qualities first emerged.

The choice of Geneva owes little to the supposedly dominant influence of Calvin. What mattered then was the city's proximity to France, as a refuge for money fleeing the French tax system (a role it has retained ever since) and as a source of funds for the French government. Yet in 1685 King Louis XIV had ended nearly a century of toleration of the Protestants and had thus sent them into far-flung exile. In the manner of the Jewish diaspora from Russia and Germany in the nineteenth and twentieth centuries the Protestant refugees, the Huguenots, enriched, intellectually and financially, the many cities, like Amsterdam and London, where they settled. But there was one important distinction. It was unthinkable for exiled German or Russian Jewish bankers to finance Tsarist Russia, let alone the Germany of Adolf Hitler. But the bankers in the 'Huguenot International', not only in Geneva, but also in Amsterdam and – surprisingly openly – in Paris itself, contributed greatly to Louis XIV's ability to conduct his money throughout Europe, mostly against their fellow Protestants.

In 1702 Geneva's foreign exchange dealers had decided not to help Louis's war efforts, but this gesture had no practical effect. Moreover, in the words of Herbert Luthy,* 'During Louis XIV's European wars, Geneva singled itself out among Swiss cities in, by and large, sacrificing the interests of its industry to those of its financial and international trading interests.' The choice was deliberate: in 1703 radicals accused the local cloth merchants of reducing their financial involvement in the textile business and diverting the funds thus released to more profitable employment with the French government. By contrast, rival cities, like Basle and Zurich, took advantage of the many restrictions on trade resulting from the wars to protect and encourage their native industries (a piece of opportunism which was to be repeated during the Napoleonic wars a century later, when the Swiss freed themselves from their dependence on England for the latest in textile technology). By contrast, Geneva turned itself into an 'offshore bank' for Louis's wars.

The Protestant bankers, above all Samuel Bernard, were so crucial to Louis's success that cynical investors preferred to leave their money with Bernard rather than directly with the French state, reckoning that when Louis was suffering one of his periodic credit crunches he would give priority to satisfying Bernard rather than his direct creditors. Bernard played such a vital role that when he fell in 1709 he brought down with him the previously mighty financial centre of Lyons. Of course Geneva was also hurt, but most of its bankers survived – a brilliant example of the historic Genevan (and Swiss) ability to profit from others' misfortunes.

Previously Geneva's bankers had provided two rather different services: they had helped to supply Louis's permanent, desperate cash requirements; and, when he had raised the money, to transmit it to distant lands at a time when the normal methods of despatching wagon-loads of gold and silver were impracticable.

The Genevan bankers were only one, and not necessarily the most important, source of Louis's finance. But because

* In *La Banque Protestante en France*. S.E.V.P.E.N. 1959, the major source for this section.

they, alone of all France's neighbours, were neutral, they fulfilled an essential and unique role in transmitting the funds; during a few decisive years at the beginning of the century, 'these neutral intermediaries', as Luthy puts it, 'appear to have completely replaced all the foreign bankers entrenched in Paris' who had hitherto handled the same business.

Another important precedent established at the time was the way the Geneva City Council, largely dominated by bankers, merchants and their families, shut the stable door only after the horse had bolted, bearing with it the savings of so many of its citizens. In 1713 it enacted a number of proposals for restoring confidence in the city as a financial centre, and in controlling the activities of its merchants/financiers. It also provided for a discretionary code that required bankers – or rather investment brokers – to keep records of their clients, but forbade them to disclose these to anyone except the client without the express permission of the City Council.

Even though Genevan finance at the end of the seventeenth century provided many precedents for the future, the city's role as a financial centre took a double leap during the second half of the next century, first when the financiers devised a new and highly ingenious system to help profit from financial problems of the French monarchy. Then the onset of the French Revolution finally confirmed Geneva's historic role as the permanent bolt-hole for the French.

The first step came with the famous 'thirty maidens of Geneva', a system which combined the very latest in medical knowledge, a great deal of ingenuity and organisational ability, and, as usual, a totally amoral and impersonal approach to business. In the last thirty years before the French Revolution the Genevans allowed outside investors to participate in what was basically a well spread bet on a field of thirty. They lent the French state money, using a well-established formula, by which interest was paid only during the lifetime of a specified individual.

But the Genevans vastly improved the odds for their clients. First they spread the risk, so that each saver had only one-thirtieth of his or her money invested on one particular life. The bankers then placed a single massive consolidated loan with the French Treasury on each of the thirty lives. They used to the full the very thorough demographic information they possessed about Geneva's upper-crust families to ensure that only girls were used (since girls lived longer than boys) and then only those from families with a good record of longevity – only betting on those who had survived the often fatal diseases then attendant upon infancy. They also drew on the very latest advances in medical knowledge, including vaccination – it was by no coincidence that two of the city's most famous doctors were both from banking families. (Theodore Tronchin's family managed Voltaire's money and Dr. Louis Odier's family is still active in Geneva's second largest private bank, Lombard Odier.) Their precautions were successful: the average life span of one batch of thirty girls was no less than sixty-three, nearly double the average for the time, and as good as many countries' today – though the premature death of one of the girls (who themselves did not benefit from the arrangement) could cause the most frightful anguish. Luthy records the general mourning when the wretched Pernette-Elizabeth Martin died at the tender age of eight, taking with her 2 million francs a year in interest payments foregone.

This ingenuity was a magnificent advertisement for the city when the French Revolution broke out in 1789 and every wealthy Frenchman with any disposable or liquid assets strove, often too late, to get them out of France.

Geneva was a natural haven, and most of the city's private banks trace their origins back to this period although many of the families involved, like the Pictets, the Odiers and the Lullins, had been prominent and financially active before 1789.

The banks they now established, even though more permanent than the often temporary, essentially trading partnerships which had been the rule before then, shared certain characteristics with their predecessors. They were not, strictly speaking, banks, in that they did not rely on the investment of the partners' own funds, but rather on the management of the portfolios of individual rich clients. So they were – and remain – partnerships, dependent on a personal relationship for their business. They were discreet: they never advertised themselves, but relied for new customers on the relations and friends of existing clients. They based their activities very largely on the funds of French families – for these, unlike the upper classes of many other European countries, often had wealth not tied up in land. The French, like their successors, were looking for security, rather than profit, which made their advisers' task much easier. In return, they expected to be kept informed discreetly, without letting slip to the French authorities, or even to possibly envious and disloyal neighbours, that they had funds abroad. So the bankers pioneered the methods that were to become routine in the Swiss banking community: letters from the banks to their clients were not posted in Switzerland, but in France itself, nor were they necessarily sent to the clients' home or business addresses – it was often advisable to keep wives, or business partners, in ignorance. And when the bankers did travel to see their clients, certain elementary precautions were taken. To this day Swiss bankers do not have 'banker' marked in their passports. Rather, they are 'lawyers' or 'businessmen'. They tried to keep the papers they carried with them to a minimum, to remember rather than record the state of a client's account. And they met them in a neutral spot, a hotel room rather than their homes or offices.

Not surprisingly, the same precautions prevailed when clients came to Switzerland. To this day, as much Swiss banking business is done in holiday villas or hotels as in offices (one reason why such fashionable resorts as Gstaad or St. Moritz have such an inordinate number of banks; though to merit a personal visit by the partner of a bank, a client must have a 'serious' fortune, and not be a mere dollar millionaire). For this reason, too, the offices of Geneva's private banks are still rather ostentatiously discreet. Their presence is generally signified only by a small brass plate outside the handsome front door of a medium-sized town house; it does not give the bank's name, merely 'H,et cie' or 'L,0,et cie' to indicate that up to a billion pounds of investments are managed within. Each bank contains a series of individual consulting rooms – still decorated in a style vaguely reminiscent of the *ancien régime*. Each contrives to have a number of entrances, some discreetly buried away behind the main entrance.

These 'bankers' were so successful that it was not until 1977 that they were forced to change the habits of two centuries. They kept to themselves: they lived richly but discreetly; they married among themselves; they kept the – Protestant – faith and excluded from their group any Jewish or Catholic institution. They symbolised the fundamental advantage enjoyed by the Swiss over other bankers, that of being next door to a major source of funds looking for a secure and tax free refuge. Not even the Dutch or the Swedes enjoyed that particular combination. But they were neither 'banks', nor 'Swiss': they were portfolio managers situated at the extreme edge of Switzerland, French in everything but nationality – and the laws and customs that governed their activities. They enjoyed all the advantages of being French and none of the irritations, like being invaded by the Germans, or having to account for their clients' or their own activities to government authorities. Real Swiss bankers often modelled themselves on the Genevans and their brothers in Basle and Zurich: but they were an upstart breed, springing up only after 1848, when Switzerland finally acquired a constitution, and goods and money could finally pass untaxed and unimpeded through the cantons.

4 / Banks: belated and local

The structure of private banking in Geneva was fixed, once and for all, during the French Revolutionary period. Three of the four banks which led the 'quattuor' of major Genevan institutions bidding for foreign loans in the 1840s – Lombard Odier, Pictet and Hentsch – still dominate the private banking scene in the city (the fourth member of the quattuor was absorbed by Pictet). But the opposite was the case elsewhere in Switzerland. Before 1848 there were effectively only two classes of banks – private banks and over 160 local savings banks, virtually all founded since 1815. A few towns, like Zurich and St. Gall, had recently founded their own commercial institutions, as had one or two cantons. These 'cantonal banks' were backed by public capital – although they usually allowed private shareholders to participate, and were regarded as a symbol of the triumph of democracy over oligarchy. They were designed to provide at least one stable, secure financial institution in each canton to tap the local savings market and employ the funds for every type of local economic activity, although market pressure through the years has led them to concentrate increasingly on mortgages and business loans, which now absorb around half their assets.

It was not until there was a federal constitution that anything resembling an ordinary privately owned commercial banking institution emerged in Switzerland. It is only in the past century and a quarter that the country has developed its banking network – the densest, most complicated and most varied in the world. In the twenty years after 1848 a hundred local banks were founded in every corner of Switzerland, as were a hundred more savings banks and nearly fifty 'land' or mortgage credit institutions. On a larger scale, the first major Swiss commercial bank, the Crédit Suisse, was founded in 1856 by a group of patriotic Zurichers as a reaction to an attempt by a Leipzig bank to establish a branch in the city. Their imitation of the French Crédit Mobilier, to be a 'steam engine of credit' devoted to the development of the country's industrial and transport systems, tapped a rich vein of local financial patriotism and was an immediate success. The wave of banks founded in the 1850s and 1860s derived its impetus from a number of sources: cantons without their own banks hastened not to be left out; foreign banks threatened to monopolise the financing of Switzerland's railway system, unless local groups could form themselves into banks big enough to cope with the steam engine's unprecedented capital requirements; and, at last, Swiss industrial concerns were of sufficient size to have to accept credit from banks, where previously they had, generally, followed a line of strict self-sufficiency.

Crédit Suisse* one of the three major banks which today dominate the Swiss scene, had a sparkling start – its first capital issue was over-subscribed seventy times by the eager citizens of Zurich and it enjoyed a virtual monopoly of the commercial banking business of Switzerland's fastest-growing city (in 1850 Zurich's population was little greater than it had been in the Middle Ages, but it multiplied eleven-fold in the next fifty years, so that by 1900 it had overtaken Basle and Geneva as the country's biggest city); the only competition came from the venerable Bank Leu, the Zurichers' own bank, founded in 1755, and reorganised several times, repeatedly preserved by local patriotism, allied to a desire to have a local mortgage bank. Crédit Suisse was also the only institution designed to be an organization of international size.

The bank that was to become the Swiss Bank Corporation** started as a loosely organised group of private bankers in Basle, who struggled for some years to free themselves loose from the influence of the German bankers who had helped found their group. The third of today's Big Three, the Union Bank of Switzerland,*** traces its origins back to two local banks, one serving the ambitious industrial city of Winterthur, the other the Toggenburg region round St. Gall, the centre of Switzerland's then thriving embroidery industry.

The requirements of Swiss industry were at the root of the sudden expansion of Swiss banking in mid-century. Previously, there were simply not enough local clients for any normal joint stock bank to be required. Such industry as existed was small scale and its owners sternly turned their faces against borrowing money – an attitude which changed as markets expanded when the internal customs barriers within Switzerland disappeared in 1848.

Although the railways were by far the most capital-hungry

---

* The French name is universally used in English. In German it is the Schweizerische Kreditanstalt (or the Anstalt for short); in Italian the Credito Svizzero.
** Schweizerischer Bankverein in German (colloquially the 'Verein'); in French the Société de Banque Suisse, in Italian the Società di Banca Svizzera.
*** In French the plural, in theory more federal, Union de Banques Suisses; in German the Schweizerische Bankgesellschaft (the 'Gesellschaft'); in Italian the equally federal Unione di Banche Svizzere.

institutions in Switzerland, the loans were spread widely among other industries. As the country's farmers increasingly specialised in dairy produce, so their requirements for capital investment grew, and soon the country's agriculture was the most capital-intensive in Europe. As more and more tourists, especially the more adventurous British, flocked to the country to climb its mountains and bathe in its lakes, so the hotel industry grew and absorbed large sums of capital. Other industries – silk, embroidery, and chocolate-making, watches and clocks, mechanical and electrical machinery – all flourished, and all required the usual banking services, the more so as they tended to export a greater proportion of their output than similar industries in countries with large domestic markets. All of today's Big Three were associated with specific industries: the SBC with Basle's burgeoning chemical industry, Crédit Suisse with the country's only natural resource, hydroelectic power and the machinery required to harness it, and the Union Bank with the textile and embroidery industries. Inevitably, Swiss banks were forced to follow their industrial customers abroad – even before they established themselves outside their native city. Such clients were typical of those in other countries, but with the difference that within Switzerland virtually every industrial activity was based on local, not national, firms, so it is not surprising that almost all the hundreds of banks founded in the 1850s and 1860s were local, serving at most a canton or a major city. The exception was the Federal Bank, appropriately based in the federal capital of Berne, which from the outset attempted to open branches throughout both German- and French-speaking Switzerland. This was doubly bold: most banks did not open any branches until the turn of the century, and those that did – like the ambitious Toggenburg Bank – confined themselves strictly to a natural economic area, their cantons, or their immediate neighbourhood – even the Bank of Winterthur did not spread to Zurich, fifteen miles away, until 1906, and no bank from the German-speaking part of Switzerland dreamt of opening in the French-speaking third of the country (the Italian-speaking cantons which include only a tenth of Switzerland's inhabitants, were, however, largely colonised by institutions backed by 'foreign' Swiss capital).

Although the Swiss banking scene has been transformed by a series of upheavals during the past century and although it is far more centralised than it was even twenty years ago – when the cantonal banks were still more important than the Big Three – yet from the start it developed a unique structure. It is far less concentrated than banking in France or in other European countries. Even a contemporary radical, dedicated to the exposure of what he perceives as a Swiss variety of imperialist capitalism, was forced to concede in a recent book that 'the existence of powerful public sector banking institutions has helped to restrain banking concentration in Switzerland, where it is less advanced than in other countries, like Belgium. The existence of cantonal banks, has, without any doubt, imposed limits on the power of the big banks in the home market.'

For the Swiss stubbornly continue to support banking institutions more varied than those in other industrialised countries. The contrast with foreign customers of Swiss banks is complete. For them the Swiss banking scene comprises above all the Big Three, and the myriad of small private bankers. The latter, of course, have very few local clients – moreover, by Swiss law, private banks, which do not publish their balance sheets, cannot solicit deposits. And until the 1960s, the Big Three, true to Swiss tradition, did not trespass on the personal banking territory traditionally left to other banks, so they rarely impinged on the consciousness of the average Swiss citizen. It was only in 1965 that they started to accept individual savings deposits. Three years earlier it was quite reasonable for Professor R. S. Sayers to state in his standard survey of European banking that the Big Three were 'purely commercial banks, almost exclusively devoted to the financing of trade and industry, international payment transactions and the administration of assets and property'. To be sure, they performed the latter service for most wealthy Swiss: but from the start the average citizen had other ideas of how to use his country's banking system. Nor were the major banks particularly interested in ordinary foreigners. When the League of Nations was established in Geneva in the early 1920s, one of the major British banks, Lloyds, opened a branch especially to cater for the financial requirements of its employees, who presumably needed the usual range of personal banking services and not the portfolio management in which the local institutions had specialised for so long.

The Swiss do not use their banks to transfer money: they invariably use their ubiquitous postal giro system, operated through local post offices. This, noted Sayers, was and still is: 'convenient, efficient and extremely cheap and is, therefore, widely used for a great variety of transactions, including even very small payments; the availability of this service inevitably limits the scope for banking of the English type where the extent of banking resources is largely dependent on the use of current accounts for a broad range of payments' and he could have added that the same applied to most other countries. It is unthinkable for the Swiss to pay their bills other than through postal giro; so postal giro payments forms are automatically attached to any bill. In addition, the Swiss are also great users of cash – the proportion of banknotes to national income is about double the figure for Britain or the United States, another feature which, in theory, limits the scope for bankers and their services.

On the other hand the prudent Swiss make the fullest use of their banks as savings institutions. They save a greater proportion of their incomes than do people in other countries, a trend encouraged by the historic absence of any provision by the federal authorities for old age or medical emergencies. But here again the Swiss are different: they tend to divide their savings amongst a variety of institutions. Since World War II they have reduced the sums they put into local and regional savings banks but have continued to entrust their cantonal banks with a substantial proportion of their savings – though not all. While virtually every Swiss male has more than one bank account, women have far fewer than elsewhere, and require their husbands' or parents' signed permission before opening an account. Moreover the period since World War II has also seen a remarkable phenomenon, the rise of the *Raiffeisen*, the credit unions named after the mayor of a German village who invented this co-operative, amateur, locally run type of financial organism in the mid-nineteenth century. *Raiffeisen* were introduced into Switzerland in 1900, but it is only since 1945 that their very Swiss attributes of self-sufficiency, local initiative and self-reliance have ensured them a definite, if modest, place in Swiss financial life.

The biggest transaction undertaken by the average Swiss citizen is, predictably, his mortgage. And until the past twenty years he relied on his cantonal bank or savings bank to provide the finance. It was only the great construction boom of the 1950s which lured the Big Three, too, into this form of financing, and even today they are far less important in it than in other financial sectors. The other two major commercial banks – Leu and the Swiss Volksbank* – have traditionally been heavily involved in the business. The loyalty of the people of Zurich to Leu, in fact, is based on this role, and the Swiss Volksbank, the co-operative bank founded in the 1860s, serves the individual customer's need for mortgages faithfully enough to have a third of its assets tied up in home finance, roughly the same proportion as Leu.

So until the last twenty years, the major commercial banks generally steered clear of the personal financial business which is the bread and butter of their colleagues in other countries. But they had other strings to their bow, which, however, required a wide range of financial talents to draw.

5 / Not bankers – entrepreneurs

Banks monopolise the financial sector in Switzerland far more completely than in most other industrialised countries. They employ the stockbrokers or jobbers on the country's stock exchanges. There are virtually no commodity traders, foreign exchange specialists, company brokers, or financial specialists other than their employees. As a result, the description 'banker' in Switzerland covers a far wider spectrum of talents than in any other country. While there are thousands of

* Banque Populaire Suisse in French.

prudent commercial bankers in the country's banks, these also employ hundreds of entrepreneurial types, who in other countries would be employed by non-banking financial operations. And if they were in the banking sector they would be safely ensconced in institutions labelled 'investment' or 'merchant' banks. English observers make the distinction that the clearing banks live off their deposits: the merchant banks live off their wits.

In Switzerland none of the banks have ever been able to live off their deposits: they have always depended very heavily on the wits of their employees. These, therefore, require a different set of talents from employees of major banks in other countries. Elsewhere the organisational ethos breeds prudent lenders and careful borrowers – in big banks anyway, since the bulk of their profits is invariably going to be derived from the spread between the cost of the funds they employ and the interest rates at which they can lend them. Other activities, if not marginal, are not central to the organisation's activities.

The banks which traditionally catered for the needs of the majority of the Swiss themselves – the cantonal, savings and local banks – did aspire to behave like ordinary 'commercial' banks. But the institutions which outsiders think of as 'Swiss banks', the major international institutions and the private banks, necessarily have different objectives. The private banks cannot advertise for deposits, and even at the other extreme the Swiss Bank Corporation, the financial institution which most nearly resembles the norm prevalent elsewhere, derives only half its profits from the money it loans to its clients (a proportion far lower than is the case with those other 'universal' bankers, the Big Three German banks).

There is a further major difference between bankers in Switzerland and those in the rest of the world, and that is the almost total absence of any form of control, external or internal, moral or physical, over Swiss bankers' activities. Everything about the Swiss, their respect for privacy, their refusal to enquire too closely about what is happening outside their *gemeinde*, their instinctive shrinking from any extension of federal control, their equally instinctive refusal to admit that the pursuit of individual profit should be confined by moral rules, points in only one direction: to the luxuriant freedom enjoyed by Swiss bankers to pursue their private profit at the expense, not only of their customers or the societies or governments from which they spring, but also of the banks which employ them. For, as we shall see, even the country's biggest banks have grown largely by absorbing smaller, local institutions; the bigger banks have, in general, tried to avoid undue interference in the affairs of their – often merely nominal – subsidiaries; even when they set up their own branches, they have been only too happy to allow the managers to pursue their own inclinations, content to see the profits (or some of them, anyway) pile up for the parent.

For there is some ambiguity in the Swiss attitude towards their bankers: great respect may be accorded to the leaders of the industry, but, at a lower level, the profession is not treated as seriously as many others. Switzerland is a country devoted to the apprenticeship system, yet this was introduced to banking, at a federal level anyway, only during World War II, far later than to other industries or trades. Even now, there still seems to be a gulf between the well regarded chiefs in the banking business and the largely ignored Indians.

Yet the employees need more supervision than they get: 'they're like fighter pilots', said one amazed British banker of his Swiss subordinates, 'basically they're not bankers at all, they're business-getters. They'll come in and ask me to take a client off their hands because they've just spent an hour with him and not earned a penny of profit for the bank.'

All this may seem totally at odds with the traditional image of the Swiss banking community as composed of persons of the utmost sobriety, caution and respectability. The contrast derives largely from the ability of the Swiss to project their image of themselves over the years – an ability reinforced in the past by the absence of anything resembling critical financial journalism. Until recently, Swiss journalists have put their loyalty to their country and its institutions before their inquisitive instincts.

As we see in Chapter VII they are now far bolder and more independent in their enquiries but the pressures on them not to enquire too closely, not to say the unsayable, remain stronger in Switzerland than elsewhere because of the narrow and close knit nature of the society. As recently as 1979, the

Zurich paper *Tages Anzeiger* published an investigation into the influence of the automobile lobby. The country's car importers promptly and simultaneously withdrew their advertisements. Two years later the official Cartels Commission published a lengthy report on the affair but refused to rule on the importers' action.

Similar pressures in other countries have bred a whole school of irreverent journals – like the *Canard Enchaîné* in France, or *Private Eye* in Britain – systematically engaged in the debunking of accepted truths, the systematic listing of 'naked emperors'. There are no such publications in Switzerland. Until recently, the exceptions to the rule of blandness and discretion over the years have usually been politically inspired. As a result the Swiss have been able to brush aside any revelations – which were often very well founded – as being of Communist inspiration. Obviously they were, but this has not lessened their veracity.

Other traditions help to protect the image: the general refusal of Swiss legal authorities to worry too much when strangers lose their money; and the absence of any federal police force capable of coping with financial frauds, which are consequently left to the usually unqualified, and always overburdened, local examining magistrates.

A rare insight into this aspect of the problem was provided by a remarkably candid interview given in 1979 by Geneva's chief prosecutor, Raymond Foex, in which he touched on the sheer shortage of examining magistrates, the complexity of financial cases, and the consequent inevitable length of time required to bring them to trial (the occasion for the interview was the trial of Bernard Cornfeld of Investors Overseas Services' fame, *ten years* after his alleged offences had been committed). He also mentioned technical problems under Swiss law, particularly the inability of examining magistrates to abandon their enquiries if they feel they are not going to get worth-while results.

But the key as Raymond Foex saw it lay with the aggrieved parties: 'They often feel, in a rather confused fashion', he said, 'that they have something with which to reproach themselves, be it their naivety, their irresponsibility, or too over-developed a taste for easy profit. At the outset, they tend to picture the person who has deceived them in the blackest hues and to maximise the losses they have suffered. Little by little this attitude changes during the investigation. On one side, the work of the examining magistrate uncovers the errors which the wronged parties have themselves committed; as a result they get a clearer idea of the situation and begin to look for specific, if limited, ways of getting some of their money back.' The result, compromise, after which 'justice stands very alone'. M. Foex did not, however, mention the single factor which has done most to ensure that the many and varied errors and frauds committed by Swiss bankers over the decades have not, generally speaking, come to light: the embarrassment which clients feel at making any complaint about their bankers' conduct.

All these factors ensured that until the crises of the 1970s the image was intact, and the amazingly lax moral framework within which the bankers operated went largely unquestioned. One point which strikes foreign bankers very forcibly is that employees of even major Swiss banks managed their own financial affairs to suit their own, rather than their employers' interests. Elsewhere in the world, these are subject to the strictest supervision; not so in Switzerland. There was a classic court case in the early 1930s which, indirectly, helped to lead to the reinforcement of bank secrecy. A devious Basle banker, Rudolf Steffen, preferred to keep his personal financial affairs separate from his professional business. So he secretly opened an account with another bank, Wolfensberger and Widmer, in Zurich. Unfortunately, his personal bankers got into such severe trouble that they had to seek help from their bigger brethren. One was Steffen's employer, and he was promptly sacked. He sued for damages, basing his case on the alleged breach of banking secrecy, but lost.

This was not an isolated instance, but other employers were not generally as severe as Steffen's. In the 1950s a small Geneva bank specialised in the 'extramarital' financial affairs of employees of other banks. Unfortunately the bank, like Steffen's, got into such financial trouble that it, too, was absorbed by a larger institution, which then discovered the infidelities of its employees and those of other banks. They were not sacked.

Nor was the late Albert Nussbaumer, one of the greatest business-getters ever employed by the Swiss Bank Corporation. In the 1950s, the attention of speculators was largely concentrated on the 'penny mining stocks' on the Canadian stock exchanges, whose prices were temporarily boosted by the world's allegedly permanent shortage of uranium. Nussbaumer's secretary was fascinated by her employer's plunges into the market, so much so that she herself invested, and formed the habit of pestering the bank's dealers for up-to-date information. Her involvement came to the notice of one of her superiors and his comment, which could serve as a symbol for the whole Swiss banking community, was: 'Maybe Mr. Nussbaumer can cut corners in his Mercedes, but you must not follow on your moped.'

This cavalier attitude inevitably breeds a general mistrust, and more specifically has led to the famous system of 'numbered accounts' – in reality 'coded' accounts, known only by a code word and numbers. In Swiss mythology, these were introduced as part of the bankers' successful attempts to obstruct Nazi efforts to get at funds deposited by German Jews abroad. In fact the system is of much earlier origin. All bank accounts, in any country, have a number attached to them. The only difference with numbered accounts is that the connection between the name and the code is known only to a few trusted members of the bank's staff. This increases the security provided to the client. The practice clearly originates in the client's (and the bankers') fears that the secret might get out if the connection were known to the bank's auditors and everyone in the bank with access to the account.

In the demure words of a senior Swiss tax official, these accounts 'are simply an internal device of the banker to provide a more efficient protection of confidentiality with regard to infringements by subordinated employees'. The danger arises only if their employers assume that 'subordinated employees' are in the habit of using the information about the accounts for their own purposes, not only for espionage on behalf of foreign powers (the usual explanation) but also for simple blackmail. If the banks had any real confidence in their employees' discretion, then the system of numbered accounts would not be necessary. But they don't, so it is.

Even with the numbers system, lapses are possible. There was an important case in the mid-1960s involving Marcel Venat, a former cashier employed by the Basle branch of the Union Bank. He had been sacked in 1960 for unidentified indiscretions, and had teamed up with Ernest Schneider, a hairdresser whose salon was conveniently situated next to the UBS's office. Together they had gone to a group of German criminals and had engaged in systematic exploitation of the list of wealthy foreign clients whose names Venat had taken with him and who were prepared to pay heavily and regularly to avoid exposure. Although the bank admitted to only one case of leakage, clearly the blackmail was extensive. Eventually one of the victims complained, but the case came to light only because the French police authorities received a request from the Swiss police for the extradition of one of the Germans involved who had been living in Dunkirk for some years. The *Neue Zürcher Zeitung* described the case as 'one of the most painful ever undergone by our country and our banks', a clear demonstration of the link between the two in the Swiss mind.

Most of the evidence we possess as to the personal financial morality of Swiss bankers is inevitably both anonymous and anecdotal. But it is remarkable that virtually every non-Swiss banker who comes into contact with them can provide numerous anecdotes illustrating their greed and lack of conscience. If the bankers are investing in American stocks then they will not only be buying in advance of their clients, at a lower price, but will also be susceptible to bribery by the brokers or bankers bringing the stock to their attention. The story is told of a banker arranging finance for a major project in an African country who comes to the directors of the company borrowing the money and says simply: 'I don't really care about the rate of interest my bank will receive, but I have this old aunt and it would be nice if she could have some money to cheer her through the winter, say $300,000.' Such shivering and hungry relatives are the stuff of too many bankers' stories to be dismissed as apocryphal.

Curiously, the most famous single individual who was once a Swiss banker, corresponds to neither the image nor the reality of the type in general. He is Paul Erdman, who has used his banking experiences when writing a series of best-selling thrillers in which Swiss banks and bankers frequently figure.

His books inevitably reflect his career: a thesis on Swiss-American relations which earned him a doctorate at the University of Basle – not a usual honour for an American; and then a crowded few years as a banker in Switzerland. For four years he ran the Salik Bank (named after its major share-holder, a San Diego businessman called Charles Salik) which was so successful that control was bought by the United California Bank, the second largest in that state (Erdman also attracted as a small shareholder the author George Goodman, who invested in the bank some of the money he had made from his book *The Money Game*, written under the pseudonym Adam Smith).

Erdman's natural self-confidence was boosted by his suc-cess in correctly forecasting the timing and extent of the devaluation of sterling in November 1967. But the next year his bank, like almost everyone else, lost money on Wall Street, and (unlike most others) by speculating in silver. Then the next year it lost $50 million, a record for Swiss banks at the time, because of uncontrolled speculations in cocoa by the bank's chief commodity trader, Bernard Kummerli.

Erdman's downfall produced a fascinating rumour. It was widely and openly assumed, without any evidence, that the Salik Bank's massive speculation in cocoa, coming so soon after the UCB had taken control, was no coincidence, and that either Erdman or Kummerli or both had made personal fortunes at their new employers' expense. This notion reveals a great deal about how the Swiss banking community expects its members to behave.

Erdman was the total opposite of the usual Swiss banker. He actively courted the press to attract attention (and cus-tomers) – and received a rebuke from the Big Three for his insolence; he refunded out of the bank's assets some of the money his clients had lost through following his advice; above all, when the crash came, he did not keep quiet even from the prison cell, where he was consigned for several months (al-though he was never brought to trial on any specific charge).

Far from it. He gave interviews (including one to Ray Vicker of the *Wall Street Journal*, who persuaded the authorities into allowing him in to his cell because he was a client of the bank and therefore had rights denied to a mere journalist). And he immortalised the ideas he had formed of the Swiss by including them in his books. The picture of them that emerges is not a pretty one. The villain in his first book, *The Billion Dollar Killing*, Doctor Walter Hofer of the General Bank of Switzerland, is clearly (and libellously) named after Doctor Alfred Schaefer, for so long the presiding genius of the Union Bank of Switzerland, although there are no other resemblances between the two.

Erdman's second book, *The Silver Bears*, obviously sprang from his unfortunate experiences in the silver market – and the name of the Mafia-controlled bank at the heart of the book, the Banca Internazionale di Sicilia e America a Svizzera, is an equally clear echo of the many ethnic banks which sprouted so freely in Switzerland in the 1950s and 1960s.

Erdman's misfortunes – and his books – are significant because he has caught so well the double sidedness of the banking community, its ability to use Swiss official bodies to help it, as well as the bankers' automatic use of secret information primarily to personal rather than institutional advantage – not to mention the need for such profits to cover up the many and costly mistakes made by his characters and their originals.

6/ The first problems

Because of their international connections, Swiss banks had to endure all the crises which regularly interrupted the onward march of nineteenth-century capitalism. Inevitably, they also suffered growing pains in their first half century of existence.

But their specific diseases only erupted early in the twentieth century, after they had been deprived of one of their major *raisons d'être* – the issue of banknotes – at the same time as they lost their major industrial customers, the country's railways.

Switzerland started building railways later than other European countries; even when construction started, the local banks were new, and Switzerland was important as the 'turntable' of the European railway system, the bottleneck through which north/south traffic inevitably poured. The construction of the tunnel under the St. Gotthard Pass was probably the single most important step in the development of a 'European' railway system. Inevitably the country was naturally seen as a highly promising prospect for financial colonisation by French and German bankers. A nationalist reaction was inevitable: 'We should have no objection to Switzerland being called the turntable of international traffic, only we should like to turn it ourselves', was the attitude of one typical politician at the turn of the century.

Because the Swiss, like so many other people, had been seized by a sort of railway madness the problem of overweening foreign influence was compounded by over ambitious and uncontrolled construction. (The UBS's ancestor, the Bank of Winterthur, got into terrible trouble in the 1870s when, fired by local enthusiasm, it helped finance the city's attempt to construct an alternative railway system across northern Switzerland, avoiding most of its major cities, an ill-fated endeavour if ever there was one.) The battle between those campaigning for national control of the railways and their opponents led to appalling problems on the Swiss stock markets in the early 1890s, upsets which did nothing to dampen Swiss nationalist fervour.

Under these circumstances it is a tribute to natural Swiss conservatism (and the power of the foreign-controlled railway promoters) that the voters turned down the first proposal submitted to them to nationalise their railway system. But a second referendum in 1898 produced an overwhelming majority in favour. In the previous year, the general attitude had been summed up in a message from the country's Federal Council, its seven-man cabinet: 'given that the ownership of our major means of communication is mostly in foreign hands, and given that foreign influence dominates in the railways' boardrooms, given that it is major foreign capitalists, together with some native-born bankers linked to them by every sort of interest and more or less dependent on them, who decide the fate of our most important railways, all this adds up to a state of affairs which is profoundly humiliating for Switzerland.'

Railway nationalisation was only one of a number of measures which together added up to an informal compact between the Swiss people and its banking community. The government allowed the introduction of the *Raiffeisen* movement and encouraged the cantonal banks, while at the same time the federal post office assumed responsibility for the clearing of domestic payments. It was made abundantly clear that the Swiss people would not tolerate the use of its banking system as a means of subverting the country's independence and control of what they generally perceived were its vital interests.

In return the banks were allowed the same freedom as other interest groups. Until 1934 they had no specific legislation devoted to them: they simply operated within a legal framework designed to regulate all sorts of commercial and industrial activities. And even when a Swiss National Bank was finally established in 1907, it steered clear of any attempt to supervise the banking system apart from the collection of statistics, an extremely sketchy business until the 1934 Banking Act.

Initially, the Swiss National Bank's major function was to provide the country with a single, unified, banknote issue. Until 1907, no fewer than thirty-six different banks had been allowed to issue their own notes and had not even required a licence to do so until 1883. The SNB has always been a different kind of central bank. At the time institutions like the Bank of England or the Banque de France were owned either entirely by private shareholders or partly by the central government, whereas the majority of shares in the SNB were held by the cantonal governments, with private shareholders owning a minority stake.

The bank's 'Swissness' extended to its structure – a three-man directorate, a Board (*Bankausschuss*) composed of influential bankers, which advised but did not control the directors (appointed by the Federal government) and a wider *Bankrat*, a forty-man bank council, twenty-five of whose members were appointed by the government. This nice balance of interests reminded Jonathan Steinberg irresistibly of a *gemeinde* – albeit one with citizenship restricted to directors of world-scale industrial companies. Nevertheless, he insisted, 'it would be hard to run the discussions in the *Bankausschuss* on lines other than those of the local *gemeinde*, especially if the members use *Schwyzerdütsch* at any time. The language naturally evokes the spirit of the *gemeinde*, the home and hearth.'

The nationalisation of the railways, far and away the most capital-intensive industry in any country at the time, released very large sums of money, far larger than could be absorbed by any other domestic borrowers. So the Swiss banks vastly accelerated their foreign lendings. These were further increased by the country's new prosperity – it was reckoned one of the richest, if not the richest, country in Europe. According to the official history of Crédit Suisse: 'between 1895 and 1906 the operations of financial consortia embraced 121 Swiss loans and around 250 foreign offerings, as well as large numbers of share issues. American railway stocks were amongst the most important issues. Subsequently a whole series of bonds issued by foreign governments were placed in Switzerland, especially those from Austro-Hungary, the German Reich, Turkey, the Balkan countries, and Russia. After its victory over the Tsarist Empire Japan, too, could issue loans on the European capital market. Finally, many issues from Central and South America were underwritten [*mises en recouvrement*] by the French and Swiss clientele of the Crédit Suisse.'

With these loans the Swiss banks returned to an old tradition, albeit on a world-wide, rather than a European, scale. But there was a new and vital difference. In the century between the 'thirty maidens of Geneva' and the nationalisation of the Swiss railways, Swiss financial institutions had lost the initiative. In general – and this has been true ever since – they have not managed the loans to which they, and more particularly their clients, were so often the largest subscribers. Yet they were enormous investors, and made a great deal of money – including a handy profit because foreign loans almost invariably earned more interest than the loans issued by Swiss public authorities to which foreigners were such eager subscribers. By 1914 the country had invested more than 6 billion francs abroad; and although this was less per head than the figure for Great Britain, the bulk of the latter's investments were concentrated in its empire (and a great chunk of the rest had to be sold off to pay the cost of the war).

Although every kind of bank participated in these loans – even the mortgage banks had two-fifths of their investments abroad, largely in Germany where interest rates were a half to three-quarters per cent higher than at home – most of the loans concerned only the big banks and the private banks. And if these two categories flourished, it was largely at the expense of dozens of other banks.

The crucial date for the change was 1905, when the Swiss agreed to concentrate banknote issue in the new National Bank, although the changeover was not completed until 1910. The unification placed a question mark on the function of many other banks that had relied for much of their business on issuing their own bank notes. They had to choose whether to liquidate, to merge with bigger institutions, or to go it alone, which generally implied expansion into hitherto unexplored areas of activity. The varied results of their decisions can be seen from the endless lists of banks which either changed their status, merged with others, or were simply liquidated in the first two decades of the twentieth century.

A steady stream of smaller banks sought the shelter of merger with the big banks, which benefited most from the transformation, and whose growth in the subsequent fifty years came very largely from takeovers of local banks. Almost all of them made their first moves outside their native cities in the years after 1905, usually through merger but sometimes by opening a branch (significantly, the first opened by the Swiss Bank Corporation had been in London in 1898). But it was able to take advantage of the troubles of its sister-bank, the Zürcher Bankverein, to absorb it completely. The Bank of Winterthur took over the Zurich branch of the Bank of Baden; and the Crédit Suisse opened six offices outside Geneva within eight years (even then, it had seven branches in its native city, more than in the rest of the country put together). This was typical – it was only after a couple of takeovers at the end of World War I that the Swiss Bank Corporation had half a dozen branches outside Basle.

The troubles of the smaller banks cannot be blamed on the upheavals produced by World War I. At the outbreak of the war the banks did indeed panic, and virtually all of them shut their offices, pleading that they could not afford to allow any cash outflow – an excuse which found a poor response from the Swiss themselves. And of course the interruption in the flow of dividends, the defaults on bonds, did create problems – the venerable Bank Leu had to be reorganised with help from the SBC because of losses incurred during the war. Contemporary observers had no hesitation in pinning the blame firmly on the banks and bankers involved, and on the fact that they were almost totally uncontrolled either by their directors, by their auditors or by the Federal or cantonal governments.

The disasters were numerous: in the four years before World War I, 50 out of the country's 300 or so banks disappeared through one cause or another. In 45 cases analysed by one expert, 17 went bankrupt, 20 were liquidated, 5 were refinanced, and 2 were taken over. Losses totalled more than 112 million francs, more than the total capital and reserves of the SBC, Switzerland's largest bank. The losses were roughly equally divided between creditors and the banks' loan and stock holders. Although the disasters were spread throughout the country, they were felt worst in the Italian-speaking canton of Ticino, where there was panic in early 1914: over 25 million francs had been lost on loans to Italian concerns and a further 17 million on local advances.

The sheer lack of external constraints on bank directors was pithily analysed in the report of the cantonal Bank of Berne for 1910:

> One can see in the small banks, and above all in the rural savings banks that the manager, or director, as he now pleases to call himself, is almost totally the absolute ruler in his domain. To be sure, he has at his side a board of directors made up of men who are completely honest,

capable and well respected, but they know virtually nothing about the conduct of the bank except what the director sees fit to communicate to them, and if the latter is persuasive and well-endowed with a good dose of self-confidence, he will bedazzle his listeners with high-flown phrases, invoking apparently sound technical reasons for his actions, so much so that none of his assistants dare interrupt so apparently competent a fellow, even when a detail seems wrong to them.

So if, as is by no means rare, the director is seized with ambition and dreams of transforming his modest savings bank into a local bank, and then into a fully-fledged commercial institution, why, then, disaster is at hand. Swept on by the desire for growth, he plunges into business circles with which he is not acquainted and which he can neither handle nor abandon. He produces continually growing deficits, which are carefully hidden until the day when, to general stupefaction, some form of crash brings them out into the light of day.

The pattern described so eloquently here has been followed by all manner of banks. The reasons for the disasters between 1910 and 1914 were many and various, but they all stemmed from the type of ignorance and over-confidence described by the Bernese. The Zürcher Bankverein, part of the SBC, for instance, was over eager to lend to property speculators who had assumed that the city's boundaries were to be extended and were building up their landholdings just outside the city limits. In many cases there was an appalling imbalance, with short-term borrowings being used to finance mortgage and other long-term obligations; risks were over-concentrated (at the Savings and Loan Bank of Eschlikon nearly half the loans outstanding were owed by one borrower, and two-thirds of the money owed to the People's Bank of Bienne was due from exactly three clients). Banks could call themselves virtually anything they liked and then actively solicit deposits. One purely local investment house, without any capital backing, was registered in Geneva under the grandiose name of the Swiss Savings Bank and promptly bombarded German-speaking Switzerland with invitations to deposit money.

If the board of directors and staff could not control an over-ambitious manager, neither could the auditors. There was a determined effort in these years to establish independent auditing companies, but these were often owned by banks, and even when they did notice something wrong, they could too easily be overridden. The auditors of the Industrial Bank of Kloten, for instance, put forward a report in which they set out a number of abuses and refused to sign the accounts. The directors simply refused to read their report to the annual general meeting and the auditors did not have the courage to take the matter further. Precisely the same thing happened when the auditors queried the accounts of the Savings and Loan Bank of Steckborn. They were not read out (there was no need in those days to produce written balance sheets) and the auditors kept quiet.

The Swiss banks' problems were compounded by a general lack of liquid assets. In the years before World War I British banks had 86 per cent of their liabilities covered by liquid funds and German banks had a 51 per cent coverage; the figure for Swiss banks varied from 35 per cent for the major banks down to a mere 3 per cent for the savings banks (even the cantonal banks, with their very varied business, were only 15 per cent liquid). No wonder the banks panicked at the outbreak of war.

Switzerland was not alone in having its problems. But whereas in Germany they led to a searching enquiry and a completely new framework of bank regulation, in Switzerland the only result was a series of enquiries. One carried a foreword by Dr. Gottlieb Bachmann, a professor at the University of Zurich, who went on to become general manager of the Swiss National Bank. In 1918 he thundered that: 'the vast majority of the mistakes are offences against the commonsense principles of banking, arising from incompetence, inexperience, lack of judgment, also out of selfishness and weakness of character, coupled with a frightening negligence on the part of the supervisory bodies and incomprehensible carelessness on the part of the wider circle of parties with interests in the banking institutions concerned'. He assumed that the result of the investigations would be a new banking law. Indeed Professor Jules Landmann of the University of Basle had drafted one, emphasizing the need for strict supervision by the auditors, who would act as the eyes and ears of the regulatory authorities. His proposals were even published by the Federal Department of the Economy in 1916 – two years before Professor Bachmann's commentary. But once the memory of the crises had dimmed in the glow of post war prosperity, the idea of bank reform faded with it. Professor Landmann went to live abroad, to die in exile in 1931. His ideas were resurrected and enacted only after his death, in the face of a crisis much more general than that of 1910–14, involving every major bank, and not only a horde of smaller institutions. The crisis of the 1930s produced not only a regulatory framework for Switzerland's distressed financial institutions, but also legal sanctions to back the country's tradition of banking secrecy. These provided foreigners with the protection they required – and the Swiss with a legend of national selflessness which has served them faithfully ever since.

PART TWO

The Swiss and the Nazis

1 / The myth

A cardinal myth about Swiss banks is that the protection they provide their clients, the secrecy with which their affairs are shrouded, results from a generous Swiss gesture: that when Nazi agents came searching for funds which had been deposited in Switzerland by German Jews, the Swiss rallied round the persecuted minority and rushed through a special provision to prevent bankers and their employees from co-operating with the Nazi efforts. The idea is exceedingly widespread. People who are otherwise totally ignorant of the history of Swiss banks are aware of the story. Yet it is simply not true.

Students of myths could do worse than study this particular example of the genre, for it seems to combine all the requisite qualities. It has been accepted without question through the years even by those most hostile to the people, the institutions (and the dubious practices) it has surrounded with its benevolent glow. It has provided the beleaguered Swiss with a rallying point, a flag of morality which they could wrap securely round themselves when they were accused of harbouring criminals of every nationality and description, and of facilitating their nefarious activities.

Yet its acceptance depends on a total lack of historical curiosity. Many Swiss bankers must be at least subconsciously aware that the story jars with known habits and known facts, that it dissolves into nothing at the first touch of historical enquiry, and that the truth is reasonably accessible, very obvious and, even though more entertaining than the myth, a good deal less flattering to the Swiss. But it was simply too important to the banks' – and the country's – standing in the world to be questioned or investigated.

The importance of this myth and its moral implications cannot be exaggerated: for the other two weapons which the

49

Swiss have used to repel inquisitive outsiders (the laws that make tax evasion a civil, not a criminal matter, and the one governing commercial confidentiality) are merely peculiarities of the country's legal system. The moral force the Swiss have been able to summon when confronted by outside criticism has rested completely on their supposed fortitude in the face of the Nazi hordes and because its origins have never been questioned, the Swiss have retained the moral initiative.

When, for instance, a team of American negotiators descended on Berne in the late 1960s to negotiate a new tax treaty, their opposite numbers started the proceedings every day with a lecture on the sanctity of Swiss banking secrecy and its sacred origins (the Americans, mostly hardened lawyers, became so weary of this lengthy and oft-repeated litany that they lodged an official complaint). The myth, so fervently believed, so often repeated, has convinced even the most implacable opponents of the Swiss, their banks and their practices. When Congressman Wright Patman was introducing a bill aimed specifically at the Swiss banks, he still felt obliged to pay obeisance: 'their current secrecy laws are a direct outgrowth of some horrible German Gestapo activities in that country shortly before the outbreak of World War II'.

The point at the bottom of this inverted pyramid of myth and legend is both small and unpretentious, consisting simply of Clause 47(b) of Switzerland's 1934 Banking Act. This sub-clause is buried in a section of the Act which sets out the pains and penalties to which those involved in banking could be liable. It provides simply that any bank director or employee or anyone involved in auditing or controlling banks who 'violates the discretion which he is bound to observe by virtue of the law on professional secrets' may be fined up to 20,000 francs or imprisoned for up to six months. As simple as that.

Despite its modesty and unobtrusiveness the sub-clause was of crucial importance. It reinforced the native tendency to discretion: and it provided foreign clients with a comforting feeling that the Swiss cared enough about secrecy to punish anyone caught violating the law. 'They don't have so much confidence in the banks of other countries maintaining bank secrecy as they do in the Swiss banks' was Robert Morgenthau's opinion. Banking secrecy is normal enough, and countries as respectable as Canada and Belgium include bankers among the professional classes whose discretion is legally protected, but Swiss law is almost unique in providing for criminal punishment for bankers who violate professional secrecy. (The only other example seems to have been Clause 544 of the penal code of Tsarist Russia, which provided condign punishment for the same offence, but numbered accounts in St. Petersburg are merely a fading memory, leaving the Swiss in sole possession of the field.)

Yet, despite the unique importance of the sub-clause, there has, until now, been no historically authenticated account of its origin. This is not because the subject of Swiss bank secrecy has been neglected. Far from it. There is an immense literature on the subject.*

The most detailed account is contained in an entertaining book by the news editor (and former economic director) of the *Tribune de Genève*, Jean-Marie Laya, *L'Argent secret et les Banques Suisses*. Laya's account was based not on documentary evidence, but on the story as told to him by the last surviving member of the 1934 Committee of the Swiss Bankers' Association. According to Laya's account the SBA was primarily responsible for introducing the clause. Laya's informant has since died, but the direct connection he provided with the alleged events of 1933–4 makes his account the most legitimate form taken by the legend.

Laya's account tells how a commando of Nazis led by an obscure former bank employee who called himself Heinrich Meinhardt infiltrated into Swiss banks in the early summer of 1933. They slipped easily enough into Switzerland because they did not carry incriminating papers. But the German consulate in Zurich provided them with full documentation provided by the *Ausland Organisation*, the foreign section of the Nazi party, and the *Volksdeutsche Mittelstelle*, the department

* This is most completely set out in the twenty-page bibliography which concludes the authoritative study of the legal implications of bank secrecy by Dr. Maurice Aubert, Jean-Philippe Kernen and Herbert Schönle. Not even Dr. Aubert can point to any direct evidence of the alleged Hitlerian origins of Clause 47(b) – though he, too, adheres to the generally accepted story.

of the SS charged with the surveillance of émigrés.

Meinhardt's men contacted a number of banks which, they had been told, employed Nazi sympathisers, and established themselves as businessmen with active accounts. They then started to worm out of their bankers details of accounts held by other Germans, who thereby contravened a new law which prescribed the death penalty for holders of undeclared assets abroad. The work was, allegedly, easier than foreseen and speeded by the judicious seduction of key female bank employees.

Swiss banks were soon confronted by a series of mysterious requests from their German Jewish clients to transfer their funds back into a Germany rapidly becoming more hostile to their race. Even more puzzlingly, these requests were generally made, not by the account-holder himself, but by another person in Germany holding a legal power of attorney. Although, on the face of it, these authorisations were perfectly valid, they nevertheless aroused the bankers' suspicions. As a result the Swiss Bankers' Association introduced the system of numbered accounts to which no names were attached; only a few senior officials in any bank would know the name that went with the number.

Now came a second wave. German Jewish clients appeared at the bank in person requesting the withdrawal of their funds but they were invariably accompanied by 'minders', who never left them. As a result Robert La Roche, a Basle private banker who was the chairman of the Association, and his colleagues set a trap: they leaked details of a non-existent German Jewish account. In short order a duly-authenticated request arrived from Germany to withdraw the funds from the account. Armed with this proof, the bankers inserted the now-famous clause making disclosure of banking details a crime, into the Banking Act, then wending its way through the Swiss legislature.

This account contains a number of minor flaws – the death penalty for possession of foreign assets was introduced only in December 1936, for instance. More crucially, this account, like all the other traditional explanations, is based on a number of highly improbable suppositions: that Nazi agents could have got to work (and thus have been discovered) in

time to affect the formulation of Clause 47(b); that rich
German Jews had deposited a great proportion of their funds
abroad; that Swiss bankers were sufficiently awake to the Nazi
menace to help Jewish clients; and that the relevant Swiss
political machinery would have been receptive to their
demands. For there is no contemporary documentary evidence to support these suppositions; the Swiss Bankers'
Association has no records of the episode, and its present
director has an open mind on the subject; nor do we know how
many German Jews had opened Swiss bank accounts,
although the evidence suggests that the German Jewish
community had not in general prepared itself for an assault in
which it could not believe until too late.

The Swiss – like so many other non-Germans – have never
been over-anxious to explore their attitude to Jewish refugees
in the 1930s and 1940s, although after the war the Swiss did at
least commission an investigation on their treatment of the
Jews and publish the results in the late 1950s. The *Ludwig
Report*, as it was called after its author, provoked an agonising
reappraisal of Swiss attitudes at the time. For Ludwig confirmed that the Swiss – like everyone else in Europe – behaved
with a notable lack of generosity towards Jewish refugees from
the very start.

In the nineteenth century the Swiss had been the last people
in Western Europe to place the Jews on an equal footing with
the rest of the population. There was a strong strand of
anti-semitism within Switzerland, encouraged by the Germans through a number of quasi-Nazi parties, called 'fronts';
there was an almost unlimited number of Jews who, if
encouraged, would flock to Switzerland – a problem which
expanded enormously after 1940 but which had been a threat
since 1933. Yet the Swiss also inherited an obligation,
enshrined in a resolution dating from the nineteenth century,
to provide a shelter for political refugees (a provision used by
Lenin among many others). The moral obligation of the Swiss
to help Jews escaping from Nazism was evaded with some
ease. In the words of Professor Edgar Bonjour, the official
historian of Swiss neutrality, 'The Swiss interpreted this
resolution with pedantic literalness so as to deny the right to
Jewish refugees from Hitler, on the grounds that they were

being persecuted on racial grounds rather than for any political activity'.

The most striking evidence regarding anti-semitism in official, rather than merely neo-Nazi, Swiss circles at the time comes from the text of an Immigration Law of 5 May 1933, and edited by Dr. M. Ruth, a senior official of the Justice and Police Department, in which he talks about the 'assimilability' of the immigrant to Switzerland. He claimed that he did not wish to evade the Jewish question, on which 'he can only express his personal opinion', as follows:

'I regard anti-semitism as a barbarism unworthy of the true Swiss ... many Jews are good Swiss citizens but there are other factors apart from humanitarian grounds to consider ... It is an undeniable fact that many Jews are not easily assimilable, especially those coming from Eastern countries. A certain incapacity to conform must not deceive us in this matter.' It was presumably in this spirit that the authorities at the time interpreted the instructions issued by the Federal Justice and Police Department on 31 March 1933: 'Jews who are caused to emigrate by events in Germany should not be refused temporary residence in Switzerland in these times of trouble for them, but that because of the over-population by foreigners here the maximum heed must be paid to this immigration.'

In this atmosphere it was highly unlikely that the Federal Finance Minister, whoever he might be, would have been prepared to help. In fact the Finance Minister at the time, J-L. Musy, was a devout, reactionary Catholic and an anti-Communist so fanatical that later in the decade he went to Germany to produce a film on *La Peste Rouge* – The Red Plague.

Suspiciously, the traditional accounts bear every sign of retrospective reconstruction. They predicate that a Nazi mechanism (or mechanisms) for banking espionage sprang into action ready-made as soon as Hitler came to power in early 1933. They also assume that the Nazis had immediately decided to conduct active propagandising and associated covert activities in Switzerland.

Yet all the evidence suggests that in their first year in office, the Nazis concentrated on repressing the internal opposition to their power. In the words of Edward Crankshaw's history of the Gestapo*: 'the Prussian Gestapo in the first year of its existence was, in effect, little more than Goering's personal terror squad ... it was only when Himmler came to Berlin [in April 1934] that the Gestapo developed into the well-loathed machine we know it to have been'.** A similar picture emerges in respect of other institutions.

It took Himmler a full year to seize control of all the country's separate police forces and, until June 1934, the energies of the SS and the Gestapo were almost exclusively devoted to the final destruction of Captain Roehm and his rival army, the brown-shirted SA. Similarly there was considerable debate within the Nazi government as to the proper attitude to take towards Switzerland, and we find Müller, the German minister in Berne, writing to his masters in July 1933 that 'any undercover police work or activity by secret services in the political or economic sphere in Switzerland' would 'effectively poison relations with Switzerland, as would any overt collaboration with the fronts'. (Secrecy would, in Müller's opinion, be impossible, since Switzerland was such a small country that everybody knew everyone else's business.) He was clearly involved in a bureaucratic battle against more activist elements in the Party, which he lost, but not in time to affect the formulation of Clause 47(b). For it was only six months later, on 15 January 1934, that an order was issued by Goering to the Gestapo and the frontier police to make a note of political émigrés and Jews living in neighbouring countries and to try and kidnap them.

The evolution of Nazi attitudes during 1933–4 did eventually result in the sort of covert activities described by Laya and others, but this was well after the formulation of Clause 47(b). For the Swiss legislators had put up the barriers before

* Putnam, 1956.
** Crankshaw also refers to 'the almost complete destruction of the Gestapo archives' and both this reference and his chronology cast a decidedly dubious light on one of the most frequently quoted sources of the origin of bank secrecy Theodore Reed Fehrenbach's book, *The Gnomes of Zurich*, in which the author claims to have found the facts in the supposedly abundant archives bequeathed to us by the Gestapo – without, however, providing any further guidance as to where these could be found, or any references to specific documents.

the Nazis were ready to attack them. As we have already seen, the first proposals to provide a framework for banking control date back to 1916. The first draft of the 1934 Banking Act is dated 17 February 1933, only eighteen days after Hitler came to power. In Section 10 of the Act, sanctions against employees giving information to third parties are already envisaged: and by the time the Federal government sent the Bill to the two houses of the Swiss legislature at the beginning of February 1934 the exact words which were to become Clause 47 were in place (as Clause 26). Most of the government's proposals were taken apart and reconstructed by Parliament in the course of 1934. One of the few exceptions was Clause 26. It was simply renumbered to accommodate the numerous clauses added to the Bill in the legislature.

So, if it was highly improbable that Swiss bankers would go out of their way to defend Jewish clients, and even more unlikely that officialdom would have helped them, their efforts would have been pointless in any case: the proposed law already contained effective provisions against the violation of bank secrecy. These proved useful later – though even this part of the legend seems greatly exaggerated – but they were certainly placed there for other reasons, with other cases in mind. To find out what they were – and indeed to explain a great deal of subsequent Swiss behaviour to foreign regulatory authorities – it is necessary to tell the full story of the crisis which led up to the 1934 Banking Act as well as the narrower circumstances which resulted in the inclusion of Clause 47(b).

2 / The grim reality

For Anglo-Saxons the Wall Street crash of October 1929 is usually taken as the harbinger of the Great Depression of the 1930s. For Swiss banks, as well as for those of Central

Europe, the starting point comes nearly two years later. In March 1931, the credit of Austrian banks was severely shaken by the announcement of a proposed customs union with Germany, then the 'sick man of Europe'. Funds were withdrawn so precipitately and on such a scale that on May 11 Austria's leading bank, the Credit-Anstalt, collapsed. For Switzerland, this crash set off five painful years for the whole banking community.

When the dust finally settled in the late 1930s only two of the country's eight major commercial banks (Crédit Suisse and the Swiss Bank Corporation) had survived without having submitted to some form of capital reconstruction. One major bank – the Comptoir d'Escompte de Genève – had collapsed completely, taking with it two other Geneva based financial institutions. Their fall signalled the end of Geneva's historic role as a major international banking centre, since the city no longer contained the headquarters of any major bank. In the rest of Switzerland five other major banks had to submit to severe capital reductions and three required substantial help from federal funds. One of the most ambitious, the co-operative Swiss Volksbank, which at the end of 1930 had boasted the largest balance sheet of them all, was pruned so ruthlessly that nearly half a century elapsed before it ventured back into the international arena. The share of Swiss banking enjoyed by the eight biggest commercial banks tumbled: where in 1930 they had forty per cent of the total funds of the country's banks, twice the figure for all the cantonal banks combined, five years later the position had been completely reversed. The total balance sheets of the major banks had shrunk by over two-fifths, they had had to write off losses amounting to over 300 million francs, and their profits had almost disappeared.

In general the deeper the dependence on foreign business, the greater were the problems (which is why Geneva, the most international of all, was so badly affected). So it was not surprising that the cantonal banks, operating entirely within Switzerland, remained generally prosperous throughout the earlier years of the crisis. Yet before the end of the dismal 1930s two major cantonal banks (in Berne and the Grisons) had been forced to face financial reorganisation.

The general crisis, however, had started in 1931, soon after the fall of the Credit-Anstalt. The first domino to fall two months later was a Berlin bank, Darmstadt und National, largely brought down by the collapse of the Nordwolle wool textile group. Within a month mistrust of banks in Germany had become so general that on July 13 the government was forced to declare a banking moratorium, close the stock exchanges, and introduce foreign exchange controls. A few months later an international 'standstill agreement' blocked foreign owned balances in German institutions, initially for only six months but it was succeeded by eight others before the outbreak of World War II. During that time, repatriation of foreign capital became slowly possible, but only through a special instrument, Register or Travel Marks. Because these could be employed for only a limited range of purposes, they stood at a discount to ordinary marks.

The longer a bank waited to redeem its debts, the worse the situation: the discount, a mere 15 per cent in early 1933, had widened to 66 per cent by February 1939 – for every year a bank waited, it lost 10 per cent of its funds.

Of all the German banks' creditors, the Swiss were the worst hit. At the end of 1929 Swiss institutions owned 3.2 billion francs of foreign securities; and although some prudent banks reduced their commitments in 1930, the Standstill Agreement revealed that tiny Switzerland held a full sixteen per cent of all the credits accorded to Germany.

Swiss banks had advanced a far greater proportion of their funds to Germany than had comparable institutions elsewhere; moreover their investments proved particularly unstable. In the 1920s the country had resumed its pre-war role as a financial entrepôt, participating very actively in international issues, trawling all over Europe for customers. Moreover the fear of bolshevism led to a renewed German interest in the possession of accounts in Switzerland. Inevitably the banks had a great deal of their money tied up in countries – not only Germany but others in Central Europe which were forced to follow the German example – where it was both blocked and steadily losing its value. The figures were startling. At the end of 1934 after many of the assets had been liquidated the seven remaining major Swiss banks had nearly a fifth of their total assets tied up in German and other blocked accounts, a sum larger than their total capital. At the same time foreign depositors in Switzerland – who were free to withdraw their funds – became increasingly anxious about the safety of their money.

These external factors were enough to worry even the most cautious Swiss bank. But an additional element was injected by the extreme imprudence, edging over into fraudulence, with which some of them had operated in the heady days of the late 1920s, none more so than the first victim of the German crash, the Banque de Genève. It was a smaller institution than the three which were to collapse later, important mainly because the city of Geneva owned nearly a third of its capital. For years a select band of the city's leading citizens, led by Alexandre Moriaud, the head of the city's financial department, had used the bank for their own purposes. The problems had started in the late 1920s when the City agreed to subscribe to a capital issue by the bank on inadequate information, despite dire warnings from the flamboyant Léon Nicole, leader of the Socialist group in the Council, and an outstanding polemical journalist.

The bank proved itself an easy touch for suspect, if well connected, local businessmen. But its principal mistake came in 1929 when it became involved with a shady Parisian 'inventor', Ferdinand Gros, who had already been bailed out by the French central bank, the Banque de France, because his unsuccessful speculations involved so many important political figures. Nevertheless, a local councillor (who was well rewarded for his efforts) introduced him to Moriaud, who was appointed to the board of Gros's holding company and ensured that the Banque de Genève invested heavily in his dubious industrial schemes. In February 1931 these had to be moved out of the limelight by being concentrated in a separate holding company (a tactic often employed by banks at the time to hide their unsuccessful industrial investments).

Although the bank was not directly involved in Austria or Germany, its situation was so precarious that it could not survive the run that was made on any bank with foreign connections, inevitable once the German banking moratorium had been declared in mid-June. At a hastily convened conference in Berne, at which Moriaud had pleaded for help from his friend, the Finance Minister, J-L. Musy, the government offered a loan at four per cent, by no means a preferential rate, provided that other local banks and the Geneva City Council would accept their share of the risk. The real rush to withdraw deposits – which resulted in the immediate closure of the bank – started the next day. But, inspired by Nicole's oratory, the upper house of the legislature refused the credit and the rescue plan fell through. So the bank was doomed and was duly put into liquidation.

The Bank of Geneva's total balance sheet was under 100 million francs but its troubles inevitably led to a run on its much bigger privately owned neighbour, the Comptoir d'Escompte, and by the end of July 1931 it was clear that its problems ran deeper than a mere shortage of cash. The attempt to save it not only cost the Federal government and the Swiss banking community a good deal of money, it also dragged down with it two originally much sounder institutions, the Union Financière (the city's leading investment trust) and the Banque de Dépôts et de Crédit. The three were formed into a bank holding company, but the Comptoir's problems ruined all three – and with them Geneva's position as a financial centre. Even more crucially, the crash led directly to the 1934 Banking Act.

The Comptoir was a relative newcomer to large scale banking. Founded as early as 1855, for the first twenty-five years of its existence it had concentrated on financing the watch trade and as late as 1916 was not counted as a major bank. It started to fulfil its ambition to be the leading bank for French Switzerland only at the end of World War I, a decade after the invasion of banks from German-speaking Switzerland. But within a few years the Comptoir, or the Banque à Genève – *The* Bank in Geneva, as it termed itself in its history, issued proudly just before the onset of its terminal illness – more than compensated for its late start. It opened branches and absorbed local banks throughout French-speaking Switzerland, as well as in Basle and Zurich.

But the Comptoir had invested extremely unwisely, with a great part of its funds tied up in Central and Eastern Europe, in countries which were among the first to follow Germany in blocking external payments. So the first loan (of 15 million francs) made to the Comptoir by its fellow major banks in mid-August 1932 was soon exhausted. The panic merger the following month with the Union Financière was counter-productive: the Union could bring to the hard-pressed Comptoir neither the cash which it needed so urgently, nor any securities which could be realised for more than a fraction of their book value. At the end of October the commercial banks made a further loan and this time Federal pressure ensured that the cantonal banks rallied round; until then they had followed the public's example and had been reducing their commitments to the Comptoir.

As the situation deteriorated during 1932 the federal authorities had resurrected the Federal Loan Board Fund (Caisse de Prêts de la Confédération) seemingly solely to deal with the Comptoir's problems. In November and December the Comptoir suffered another severe run, set off by rumours that it, like the Basler Handelsbank, was in trouble with the French tax authorities (no ordinary problem, as we shall see). By the end of the year the Comptoir had exhausted all its cash resources and was in a critical state. At that point a revolutionary rescue plan was evolved: a new class of capital was to be created to which the Federal government would subscribe in order to persuade the country's banks to increase their committment to the Comptoir. This partial nationalisation was put forward by Musy (to the bankers if not to the public) as an alternative to the long overdue creation of a special legal framework for the banking community.

When the outline of a new banking law started to emerge early in 1933 the banks felt that Musy had broken his promise but by this time legislation had become inevitable. Although the Federal government had avoided referring its loans to the Bank of Geneva to the legislature, its involvement with the Comptoir was so deep that unfettered executive action was no longer possible. There had been sporadic demands for legislation since 1931, linked to pressure for reduced interest rates (which, like the export of capital by the banks, were a favourite bugbear of the powerful rural cantons) or, from the Socialists, to a demand for bank nationalisation. But the legislation which began early in 1933 as a narrow measure designed to help in cases like that of the Comptoir became a much broader affair within a year under the pressure of public and parliamentary opinion. The government's aid to the Comptoir received only grudging parliamentary approval at the end of May, arousing some opposition and a great many abstentions among the ruling majority.

The rest of 1933 was spent in the consultations inevitable in the formulation of any piece of Swiss legislation. After two committees – both of which included bankers – had revised the projected law, it was sent to Parliament at the beginning of February 1934. But such was public interest that it was raked over and extensively modified in both houses before it finally became law in November 1934.

The two years which elapsed between the plan for partial nationalisation and the final passage of the Act were dreadful ones for the Swiss banks. During 1934 it was not only the banks which had invested too heavily in Germany and Eastern Europe which suffered. The devaluation of sterling in October 1931 stopped an inflow of capital which had kept the Swiss economy surprisingly buoyant for two years. Although Switzerland's economic difficulties had started after the Wall Street crash and both exports and employment had suffered, yet it was only in 1932 that the situation became critical.

Under these conditions the Banking Act bore every sign of being a series of compromises, born out of a series of panics, themselves resulting from a series of specific problems. Even under the pressure of events the Federal government was not prepared to be directly involved in inspecting the banks' accounts, a task which was still delegated to the (supposedly independent) bank auditors; any federal supervision would be at one remove.

The new Banking Commission was authorised to supervise only the banks' auditors, rather than the banks themselves (an ungrateful task which both the Swiss National Bank and the Federal government had refused to perform). The Commission's direct powers were decidedly limited. Even forty-five years later, when Dr. M. Magdalena Schoch was giving evidence on the subject to the U.S. Senate, she could assert that 'no charter or license is required for establishing a bank. The Commission does not decide whether the basic capital is adequate; it must merely examine whether the proposed bank has a proper internal organisation'. She could have added that, because of the prevalence of 'bearer' shares*, even the ownership of banks was often obscure. There were to be five members of the Banking Commission. They were not supposed to be directly involved in banking yet had, legally, to be banking experts; the result was that for forty years the Commission was effectively dominated by former employees of the major banks, who alone had the requisite knowledge.

Many of the other provisions were so elementary that it seemed surprising that Swiss banking had managed for so long without them. Even so, bankers denounced them as constituting an intolerable intrusion on financial liberties. Yet provisions like the requirement to file annual accounts to the National Bank (quarterly statements in the case of major banks) or to maintain 'appropriate' liquidity and capital ratios (no figures specified) were designed merely to ensure that the whole financial community conformed to habits already prevailing amongst the country's more responsible banks.

Nor were the National Bank's powers greatly strengthened: even after the Act it was unable to counter the growing effects of the Depression by buying up government bonds to release funds for investment elsewhere in the economy. Major banks did, however, have to inform it in advance if they intended to increase their interest rates and the Bank had the legal duty to try and prevent them. More real was the power to veto foreign loans of any size if they were thought contrary to the national economic interest, a clear case of shutting a stable door through which horses had been escaping (mostly in a northerly direction) for too many years.

But most of the Act's provisions were designed to remedy more specific failings in the system revealed in the previous couple of years. A number of clauses were included to adapt the Swiss legal system to control bank failures. The numerous provisions to deal with banks in trouble were designed to prevent a recurrence of the problems the Federal government

---

* Banks or other companies issuing 'bearer' bonds or shares, then the usual practice in continental Europe, had no means of knowing the actual owners of these securities.

had encountered in its attempts to rescue Geneva's banks. A carefully graduated system of bank moratoria was enacted, ensuring that an irreversible commitment to salvage an ailing institution could not be entered into unless the rescuers had previously made sure that the situation was not irretrievably lost. Conversely, the system was designed to provide help for fundamentally sound institutions suffering from temporary difficulties – the problem which faced most of those Swiss commercial banks which were then in trouble. (The Swiss Volksbank merited its own clause, forbidding any other co-operative banks from engaging in commercial banking.)

Finally, a dozen or more clauses were included to pin legal responsibility on bankers in respect of the many and various misdeeds of which they had been guilty in the preceding few years. Issuers of false prospectuses, founders of banks deemed to be negligent in their duties, bankers and bank liquidators were all held personally responsible for any financial damage caused by their actions. Infringement of many of the clauses in the Act could lead to a fine of up to 20,000 francs and imprisonment of up to six months. Clause 47(a) provided that the same punishment could be meted out to auditors found 'gravely deficient' in their duty, and in 47(b) we find the same standard format applied to bankers or bank employees who violated professional secrecy. Like so many of the Act's other provisions, Clause 47(b) was merely a hasty answer to a specific, unforeseen problem which had suddenly cropped up in the first troubled years of the 1930s.

3 / The little list of Fabien Albertin

The decisive moment when the reinforcement of Swiss banking secrecy with criminal sanctions became inevitable can be pinpointed with some accuracy. It was at 4.10 p.m. on

26 October 1932 that a squad of Paris policemen, headed by one Commissioner Barthelet, raided the elegant offices of the Basler Handelsbank in a five-room apartment on the first floor of a house in the Rue de la Tremoille, near the Champs Elysées. In the waiting-room they found a small group of the bank's clients, the last of the many hundreds who had visited the office in the previous ten days to cash the dividend coupons, which with bearer bonds were physically attached to the bond. M. Barthelet was well armed with precise information. Someone high up in the bank had provided him with a list of the bank's French customers, numbering over 1,300 – a figure rumour soon swelled to nearer 2,000.

Although so many clients had already been paid, the police also seized 245,000 French francs due to be handed over in the couple of hours before the payment sessions were due to end.

Because the evasion of a number of French taxes was at the heart of the affair the raid was, politically, highly convenient. The coalition government then in power, headed by the radical Edouard Herriot, was known to be preparing an exceedingly tough budget, designed to hit all classes of the population, so it was obviously timely to show that the government was cracking down on tax evasion by the wealthy. Within a few days the police had started legal proceedings against Georges Jean Berthoud, the bank's responsible director, and the head of the agency, M. Renaud (according to one rumour, the bank had opened a credit line of up to 100,000 French francs a day with the Paris branch of an English bank to take care of its employees' defence).

Just how many wealthy citizens were involved, and just how powerful they were, was revealed, in part anyway, in a stormy debate in the lower house of the French Assembly a fortnight after the raid, on 10 November. The debate was opened, ostensibly on a point of order, by a Socialist deputy, Fabien Albertin, who was armed with a list of the bank's clients – a list whose fame had already spread through Paris, and with full details of the raid. Both right- and left-wing papers noted cynically that his initiative had clearly been orchestrated with the relevant ministers so as to demonstrate the government's even-handed attempts to dispense fiscal justice.

Albertin was the ideal vehicle for the protest: the son of a lowly customs inspector, after obtaining a doctorate in law he had worked with the union which represented many sections of the civil service including customs officers. He was running their newspaper before his thirtieth birthday and maintained his connections with what he called rather patronisingly '*mes petits douaniers*' – 'my little customs men' – even after he became a deputy. The civil service unions had been complaining vociferously of the government's petty economies, although no real efforts were being made to make the collection of taxes more effective. Clearly the list had been slipped to Albertin through one of his 'little friends' involved in the raid.

His oration was his first hour of glory in the Assembly after his election three years before and he relished the opportunity. He mercilessly teased the opposition parties by responding to general cries for 'names, names' only sporadically, conducting a kind of strip-tease. He did not provide a complete list, only titbits from it. One of the juiciest revealed that two bishops, including M. d'Orléans, were evidently clients of the bank. 'Their kingdoms are surely not of this world,' he said, a remark which created the first of the day's many disturbances – described in the demure words of the official report as '*mouvements divers*' ('general bustle'). He made much play of the fact that a number of generals, the army's comptroller-general, and several super-patriotic public figures were also on the list. Yet, as Albertin pointed out, the money they had deposited in a Swiss bank was most likely being employed to help the historic enemy, Germany. He also revealed that both the present and the previous Madame Coty were on the list. By no coincidence M. Coty, owner of the famous perfume concern, was a leading right-wing political figure, as well as the owner of a leading newspaper, *Le Figaro*. The managing director of another leading right-wing paper, *Le Matin*, was also on the list, as were three senators.

The whole speech was a mixture of serious analysis and political point-scoring. Behind the gossipy facade his case was a solid one, with disturbing implications for the Swiss banks because he spelt out very clearly the reasons why so many foreigners had accounts with them, revealed the cynicism of their attitudes, and provided a persuasive estimate of the vast amount of tax being evaded. To make matters worse, the attack implicated every major Swiss bank, for the Basler Handelsbank was not the only one involved, nor even the most important even though, he reckoned, it had deposits of 2 billion French francs from its French customers. Yet Albertin claimed that at least five other banks, all well-known names, had even more French customers.

The taxes they were evading were important ones. The most obvious was the twenty per cent withholding tax that should have been paid on the coupons they had been presenting to the bankers, as well as taxes on deposits and foreign investments. As Albertin pointed out, the bank would not have agreed to clip its clients' coupons unless they were already customers with substantial amounts deposited with the bank, which would also be managing their portfolio of securities. Foreign banks (not just Swiss but Dutch banks also) used a kind of code when advertising their services, saying that they would 'pay any kind of coupon', a sign that they would also arrange for illicit accounts to be opened. Albertin compared their code with the one used by midwives who had been prepared to arrange abortions before the French law on contraception had been tightened up. 'Avoidance of all delay' had been the midwives' code. 'I believe their readers knew what the words really meant,' he observed to appreciative laughter.

Although substantial sums were being lost in income taxes, yet the biggest drain was through the avoidance of succession duties. Albertin made a telling point when he quoted from an official document issued by the biggest Swiss bank, the Swiss Bank Corporation, which spelt out just how little the bank wished to know about joint accounts opened by '*M. Tel et un autre*' – 'Mr. So and So and another' – provided that the documentation was legally sound. The banks were not concerned over the relationships, if any, between two or more depositors each of whom had separate access to the account, nor as to the relationship of heirs or survivors to a deceased. As the document said, 'Swiss banks are not obliged to inform any government department of the existence or state of a deposit account after the death of one of the depositors, nor to provide anyone with a list of joint or collective accounts.' To provide customers with further protection, one of the provisions common to the – otherwise often very different – cantonal Swiss tax laws was that securities deposited by non-resident foreigners were exempted from all Swiss income taxes and succession duties. Albertin estimated that the French authorities were losing up to 4,000 million francs a year in revenue, an enormous but not surprising figure considering that his list contained such notable names (back to the specific) as M. Levitan, France's biggest furniture manufacturer, and the Peugeot family, makers, then as now, of cars and cycles, and natural customers for a bank based in Basle, only a few miles from their factories in Mulhouse.

The bank's clients, concluded Albertin, were clearly guilty both of tax evasion and of breaking a 1926 law which required French taxpayers to declare assets held abroad. If convicted Messrs. Berthoud and Renaud faced prison sentences of up to a year, under a law passed before World War I designed to prevent agents of foreign banks without official branches in France from paying the dividends on coupons on which stamp duty had not been paid. This was a clear indication that this type of fraud was not a novelty. It had been practised in pre-Revolutionary times, and even before World War I, the French Press had inveighed against Switzerland as the 'Eldorado of French Capitalists'. The accusation had so alarmed the Swiss Bank Corporation that it was forced to reply, claiming that 'French banks have been competing against us in Switzerland for many years and opened branches here before Swiss banks sent representatives to France'. Moreover the bank claimed that for several years previously, the bank had 'stopped any publicity and only accepted the deposits which were offered to us'. Clearly the subject was a sensitive one, but this had not deterred some, at least, of the Swiss banks – the Basler Handelsbank had opened its office in the Rue de la Tremoille over seven years before it was raided.

Most of the subsequent speakers supported Albertin, while often embroidering on the theme that the rich should pay because the poor had suffered for too long. One deputy pointed out that the subject had been raised eighteen months earlier when there had been rumours that six deputies were involved in tax evasion. A Communist contrasted the treatment of rich tax dodgers with that of a small tradesman recently sentenced to three years' imprisonment for defrauding the social security system. A Socialist deputy (and future President), Vincent Auriol, remembered that a similar flight of capital abroad had led to the fall of the franc in 1925 (hence the 1926 law requiring the declaration of foreign assets). But at least two of the accused found a defender when a Catholic deputy rose to defend the bishops. He was authorised to state in their defence that the money was not their personal property but funds entrusted to them 'for educational purposes'. Moreover, 'these funds were all that remained of possessions which have undergone waves of depredation by the state and that it was therefore altogether natural to protect them from the ravages of the tax authorities.'

The Socialists wanted the total suppression of bearer bonds, and at that year's Radical Party congress, held only a few days before the debate, a very young delegate, Pierre Mendès-France (to become famous in the 1950s as the Prime Minister who extracted France from its bloody and prolonged involvement in Vietnam) had put forward a sensible plan – quoted approvingly by Albertin. He had suggested an end to anonymous stock certificates. Under what he called '*la nominalisation des titres*' they would all have a name attached; even worse from a Swiss point of view, he proposed a form of 'fiscal extradition' on the lines of a recently signed Anglo-French agreement over succession duties. This was bad enough: but for the Swiss the most sinister element of the situation was not the list of names, nor the proposed measures, but the way it had been obtained. For previous attempts to nail Swiss banks had failed for lack of precise information, and both Albertin and the Minister of Finance made it abundantly clear that what distinguished the affair of the Rue de la Tremoille was that someone high up in the bank had provided the police with a list which combined the names of clients and the numbers of their accounts.

Although the Speaker of the Assembly had shown some token resistance to Albertin's desire to turn his point of order into a full-scale debate, it became abundantly clear that this result had been carefully prepared. The Prime Minister wandered into the chamber during Albertin's speech, and although he deplored the fact that names of some of the bank's clients had been mentioned, he and M. Germain-Martin, the Minister of Finance, were only too happy to fall in with many of Albertin's suggestions (though Germain-Martin got into terrible trouble when he claimed that, because of a scrupulous application of the doctrine of the separation of powers, he had never seen the famous list, which belonged, he said, exclusively to the judicial branch). Albertin, too, was eager to improve fiscal discipline; ominously, he said that the government was seeking to obtain from the Swiss the right to inspect foreign held accounts through a system of *commissions rogatoires* – a feature of Roman law best translated as 'official summonses' backed by legal sanctions.

The French government suited its actions to its words. In its 1933 budget, published a few days after the debate, it proposed an elaborate system of controls: companies could pay dividends only if the beneficiary produced evidence of his or her identity, and they were obliged to furnish tax offices with a monthly list of payments. For their part, banks were obliged to certify the true ownership of the stocks or bonds involved, to notify the tax authorities of the deposit of documents or bonds, the opening of new accounts and the contents of strong rooms. The tax authorities were to be allowed extensive powers to investigate the banks.

At the same time the prosecution of the Basler Handelsbank's clients was vigorously pushed ahead. All thirty-eight examining magistrates in Paris devoted their energies to prosecuting the 1,300 or more French citizens accused of tax evasion; a week after the debate an examining magistrate summoned Berthoud and Renaud to a hearing and placed them under arrest, charged with not registering their Paris office with the police and with the non-payment of taxes on the coupons attached to foreign securities. They were repeatedly asked to provide the French authorities with access to the bank's books in Basle so that their clients' accounts could be examined. In reply the bank routinely relayed the unanimous opinion of Switzerland's Federal Council that in accordance with the established attitude of the Swiss Federal Supreme Court (itself merely confirming the relevant Swiss law on the subject) Swiss banks had a duty to absolute silence about their customers' affairs. The Council added, rather gratuitously, that in their view voluntarily to allow foreign authorities access to a bank's books would be an immoral action.

The two countries were obviously separated by an unbridgeable gulf. A week after the debate the *Tribune de Genève* reported with approval the opinion of one Swiss broker who had exclaimed that it was revolting the way the revelations against Swiss banks had been exploited. In France the Swiss were supported (in public anyway) only by M. Coty. *Le Figaro* belaboured everyone connected with prosecuting its owner and his wives past and present; the deputies were hypocrites because they paid tax on only half their parliamentary salaries, it said, and the debate as a whole had been useless – as the government had already announced that it had initiated legal proceedings. As for the government, despite Germain-Martin's protestations, it had been guilty of a breach of the separation of powers by telling the examining magistrates what to do. Finally came the eternal pleas of the well-heeled, that they were bearing more than their fair share of the tax burden: according to the 1931 figures quoted by *Le Figaro*, the 8,600 French tax-payers whose income was more than 300,000 francs paid half the taxes received by the government.

For all Coty's indignation, it was the Communist *L'Humanité* which best understood the essential theatricality of the whole affair. The day after the debate it remarked sardonically: 'fraudsters, sleep peacefully. Strengthened by the confidence shown in it by the Chamber of Deputies, the Herriot government has taken upon itself ... to let you sleep in peace.' Whatever Herriot's ministry might have done will never be known (although the French historical form-book suggests that *L'Humanité* was right), but the Herriot administration was defeated just before Christmas, to be succeeded by a right-wing administration less eager to pursue rich and influential tax evaders. Before the end of 1932 a special commission had decided not to prosecute the three senators involved. In the following May the charges against the French customers were dismissed on a technicality (that no individual claim had been filed against any of those charged). They were merely sent a routine request to fill in their tax forms more correctly in future. Nor, seemingly, were the Swiss bankers implicated in the affair convicted of any offence.

Five years later, the specific 'French gap' in the Swiss defences was filled, when the Swiss government took advantage of the financial needs of the then French Socialist government. The official history of the Swiss Bank Corporation tells the story succinctly:

'A typical example of the way financial and commercial interests are closely interlocked in foreign trade is provided by the treatment of the requests for credit made by France to Swiss banks in Autumn 1937. There was readiness on the part of the banks to accede to these requests but the credits were made dependent on two conditions of general interest: the French import quota system had to be modified in a manner favourable to Switzerland and an acceptable double taxation agreement was stipulated as a *conditio sine qua non.*'

Not surprisingly, the Treaty which emerged provided specifically that Swiss laws, regulations and administrative custom and practice would be scrupulously respected by the French. In the meantime the general problem of banking secrecy raised by M. Albertin's little list had been dealt with, in a form which has achieved an importance quite out of keeping with the modest political scandal which sparked off the legislative process.

4/ Secrecy: Challenge and response

Within Switzerland the importance of the Basler Handelsbank case was obscured for a few days by more pressing news. For the debate in the French Assembly took place on the Thursday of an historic week. On the Tuesday the American people had voted overwhelmingly to elect Franklin Delano Roosevelt as their President for the first time. On Wednesday 9 November the political tensions within Geneva culminated in the bloodiest disturbance Switzerland had witnessed for a century: that evening a regiment of raw recruits fired on a crowd assembled to protest against a Fascist demonstration. Twelve of the Socialist protestors were killed and the next day the firebrand Léon Nicole and another Socialist leader were arrested. It was only the following week that the Swiss public – and the authorities – started to consider the damage that had been done.

At the centre of the storm was the Federal Finance Minister, J-L. Musy. All the support he had organised for the Comptoir de Genève (now dignified with the name of the Swiss Discount Bank following its two takeovers) crumbled. It was rumoured to be the next target of the French taxmen and almost all its foreign deposits were withdrawn. This was the beginning of the end for the bank which finally collapsed in April 1934 (by that time Nicole was master of the Canton of Geneva and refused to honour the commitment made during the rescue negotiations in December 1932.*

At a personal level Musy was deeply involved with the Basler Handelsbank itself. Following the bank's final collapse after World War II disgruntled employees traced its troubles back to Musy. They claimed that he had exerted an undue influence over the bank in the early 1930s, had encouraged it to over-extend itself in Central and Eastern Europe, and had abused his office to provide verbal guarantees of Federal help if the bank suffered losses as a result. The employees also claimed that the bank had a higher proportion of its assets invested abroad than in Switzerland itself.

But the Basler Handelsbank case did far more than lead to a run on those banks suspected of being targets for the French. It struck simultaneously at the very foundations of the Swiss banking system: secrecy – and the fundamental difference

* The Canton had then agreed to invest up to SF 5 million if the other funds – pledged by banks in Geneva and in the rest of Switzerland, as well as by the Federal authorities – were not sufficient. By April 1934 the financial situation of Geneva (as well as of the banks) was desperate, and the Federal government suffering from a major political crisis.

between the Swiss attitude to tax and that of any other Western European country. For the Swiss – as for the Americans – the ability to control one's own taxes lay at the very heart of their historical tradition. If the Americans remember the Boston Tea Party and the slogan 'no taxation without representation', then the Swiss have an even more fundamental legend, that of their national hero, William Tell – or rather Gessler, his implacable opponent, the man the Swiss have loved to hate for six centuries. He was the very image of hated alien authority and his main job, inevitably, was to levy taxes. For nearly seven centuries since his day the Swiss have held sacred the idea that they should be allowed to levy their own taxes; so the right remained in general with the canton or even the commune. It was extended only grudgingly to the federal authorities; crucially, tax evasion was not a matter for the criminal law (if it had been, why, their national hero could have been condemned as a tax evader). This does not matter so much within the country. In modern times there has been a stiff withholding tax on interest and dividends payments, and in the words of an American jurist, John L. Lannan, 'Despite the absence of any criminal sanctions Swiss tax authorities nevertheless are able to extract revenues by virtue of the device of *Ermessenstaxation*, or *taxation d'office*.' This is an assumption of income or wealth which the taxpayer can rebut only by producing evidence of his debts and expenses, such as bank statements. A taxpayer who does not supply true information to verify his tax liabilities, is taking a considerable risk. The – deliberately exaggerated – estimate 'may in certain cases be combined with the withdrawal of the right to appeal and with a penalty for tax evasion'. The system may suit the Swiss, but it is profoundly inconvenient for foreign governments whose money has taken sanctuary in Switzerland. In Swiss eyes it was up to other countries to organise their own tax systems, and not expect the Swiss to help if these resulted in tax evasion.

In John J. Lannan's words: 'like most nations, Switzerland extends assistance in civil and criminal matters but not in matters of administrative law ... Tax evasion, securities, and foreign exchange violations are considered fiscal or administrative offences, therefore the Swiss refuse legal assistance in these areas.' A Swiss lawyer, Carl Mueller, put the point succinctly: 'Switzerland takes the view that it is the duty of the internal legislation of each country to provide effective measures against tax evasion'. In his standard work on the banking system in Switzerland Hans Baer, himself a distinguished banker, emphasised that 'from the client's point of view, the most important aspect of the Banking Secret is that neither the tax nor the exchange authorities can obtain any information whatsoever from the banks.' The banks were obviously fully aware of the attractions of secrecy. In the early 1920s, for instance, when the UBS opened a major new branch office in Aarau it deliberately chose as decoration for the façade a bas-relief of three sphinxes, symbolising, indeed proclaiming, the discretion to be found within. Yet this secrecy, as the revelation of the Albertin list showed, could be undermined, with fatal results.

The point was taken almost immediately. In late December 1932 and early January 1933 the *Neue Zürcher Zeitung*, then as now a reliable indicator of official Swiss thinking, carried two lengthy articles on the subject, signed simply FHz. They were clearly inspired by the unfortunate events in France. 'Unusual events in recent times have brought the problems of banking secrecy back into the foreground of public interest,' was the coy way FHz introduced his first article. 'It has become more important as Switzerland has become more significantly involved with the economies of other countries in the field of transfers of capital and possessions,' and the writer went on to regret that the current trend was to concentrate on 'the right to refuse information ... instead of the duty to preserve secrecy'.

The second article emphasised the importance of banking secrecy. 'It is essential to Swiss banking and to the Swiss international position in finance ... because the banks are so important in the national economy, the state has an interest in preserving bank secrecy, and therefore the state should also respect and take some of the responsibility for bank secrecy. This has been pointed out very recently in connection with certain foreign attempts at bank espionage in Switzerland. Such attempts, which in any case can be vigorously countered by the Swiss banking community, quite obviously present a threat to the national economy and in effect to the financial and economic independence of our country ... thrift and bank secrecy go together and cannot be separated'.

The threat was pictured almost as an international conspiracy: 'The touchstone of the state's relationship to the banking secret is tax legislation', the first article had observed sagely. 'A series of European states have since the war broken the banking secret in favour of fiscal authorities rather than the banks. One need only point to the withdrawal of German capital, and the laws regarding foreign currency, which Austrian legislation also follows in its essence. For tax purposes, banking secrecy has been lifted to the greatest extent in Czechoslovakia. France imposes duties to register for the assessment of tax on inheritances, on the renting of deposit-boxes, restrictions on capital exports and duties to reveal any dealings in foreign currencies.' The article was published two days after the fall of the Herriot ministry, but the *Neue Zürcher Zeitung* clearly took the new threats seriously as the writer added ominously, 'Further inroads into bank secrecy are imminent'.

Even at home there were worrying signs that banking secrecy was being eroded. In the canton of Fribourg, both commercial and savings banks were obliged to provide the cantonal authorities with a list of deposits with names attached. The Federal Supreme Court had upheld this regrettable decision, which had induced even the upright Fribourgeois to use banks outside their native canton. The article went on to note another unfortunate exception, also based on a recent decision of the Supreme Court. This related to the law concerning bankruptcy. Until 1930 the Court had ruled that every item demanded by creditors of a bankrupt person should be listed individually. Hidden assets were, therefore, safe from sequestration. It changed its mind in 1930 and obliged any third party, including bankers, to provide information to the liquidator regarding any assets in their charge belonging to the bankrupt. This worried FHz no end: 'A confiscation can therefore easily be an attempt, assisted by a feigned claim, to deprive the banks of the professional secrecy incumbent upon them, and in particular become a means of foreign bank espionage in Switzerland'. This theme is taken up in some versions of the traditional story about bank secrecy, in which Nazi agents enquire about accounts belonging to German Jews on similar pretexts – except that FHz was writing two months before the Nazis came to power. 'The damage to the national economy from such a stance is obvious,' he went on. 'Abroad, the new stance of the Federal Court has also been widely and exaggeratedly used in a campaign against Swiss banks and in mountebank-like press articles which have declared that the banking secret has been partially lifted'.

The writer's theme is expressed even more clearly by a Geneva lawyer, Georges Capitaine, in a book on bank secrecy published in 1933. He quotes two other recent rulings by the Federal Supreme Court that secrecy was not a formal legal obligation on bankers, but merely a matter of custom and practice. Capitaine's most pertinent example concerned a French shopkeeper named Charpiot who lived near the Swiss frontier and had been in the habit of using a bank just across the border in Bassecourt to change French banknotes into Swiss ones. But he did not always slip across himself; he had introduced to the bank a young lady he employed as his representative and she carried out most of the actual trans-actions (he even used to telephone her while she was in the bank's offices). Two years later, after she had been sacked by M. Charpiot, Mlle M. took her revenge. She asked for and received from the bank – which had not been told of her dismissal – a summary of the foreign exchange transactions she had undertaken on her former employer's behalf, ostens-ibly to help him complete his accounts for the relevant period. In fact she took the document to the French customs. They prosecuted the wretched Charpiot for illegal capital exports and he was condemned to pay a fine – plus accrued interest. In both these cases the Federal Supreme Court emphasized 'custom and practice' as the only existing legal basis for bank secrecy and had thus left the door open for further inroads.

By contrast the authorities of the tiny Duchy of Liechten-stein, tucked away between Switzerland and Austria, had been reinforcing the opportunities they provided for total secrecy. Inspired by the collapse of the local textile industry after World War I and a tax treaty with its bigger neighbour in

1924, the Duchy's government introduced a system of 'trusts' which enabled any individual to transform himself easily, quickly and inexpensively into a legal entity and thus gain complete anonymity. Other advantages included an absolute guarantee of tax and banking secrecy. These trusts were immediately used on a large scale by Swiss lawyers acting for German clients anxious to escape from the stiff exchange controls introduced by Dr. Schacht in the wake of the hyper-inflation of 1923.

What with the Liechtenstein example, the court decisions, and the Basler Handelsbank case, the inclusion of pains and penalties for violation of banking secrecy in the upcoming Banking Act was a foregone conclusion. The only debate – which sometimes seemed more metaphysical than legal – concerned the concept of secrecy. To Capitaine the key was the 'confidence required for the practice of the profession involved'. To Mr. FHz the 'banker's duty to preserve secrecy arises from the business relationship between himself and his customer ... a relationship of trust exists ... the unspoken obligation to silence is part of the contract and is characterised as a contractual duty of the banker ... the holder of this right to secrecy, however, is in fact the customer ... the right to preserve secrecy is therefore highly personal and not transferable' by the customer to the banker. Moreover, the customer's right extends naturally to details of his property and, even further, to the relationship as a whole, so 'the banker must not therefore inform a third party that the customer has concluded business of a specific nature, has deposited any sum with the bank, etc.'

The disturbance resulting from the court decisions of the early 1930s was the greater because the 'custom and practice' dated back a long time. According to John J. Lannan. Swiss courts had 'traditionally held that confidentiality is an implied contractual obligation not dependent on an express agreement'. To Hans Baer:

> The banking secret is in effect simply another phase of the professional secret, as it was known in Roman law as *actio iniuriarum*. The entire concept is based on the ethical law of secrecy for all those professions where facts and conditions

of a personal nature must be disclosed by the client. It is obvious that the banker is more or less in the same position as a lawyer, doctor or clergyman, each of whom must guard the personal interests of his client. Much of the confidence which a customer must place in his banker is based on the knowledge that the facts related to the banker as regards his business and finance will be kept in strict confidence.

The basic obligation to professional secrecy can be traced back to the code imposed by the Emperor Napoleon on the French in 1810. Capitaine quotes Article 378 of the French penal code listing various professions, doctors, midwives, pharmacists, as among those who can be awarded up to six months' imprisonment if they reveal professional secrets. This Article was repeated almost word for word in the Cantonal penal codes in Geneva and Berne, and Capitaine points to another similar article (which brought clerics and lawyers into the net) in a projected 1918 Swiss Federal penal code. The only distinction is that whereas the obligation of professional secrecy of lawyers and doctors was absolute, with the bankers it could be – and was – qualified in specific instances. This distinction derived from the fact that Swiss lawyers did not trust the bankers' capacity to discipline themselves. Unlike lawyers or physicians, wrote Carl Mueller, 'They are subject neither to a special code of ethics nor to a supervisory authority which may take disciplinary action in case of suspect or illegal transactions' – and Mueller was writing thirty-five years after the installation of the Federal Banking Commission.

For obvious reasons the terms and conditions applied to professions were adapted to fit the bankers' requirements. As Dr. Aubert pointed out in his standard work on banking secrecy, 'whereas the violation of other professional secrets is punished only as a result of a complaint by the injured party, that of banking secrecy can be punished as a breach of professional obligations'. The legislator, as Aubert says, excused the victim from having to lay a claim in view of the 'inconveniences' which might arise, and thus avoiding the situation where a breach of the law would remain unpunished because the plaintiff was afraid to go to court himself. There were two other major differences from the usual laws regarding professional secrets. The penalties were rather greater, and whereas other professions could not be pursued simply because they had been neglectful of their professional duties, negligence in a banker was considered an indictable offence in itself.

Although no documents have survived showing the actual process by which Clause 47(b) emerged, the circumstantial evidence pointing to the course of events described in the last sections is surely overwhelming. The Basler Handelsbank case, following on the earlier decisions of the Supreme Court (and the way they had been misunderstood and exaggerated abroad), the threat from possible new French legislation, and the application to the Swiss authorities to agree to a 'fiscal extradition' treaty were reason enough to act. But they were compounded by the looming bankruptcy of a number of major banks because of the withdrawal of foreign funds. The case of the Swiss Discount Bank had shown that the rush would be greatly accelerated if foreign depositors' confidence in the impregnability of Swiss banking secrecy was not restored by some positive measure. All these elements point to Clause 47(b); and its wording is closely related to the normal run of legislation protecting professional secrecy, adapted to ensure that the foreign clients of Swiss banks would not have to go through the embarrassing process of making a legal claim if they felt secrecy had been broken.

There remains only one major question: when the Nazis *did* start trying to put pressure on Germans with Swiss accounts, how did they go about it, and how did the Swiss cope with the problem?

5/In the front line

In the mid-1930s the Swiss banking community had one overwhelming worry, and it was emphatically not about German espionage.* It was simply how to survive. For the major immediate impact of the Banking Act was to allow a number of banks to admit their financial troubles and use some of the Act's provisions to adjust their financial structures (to put it mildly). For the two years between the devaluation of the dollar in April 1934 and that of the Swiss franc two years later marked the depth both of the financial and economic depressions in Switzerland. Economic life was paralysed by the over-valuation of the Swiss franc and growing world-wide protectionism; the combined impact of currency uncertainties and worries over the banks' own solidity (and their clients' cash requirements) reduced the sheer size of Swiss banks. In the two years that followed the passage of the Act the Swiss Volksbank, Bank Leu, and the Basler Handelsbank all underwent surgery involving the injection of federal support; another of the Big Seven (as they had become following the final disappearance in 1934 of the Swiss Discount Bank), the Union Bank, had to reduce its capital base very severely, although it never had to declare any form of banking moratorium.

Under these circumstances the first signs of German interference in Switzerland did not affect the banks directly. It was only early in 1934, following the decree to the frontier police mentioned on page 55, that German 'snatch squads' started to operate against German refugees.

The first widely reported case of kidnapping by the Ger-

* Prior to 1933 it had not been German espionage which worried the Swiss so much as Italian interference in the Ticino region. (Typically, in November 1932, a long-time Italian agent was accused of planting explosives on Italian political refugees to incriminate them with the Swiss.)

mans was that of Rudolf William Sprenger, a German tech-
nician living in Zurich. At the end of August 1934 he was
kidnapped in a taxi, chloroformed, and whisked over the
frontier to Jestetten in Germany. He stuffed some apparently
vital papers he was carrying into the taxi's upholstery; and
although the taxi-driver scrupulously handed the papers to
one of the kidnappers Sprenger nevertheless managed to
smuggle a letter to the Swiss police. There was a popular
uproar but, at the time, the newspapers seemed resigned to
the fact that Switzerland was helpless in the face of this and
similar less widely reported incidents.

The attitude changed dramatically in March 1935 when the
Gestapo kidnapped a German journalist also living in Zurich,
Berthold Jacob. The Swiss were able to show that the
kidnappers had acted with the knowledge and co-operation of
the German authorities. After an enormous popular and
diplomatic row, Jacob was returned.

The result was that the Swiss Parliament passed a Bill
(which had been rejected as recently as March 1933) providing for the creation of the crime of 'economic and political
espionage'. This, astonishingly, had previously been absent
from the Swiss statute book, and as a result the Swiss
accomplices in the Jacob kidnapping could not, effectively, be
prosecuted. Clause 4 of the new law, popularly known as the
Spitzelgesetz, Espionage Act, created the crime of economic
espionage and this also covered the disclosure of a 'manu-
facturing or business secret'. This was later enshrined in
Article 273 of the Swiss Penal code, used widely after the war
against any foreigner thought to be showing too close an
interest in Swiss affairs, financial or industrial. Comparison
with Clause 47 of the Banking Act passed the previous year is
instructive. Both were drawn up as a result of specific cases;
and both reinforced existing Swiss traditions. For just as the
banks were traditionally reticent about providing information
about their customers to third parties, so their customers in
the Swiss industrial and commercial community were habitually unwilling to provide any information to their bankers. As
Hans Baer noted, Clause 47 prevented 'any closely-knit
system of credit information such as exists in the United
States ... It is of course a not inconsiderable disadvantage for

a bank to be unable to obtain information concerning a client's relationship with other banks except from the client himself'. And he may not be any more forthcoming. In Professor Sayers' words: 'it is impossible to break down the secretive attitude of the business borrower ... the bank may not even be allowed to look at the books'. These attitudes, these habits, spring from a very deep element in the Swiss character – refusal to provide any information to anyone outside the *gemeinde*: for a people as diverse as the Swiss the right of refusal was always essential for the right to privacy, the right to live undisturbed by external authority. In the 1930s the legal reflection of this fundamental trait proved most helpful in combatting Nazi agents.

By the time the *Spitzelgesetz* was passed, German agents had become very active in trying to stir up Nazi sympathies within Switzerland. But their reliance on a rebirth of the pro-German sentiment which had been so widespread during World War I quickly proved unfounded – though not for want of trying, and not before the wildest rumours had gained credence (as, for instance, that a pan-German league was being founded in St. Gall to help annex the areas of Switzerland with a German-speaking majority to the Reich).

These rumours started even before Hitler moved into the Saar, Austria, and then Czechoslovakia in his expansionary attempts to create a thousand-year Reich. But the Swiss took the threats seriously from the very beginning: in the late 1930s at least one banker was prepared to break the banking secret to tip off a relation in the police when the Nazis deposited funds in favour of neo-Nazi groups (he excused his action by describing this emergency as an *übergesetzlichte*, an emergency which overrode narrow legal considerations).

German espionage attempts do not seem to have affected the banks until 1937. The decisive sign that the Nazis had turned their sights on the assets of Germans abroad was the law against economic sabotage enacted in December 1936. In part this was aimed at enticing Germans to repatriate their foreign nest-eggs: those prepared to admit they had assets abroad could keep a third of them after they had handed over the remaining two-thirds to the Reichsbank, which would repay in Deutschmarks (alternatively, those wishing to retain their anonymity could hand over one third of their funds to the Reichsbank and retain the other two-thirds).

But the overwhelming motive was political. This is shown by the emotional and flamboyant language of the law: 'Any German national who knowingly and having as a motive vulgar self-interest and other low motives acts against the law in transferring assets abroad or keeps them abroad and thereby damages the German economy is punished with death'. Moreover the act was to be implemented not in the ordinary courts, but in the Nazis' own dreaded People's Courts. If the guilty party did not take advantage of the amnesty all his assets were to be confiscated, and the law also applied to Germans living abroad. This was an unprecedented extension of foreign jurisdiction to people living on Swiss soil, or those with assets protected by the recently reinforced Swiss banking laws; and the precedent furnished the Swiss with a great deal of moral comfort in the 1960s when American investigators embarked on their attempts to extend their jurisdiction over assets held by American citizens in Swiss banks.

Legally, the Nazis' efforts constituted no more than a reinforcement of the regulations against transferring or keeping assets abroad that had first been passed in 1924 when Dr. Schacht imposed draconian measures to stabilise the German economy following the hyper-inflation of 1922–3. Nor – contrary to legend – do the Nazis seem to have relied on their own special agents, from the Gestapo or the Party's foreign section, to conduct the actual espionage. We know this because there is at least one witness able and willing to tell us of the efforts made by Swiss banks to protect their clients against Nazi espionage. He is Dr. Max Homberger, a sprightly septuagenarian who retired in the early 1970s as a senior manager with the Swiss Bank Corporation. When he was first employed as a young lawyer by the SBC in the mid-1930s he quickly became the bank's expert on counterespionage and was consulted by branch managers confronted by unusual problems with German clients (the way he seemingly drifted into this specialised niche which had not been filled before, provides another, albeit indirect, indication that the problem had not been serious before 1936). But later in the decade as he told me 'we really felt we were in the front line of the fight against Fascism'.

Before the young Homberger was entrusted with his delicate task he had proved his qualities on a hazardous journey to Germany to contact a client – not a Jew, nor an industrialist, but simply an *Uberlehrer*, a high school teacher. He had 45,000 francs in his account and the bank was puzzled to receive from him a letter asking them to hand over all his assets to the Deutsche Winterhelfe, in theory merely a charity, in practice well-known as a fund, under Hermann Goering's control, used for rearmament.

The teacher had left the address in Nuremberg from which he had given his instructions; and when Homberger tracked him down to a new address in the smaller nearby town of Bamberg and rang the bell, there was no reply. But Homberger was convinced that his client was simply hiding from undesirable callers, so he went to a nearby public telephone and eventually got through. When he was finally allowed in and announced his name and the purpose of his visit, 'the man literally went white and trembled,' says Homberger, 'I'd never believed that people actually reacted like that.' After giving all the details he had learnt by heart, Homberger told the wretched client that either he was in the presence of a Gestapo agent, in which case the game was up, or that Homberger was indeed a real live Swiss banker. Not surprisingly, the teacher preferred the second alternative, and confessed that fear and pressure had led him to make his request.

Homberger and the head of the SBC's legal department devised a graduated series of responses to implausible requests for funds to be repatriated to Germany, or for information about an account held by a German. Under these circumstances Clause 47(b) provided a useful basis for the regular form letter which the bank sent out declaring simply that under its provisions it could neither admit nor deny the existence of an account in favour of a particular individual, let alone give out specific figures.

But this was only a first line of defence; and others were

needed after 1936, when a number of SBC branches began to receive visits not from Gestapo agents but from customs officials. This was not unexpected. Other countries, like France, relied on customs agents for policing currency smuggling; and the Germans had also relied on them since Dr. Schacht's first restrictions in the 1920s. They did not announce their identity, but simply produced legally valid powers of attorney duly signed by the depositor. To confront this challenge Homberger used not Clause 47(b) but Article 271 of the Swiss Penal code, which specifically envisaged such emergencies. Article 271, another result of the *spitzelgesetz*, provided that agents of a foreign state who operated anywhere in Switzerland in an official capacity without first asking official Swiss permission could be imprisoned; the seriousness of the crime was emphasized by the provision that they could be imprisoned in a *Zuchthaus*, or maximum security closed prison, for life. Homberger simply reminded them of the legal position, said he would leave the room for one minute, and that if they were still there when he returned he would call the police. He had only to use this technique a few times before the visits ended as suddenly as they had begun.

Article 271 was also employed officially against the Germans. In the Kaempfer case, in 1939, a German auditor went to Switzerland to examine the books of a subsidiary of a German firm. Because he was acting on the orders of a semi-governmental agency he was arrested, his report was impounded, and he was expelled from Switzerland. But the bankers could not rely entirely even on their newly strengthened legal support. They also had to devise solutions tailored to specific clients, only a proportion of whom were Jewish. The devices were often ingenious. Homberger remembers one client called Weiss: if the bank received any letter in which he had left the dot off the i in his name then the bank would ignore any instructions it contained. Another client gave the bank half a torn card: if anyone arrived claiming a power of attorney without the other half then the bank was to refuse payment.

But the most delicate case Homberger recalls concerned a German client who was apparently not satisfied with the routine reply citing Clause 47(b) but sent a second request (from a prison cell)* for all the money he had deposited to be handed over to the *Zollvandstelle*, the customs authorities. The letter was peremptory, holding the bank responsible for any loss or personal harm that might be caused if it did not comply. Homberger and his boss sent a carefully phrased letter which still stonewalled on the request. In reply they received a third demand, stating that the client was disputing the terms of an inheritance with his uncle and would therefore be grateful for details of the state of his account. Homberger and his superior agonised over this request for some time, since non-compliance could so clearly involve the client in grievous bodily harm. But they stuck to their original defiant attitude. Their reply stated that they knew the uncle and could, therefore, only repeat what they had previously written.

Some months elapsed before they received a simple post-card from a small town just inside Czechoslovakia, then still unoccupied by the Nazis. The writer thanked the bankers effusively, confirming what they had suspected all along, that he had been writing under compulsion, as without information from the bank no crime could be proved against him.

It was experiences like this, multiplied a hundred-fold, which hardened the hearts of a whole generation of Swiss bankers and led them to show a similar spirit in the face of investigations which had nothing in common with the Nazi efforts, except that complying with them would have involved breaking Swiss law.

---

* After the war the Communist government in Rumania copied this technique. With the help of an agent within the UBS they managed to obtain a list of over a hundred and fifty of their citizens with accounts at the bank, who were then locked up until they authorised the release of the assets.

PART THREE

A Profitable Neutrality

1 / 'Gallant little Switzerland'

For thirty years after 1945 the British comforted themselves with the delusion that the evacuation at Dunkirk had been a triumph. The French, for their part, enjoyed the comforting pretence that their country was buzzing with resistance from the very beginning of the German occupation. The Swiss equivalent was the idea of 'Gallant little Switzerland', expressed most cogently by Sir Winston Churchill in December 1944:

> Of all the neutrals Switzerland has the greatest right to distinction. She has been the sole international force linking the hideously sundered nations and ourselves. What does it matter whether she has been able to give us the commercial advantages we desire, or has given too many to the Germans, to keep herself alive? She has been a democratic state, standing for freedom in self-defence among her mountains, and in thought, in spite of race, largely on our side.

In the past few years these myths have been called sharply into question by a younger generation of historians, lacking the psychological need to accept previously received ideas as to their countrymen's behaviour under the extreme conditions imposed by the last war, although, typically, the questioning has not gone as far in Switzerland as it has in France, Britain, or in Germany.

Even Churchill had inserted a qualification in his panegyric, and officials in the Ministry of Economic Warfare who were involved in negotiations with neutral countries at the time had been far more critical: 'In 1941,' according to W. N. Medlicott, 'there was a majority (not unanimous) opinion in the Ministry of Economic Warfare that Switzerland should be treated purely as in the Nazi sphere of influence.' This hostility was 'buttressed by bitter experience in the first years of the war when Swiss commercial banks, among others, anticipated an Axis victory.' Paradoxically, the majority of the Swiss people were staunchly anti-Nazi right through the war, yet Swiss policy was – to put it mildly – overly influenced by the complete Nazi encirclement of the country from June 1940 to late 1944, especially after November 1942, when the Germans occupied Vichy France, and thus tightened the ring round the Swiss. They were totally dependent on the Axis powers for their fuel supplies, and relied almost entirely on the railway line from Genoa for the raw materials and foodstuffs they were able to transport in foreign ships registered as nominally 'Swiss' and therefore treated as neutral territory.

But, for once in their history, the Swiss did not fully exploit their major strategic asset, their control over the St. Gotthard route across the Alps. While Swiss neutrality precluded use of the route for the transport of war material, yet the rail tunnel in particular was crucial in supplying the German war effort in the Middle East, Italy and the Balkans, especially with coal and oil. The route became even more vital to the Germans when the Allies invaded Sicily and then Italy in 1943, and when the alternative route via the Simplon Pass was threatened in late 1944 by the Allied advance.

Nevertheless Swiss policy was dominated until the very end by the assumption that the Germans would win the war. It was only in October 1944 that the Swiss finally banned the export of all war materials to all the belligerents, and it was only a few weeks before the German surrender (and then only under extreme pressure, especially from the Americans) that the Swiss took any steps to limit their trade with the Germans and the Italians. The figures are telling: in 1938 less than a quarter of Swiss exports went to the two countries. By 1941 the two were receiving more than half – and even in 1944 exports to Germany accounted for a full quarter of the total as against sixteen per cent before the war). Moreover, the Swiss were providing the Germans with advanced arms and equipment, and with equally sophisticated financial services, unavailable elsewhere. In effect the 'neutral' Swiss were of far greater importance to the Axis war effort than all their supposed allies in the Balkans, Bulgaria, Hungary and Rumania, together. The scale of the contribution made by the Swiss to the German war effort is best attested by the size of the 'clearing debt', the surplus accumulated by the Swiss in their trade with the Axis powers. In Medlicott's words: 'the enormous size of the clearing debt at the end of the war showed clearly the failure of the policy (if it had ever been seriously intended) of encouraging a *reduction* of the clearing balance by getting the Germans to export more to Switzerland than the Swiss exported to Germany.' The sheer blindness of the Swiss, and the build-up of frustration this produced is best described by Dean Acheson, then an Assistant Secretary of State:

If the Swedes were stubborn, the Swiss were the cube of stubbornness. In June 1941 the British gave up argument and placed a total embargo on all goods 'capable of benefiting the enemy's war effort', while continuing, however, the existing rations of foodstuffs and fodder. Long months of talks in London between American and British negotiators and the Swiss finally produced an outline of possible agreement in December. But German pressure resulted in Swiss refusal to meet allied demands for reduction of Swiss arms and ammunition going to Germany, and nothing came of it.

Our successes in North Africa in 1943 registered slowly in the Swiss mind. They gave greater weight to the more immediate German presence on their borders, allowing the Nazis further clearing arrangements in return for promised coal deliveries. In mid-August, however, the allies thought that concessions were in the offing. They agreed to open half the foodstuff quotas which had been closed off in May in return for Swiss reduction in the arms traffic to Germany. Almost at once they learned the shocking truth that, instead of reducing exports to Germany in the second quarter of 1943, the Swiss had actually increased them over the first quarter by from fifty to a hundred per cent. They also withheld the figures from the British and ourselves until after the agreement was made. Winfield Riefler, our Economic Minister in London, described this Swiss performance, moderately, as a 'flagrant violation of good faith'. In the remainder of 1943, while the allied advance was stalled at the Gustav line, Swiss trade with Germany increased further. After months of stubborn argument, we and the British threatened post-war retaliation and cancellation of all import permits, and began to place individual Swiss firms engaged in important German trade on the blacklists, threatening to extend the practice to all firms in the trade. The Swiss wavered at the year's end sufficiently to warrant a *modus vivendi* with them pending further talks.

When discussion was renewed in February (1944), the Swiss were if possible less malleable.

Even after Stalingrad, even after the invasion of Italy, they were still obsessed with the – to them – apparently overwhelming nature of German power, and felt helpless, surrounded as they still were by Nazi-occupied Europe. There was also a cold-blooded element in their policies. As Urs Schwarz put it, they knew that 'both belligerents had an interest – at least a marginal one – in avoiding steps that would jeopardise continued neutrality and make life impossible for the nation surviving in the eye of the hurricane'. The credibility of the stance depended almost completely on the Swiss army's plan to retreat to an Alpine redoubt and blow up the crucial tunnels under the Alps if the Germans invaded: but this fact seems to have escaped the majority of the Swiss official classes. For these were largely wrapped in an overwhelming sense of unreality, superbly expressed in a famous despatch by W. E. Norton, the British minister in Berne, on his return to Berne after a visit to London in 1944. It 'was like a return to the air-conditioned saloon of a liner ... one could see through the porthole the storm and stress of the weather or the heat of the tropics, but it was only by going on deck that one appreciated the conditions which the captain and crew were facing and by which they were being hardened and influenced.'

The policy of appeasement towards the Germans was personified by the Federal Councillor responsible for foreign relations between 1940 and December 1944, Maurice Pilet-Golaz. Indeed until quite recently the whole blame was pinned on his shoulders. Like Neville Chamberlain in Britain, Pilet-Golaz invited blame by his arrogance and by his consciousness of superiority over admittedly inadequate colleagues. Pilet-Golaz made matters worse by an over-indulgence in inappropriate 'flip' adolescent witticisms. Sir David Kelly, Norton's predecessor as British minister in Berne, bluntly called him a 'Swiss Quisling', and Edgar Bonjour devotes a whole chapter of his history of Swiss neutrality to explaining Pilet-Golaz's isolation from his colleagues, his unwillingness to listen to the evidence (or even receive Swiss diplomats returning from the 'deck'). Bonjour also emphasises that his own party, the radicals, did not want him re-elected in 1943 to a post which he owed to the sudden death in early 1940 of the pro-German Giuseppe Motta, who had dominated Swiss foreign policy for the twenty preceding years. For within Switzerland the Germans' key supporters were relatively few in number: the majority of the seven-man Federal Council, some major industrialists – and virtually the whole Swiss banking community.

The classic contrast between the appeasers and the sturdy Swiss people was best expressed in 1940 in the dark days following the fall of France. In times of war the Swiss elect a single General, in this case Henri Guisan – so pro-Allies that he had encouraged talks between his staff and the French (news of which leaked to the Germans and haunted Guisan for the rest of the war). His response to the otherwise all-conquering Nazis in the dark days of June 1940 was to summon his officers to the sacred Rütli meadow and deliver a magnificent oration echoing the defiance being hurled by Winston Churchill in Britain. But while Guisan was declaring that the Swiss would fight for their freedom, if necessary retreating into their 'Alpine Redoubt', Pilet-Golaz was giving the Germans the clear impression of a man hell-bent on accommodation, and prevented from bending to the Germans' wishes 'only by a sick Swiss people who refused to understand that times had changed, by politicians and political parties who made life hard for him, by recalcitrant fellow Federal Councillors, and by a General who torpedoed his every effort of accommodation with the Reich.' Pilet-Golaz's true feelings emerged during an infamous broadcast when he talked of the need for the Swiss people to adapt themselves to the new reality. For Pilet-Golaz never wandered far from his vision of a Europe dominated for the foreseeable future by Hitler's armies.

There was, of course, another strand in the thinking of most Swiss statesmen, a fundamental anti-communism, expressed in Switzerland's lack of normal diplomatic relations with Soviet Russia. In late 1944, the Swiss approached Stalin to remedy this state of affairs; he rejected the approaches with characteristic brutality – a rebuff which led to Pilet-Golaz's departure (and to Churchill's eulogy, uttered in response to a suggestion by Stalin that the Allies ought to ignore Swiss neutrality and invade Southern Germany through Switzerland). The suddenness of the revelation that one of the Allies thought of their country as just another enemy came as a terrible shock to the Swiss, who had been shielded from any news inconvenient to the ruling clique during the war. As a maverick British diplomat, John (later Sir John) Lomax wrote in his book *Diplomatic Smuggler*: 'The Swiss people would never have submitted to support the German war effort if the facts had been squarely placed before their public opinion ... the small ruling group were far from representing the pro-Allied sentiment of the Swiss people. One or two were pro-Axis; others were convinced that Britain would be beaten and were therefore disposed – as the French put it – to run to the help of the victors'. For Lomax, as for everyone else, the symbol of ultimate resistance was Guisan, and 'he was kept in the background and never allowed a say in, or even a knowledge of, diplomatic affairs.'

But it is altogether too pat and convenient to blame Pilet-Golaz alone for a policy which inevitably reflected the feelings of a majority of the Federal Council. Lomax blames the Foreign Office for not spelling out the truth to the Swiss people. Because· of press censorship there is only indirect evidence available regarding the attitude of the Federal Councillors in general. At a press conference given by one of them, the Minister of Justice, Dr von Steiger, in May 1942, he went out of his way to emphasise the sternness and impartiality of his government's attitude towards spies and agents, whoever their masters. According to a 'well-informed Swiss journalist, well acquainted with Dr Steiger,' quoted by the Counsellor to the American Legation, 'the Federal Councillor was really aiming at the agents in Switzerland, often Swiss themselves, of Nazi Germany ... he was one of only two (the other being Stampfli) of the seven Federal Councillors who were actively defending Swiss independence with considerable courage and opposing to the limit all German attempts at intrusion in Swiss affairs.'

However 'well-informed' the journalist, he had virtually no opportunity for practising his craft since the ability of the ruling group to impose their policies depended very largely on the press censorship.* Had the newspapers been freer, there is no doubt that they would have been immensely critical of the government's policy. A British despatch in 1944 noted how the German-Swiss papers were solidly pro-Allied, and, as the diplomat elegantly expressed it, those of French Switzerland 'gradually put less Vichy water in their wine once they had recovered from the shell-shock caused by the French collapse.'**

Thus only through the strictest (and most undemocratic) control could the country's rulers keep Pilet-Golaz in office. Edgar Bonjour notes that already in 1940 the head of the Political Department (which included foreign affairs) no longer retained the people's confidence. And he was not subsequently able to regain his credibility.

The contrast between the collaboration with the Germans and their friends and the 'negative neutrality' displayed towards the Allies in official quarters was bad enough. But

* The Nazis were always terrified of the German-language Swiss papers. From their earliest days in power they had clamped down on the import of these papers into Germany, because of their objective reporting of events within the country.
** The news blackout required to prevent any eruption of popular feeling ensured that news-gathering was always a difficult business for Allied diplomats – to get copies of the directive to Swiss banks issued by the Federal Council in early 1943, an enterprising diplomat had to resort to trickery. He pretended to the Swiss Compensation Office, which was in charge of policing external financial matters – like the clearing with Germany – that the Americans (naturally) already had a copy of the directive in German and merely wanted one in French to obviate the need to translate it.

official attitudes turned to active hostility when dealing with refugees. Despite Steiger's personal staunchness in standing up to the Germans, the Swiss Federal Police became notorious for their heartless treatment of Jewish refugees. In his report, Dr. Ludwig published a number of stories of Jews, spurned by the Swiss, committing suicide rather than face returning to Germany. And when Jews were admitted they were subjected to exceptionally strict treatment. One standard form even provided for the breakage of banking secrecy. In return for being granted residence the refugee was forced to agree, among other conditions, to 'give the authorities precise and truthful information about my financial situation and to give prompt and unsolicited notification of any change in my circumstances. I attest that I have given the authorities full information about my financial circumstances. I empower all persons who professionally or legally have or have had financial dealings with me, viz, banks, repositories, lawyers, etc., to disclose details of my personal finances.'

An American official document provides a complete contrast, describing the kid-glove treatment accorded to a certain Leopold Egon Winkler who:

from 1938 on had the reputation, amongst Austrian and other anti-Nazi refugees, of being a German agent. An Austro-German national, Winkler established himself in Paris some time subsequent to the German occupation. He was known and feared as a German police informer and spy. He was probably an SS man ... he entered Switzerland with his wife and two cars in the summer of 1943. He is alleged to have brought in some forty trunks containing jewelry, furs, dollar notes, Swiss francs and gold coins. The foreign exchange and gold were deposited by him in a safe deposit box in the Banque Cantonale Vaudoise, Lausanne ... shortly after Winkler's entrance he was denounced to the Swiss authorities as a German espionage agent. In any event he was incarcerated in the prison at Bois-Mermet and his assets in the bank sequestered by the Swiss Military Police. According to our informants, the evidence of Winkler's espionage services was so strong that ordinarily he would have been shot. However the Swiss government allegedly may not have felt secure enough *vis-à-vis* the Germans at that time and simply ignored Winkler's espionage. There is the possibility that Winkler's associates included certain highly situated Swiss officials as well.

In the event Winkler's partner in his nefarious activities in Paris sued him in the Swiss courts in a successful effort to have all the funds he had deposited sequestered (it was only later that the Swiss Compensation Office blocked the assets). The disgust aroused by this blatant contrast between the treatment accorded to Jewish refugees and to rich Nazis was expressed by a Vaudois paper at the end of the war, when Swiss censorship restrictions had been lifted: 'Refugees', it wrote, 'are subjected to a rigorous interrogation before being allowed to benefit from the right to refuge on the soil of the Confederation. Capital benefits from the right to asylum without any enquiry.'

The picture that emerges is of a ruling group largely insulated from the moral implications of their actions, and still pursuing their narrow personal financial ends even in wartime. The absence of patriotism went to great lengths. In Dr. von Steiger's press conference 'he indicated that the number of cases of spying and treason, in which even Swiss army officers were implicated, was growing, and that they were often caused by a simple desire for gain' – a damning indictment when it is remembered how closely the officer and executive classes were knit together. More general than spying was the simple pursuit of a personal career at the expense of public service. In 1943, Fritz Schnorf, then a senior official of the Swiss National Bank, left his post to join the Swiss Aluminium Company at three or four times his official salary. His change of jobs was widely regarded as desertion and, after the war, his appointment as President of the Bank was vetoed by Bernard Nobs, the first Social Democrat ever to join the Federal Council.*

Schnorf's pursuit of personal gain was widely imitated in the Swiss banking community, which enjoyed undue influence

* Schnorf's move didn't help the Aluminium Company much either: when he joined as general manager, the shares stood at 4,000 francs, and by 1946 were down to a mere 1,600.

over the government in the first few years of the war, before the Federal Council was strengthened in 1943 by the inclusion of new, younger blood, including Nobs. In those years there was no gainsaying the truth of the saying (which passed for a witticism in the original *Schwyzerdütsch*) that the country was ruled by the Federal Council (*Bundesrat*) with the help of the *Vorort* (the Executive Office of the Association for Swiss Commerce and Industry), and no denying, either, that this influence was employed wholly on the side of the Germans.

2 / Hard-faced men who did well out of the war

This description was coined to describe the many war profiteers sitting on the Conservative benches in the House of Commons in the years immediately after World War I. But at least these men had made their money from the winning side. It was the peculiar genius of the Swiss banking community to emerge relatively unscathed – morally or financially – from the second global conflict in which they retained their prized neutrality while providing systematic (and highly profitable) aid and comfort to the losers. Their victory was not, however, primarily financial: the declared profits of the Swiss Bank Corporation, for instance, barely changed at all during the war, and two of the many banks which had been so badly damaged in the 1930s finally collapsed in 1945. Rather, their victory lay in preserving their traditional weapons of secrecy piled upon discretion, in the face of an unprecedentedly fierce series of assaults, and in thus advertising their uniqueness as a refuge for the world's wealth.

The imbalance of the banks' committment cannot be exaggerated. For many Swiss banks, especially in Zurich, Germany had always been the natural financial and economic partner. But during the war the imbalance grew greater – victory for Germany would have been a cause for virtually unalloyed joy in the country's banks, financially, and, in many cases, politically as well.

To be sure, Julius Baer, then a relatively small private bank – and one owned by a Jewish family – greatly helped the OSS by arranging for the foreign exchange it required. And one famous Geneva-based concern, the Société Générale de Surveillance, extended its basic business 'of inspecting merchandise in transit through Switzerland and of freight forwarding' to 'holding funds representing profits realised by its Balkan customers on shipments of merchandise to neutrals and to enemy territory ... these funds and other property are beneficially owned by Jewish persons who are nationals and residents of' various Balkan countries. They were naturally anxious to 'move funds out of their home countries and to ensure that their funds would be safe from confiscation'. (They were also anxious to profit from the local black market in foreign exchange.) The Swiss also provided a refuge after the war when the Russians tried to seize the accounts of Hungarians, Rumanians and Bulgarians who had deposited money or valuables in their banks. Nevertheless, for every such genuine 'refugee' there were a hundred German customers. In the words of an unpublished American official history: 'their aid to the enemy in the banking field was clearly beyond the obligations under which a neutral must continue trade with a belligerent and dictated solely by the profit motive ... The use of the Swiss banking community by the Germans is difficult to exaggerate. By early 1945 German investments and accounts in Switzerland amounted to 600 million dollars'. It was also believed that: 'considerable amounts of German assets were represented in securities, currencies, works of art etc., held in Swiss safety deposit boxes. German real estate holdings in Switzerland were thought to be worth 62.5 million dollars and insurance policies and annuities were estimated to represent 50 million dollars. Privately owned German accounts were reported to be in excess of 500 million Swiss francs.' At the end of the war, Albert Nussbaumer of the SBC estimated that the Germans had added between 1 and 1.5 billion francs to their Swiss holdings during the war – a substantial proportion of the total estimated by the Americans. But they were not merely depositories. No deal was too convoluted – and no client too disreputable – for them. (There was even a persistent rumour that Hitler himself had an account in the Union Bank under the name of his man of business, Max Amann.) The circumstances varied wildly; if Gestapo agents were bribed to stop the transport of the Jewish population of Slovakia to Poland, then the money required was deposited in the Union Bank; if the Reichsbank wanted to get funds to a German agent in Dublin, another neutral capital, then the Swiss Volksbank and the SBC obliged by transmitting money to one 'William Greene'.

Swiss banks were not alone in their activities. The name of the Enskilda Bank of Stockholm occurs more than any other in the British and American archives as providing a range of services to the enemy. German groups like Robert Bosch and I. G. Farben channelled many of their transactions through the bank, which also worked actively with a number of its Swiss brethren (the Dresdner Bank's foreign exchange transactions were conducted, seemingly, through both the Swedish bank and the SBC). One American diplomatic document* mentions the 'close co-operation between the Stockholm Enskilda Bank and enemy banks in the Far East, especially the German colony in Shanghai' – where the Swiss were unable to help. But the Swedish bank differed totally from the Swiss in two respects: while Jacob Wallenberg, one of the two

---

* The cooperation between the Swiss, the Swedes and the Germans can be seen from the following convoluted, if typical, transaction:
'To the account of Dresdner Bank, Berlin, the Swiss Bank Corporation credited Enskilda with 463,000 Swiss francs, July 22, 1944. Dresdner Bank, Galata, authorised Enskilda to sell 315,000 Swiss francs, reimbursing Dresdner Bank, Berlin, with an equivalent amount. Dresdner reimbursed Crédit Suisse with 215,000 Swiss francs, and the Swiss Bank Corporation, Zurich, in the amount of 100,000 Swiss francs, June 25, 1944. Dresdner Bank told Enskilda, March 5, 1944, to sell 157,000 Swiss francs to the Swiss Bank Corporation and to pay counter value to Dresdner, Berlin. On July 13, 1944, a like transaction was authorized by Dresdner Bank, Galata, for the Swiss Bank Corporation to sell 100,000 free marks, reimbursing Dresdner Bank, Berlin. Enskilda was to be reimbursed, account of Dresdner, Berlin, in the amount of 80,000 Swiss francs. On August 28, 1944, on authorization of the Swiss Bank Corporation, Enskilda credited 29,513 kroner to Gewerbekasse, Baden.'

remarkable men who ran it, concentrated on the bank's German connections, his younger brother, Marcus, was equally active on the Allied side (while a cousin, Raoul, became one of the war's heroes for his efforts to save the Hungarian Jewish community). Moreover the Swedes, as we shall see, did not defy the Allied efforts to pursue German war criminals nearly as tenaciously as did the Swiss.

Even within Switzerland the bankers were not alone. Many Swiss lawyers lent their talents to devising covers for German interests. Others helped form trusts and companies for the same purposes. Numerous other covers were used: the German Sanatorium at Davos became notorious as a bolt-hole, while even the sacred name of the International Red Cross was employed at the end of the war to cover the export of watches made by a German owned concern. But most German business inevitably passed through the banking system, and the British and American archives* provide fascinating, if episodic, glimpses of its size and diversity as the Allies gradually grasped its significance. 'It was generally known that Swiss banks acted as Germany's international bankers prior to the war,' says the American official history, 'the extent of Germany's use, however, during the war of Swiss commercial institutions was uncovered only through investigations after the war had started.'

The banks' activities were largely devoted to their German clients although, as the tide of war turned, they felt increasingly obliged to preserve at least a nominal balance. Sam Woods, the well informed American consul-general in Zurich, wrote in 1944 that all the banks 'without exception, are engaged in activities from time to time which do not coincide with our interests. The best that can be said of them is that several of them have members of their staffs who are very friendly to, and co-operative with, the Allied cause. It is believed that these men are picked for their abilities to maintain contact with the Allied countries while other members in the past have been picked in the same manner to maintain contact with Axis countries.' Woods mentioned as pro-Allied Walter Fessler, of the Crédit Suisse, who had an

*For details of the archives I have used see notes.

American wife, and Ernest Hoch, of the SBC – the same institution which employed Albert Nussbaumer, the banker who had most contact with the Americans. ('I always find Nussbaumer a pleasant conversationalist' wrote the American diplomat, 'and my evaluation of him is that he is sincere, honest and forthright in his dealings, at least with me. He is probably subject to the common Swiss failing of placing undue value on money and may be inclined to give himself a cleaner bill of health than the actual full record of past transactions would warrant. But I would be inclined personally to trust him').

Poor Nussbaumer was the man in the middle, negotiating with the Americans on behalf of his obstinate and ungrateful fellows over black lists and blocked assets, eternally misunderstood by both sides, worried that he would not be allowed into the United States because of his alleged involvement with his bank's activities before 1939 in helping German companies 'cloak' the real ownership of their foreign subsidiaries, held up in Lisbon on a projected visit in June 1944 because of the imminence of D-Day (a delay he attributed to his links with Pirelli's interests in Latin America), unable to persuade his conservative fellows of the need to co-operate more freely with the Allies.

The uneasy balance within Swiss banks came into the open in 1944 when Dr. Rudolf Speich succeeded Dr. Max Staehlin as Chairman of the SBC bank. The American consul at Basle explained that Speich had 'until recent years been singularly successful in Central Europe and the Balkans for his bank. In countries where others had often failed, Dr. Speich, it seems, had always been able to operate without losses. But his work, too, was destined to come to grief in those parts, with the result that Dr. Speich's department ... had become known as the "cemetery" within that organisation.' It was this knowledge of German affairs which led to his elevation, in preference to the candidate from French Switzerland, Maurice Golay, whose appointment, it was thought, 'would have been more pleasing to London and Washington' because of his 'long and successful connection with the bank's large English and French interests'. But in competing for 'what is generally considered as the biggest plum in the Swiss banking world,

Golay's French-Swiss background was more of a handicap than a help in German-speaking Basle and Zurich' where he had never been truly accepted. 'Moreover the successful Dr. Speich, who is a colonel in a Glarus regiment, has been a prominent figure in Swiss military circles for years, and it is perhaps revealing no secret to say that he was not "heroic" in his attitude to Nazi military might'. In this context the adjective 'heroic' is a code word, signifying those who were true to Guisan's ideal of armed, impartial, Swiss neutrality. To be 'unheroic' was simply to follow the path of least – and most profitable – resistance, working with the Nazis.

(But the balance was always shifting: Dr. Staehlin moved from the SBC to its biggest industrial client – and itself a major shareholder in the bank – the chemical group CIBA, where his appointment spelt disappointment to a strong, and strongly pro-Nazi, opposition group. But Staehlin, a 'close friend and brother Mason' of the former chairman, prevented a pro-Nazi takeover.)

The underlying tension within the Swiss banking community is best summed up in the person of a private banker, Johann Wehrli. His family had been established in Zurich for centuries, and was distinguished enough to have entertained the Kaiser when he visited Switzerland in 1912. Johann Wehrli, a close personal friend of Pilat-Golaz, was a millionaire in any currency. But only a quarter of his fortune – reckoned at between 30 and 40 million Swiss francs – over 10 million dollars – was invested in his bank, and by the outbreak of war he was sixty-five and anxious not to be actively involved with it. His son concentrated on the very large business the bank had built up in Latin America, taking care of the interests of wealthy Germans, but the bank's domestic banking activities were left to the charge of a long-time employee, Karl Kessler, a Swiss so devoted to the Nazi cause that he was not even prepared to share a hotel lift with his American or British fellow guests.

Wehrli's most trusted employee may have been a fervent Nazi but his son-in-law was a British officer, Max Binney. Formerly a businessman in Zurich, and brother of Sir George Binney, a distinguished Arctic explorer employed by British Intelligence, Max Binney went back to England in 1939 to take up a captaincy in the Grenadier Guards. His return in 1942 to become the British vice-consul in the key listening post of Lugano was marked by great diplomatic whisperings (not least how a serving British officer could have been allowed safe transit through Spain and Vichy France).

Before Binney's return the Americans were exerting considerable pressure to have both Wehrli's bank and Kessler himself placed on the Allied Black Lists and thus forbidden from doing business in countries controlled by the Allies. The Americans were blunt: 'Wehrli is believed to be fairly neutral in his political views, but perfectly willing to leave Kessler and Reutter in charge so that the firm works one hundred per cent for the Axis countries, and he, Wehrli, without taking active part, reaps large profits.' The British were cynical. In a letter to the ever-bristling John Lomax, Eric Cable, the British consul-general in Zurich and himself a friend of Wehrli, wrote that 'it seems to me that if we blacklist a firm like Wehrli and Co on the flimsy material available and in the teeth of arguments to the contrary, it is difficult to see how we can avoid blacklisting practically the whole of Switzerland.' His case for Wehrli was that he was a 'man of the old school', a true Swiss patriot, and 'though his wife is of German origin she too is completely out of harmony not only with the present regime but also with Germany going to war at all, as she was in the case of the previous war.' Kessler was a different matter entirely and quarrelled so violently even with his fellow manager, the supposedly pro-German Max Reutter, that the latter had a serious heart attack.

Of Kessler's German connections there was no doubt. He was German-born, his wife was German, his brother lived on the family's estates near Hamburg. 'He has kept in touch with German industry for many years', reported the American consulate in Zurich. 'The firm under his direction dealt in German marks after the last war and was engaged in bringing marks out of Germany. The firm tried to push German industrial shares and held large numbers of shares in German industrial concerns. Furthermore Mr. Kessler is on the boards of many German firms and spends part of each year in Germany. He is reliably reported from various sources to be a very close friend of Von Ribbentrop and the latter's brother-in-law, Henckel' [*sic*]. In the same account based on 'reliable information' from a 'well-known Swiss business man' came a report that Kessler 'may probably be the person who administers Goering's private financial interests in this country, reported from other sources to be in the neighbourhood of four million dollars.' Not only Kessler was involved. 'Dr. von Stauss, vice-President of the Reichsbank and a man who played an important role under the last Emperor and Hindenburg, comes to Zurich frequently where he has business connections with Mr. Johann Wehrli. Dr. von Stauss is a director of Lufthansa, Ufa, Mercedes, the Dresdner Bank, and many other of the largest German business enterprises.'

Because of Wehrli's friendship with Eric Cable, the Americans did not share this particular titbit with the British – but the Ministry of Economic Warfare nevertheless put Kessler's name on its Black List, although they firmly stuck out against inclusion of the bank itself. The affair became murkier when Binney returned, for he boasted to an American diplomat at a cocktail party that he was a personal friend of the British Foreign Secretary, Anthony Eden, and that 'he should at least be given credit for having prevented the listing of his father-in-law's bank and his "Nazi in-laws", even though he had been unable to keep Kessler off the list.' (How far this remark was merely a camouflage for Binney's own intelligence activities is unclear.)

Clearly the British were hoping to use Wehrli to obtain information about Nazi activities. Wehrli encouraged this belief, but never, apparently, came up with any information. In the end, however, Wehrli's bank was one of the five institutions named by American investigators as those which had done most to help the German war effort (a comparatively limited and ingenuous list). Wehrli himself seems to have spent the entire war unable to reconcile his desire to allow Kessler (whom he steadfastly refused to sack) to continue to earn profits and his genuine distaste at his personality and methods. In a pathetic letter to his son Peter (which was never actually sent, following the advice of the British Legation) Wehrli wrote of the funeral of a cousin and the illness of virtually the whole of the rest of the family, of the deceptions practised by Kessler and of his desire to run down the bank's operations. But still the indomitable old man dreams that 'representation for Switzerland, etc., of an American private banking house might possibly be entrusted to us after the war'. But the dream came to nothing, and Wehrli liquidated his bank in 1945.

Less ambiguous – but even more startlingly illustrative of the Swiss attitude to collaboration with the Nazis – was the case of Edouard von der Heydt, probably the single most famous Nazi supporter within the Swiss banking community. Von der Heydt came from a rich family, was financial adviser to the former Kaiser, and had sheltered him on his estate in Holland. His connection with Switzerland began in 1926 when he bought Monte Ascona, a fabled property in the Ticino, and he prudently acquired Swiss citizenship in 1937, settling permanently in the country on the outbreak of war.

He had joined the Nazi Party in Germany in 1933 and throughout the war he served the Nazi war effort in two ways: he was on the board of the bank created by the Thyssens, owners of one of Germany's biggest steel groups, to control their financial dealings – characteristically the bank had a branch in Zurich; and von der Heydt's own bank in Locarno was used by the German High Command to channel payments to their information network outside Germany – nearly a million francs passed through in 1940–3. He naturally became connected with the mysterious figure of Hans Gisevius, nominally the German vice-consul in Zurich, in fact a member of the German Intelligence service and thus closely linked with the group round Admiral Canaris which became deeply – and eventually conspiratorially – estranged from the Nazi regime. Gisevius even succeeded in setting up a secret cache of easily realisable assets (mostly gold coins) using army funds, which was kept with von der Heydt (unfortunately, an informant managed to break the secret and Gisevius had to return the funds).

After the war the Swiss arrested both Gisevius and von der Heydt. Gisevius was charged with 'subversive financial dealings' – presumably with von der Heydt, while the banker was charged with 'conducting military intelligence for one foreign state directed against another foreign state' and stripped of his Swiss citizenship. Unfortunately for him, soon after they had entered the war, the Americans had picked up a number of German agents who had admitted that they had received their money through von der Heydt's bank. On hearing this, the Americans had promptly impounded the selection of works from his famous collection of Asian art, which he had lent to a museum in Buffalo.

But it was this taste which was the salvation of von der Heydt. In January 1946 he gave the bulk of his collection to the Rietberg Museum in Zurich, where the city fathers, aware of its importance, welcomed it gratefully. Within a year he had been acquitted of the charges brought against him, and, albeit grudgingly, his Swiss citizenship had been restored to him. The trial of Gisevius was postponed *sine die*, because, it was surmised, any publicity might have led to unwelcome revelations about Swiss collaboration with the German army during the war.

Although the von der Heydt case is famous in Switzerland, he and Wehrli and indeed the other private bankers engaged in similar practices were providing only specialised services for a relatively small group of customers. Most of the transactions with the Germans involved the bigger banks and relatively routine transactions. Curiously, few of these were concerned with the massive flow of Swiss-German trade which so distressed the Allies. The major banks had far too great a proportion of their assets tied up in Germany for comfort, so they shifted the burden. They simply imposed intolerable conditions on credits granted for exports to Germany. Swiss industrialists turned to the government to provide the backing they required. This in turn boosted the trade imbalance during the war so that the accumulated deficit weighed heavily in the arrangements made for the repayment of Germany's debts after the war. The banks' routine activities largely concerned foreign exchange and gold. The very regularity of these activities tended to obscure their importance, although not from the Germans. In June 1943, Walther Funk, then the German Minister of Economics, declared bluntly that the Nazi government could not afford even a two-month break in the Swiss financial connection. A year later an American official made the same point: 'German gold exports to Switzerland are the lifeline of Germany's war potential abroad, furnishing about ninety per cent of her foreign exchange requirements, and the number one facility suitable for *official* German capital flight as far as the western hemisphere'. By acting as a conduit for the German gold the Swiss banks were aiding and abetting not only the German war effort, but also German looting of occupied countries. Recent Swiss research estimates that the Germans sold 1.6 billion Swiss francs worth of gold through Switzerland during the war. This figure was ten times the official German pre-war gold reserves. Even though Dr. Schacht and other German officials had played down the real figure to impress foreign bankers with Germany's poverty, it is difficult to disagree with one American opinion: 'Even allowing for private German holdings and possible purchases of bullion from Russia early in the war, the conclusion is inescapable that most of this was looted gold – from government stocks of the invaded countries, from private hoards, or perhaps from the teeth of concentration camp victims.'

Inevitably, given the multiplicity of sources, most of the non-official gold simply disappeared. The Allies never succeeded in reclaiming even the official gold holdings which had passed into or through, Swiss hands. (The most famous case concerned nearly a hundred tons [115 million dollars] worth of Belgian Government gold, diverted to Dakar in West Africa and then handed over to the Germans by the Vichy government. Like so much more, its identity became blurred when it was melted down and sold, often through the Swiss National Bank, to anonymous and untraceable destinations.)

The quantities were enormous. In September 1944 when the flood was at its height, one American intelligence report stated that 'a number of Swiss banks are now embarrassed at having so much stolen gold'. The principal beneficiary of this *embarras de richesses* was the Bank Leu 'whose director, J. H. Pfeiffer, has done the larger part of handling these German manipulations'. Pfeiffer and the others were 'doing their best to sell it to "sure persons" in spite of the fact that this constitutes a breach of the country's law forbidding the export of gold'. By that time, gold had become a major vehicle for Nazis eager to smuggle assets abroad: 'some of the identifiable German gold sent to Portugal', according to one authority, 'was sold to goldsmiths to be melted down and turned into ornaments. German agents even managed to exchange their looted gold for some that was demonstrably untainted, having been resting in vaults in the western hemisphere through the war, by selling gold to Switzerland for free Swiss francs, using the francs to establish a credit in Argentina, and buying the gold there.'

Earlier in the war, gold had been used for a bewildering variety of financial and commercial transactions, in virtually all of which Swiss banks played a profitable part. The Italians blazed a trail which was followed after 1945 by thousands of their fellow countrymen seeking the anonymous security of Switzerland. Until virtually the end of the war: 'a substantial number of gold pieces was being smuggled daily from Switzerland to northern Italy. These were paid for by lire banknotes, which in turn were smuggled into Switzerland and found a ready market against Swiss francs. The gold pieces were purchased in northern Italy in part by "harmless" speculators or investors and in part, undoubtedly, by war criminals and other undesirables. The lire notes dealt with in Switzerland eventually found their way back into northern Italy in payment for Italian goods, such as silk and rice.'

Gold was, however, principally a medium of exchange not for lire, but for Swiss francs. Despite its soubriquet of 'almighty', during the war the dollar was far less desirable than the Swiss franc, then the standard currency used for hoarding. Hans Baer estimated that in 1943, 'between 1 and $1\frac{1}{2}$ billion francs in banknotes out of a total circulation of roughly 3 billion were not actually circulating, and that several hundred million were probably in foreign countries.'

In the 1930s currency uncertainties had led to a series of tidal waves involving massive Swiss investment in the United States followed by equally sudden withdrawals. By 1941 the Swiss National Bank was awash with dollars, as a result of these movements, would not increase its holdings of the currency, and organised a 'gentlemen's agreement' with the country's banks to impose a strict distinction between 'commercial' and 'financial' dollars, to confine its transactions to the limited amount of currency required for trade purposes. The result was a flourishing market described by the

Americans in 1942 (largely from British sources): 'Germany has systematically collected large amounts of hoarded dollar notes in Germany and occupied territories. They have been confiscated, purchased on the black market, or looted ... since Switzerland is a free gold and foreign exchange market there are few difficulties in selling dollar notes' – albeit 'at approximately 50 per cent of their parity' (the same documents list other sources of Swiss francs as gold, foreign securities, and the 'free' Swiss francs available as a result of the 'clearing agreement').

One specific source of profit involved the escudo, the currency of another neutral, Portugal. The escudo was in great demand from both sides because Portugal was the key source of wolfram, which, when refined as tungsten, was essential for hardening steel. The Swiss banks participated with enthusiasm in a traffic which gave them handsome and virtually risk-free profits (the dollar bills they had purchased at a discount of forty per cent in Switzerland could be sold at a discount of only thirty-two per cent in Portugal).

The leader was the Basler Handelsbank, which was also a principal agent in 'laundering official German funds'. A message from the American ambassador in London spelled out the form: 'the bank has been very active in selling sterling, Italian lire and French franc notes to Portugal. The suspicion of enemy taint in these notes, which are mainly handled by the bank's Zurich branch, is strengthened by the rather remarkable synchronisation of this activity with the same branch's transfers of escudos to the Reichsbank ... it may of course be purely coincidental but it does lend itself to the sinister interpretation that the escudos are the proceeds of notes sold by the Zurich bank as agents for the enemy.'

Another neutral currency much in demand from the Germans was the Spanish peseta. The Germans used the Wehrli Bank as an intermediary. According to one British report, 'almost all peseta notes coming to Switzerland are sold by an electric factory in Andorra whence they find their way to the Wehrli Bank and Kessler is then said to take them to Stuttgart', where they were returned to Spain as directed by the German High Command. These transactions came to light in September 1942 when the Crédit Suisse told the

British consulate about the transfer of the million francs used
to buy the pesetas. Questioned by the British consul, Wehrli
stated that the money was used for buying pesetas on behalf of
the Reichsbank for the Vatican, 'which', added the consul,
'does not make sense to me' – in fact it was used for buying
foodstuffs for the Germans.

In hundreds of similar transactions the Swiss played a
central role in the movement of German funds, even when the
business was being carried out in another country. For
instance, Istanbul fully lived up to its historic reputation as a
centre for intrigue. It was an important market for the sale of
gold in exchange for Swiss francs; the Deutsche Bank, for one,
used its Istanbul branch to hold its accounts with the major
Swiss banks. Black market operators also used a Swiss bank to
transfer funds in favour of local Germans; and the German
banks in Istanbul also used a complicated scheme involving
cheques drawn on an account with the Union Bank's head
office in Zurich on behalf of the former Bulgarian consul in
Istanbul.

None of these transactions was subject to any restrictions.
'The Swiss National Bank', asserted the Americans, 'has
practically no authority over gold and foreign exchange
transactions and cannot prevent the Swiss commercial banks
from undertaking certain types of transactions.' The only
exception was the dollar agreement between the Swiss
National Bank and the banking community. In that case:
'because it is the only large buyer of dollars, it can lay down its
own conditions. In regard to other transactions, no such
one-sided advantage exists'. Moreover, because of banking
secrecy, 'it is possible that the Swiss National Bank and the
Swiss government are not fully aware of what is actually going
on' – although the author was probably being over charitable
to the Swiss authorities, banking secrecy did at least enable
them to proclaim their official ignorance of what their
country's financial institutions were up to.

Trading in gold and foreign exchange were, if not routine,
at least regular transactions, derived either from long-
standing correspondent relationships between major banks in
different countries, or natural for financial institutions based
in a country always largely dependent on international trade

and foreign exchange. Even when the banks were helping the Germans dispose of looted gold, they could at least pretend that this was merely 'business as usual'. Their truly 'collaborationist' activities lay in three other fields: the way the whole Swiss financial and legal community rallied round the efforts of German industrialists to conceal their foreign interests behind a neutral cloak; the equally neutral cover the Swiss banks provided for securities held by the Germans; and the bolt-holes they organised for German capital.

Because of the confiscatory measures supervised by the Alien Property Custodian in the United States during World War I, German industrialists were active in the 1920s and 1930s in devising apparently neutral 'holding companies' and trusts to cover their foreign interests. Although the Dutch and the Swedes enjoyed some of the business, most of it was channelled through Switzerland. There was a rush of capital to Switzerland as war grew nearer, according to official figures recorded by the American consul in Basle: 'on the eve of the great conflict in 1939, no less than 260 international financial corporations with 250,000,000 francs capital were registered in Switzerland, bringing up the number of such institutions to 2,278 with assets of approximately 4 billion Swiss francs ... The number of holding companies, independent trusts and personal corporations which are often organised here for the care or management of private fortunes of Germans, French, Belgians, and others number approximately 2,026 and represent a capital of approximately 2,200,000 Swiss francs.' The most elaborate scheme was that devised by the German chemical cartel, I. G. Farben, using a small Swiss bank founded in 1920 expressly to carry out the convoluted transactions involved. This was so important that it deserves separate discussion (see Part IV).

Most of the precautions had been taken well before the war – for instance the Schering pharmaceutical concern used the Swiss Bank Corporation to safeguard its interests through the establishment of holding companies with curious names like Chepha and Forinvent. The Swiss nominally owned the companies, but German interests were secured, through a legally binding option by which the real owners could repurchase the shares at any time.

With the German occupation of Holland, however, nominally 'Dutch' holding companies were classed as enemy owned by the Americans and therefore also subject to confiscation. So even in the middle of the war the Germans were often looking for active collaboration from the Swiss. And their requirements for help from their banks were elaborate and sophisticated. When, for instance, the steel group Vereinigte Stahlwerke was trying to 'cloak' its Argentine subsidiary, Thyssen Lametal (Thyla), by introducing a nominally Swiss firm into the ownership chain the Germans stipulated that 'a way should be found which will make it possible for the Swiss firm to appear vis-à-vis a third party with full authority as unrestricted owners of the shares. Besides the firm in question must be ready to uphold this standpoint, if necessary, not only with the Argentine but also with the Swiss authorities ... it should be guaranteed that the Thyla shares could be reconveyed at any time at your request to the ownership of the Cehandro' – a Dutch holding company. Ernst, a private bank in Berne, collaborated with a will. 'It has notified the entire payment of the purchase price by wire to Argentina in order to render credible the change of the shares to Swiss property.'

If these cover-up operations went wrong then the Swiss bankers could suffer, both materially, and, in a society where money and prestige were so intimately linked, in their reputation as well. The American consul-general in Basle recorded that: 'the prestige of even Dr. Max Staehlin, the eminent lawyer and chairman of the SBC, had suffered not a little following the losses of some 15 million francs or more in the Metallwerke, Suchard and Schering Corporation, New York, cases in the last years of his presidency. The Suchard and Schering collapse apparently cost Dr. Staehlin a considerable part of his fortune ... the sale of Dr. Staehlin's large residence here ... seems not unconnected with the losses sustained by him in the above-mentioned cases'. (His colleague, Samuel Schweizer, was placed on the Americans' confidential list of suspects because of his role as sole administrator of Atlantis AG, a Panama holding company concealing Schering interests abroad.)

Providing cloaks for major industrial groups merged into

providing the same service on a wholesale basis for families as well. In 1939, Johann Wehrli, Kessler and Reutter 'withdrew cash sums from their personal accounts in the Wehrli Bank and transferred part of them to Argentina to form the three "S" companies' – Securitas, San Juan and Stella. By 1943 the real value of the assets of the companies had multiplied several times: 'these companies maintain secret numbered accounts that are owned by Germans', reported the American Foreign Economic Administration department, 'and evidence shows that accounts ostensibly held for various neutrals are actually cloaking German interests ... another account, held in the name of Moriz Carl Bunge of Zurich and containing assets in excess of 3 million pesos, actually is proved to belong to the Henkell family of Wiesbaden, Germany, of which the wife of Joachim Von Ribbentrop is a member. In establishing these accounts in Argentina, Wehrli and Company transferred assets held in their name from throughout the world.'

Johann Wehrli's son, Peter, had originally gone to Buenos Aires to supervise these interests – as well as the family's extensive land holdings in Argentina, but he was subsequently trapped in New York, unable to obtain an exit visa (consoling himself by marrying an American wife). But his family's transactions were as nothing compared to the wholesale faking of bonds, shares, and dividend coupons by a number of major banks after the German occupation of France, Holland, and Belgium. The international criminal underworld, enthusiastically backed by the Germans, and using a number of Swiss banks, ensured that dividend coupons belonging to shares (especially in that old Continental favourite Royal Dutch Shell) owned or looted by Germans or in the hands of citizens of occupied countries, were recertified as being in neutral ownership. The dividends were then duly paid, to the tune of millions of francs. According to the British consul in Lausanne, who 'had an enormous file in hand', 'the organisation at the root of this traffic is the famous Caduff, native of Graubunden, in Geneva, a notorious international swindler who was expelled from France before the war'. He had agents all over Switzerland, including fifteen notaries in the Canton of Berne alone, all busy attesting to false affidavits (not to mention another who was the son-in-law of the *Juge d'Instruc-*

tion, the district attorney of the canton of Valais). These swindlers employed 'innocents', irresponsible people, who signed blank affidavits ('Leon Giroud of La Batia, for example ... is an inconsequent peasant of no means, who signed affidavits just to please a pal'). The traffic was largely conducted through the Berne branch of the Federal Bank, but it was only in early 1943 that the bank, swearing it knew nothing of the matter, dismissed the head of its coupon clipping service, and the police, at least in the canton of Vaud (in which Lausanne is situated) got their teeth into the case (things were rather different in the Valais, where the *Juge* was naturally reluctant to pursue his son-in-law).

There was an even bigger traffic in looted shares. Again the traffic was largely concentrated in those issued by Royal Dutch Shell (the Reichsbank helped matters along by changing them from named 'nominal' shares to the far less traceable 'bearer' shares after the Germans had occupied Holland, the firm's former home country). It was 'known for a fact' by the American Legation in Berne that 'such German agents as Wilhelm (Will) Lein and Leon Benaroya (now living in Geneva) were arriving here with Royal Dutch and other shares within a few months after the occupation of Holland and France and continued unloading foreign shares and currencies in this market against gold for the account of the Reichsbank, Berlin.' The shares were transported by diplomatic bag, often by Latin American diplomats accredited to the Vichy government, 'with the assistance of the French and German authorities'. The biggest – nominal – seller of these shares was, again, the Federal Bank, and the biggest buyer was the Union Bank (which could at least claim that it was unaware of their origins).

The worst scandal hung over the Swiss Bank Corporation: the manager of their Zurich branch was involved, as was the young nephew of one of their general managers. But the SBC employee most heavily implicated was one Werner Hurter, who had previously worked for the Bank for International Settlements. When Hurter was arrested 'he was found in possession of hundreds of thousands of Swiss francs hidden under carpets at his home in Zurich'. Nevertheless he did not go quietly. He went straight to the American consulate, accompanied by his lawyer, Dr. Zundel.* There Hurter informed on the whole Zurich hierarchy of the SBC and denounced the *Commissaire de Bourse*, Walter Amrhein, who had first investigated the false affidavits, as being pro-German – not surprisingly as Amrhein had thrown Hurter into jail for four and a half months. Although the consul concluded that Hurter had 'come in out of spite to make charges against the bank' he had made one telling remark: if a particularly infamous art gallery, Galeries Fischer, 'was listed for disposing of stolen art, the banks that dispose of stolen securities and currencies should also be listed'.

By May 1944, when Hurter hurried to the consulate, the Germans, aware of impending defeat, were employing Swiss banks in a slightly different game, proving that assets which had, in reality, been owned by Germans at the outbreak of hostilities were legally owned by neutrals. The single most spectacular instance of this type of cover up is, again, provided by the case of I. G. Farben.

But it was not an isolated instance. By 1945 Herr Ruegg, a director of V. Ernst, who was married to a German wife and had spent some years in Germany before the war, was conducting a wholesale business in false affidavits, designed to prove that German assets in Sweden – mostly shares and loans – were Swiss. 'Ruegg', the Americans discovered, 'finds Swiss who, in return for bribes sign "affidavits" declaring that they were in possession of those assets in Sweden before a certain date in 1940–1 (these orders were alleged to have been deposited in the bank as early as 1939) and that they hereby authorise the bank to sell them. The bank then sends the papers to Sweden where they are sold and the money goes to German capitalists'. With the help of two Swedish banks, 'the V. Ernst bank has already transferred over 10 million Swedish shares of German ownership'. Another source described how he 'was invited to meet Ruegg at the Café Parade Platz in Zurich' – in the heart of the banking district and as conspicuous a spot as it was possible to find – 'Ruegg explained to source that he would give him the chance to earn easy money,

---

* According to the consul: 'Dr. Zundel seemed all right and though he had a curious accent it showed definite American influence. He claims to have gone to Columbia Law School after finishing law in Zurich.'

whereby no risk was involved and the bank secrecy code would safeguard the details. Ruegg required signature of source (who is a Swiss, well-established and resident in Switzerland) to one order for sale and two affidavits. He was willing to pay for this Swiss francs 200 per signature ... it was observed by source that Ruegg interviewed various other individuals at the Cafe Parade Platz in the course of the afternoon, with whom he exchanged documents and to whom he paid out money.'

Most well-heeled Germans, were, however, much more foresighted than Ruegg's clients. As early as December 1941, 'the Berne manager of one of the leading Swiss banks' told a British diplomat 'that to his personal knowledge every leading member of the governing groups in all Axis countries have funds deposited in Switzerland. Some of the leaders have fortunes here and even some of the smaller fry have considerable sums, i.e. upwards of half a million Swiss francs ... the accounts were originally in dollars then in Swiss francs, later on banking advice on "gold account". This switch had a considerable influence on the rate of exchange between the Swiss franc and the dollar ... recently they have been closing their "gold accounts" and keeping actual gold in a safe deposit box'. Italian Fascist leaders also took precautions. In late 1944 an Italian newspaper, still Axis controlled, quoted by the Italian radio, spread the story that the country's former leaders, including King Victor Emmanuel, had stashed away up to 500 million francs in Switzerland (a story obviously designed to blacken the name of figures who had 'deserted' to the Allies). The Duce's son-in-law, Count Ciano, allegedly employed the former Swiss minister to Rome, Mr Vieli, to 'take charge of the clandestine transfer of Ciano's capital to Switzerland. Vieli formerly belonged to banking and high Swiss financial circles and could accomplish the transfer without arousing suspicion in Italy or Switzerland.'

The general pattern was of individual transfers arranged for specific customers. In many instances banks charged a fee of five per cent to buy property in Switzerland on behalf of (but not in the name of) German clients. The same figure was mentioned when a group of German industrialists met in August 1944 in Strasbourg, to plan a recovery from the defeat they perceived was by then inevitable. They were relying on the Swiss banks to provide a secure refuge for the funds required to finance the come-back. To help these plans the Nazis were relaxing the rules against the export of capital – previously the Swiss had proved equally useful in breaking the rules against capital exports imposed by the nationalistic Nazis. In his book advocating a deindustrialised Germany, Henry Morgenthau, then the U.S. Secretary of the Treasury, explained that 'these funds will be at the disposal of the Nazis in their underground campaign (but the industrialists will be repaid by concessions and orders when the party candidates come to power). Two Swiss banks through which operations may be conducted were named, and the possibility of acquiring a Swiss dummy at a cost of five per cent was noted.'

The Strasbourg meeting has become famous, but it gives a slightly misleading picture, for the evidence suggests that the better organised German underground movements simply did not trust the Swiss banks. As Werner Brockdorff pointed out in his book on the organisation and financing of German escape routes: 'Martin Bormann – the movement's mastermind – had deposited no money in Switzerland because he knew that the Allies would concentrate their efforts on Switzerland and Austria.' The situation was crisply summed up in a note from 'C', the head of the British Secret Service, MI6, in February 1945. 'The German underground movement disposes of considerable funds in Switzerland. The assets consist chiefly of *Devisen*, mostly in Swiss banknotes, and of diamonds, probably also of other precious stones. From the beginning of its activity in Switzerland the underground movement had avoided opening bank accounts with Swiss banks and not even bank safes were used. The assets at the disposal of the movement are deposited in safes belonging to private individuals.'

Less exalted Germans did not, however, share their leaders' fears. As the Allies advanced across France following their landings in Normandy on 6 June 1944, the formal meeting at Strasbourg was paralleled by a panic by less exalted Germans. Typically, an intelligence report from a 'reliable French source' reports how 'mail cars accompanied by two or three German policemen arrived in Switzerland in mid-October from Nuremberg and Munich via Buchs-St. Margarethen. These cars were transporting large sums of money and securities which have been deposited in two banks in Davos. Other similar deposits have been made here in the past.' These and other deposits were looking for a safe haven, and the Allies' attempts to deny them their repose was to lead to one of the stormiest episodes in the history of Swiss banking.

3 / How safe a haven

Stalin believed that Switzerland should be used as a stepping-stone towards an invasion of Germany. In the early years of the war, the British official attitude to Switzerland had varied between impatience and hostility. But once the tide had clearly turned, the Foreign Office line softened, and the value of Switzerland as a neutral to be courted clearly outweighed its services to the German war effort.

The Americans, however, having caught the earlier British attitude, stuck fast to it. They believed that justice should be done, and that the Swiss should 'pay their passage home' in the words of one official. They should recognise and compensate for their previous unbalanced 'neutrality' by the fullest possible co-operation with Allied efforts to punish war criminals, to restore looted assets, and to thwart German efforts to shelter their industrial interests from sequestration.

It was ironic that the Swiss should have found themselves so fundamentally at odds with the Americans that the two sides were often, seemingly, talking about totally different situations. For, not only had the Swiss constitution been based on the American, but also in the mid-nineteenth century, America had engaged the emotions of the Swiss people as no other country ever had before or since. In the Civil War, Switzerland was 'almost the only European state to have sympathised entirely with the Union and acclaimed its cause as the cause of justice'. The assassination of President Lincoln, 'proclaimed as the martyrdom of the apostle of liberty', gave birth to an unprecedented and spontaneous movement, the *Adressenbewegung* in which hundreds of addresses of sympathy were drawn up and presented to the Americans. In Glarus, 'the whole free community of the people, in one of those solemn ceremonies which are peculiar to it, bared their heads in solemn silence as an expression of their respect and sympathy for the self-liberation of the noble American people'. All this was long forgotten when the Swiss were grappling with the Americans' unprecedented demands during the last two years of the war.

Negotiations to prevent Swiss assets being used to help the Germans started in 1944, because of Switzerland's position as one, if not the biggest, of the foreign holders of US dollar assets – the estimate of nominally Swiss assets in the United States was raised from 6 to 8 million francs before the war ended. These holdings had been blocked in June 1941 – although they were not sequestrated and no attempt was made to discover the real as opposed to the nominal ownership of the blocked funds. The situation changed in October 1943 when the American Treasury Department issued General Ruling No. 17, asking for full identification of the beneficial owners of these funds. Unless the ownership was revealed, they were treated as though they were enemy assets – and they provided a marvellous hostage for the Americans in dealing with the Swiss. It was only their release, following the Washington Agreements of May 1946, which relaxed the stranglehold and returned the assets – and thus their freedom of action – to the Swiss banks.

The Bankers' Association responded within a couple of months with a circular to its major members asking for details of their connections with the Axis countries. The list was quickly narrowed down to the country's twenty leading banks, on the grounds that they accounted for a third of all the assets involved. Even so there were problems about the clearing organisation through which the information should be passed. The Crédit Suisse promptly went into a sulk and refused to co-operate with the SBA, because one of its senior officials,

Adolph Jann, was about to leave the SBA to work for the Union Bank. Naturally the Crédit Suisse had no desire to add to his knowledge of their most closely guarded secrets. In the end the wretched Nussbaumer acted as honest broker and a report was submitted – though, of course, the unidentified or enemy assets remained frozen.

In September, American pressure to try and reduce or even eliminate the banks' dealings with the Axis countries led to a much more controversial circular from the SBA, designed to restrict dealings in foreign currencies and securities. Although no sanctions were envisaged, every member of the Association was to bind himself in writing to observe the Convention faithfully. The prospective inability to deal 'acted like a bombshell in banking and commercial circles' in the words of the American consul in Basle, Walter Sholes.* Sholes's problem was that the dollar promptly collapsed because, with the removal of German demand for dollars, the flood within Switzerland would impose an unendurable strain on the exchange rate. On September 15, the rate had been 3.20/3.30 francs to the dollar.

On Saturday, September 23, 'private persons' in Lausanne were quoting the dollar at Fr 2.25 to 2.50. The previous day a Zurich banker, in discussing the circular with a Basle financier over the telephone, remarked: 'we might as well close our doors now' – clear evidence of the bankers' dependence on German business.

The circular seemed to have unleashed tensions which until then had been restrained by normal banking urbanity. The SBA was forced to threaten with suspension Paul Dreyfus, the head of a large private Basle bank, because of his explosive reaction to the circular at a reception held in the house of one of Sholes's colleagues. According to an American diplomat:

> I was standing talking to Dr. Jann and Dr. Ernst in your living-room before dinner when Paul Dreyfus rushed up to us and addressing Jann and Ernst in an excited tone of voice said that the circular issued by the Bankers' Association was an excellent piece of work and that the

* The quotation comes from a letter annotated in his own hand 'trouble again for WHS'.

only trouble with it was that it had not been issued two years ago. Had it been issued earlier, he continued, all the dirty business in which the Swiss banks have been indulging, with the one exception of his own bank, could not have been possible. It was the big banks who had been the principal offenders, everybody knew it, and addressing Ernst and Jann, 'you know it as well as anybody else'. It had been an outrage but now a stop had been put to it. 'My bank', he went on, 'which as many would say belongs not to a good Swiss but to an international Jew, has been the only one which as far back as two years ago imposed upon itself the restrictions which now at this late date have been adopted by all Swiss banks, now, when every child in Switzerland knows who is going to win the war. It's the same as with the Swiss reaction toward persecution of the Jews and other Nazi atrocities.'

Dreyfus' harangue, which was obviously most embarrassing to Jann and Ernst, was halted only when the guests were invited to proceed to a restaurant for dinner.

The tensions so vividly illustrated by Dreyfus' outburst were further exacerbated by the SBA's belated attempts to impose some controls over its members. In May it had finally clamped down on the affidavit scandal, by trying to ensure that only those persons who had been living in Switzerland uninterruptedly since September 1939 could collect dividends – even then the ever-suspicious Americans noted a loop-hole, in that the circulars referred to the 'possessor' of the shares – who in the original German need not have paid for them – rather than the 'beneficial owner'.

Swiss attempts to cope with the American problem included an abortive mission to Washington, led by a Genevan private banker, M. Barbey (the wretched Nussbaumer attributed his exclusion from the mission as proof of his colleagues' jealousy: he correctly predicted that the mission would come to naught). But during 1944 the pressures on the Swiss bankers – and their government – started to mount.

The first problem the Americans tackled at a governmental level was the glaring case of Germany's gold transactions. At the end of February 1944 Henry Morgenthau – supported by the Allied governments – issued a formal statement warning that the United States would not recognise the legitimacy of the transfer of looted gold and would not buy gold from any country which had diplomatic relations with the Axis governments unless the Allies were sure that it was not tainted. The only people to take any notice of the warning were the Germans. They immediately intensified their efforts to disguise the origin of the gold they were selling. They melted it down and recast it, stamping pre-war dates on it. Officially, at the time, the Swiss merely asked the Germans to produce a certificate that the gold they were selling actually belonged to them. They later professed themselves deeply shocked at the idea that the Reichsbank's guarantee might not have been completely reliable. (After the war, the left-wing Swiss press alleged that the Swiss National Bank copied these tactics and marketed 20 franc Swiss gold pieces nominally dated 1935 or 1937, but which had been minted from gold bought from the Reichsbank during the war.)

If anything, the six months following the gold declaration actually saw an increase in the rate of gold sales by the Germans. The holdings of the Swiss National Bank rose by more than 40 million francs a month during the first half of 1944. According to one American document, 'as late as the end of May 1944 an agreement was concluded between Mr. Puhl, Vice-President of the German Reichsbank, and Mr. Weber, President of the Swiss National Bank, who is said to be a personal friend of Mr. Puhl. It was reported that at this meeting a monthly quota of imports of gold from Germany valued at about 30 to 40 million Swiss francs was fixed.'

But gold was only a small part of a problem summarised in Resolution VI passed at the international monetary Conference held at Bretton Woods in August 1944, which became the basis for all subsequent negotiations. It called on neutral governments to immobilise looted assets, to uncover and control enemy property, and to hold German assets to be disposed of by the authorities who would be running a defeated Germany.

The three targets came to be summarised under the single word 'Safehaven', to describe the operation designed to secure German loot and German controlled assets and to prevent their use in any future aggressive activities. The operation brought together three American departments, only one of which, the Foreign Economic Administration, thought of it as a central part of its *raison d'être*. Although it was probably Samuel Klaus, a treasury official, who first thought up the idea of Safehaven, his department was interested only in the surveillance of German controlled funds and financial transactions; the State Department naturally looked at the operation country by country. Although the FEA was in charge of the programme (and even it was rent by the bureaucratic in-fighting endemic to Washington life), State was inevitably going to be a softening influence – in Britain, after all, the Foreign Office's no-recrimination policy was virtually uncontested, and the Ministry of Economic Warfare, the FEA's equivalent, was unable even to put forward its rather more militant views. Safehaven developed from the talks held early in 1944 between the American Treasury and the Swiss Bankers' Association. The Americans 'initially emphasised objectives connected directly with the prosecution of the war', but as they progressed, 'tended to shift their direction and to concentrate on preventing the Nazis from caching their spoils for post-war use.'

The Department of State 'took the position that continuation of economic blockade against the neutrals or of exchange control or freezing regulations for the purpose of giving effect to the policy would not be warranted.' It took four months 'and a vast amount of consultation and compromise' for the three American departments to hammer out an agreed policy, and it was only in January 1945 that the State Department circularised its detailed instructions on implementing Resolution VI to its missions abroad. The previous month, formal negotiations had started with the Swiss over all aspects of their 'neutrality' as it affected finance and trade, but it was not until February that a delegation from the United States got down to business with them.

In the meantime a major confrontation at official level was building up. As the Allies advanced against Germany, so the Swiss found it increasingly difficult to import food and raw materials as they had previously done via Spanish and Italian ports – especially Genoa. Nor did they receive the same sympathetic treatment as in World War I. Then it had taken only a few months after the Americans entered the war for the Swiss (helped by personal ties to President Wilson's key aide, Colonel House) to secure their supplies of foodstuffs. Things were very different in 1944. Dean Acheson put it succinctly:

Negotiations with the Swiss moved at their glacial rate. We took advantage of the uncertainty the military situation had created in communication with Switzerland to suspend shipments. Even Mr. Hull* entered the fray, saying to the Swiss Minister that 'neutral aid to the enemy in order primarily to gratify some businessmen ... presented a most serious question to this country ... that one of these days the stand of some of the Swiss businessmen in question would be uncovered as in these [*sic*] cases of certain people in Sweden, resulting in inevitable friction between our countries.'

At length, in August, the Swiss put a ceiling on exports to Germany. When we pressed them to end transit of enemy goods across their country, their reply concluded with a delightful and typical Swiss statement of policy: 'It goes without saying that the war as it nears the Alps changes the aspect of the transit problem and has a bearing upon its solution. For this reason the federal authorities keep their problem under constant and careful watch. They have thus been able to observe that traffic in both directions has in general decreased and not increased since spring. In the spirit of true neutrality which guides them they will see to it that it follows the trend circumstances demand.'

On October 1 the Swiss prohibited the export to Germany of all arms, munitions and military supplies. At the end of the month they closed the Simplon routes to transit traffic, though not the Gotthard.

The negotiations held in late February and early March 1945 in Berne have become famous as the 'Currie Mission' after its American leader, although the delegation also included a junior British minister, Dingle Foot, and a French official. Laughlin Currie was a classic New Dealer. In the

*Cordell Hull, US Secretary of State.

1930s he had been a colleague of John Kenneth Galbraith in the Economics Department at Harvard, where, according to his friend: 'he failed of promotion partly because his ideas, brilliantly anticipating Keynes, were considered to reflect deficient scholarship until Keynes made them respectable. Economics is very complicated.' Later he moved to Washington as assistant to Mariner Eccles, Chairman of the Federal Reserve Board and, surprisingly, a pioneering Keynesian. Currie became 'a skilled and influential interpreter of Keynesian ideas in the Washington community'.

Currie had served as deputy head of the FEA and in early 1945 was working as one of President Roosevelt's assistants. He was thus ideally equipped to negotiate. (This did not prevent the Secretary of the Army Henry Stimson from objecting, partly, one suspects, because of his close attachments to Henry Morgenthau). His arrival – on the first through train from Paris to Berne since the Germans occupied France – was greeted by a crowd of several hundred people, all celebrating what seemed like the lifting of a siege.

But Swiss officialdom knew full well that he was by no means friendly. 'He arrived here with exceedingly sceptical, not to say hostile feelings regarding our future neutrality,' said one minister. He and his colleagues were wined and dined and shown the beauty spots of the Bernese Oberland. More importantly, they were treated to a day's demonstration of the Swiss army at manoeuvres, and an explanation of Swiss strategy, after which Currie told Professor Rappard, the veteran Swiss negotiator: 'I now have a new idea of your idea of neutrality. Overall it is nothing more than a veil behind which is the defensive force of your army.' (Currie's attitude swung so far towards Switzerland that he was back the next year with a former State Department official, Malvin Fagen, to help American companies recuperate assets of theirs sequestrated during the war as German owned.)

The three weeks of negotiations represented the low point for the Swiss – in the words of Hans Meier 'a terrific diplomatic defeat for Switzerland ... the inevitable consequence of the failure on the part of the Swiss government to adjust its foreign economic politics to the very obvious political realities of the times.' Not that the Swiss saw it this way. To this day they cling to the idea that the Americans were blackmailing them. They simply lack the imagination to perceive that their stubbornness looked like hostility to the Allies. In practical terms the Swiss had to agree to cut their trade with Germany (and the traffic they allowed to cross their territory) to a trickle. Even before the negotiations began they felt obliged to make a gesture by blocking German assets (despite ferocious opposition from the Swiss Bankers' Association they then had to block those belonging to other enemy countries as well). They had to stop trade in, and the export or import of, foreign banknotes. The Swiss National Bank was to limit its purchase of gold from Germany to the minute quantities required for the use of the German Embassy and other specific purposes. And the Swiss promised complete co-operation in helping the Allies return looted property to its rightful owners. They obtained a limited lifting of the Allied blockade but this was a mere trickle, enough food and fuel to cover only one tenth of the country's requirements.

But the Swiss did not give way on two important points of principle: they insisted on conducting the census of German and other enemy assets in Switzerland themselves, for no foreigner was to be allowed to penetrate Swiss banking secrecy; and they refused to sign Resolution VI of the Bretton Woods agreement, because its use of the word 'enemy' offended their conception of neutrality.

Given that Germany was collapsing, it is surprising that the Swiss thought – and still think – of the agreement as such a defeat. The most dramatic view is that of Paul Erdman, who had written his doctoral thesis on the subject. In his thriller *The Crash of '79* he gives a splendidly romanticised version of events, beginning with the miseries endured by the Swiss the previous Christmas, and continuing with their 'complete diplomatic surrender'. But, he goes on, 'to be sure the whole affair had a somewhat happy ending, the Swiss eventually reneged on almost every commitment they had been forced to make. They just stalled until the inauguration of the Cold War, when America's attention was diverted to much more pressing matters in Europe.' Erdman may have exaggerated earlier events, but he was telling little more than the plain truth about the eventual resolution of the argument.

4 / A lesson in stubbornness

In the seven years after the seeming humiliation of the Currie Mission, successive Swiss governments showed exactly how useful national stubbornness and insensitivity could be in protecting the country's banks and their clients from external pressures. The Swiss soon made it clear that their acceptance of anti-German measures was perfunctory, a mere facade behind which business would go on as usual.

The contrast with the other neutrals was complete. Where the Swiss eventually managed to wear down the Allies by sheer stone-walling and stubbornness, the Swedes, the Portuguese and even the Fascist Spanish government of General Franco jumped to do the bidding of the triumphant Allies. All three signed Resolution VI of Bretton Woods; all three co-operated in compiling an openly available census of German interests. By July 1945 the Swedes had changed their civil law and established special administrative courts to track down assets looted by the Germans; and in Madrid Allied diplomats assumed direct control of all German-owned or controlled companies. It was very different in Switzerland. It immediately became clear that the freezing of German assets was nominal and that the Swiss had absolutely no intention of taking any positive steps in line with the spirit of the Currie agreements. A mere week after the freezing decree, the head of the British Secret Service noted that 'the blocking of German bank accounts in Switzerland has therefore not affected the movement [of German funds]. Incidentally this Swiss move had long been expected in Germany ... the Swiss could cause serious embarrassment to the underground movement only by a sudden change in their banknote issue involving the immediate calling in of their present notes. None of the funds held in banknotes by German agents have, of course, been declared in connection with the Swiss capital tax. The belated disclosure of large amounts in notes would certainly arouse the lively interest of the competent Swiss authorities.' At the same time the OSS pointed out that the Swiss were not taking any positive steps to block the movement of enemy funds. Blocking the export of Italian currency meant only that 'a person leaving Switzerland for Italy would be in real trouble if he tried to conceal even 500 lire, but he can carry large sums of Swiss banknotes without being molested by the customs officials.' Yet, the OSS report continued, the Swiss could easily have blocked the traffic with Italy by asking travellers for the reason why they were carrying Swiss currency out of the country and prohibiting the export if the alleged reason was unacceptable. 'No new Swiss legislation would be required . . . a new decree could probably be issued as a logical sequence to other protective measures already adopted by the Swiss'.

There was to be no nonsense about a 'logical sequence' so far as the Swiss were concerned. It took another fifteen months for the two sides to reach a supposedly final accord in the Washington Agreement of May 1946 designed to dispose of the question of German assets once and for all. This period was devoted to almost uninterrupted arguments between the Allies, and within Switzerland itself. But the basic quarrel was between the Americans and the Swiss government. Although Pilet-Golaz had departed, the new Swiss government inherited the burden of Allied suspicion from him – and did nothing to shake it off. In July 1945 Albert Nussbaumer admitted to an American diplomat that his government should have completed its census of German assets. But it was September before any sort of report was presented to the Allies. Early in August Herr Schwab, the head of the Compensation Office (which was handling the census) told the economic counsellor at the American embassy that there was a complete report in course of preparation. For six weeks the Swiss fended off the increasingly impatient Americans. The report, they said, was being translated into French, and the translation had to be checked by Herr Schwab, who had gone on holiday for a fortnight. At the end of September, the Americans smelt a cover-up: 'the report prepared by the Swiss Compensation Office and intended for this and the

British Legation and the French Embassy was censored and a perfunctory résumé substituted therefor. The enclosed report, it is hardly necessary to state, represents a failure on the part of the Swiss to carry out their promise to acquaint us with the interim result of the census.'

The same tactics were employed to prevent any mass restoration of looted property to its rightful owners. The conclusion was obvious: 'the Swiss government is pursuing dilatory tactics to test the sincerity, firmness and unity of the Allies with respect to the German assets in Switzerland ... these tactics are being employed, it would appear, in the belief that, in the interim, the Allies will become so preoccupied with other affairs as to neglect to press for further execution for the March 8 Agreements', the point of the Currie Mission.

It was a Polish lawyer, Dr. Philipp Rossiez, author of a standard study on the weaknesses of financial regulations in European countries, used even by the Nazis, who best ana-lysed the position. By 1945 he was practising in Switzerland, and he submitted a lengthy memorandum to the Americans on how the Swiss could – and should – have collaborated. As a poacher turned gamekeeper the good Doctor knew precisely what the Germans had been up to. They had been selling off (or nominally disposing of) their assets at a great rate, taking advantage of the Swiss Compensation Office's vaguely defined permission for sales required to raise funds for 'current operations' or 'ordinary living expenses' – phrases which could not have covered, say, the well publicised disposal of the German sanatorium at Davos. And these disposals were the easier because the freezing of enemy assets was not followed by the necessary decree providing for compulsory registration for several months (and even this decree was 'not suitable for achieving the ends desired by the Americans'). The decrees allowed Germans who had taken out Swiss nationality after 1940 not to register – and as for the hundred thousand or so German nationals in the country 'their position today in Switzerland is almost more favourable than it was during the war; not of least importance is the circumstance that today they enjoy a remarkably far-reaching protection of the Swiss state with respect to their assets. This favourable position of Germans in Switzerland bears no comparison with the very precarious one of Allied nationals during the war, even of those who had lived at length in Switzerland.'

Even worse was the position of people trying to retrieve property which the Nazis had looted and stashed away in Switzerland. Following a talk with the chief Swiss negotiator in September 1945 the British commercial counsellor wrote indignantly: 'It transpires that the Swiss had no intention whatsoever of doing anything governmentally about it. The standpoint was that their existing civil law provided machinery for this purpose and that therefore it was up to each dispossessed owner to take individual action in the Swiss courts. It was pointed out to him that the five year statute limitation would operate to prohibit action in respect of loot disposed here in 1940, but he did not appear to be open to argument, nor at all interested in the implementation of the Swiss pledge in the March 8th Agreement that every facility would be accorded.'

Besides providing ample time and opportunity for the Germans to escape the net they were, ever so slowly, throwing over their assets, the Swiss also indulged in some splendid legal quibbling. In August 1945, after the Potsdam Conference, the Allied Control Commission in Germany claimed jurisdiction over all German assets, wherever located, thus implementing part of the Bretton Woods agreement. The Swiss retorted that the German government might have disappeared on 8 May 1945, but that a German state still existed and that the Allied Control Commission were merely its military occupiers. According to Professor E. D. von Waldburch, the Allied decrees 'could under no circumstance apply to assets or property outside Territory actually occupied.' The Americans replied that 'the occupying powers have supreme authority in Germany by virtue of the terms of the unconditional surrender'.

But by this time the British and the Americans had drifted far apart. An American treasury official, Orvis Schmidt, set Switzerland alight by a speech in which he claimed that the Germans had 16 billion francs hidden in Switzerland, that the banks had invited them to deposit their funds, and that not even the Swiss government knew the names. This was pretty extreme, but by the middle of the year the British were objecting even to the milder policy being pursued by the State Department. As W. A. Brandt of the Foreign Office put it: 'Is our primary object to eliminate German influence or to make as much money out of it as possible? I think we have all come to the conclusion that the elimination of German influence is our target number one.' Brandt was not even prepared to admit that there were loopholes in the Swiss legislation. In August both the State Department and the U.S. Treasury were 'bothered by the apparent relaxation of British control over Swiss accounts and feel that such action may be premature at this time ... we have found the Swiss extremely sensitive to our suggestions if they feel their assets in this country are in any way prejudiced and probably Allied control over Swiss assets is the most potent weapon we have with which to obtain Swiss compliance on Safehaven.' Nevertheless, the British influence was limited – the British member of the Allied Control Commission did not object to the claim of sovereignty over German property in Switzerland. Even the British objected to one blatant and overt act of defiance – the purchase of three tons of gold by the Swiss National Bank from the vice-president of the Reichsbank, Emil Puhl, in the dying days of the Third Reich. Unfortunately for the Swiss, the letters Puhl wrote to his president in Berlin during his visit to Switzerland were found by the Americans and were made very public by a maverick senator, Harvey Kilgore, a staunch radical opponent of monopoly capitalism. The Senate sub-committee on 'Military Preparedness', of which he was chairman, spent much of the year conducting widely reported hearings into Germany's potential for future military aggression. The Swiss were furious at the leak, which was very damaging. Puhl contrasted the hostility of the press, and the increasing preparedness of the government to intrude on the banker's prerogative of secrecy, with the friendly reception he found in banking circles. It was obviously in Puhl's interest to prolong his absence from the flaming ruins of his home country, and to exaggerate his success, but his tone was unmistakable: 'The personal relations are now as before of greatest cordiality ... it is pleasing to note how strong the cultural ties are that connect our two countries'.

Puhl's indignation was echoed in banking circles. Far from expressing gratitude that their government was prepared to renege on its pledges wholesale to defend them and their clients, all the Swiss professional classes violently opposed the idea that even the government's Compensation Office should be permitted to intrude on banking secrecy.

In September the Federal Council finally ruled that the obligation to give information to the Compensation Office overruled even lawyers' duty to secrecy. A British diplomat noted that: 'The lawyers' Association had contended that the original decree was too general in its working to absolve them legally from their duty of secrecy. The leading spirits behind the lawyers' opposition were reported to be the Association's President, Dr. Robert Blass, and Dr. Frick, both of whom are said to administer very large German holdings. Later this month we learned that Dr. Frick is about to suffer eclipse owing to the institution of a lawsuit against him for embezzlement of a client's money' in connection with an industrial investment trust.

The two learned lawyers were not the only victims of the fall of the Third Reich. Too many banks had been too involved with Germany, before and during Hitler's regime, for that. Three of the country's major banks were badly affected. Leu, that seemingly everlasting black sheep of the Zurich banking family, had to be rescued yet again, this time by the Swiss Bank Corporation, which underwrote a major share issue. But Leu's troubles were merely an echo of the collapse of two major banks, the Federal Bank and the Basler Handelsbank. Nearly half of the latter's assets were still tied up in Germany and the Balkans in loans granted before 1931. The banks had tried to reduce the burden but the investments amounted to nearly 40 million francs (they had been 55 million in 1937) out of a balance sheet total of less than 100 million.

The SBC came to the rescue of its local rival – with which it had nearly merged forty years before. The Basler Handelsbank was not bankrupt, but its 'free' assets were embedded in apparently everlasting permafrost. For while its liabilities were – just – covered by realisable assets, the bank and its shareholders had to their name only holdings in Central and Eastern Europe which seemed valueless at the time. The bank could survive in wartime, when it was receiving 1.8 million francs a year from these loans and was supplementing this income through innumerable transactions involving German clients (helping the Italian subsidiary of the Robert Bosch group to be 'neutralised', and trying to transfer dollars – illegally – to the pharmaceutical company Hoffmann-La Roche were among the dubious transactions noted by vigilant American diplomats). But all these sources of income disappeared when Germany surrendered. In July 1945 the bank's president, Max Brugger, committed suicide, and three months later the SBC took over all unblocked assets and liabilities. Within ten years the Handelsbank's shareholders had recuperated an undreamt of 31 million francs – three-quarters of the blocked assets. But they were greedy. In the dry words of the SBC's official history: 'The Basle Board of Directors, which wished to carry the successful liquidation through to a conclusion, resigned and was replaced by an outside group which was to restore the firm to an active role by converting it into a finance and holding company. However in the very first year its speculative investment policy resulted in such a loss that again a new board was appointed under a Basle chairman.'

The Federal Bank was less badly off than the Handelsbank, with about 17 million in 'free' assets over and above its blocked loans and its liabilities. But its directors, faced with the need to reduce the capital for the third time in fifteen years, had lost heart, and were open to the blandishments of the rising star of Swiss banking, Dr. Alfred Schaefer of the Union Bank. The son of a wealthy building contractor, Schaefer had qualified as a lawyer, and had nourished an ambition to teach history. But in 1931 he joined the then struggling Union Bank on a year's temporary assignment. Within a very few years he had emerged as the dominant force with the bank, and was a general manager at the age of thirty. (Hans Strasser, the present chairman of the Swiss Bank Corporation, was forty-four when he became a general manager, and he was far the youngest in his bank's history.)

Schaefer provided the drive which transformed an institution of relatively modest size, apparently crippled by the shocks of the 1930s, into the country's biggest within a quarter of a century. He was lucky in inheriting a clean slate since his predecessors had written off a far higher proportion of the blocked assets than had their fellows in the other troubled major banks. Schaefer's drive had started in wartime: the bank hired key executives from the National Bank and from its rivals, at a time when such moves were most unusual; and in 1944 it achieved its first breakthrough into Central Switzerland by taking over a bank in Lucerne. But the absorption of the Federal Bank was another matter altogether. Absorbing its free assets increased the size of the UBS's balance sheet by forty-two per cent. But because of the Federal Bank's weak position, its shareholders received only three shares in UBS for every ten of their own, thus increasing UBS's capital by only a quarter. In partial compensation, the Federal Bank's shareholders retained their rights to the bank's German assets, which increased ten times to over 500 francs a share within fifteen years.

Schaefer also emerged as a major public spokesman for the interests of the banking community as a whole, a role he was to fill for the next quarter of a century. In a lecture at the University of Zurich he defended the banks, and the importance of bank secrecy which, he said 'resulted in giving an extraordinary impulse to the banking organisation and securing for it a large foreign clientele'. But he was a political realist, and admitted that Nazi money 'should not' be found in the country's coffers (he never said it *wouldn't* be found). By that time, too, the American consul-general in Zurich was finding him 'quite co-operative'.

The banks needed defending, for the war years had seen a number of attacks on bank secrecy. It was, indeed, during the war that the Swiss Bankers' Association adopted the position which became standard over the next decades: that abolition of secrecy would lead to a wholesale withdrawal of funds by foreigners and that any such withdrawal would prevent the banks' supporting the many bond issues required to cover the government's unprecedented wartime deficits.

The attacks concentrated not on the international morality of the bank's actions, but of local fiscal honesty. The object of bills introduced in the Swiss legislature in 1944 was to remove banking secrecy so far as federal, cantonal and municipal tax authorities were concerned, in order to prevent tax frauds 'and thereby establish a more equitable distribution of the tax burden in Switzerland'. These efforts came to nothing, thanks to conservative opposition led by a Federal Councillor, Franz Wetter. He did not deny the need for more effective taxation, but opposed the idea that the best way to reach untaxed income was through allowing banks to disclose information to third parties. He preferred to devise improved means of taxing incomes at their source. In the sardonic words of the American consul in Basle: 'It is significant that no mention was made of the country's large frozen assets in the United States, although everyone present was aware of the American government's interest in an identification of those assets – on many of which no taxes have ever been paid – and in the bank secrecy law.'

There was even debate at the end of the year within the bankers' ranks about the Swiss assets frozen in the United States anyway. Dr. Ernst Bartschi, a leading light in the banking committee of the Swiss Parliament (and President of the canton of Berne), was reported by the American consul 'to be among those who favour a speedy settlement of the frozen assets problem without further delay'. Assets owned by Swiss nationals would be treated differently from those owned by foreign – mainly German – clients. He was supported by Nussbaumer, but they were opposed by the 'controlling conservative faction' within the Bankers Association. So it took a shove from the Federal government to induce the bankers even to agree to the minor modification required to provide a rough division of the assets' ownership – and even when the final agreement was reached, the real ownership of the funds which the American Treasury had blocked as not definitely being Swiss was decided by the Swiss Compensation Office. Nevertheless, and whatever the Allies may have thought, in the summer of 1945 the Swiss government, however belatedly and inadequately, did try to compile a census of German assets (the Compensation Office had a good start, having already compiled extensive files following the declaration of Allied 'Proclaimed Lists' of undesirables).

To a correspondent in the *Neue Zürcher Zeitung*, all this federal activity and breakage of bank secrecy represented a regrettably necessary 'far-reaching interference by the state in a purely private economic sphere', and the paper was in the van of the right-wing press which demanded that German assets should be used primarily to provide 'a full satisfaction of Swiss claims, namely compensation with our assets in Germany, indemnification for the damages suffered by Swiss who have returned from Germany and further claims'. Moreover, the right-wing press was thunderous in its denunciation of the impertinence of the Americans, in particular, for treating the Swiss so shabbily, and for not accepting their version of neutrality.

These papers enjoyed a field-day, whipping up a scare campaign asserting that if banking secrecy were abrogated then this would frighten even Swiss peasants from placing their money with the banks. Walter Stampfli, the head of the Federal Economics Department, joined in the attacks, as did the 'stormy petrel' of Swiss politics, Gottlieb Duttweiler, founder of the Migros co-operative chain, which had become a powerful competitive force in the previously cosy world of Swiss retailing. Politically Duttweiler was a maverick populist with his own party. He organised petitions to ensure that any money received from the Americans be used to satisfy Swiss claims on the Germans.

But none of this impressed the left, suddenly luxuriating in a press freedom denied to it for five years. In July 1945 the *Volksrecht* asked, 'How long does the Federal Council intend to hesitate and allow Swiss bankers to lead it by the nose until we are starved and frozen?' (Within a couple of months the writer had his answer when the Americans increased the quantities of food and fuel they allowed through to Switzerland, despite the lack of diplomatic progress in negotiating over the German assets.)

The Swiss Workers Party demanded bank nationalisation and controls over the export of capital. One anonymous journalist made a telling comparison when he wrote in November 1945: 'Sweden has shown her desire to do the right thing whilst we allow receivers and gangsters to roam at large'. But the left overplayed its hand by claiming that the banks which had gone under had done so through lending money to further Hitler's rearmament plans. In fact, of course, they were desperately trying to withdraw funds from Germany, not pouring good money after bad. And the right could also attack the Communists by classing them with other 'war criminals' because of the Nazi-Soviet Pact of August 1939.

In December 1945, nine months after Currie's departure, the Swiss Compensation Office finally produced the result of its enquiries. It explained the delay convincingly enough: special powers had to be created by Parliament to compel Swiss lawyers to disclose confidential information, and indeed also 'to look at the contents of safes and safe deposit boxes.' In addition, 'the technical staff was difficult to assemble and many completed forms returned by August 31st turned out to be incomplete and many questions wrongly answered'. The total the Office came up with was around $250 million (a billion francs), half the official U.S. estimate and suspiciously close to the Swiss claim for 973 million francs in compensation for their citizens' assets lost in Germany. Only 371 million related to the assets of Germans living in their own country; Austrians had a mere 41 million in Swiss banks, and Germans living outside Germany, Switzerland or German-occupied territories had 79 million – a total of under 500 million francs which the Swiss admitted as falling unquestionably within the scope of the negotiations. A further 235 million was deposited in 400 accounts where ownership was still undecided, 254 million belonged to Germans living in Switzerland, and 'by Swiss law the assets of Germans long domiciled in Switzerland cannot be alienated'.

At the end of 1945, within a few weeks of the announcement, the Swiss told the Americans they were ready for negotiations over the assets. This untypical burst of speed was the work of the man who led the Swiss delegation to the talks, Walter Stucki, the senior official at the Swiss 'Political' Department. During the war, he had been Swiss ambassador to Vichy France and had displayed impressive diplomatic skill when he successfully negotiated for the safety of the whole diplomatic community when the Vichy government collapsed. Unfortunately he shared his countrymen's delusion that they alone understood the true meaning of neutrality: 'one cannot expect off-hand an American to know what neutrality means' was his disdainful pronouncement at the conclusion of the Currie Mission. His team included senior people from all the institutions involved, and was matched in depth by the American delegation headed by Randolph Paul, a former general counsel to the Treasury Department, and a close and trusted associate of President Truman – by contrast the French and the British were represented only by token delegations.

The opening Swiss position was pretty negative. They refused to recognise the legal status of the Allied Control Commission in Germany, which had claimed jurisdiction over German assets abroad. They refused the Allied demand to return stolen gold until and unless proof were provided as to its original ownership. They would liquidate only the assets of Germans resident in Germany, and even these assets were to be earmarked to cover the – even greater – Swiss claims against the Germans.

The first breakthrough came over gold, when the Swiss realised that the Americans, through a simple court order, could seize the vast amounts of gold held in the United States on Swiss account. After a lot of haggling, the Swiss agreed to pay 250 million Swiss francs compensation for the stolen gold they had received. But, as a result of this pretty piece of plea-bargaining, the Allies renounced any further claims over the – far larger – amounts of gold processed through the Swiss banking system during the war (as the Dutch government discovered the next year when it tried to track down gold stolen by the Germans and traded through Switzerland).

A similar compromise was eventually reached regarding the German assets in time for the two sides to reach agreement at the end of May, only two months later. When these German owned assets were sold, the Swiss and the Americans were to divide the proceeds fifty-fifty, although the Swiss government had to stump up 20 million francs immediately to help refugees. But the Swiss had gained three crucial points: their assets in the United States were to be unblocked – and Swiss companies were taken off Allied black lists – *before* the Swiss had fulfilled their obligations under the agreements; the only property covered by the agreement was that belonging to Germans living in Germany or to the few criminals who were due for repatriation – all other German property in Switzerland was protected; and the Swiss retained virtually complete control over the process of identification and confirmation of ownership.

By these terms the Americans surrendered the hostages they had held, control over Swiss assets in the United States and the black listing of unco-operative banks and companies. Even before the agreement had been ratified the Swiss names on the Black List had been removed. The unblocking of Swiss assets started before the end of the year and was largely completed within the next eighteen months. Nevertheless the Swiss clearly felt they had been defeated. By the end of 1946 Stucki had been removed from his post – although this was probably due to the unwillingness of Max Petitpierre, the man who was to dominate Swiss foreign policy in the first two post-war decades, to share power with such a strong-minded and independent subordinate. In addition, as an American diplomat put it: 'Sources within the Swiss government have intimated that the retirement of President Weber (of the Swiss National Bank) was actuated in part by discontent in official and banking circles with the manner in which the SNB had operated with regard to looted German gold and specifically through the "bungling" of this question by the representatives of the SNB during the negotiations at Washington'.

The same – largely unjustified – attitude permeated the parliamentary debates on the subject. There were predictable laments that 'the inviolability of private property is no longer the absolute rule' and references to the ingratitude of the Allies despite the fact that the Swiss had introduced bank secrecy to protect German Jews (probably the first occasion on which the myth had surfaced). But the average Swiss reaction to the Agreement was close to that of Gottlieb Duttweiler. He acknowledged – and regretted – the importance of Swiss anti-semitism, as well as the 'total loss of confidence in Swiss banks' which he felt had resulted from the access secured by the Swiss Compensation Office to the banks' records and the safe deposit boxes of some, at least, of their customers. (With typical insularity the Swiss did not realise that their stubbornness had earned them the increased trust of those anxious for a secure place for their funds: if the

Swiss were prepared to put up such a stout defence on behalf of such universally detested clients as rich Nazis against such overwhelming odds, then it was clear that less undesirable clients, faced with enemies far less all-conquering and implacable than the Allies, were safer with Swiss banks than with comparable institutions in other neutral countries which had shown so much less resistance to Allied pressure.)

But Duttweiler also expressed typical Swiss disquiet at the way the banks had dragged down the country's international reputation:

> I would like to point out an error on our Swiss foreign policy [he said] we waited for too long to determine the amount of German assets in Switzerland. These assets were only a fifth or a sixth of the amount attributed to us in the American press. If it had been known that we were dealing with a maximum of 500 to 1,000 million francs the whole affair would long since have lost its sting and our credit would have suffered less. It was therefore a mistake to pay too much heed to advice in the interest of the banks, and to transfer for so long sole responsibility for Swiss foreign financial policy or at least tacitly allow them to exercise such responsibility.

He went on to blame the banks for the financial cost, of around a billion francs, attributable to their refusal to allow Swiss retaliatory measures when the Germans introduced a compulsory clearing system against the Swiss.

But it did not require any pressure from the banks to ensure that the Swiss relentlessly refused to carry out their obligations under the Washington Agreements. The same spirit of stubbornness was displayed even when both sides were agreed, as they were over the compensation to be paid for the accidental bombing by twenty American bombers of the Swiss city of Schaffhausen in 1944. In the words of a Swiss journalist, Urs Schwarz, 'the blunders were immediately admitted and compensation was promised, including reparations for valuable works of art that had been destroyed. An amount of $62 million was paid by Washington in 1949. Some unpleasant haggling, for which the Swiss were responsible with their ludicrous insistence on payment of interest from the day of the bombing, preceded the settlement.'

This piece of pedantry was as nothing compared with the implacable petty-mindedness displayed over the supposedly equal division of the assets. It took six more years for final agreement to be reached. The Swiss opening gambit was to dispute the rate of exchange between Swiss francs and German marks, a point not covered in the Washington Agreement, but which took over five years to clarify. By that time, Germany had been restored to the status of an ally in American eyes, so the final agreement provided for some compensation for the Germans involved: it was the German government which bore the burden – and paid the Allies and the Swiss through a loan raised from Swiss banks.

Finally, in 1952 the Allies half-share was valued at a mere 135 million francs. But they did not receive even this much-reduced sum. Ten per cent was deducted because the money was paid in cash, and a further twenty million was accounted for by the advance payment agreed six long years earlier. There could have been no better tribute to Swiss stamina, the national determination to stonewall in the face of overwhelming odds, and of the banks' consequent ability to protect their clients and their own interest.

But the final proof of the Swiss ability to defy would-be violators of banking secrecy came from the one piece of business left unfinished even in 1952, the question of the real ownership of the American companies originally owned by the German chemical groups which joined together to form the I. G. Farben cartel. It took another decade for the Swiss banks to gain their final victory over the Americans.

PART FOUR

The Greatest Conspiracy

1 / Spider's web

The keynote for this extraordinary story was struck in 1912 when Alfred J. Keppelmann, paymaster for the German Bayer Company in its successful efforts to bribe American customers to purchase their dyestuffs, was due for indictment in Philadelphia. In the event he divorced his wife (paying her $100,000 alimony, a fortune at the time), and the day before the trial married his confidential secretary who was due to testify against him the following day. This cunning move completely stymied the local district attorney, who told his assistants: 'It's no use, boys, it's all off, the defendant has married the evidence and it's not admissible.'

This master-stroke established a pattern, of American authorities foiled at the last minute by the wiles of wicked foreigners, which was to be repeated for half a century to come. The end result was the biggest single triumph ever achieved by Swiss banks and bankers – over the American interests of the German chemical cartel, I. G. Farben. Following twenty years of *Sturm und Drang*, Swiss banks and government finally confirmed that not even the American government could penetrate bank secrecy. More narrowly, the Union Bank of Switzerland emerged in 1967 with sufficient profit from the affair to leap-frog the country's other major banks and to become the country's biggest.

The saga involves an enormous cast from John Foster Dulles to Robert Kennedy. The case itself lasted a mere eighteen years after World War II – but the story covers half the twentieth century. It is generally called the 'Interhandel' affair, after the post-war name of the Swiss holding company used to cloak I. G. Farben's activities before its subsidiaries were seized by the American government as enemy property in 1942. Yet even the name can be construed as misleading.

In 1958 Malcolm Mason, formerly general counsel to the

U.S. Government's Alien Property Custodian, made the point firmly during a debate organised by the American Society of International Law. To Mason the problem was simple: 'Here is an important company in the United States called General Aniline and Film Corporation. Who at the time we seized it owned that company? Who controlled it? And what should now be done with it? When we say the Interhandel case we sound as though we were talking about what should be done with Interhandel's property in the United States, and, of course, that is the way Interhandel wants us to talk about it. In fact the United States expressly denies that GAF is or ever was Interhandel's property, so this is not the Interhandel case but the GAF case.'

Whatever the case is called, its origins dated back further even than the abortive attempt to indict Alfred J. Keppelmann, to the earliest days of industrial chemistry in the United States, when the Germans held an undisputed lead in the technology of such vital new products as chemical dyes made from coal tar rather than from natural sources. The chemical conglomerate General Aniline and Film was, in fact, a merger of a number of companies dependent on such discoveries. The 'Aniline' in the title came from a company originally established in 1868 to pioneer coal tar dyes in the United States, and bought by Bayer fourteen years later. The Film referred to a company founded in 1842 by one of the pioneers of American photographic manufacture, Edward Anthony, who had supplied materials to such noted photographers as Mathew Brady. The group included the Ozalid company, which made the light-sensitive diazo compounds used for prints before the arrival of photo-copiers. Even before World War I, as the Keppelmann prosecution shows, German companies had been working closely together to monopolise the dyestuffs market in the United States. Nor did the confiscation of their companies in 1917 as enemy assets disturb them permanently. Bayer's American assets were all sold off to Sterling Products, but an undercover agent of Bayer bought back the crucial dyestuffs division in the early 1920s, thus thwarting a basic condition of the sale, that no part of the business should ever return to German hands.

But the affair took on another dimension entirely with the

merger of virtually the whole of the German chemical industry into one giant cartel, I. G. Farben, in 1925, and the arrival on the scene of Farben's financial genius, Hermann Schmitz, one of whose tasks was the organisation of the cartel's overseas interests. The late President Roosevelt was paying tribute to Schmitz's ingenuity when he made his famous comment 'the history of the use of the I. G. Farben Trust by the Nazis reads like a detective story'.

Schmitz had started his career working for the German metallurgical group Metallgesellschaft under its founding patriarch, Wilhelm Merton. Schmitz was so brilliant that he became head of all the group's foreign interests before his thirtieth birthday. It was in that position and before World War I that he discovered the usefulness of establishing a holding company in Switzerland to own his group's foreign subsidiaries, thereby avoiding German taxes on their profits. After America's entry into the war in 1917 he stumbled on another use for them, as shelters behind which their true ownership could be concealed, and thus avoid the sequestration which was the fate of openly German-owned concerns. 'This period', in the words of Joseph Borkin,* 'also marked the beginning of Schmitz's love affair with Switzerland.'

After World War I the corporate fun and games really started. Merton's son Richard tried to disguise the ownership of his group's subsidiary, American Metal, by lodging the stock in the names of the company's American executives. But they informed the US government of the attempt, and the shares were duly sequestrated as enemy property. In 1919 the Alien Property Custodian sold the shares by auction to a Wall Street syndicate for $5.5 million. Merton claimed that the sale was void because the shares had been sold by Metallgesellschaft to a Swiss company, Société Suisse, five days before the auction. This was laughed at, but Merton was saved by the arrival of the Harding administration. Ignoring the advice of his lawyer, John Foster Dulles (whom he had met in the course of his wartime manoeuvrings), he bribed the new Alien Property Custodian and his boss the Attorney-General, Harry Daugherty, to accept that the shares had in

* *The Crime and Punishment of I. G. Farben*, The Free Press, 1978.

fact been sold to the Swiss company just before the outbreak of war between Germany and the United States, and thus were neutral property, which should be handed back to their 'rightful owners'. The transaction was rushed through, relying on a false affidavit sworn in front of a young Swiss lawyer employed by Société Suisse, Felix Iselin. The suddenness of the sale soon attracted the attention of the American press, the case was investigated, and eventually the officials were brought to trial. The Attorney-General escaped, but William Miller, the Alien Property Custodian, was duly convicted. Despite the trial, the perjury, and the bribery, Merton's group still owned the shares. And all would have been well if Merton had not sued the American government for the interest on the funds between the sale of the assets in 1919 and their return in 1921. A welter of trials, claims and counterclaims followed: eventually – in 1938 – the U.S. government was awarded judgment for $15 million. But by that time the Swiss holding company had become a mere shell. So the government had to content itself with suing their bankers, the Swiss Bank Corporation, as a party to the original conspiracy and eventually had to be satisfied with a mere $3 million.

This was only a rehearsal for what was to come. In 1919 Schmitz had met Carl Bosch, who was to become the first head of I. G. Farben, at the Versailles Peace Conference, and a few years later Schmitz went to work for him. Given his background it is not surprising that he soon started to organise a series of foreign holding companies established in neutral countries (not just Switzerland, but also Holland, which had been neutral in World War I). Although the corporate structures involved were impenetrable, Schmitz relied on a handful of people, notably Iselin, Eduard Greutert, another alumnus of the Metallgesellschaft school, Greutert's family connections, and the Greutert bank in Basle, established in 1920 basically to conduct Metallgesellschaft business.

I. G. Farben's major foreign companies were organised in 1929, not primarily because Farben wanted to conceal its foreign investments, but to avoid German tax and to raise capital on the Swiss and American markets. Both these incentives sprang from a major deal with Standard Oil that year. The Americans acquired the rights to a new process being developed by the Germans to convert coal into gasoline; in return, the Germans were allotted two per cent of the corporation's equity, worth $35 million, and making them the second largest shareholders after the Rockefeller interests. The scheme was very much the pet project of Standard's chairman, Walter Teagle, who became closely involved with Farben's American interests in the 1930s.

From the American point of view the deal was a disaster, since the process involved – although it proved invaluable to the Germans in World War II – was by no means as fully developed as the vendors pretended. Moreover, as critics have never ceased to point out since, it represented a major step in the Germans' attempts to eliminate competition in as many products as possible; for instance Farben made sure that Standard would not increase its research on synthetic rubber. This was not the only such deal. As one American critic put it, the Germans made a series 'of secret and illegal agreements with American industrialists to discourage or control all developments here in synthetic rubber, magnesium alloys and other war essentials.' In these, as in so many other instances, the interests of Farben, whose boss, Carl Bosch, was one of the few major German industrialists to be firmly anti-Nazi, chimed in very well with Hitler's militaristic ambitions.

The tax problems created by the size of the deal, and the growing cost of the hydrogenation process, led Schmitz to create two holding companies. The American, General Aniline, was an ordinary industrial holding company bringing together the cartel's American interests which by this time had grown to include the country's second largest photographic concern and one of its biggest dyestuffs operations. Bosch and Schmitz were joined on the board by a galaxy of leading American industrial and financial personalities, including Teagle and Edsel Ford. They promptly raised $30 million in debentures convertible into common stock whose appeal to investors rested largely on the unconditional guarantees provided by I. G. Farben. But, in Borkin's words, 'Schmitz had no intention of surrendering an iota of control'. So he arranged that the opportunity presented to the American public stopped short of allowing them votes if they converted their debentures into stock. The voting shares were all issued to Standard Oil, to a Dutch company controlled by Farben, and to other individuals and institutions Schmitz could control. During the next few years the shares all found their way back to Zurich, where they were securely lodged with an obscure concern, Mithras AG, with suspiciously close ties to Greutert.

The Swiss 'banker' – who owned his financial eminence entirely to the backing provided by the Germans – together with that other Metallgesellschaft loyalist Felix Iselin, were the crucial links in the tangled chain. It was, indeed, useful for Bosch and Schmitz to be able to entice American investors by including tame luminaries like Teagle and Ford on their American board, and Dutch holding companies may have come in handy. But to carry out their conspiracy, they depended acutely on reliable neutrals. In the words of I. G. Farben documents captured after the war: 'If the shares or similar interests are actually held by a neutral who resides in a neutral country, enemy economic warfare measures are ineffectual; even an option in favor of I.G. for the eventuality of war should not substantially interfere with the conduct of business in normal times. For a variety of reasons it is of the utmost importance ... that the officials heading the agent firms which are particularly well qualified to serve as cloaks should be citizens of the countries where they reside.'

The holding company Schmitz organised in Switzerland for the group's foreign interests was Internationale Gesellschaft für Chemische Unternehmungen – universally known as I. G. Chemie. Like its brother in the United States, it was designed to raise money, largely on the Farben guarantee, without giving control to outside investors. The idea was announced by Schmitz at a special meeting of Farben's shareholders in February 1929. In Borkin's words, 'Schmitz proposed that I.G. back the project by guaranteeing the purchasers the same dividends as those received on I. G. Farben shares. In exchange, I.G. would retain control through an old and trusted device, an option to buy the assets of I. G. Chemie at any time at market value. As an inducement to vote for the dividend guarantee proposal, I. G. Farben stockholders would have the right to purchase I. G. Chemie shares at half price. Attracted by the chance to buy the Swiss company's shares at a bargain price, the I. G. Farben stockholders overwhelmingly approved Schmitz's plan.'

Whatever the merits of the investment, they did not include control of I. G. Chemie. The owners of the ordinary shares, who had paid the full price of 500 Swiss francs each, had one vote, but then so did the owners of each of the six per cent preference shares, of which 100,000 had been issued to the board of I. G. Chemie and its friends, at the knock-down price of 20 francs per 100 franc share (as a result the owners of the preference shares bought twenty-five times as much vote with their francs as did the ordinary shareholders).

During the 1930s the whole set-up was refined. The vast majority of the non-voting as well as the voting stock in GAF was bought up (cheaply) and transferred to a multiplicity of companies, banks and trusts, in Holland and Switzerland. The only common factor linking these purely nominal concerns was their control by I. G. Chemie – which admitted in 1940 that it controlled ninety-one per cent of the GAF stock. By that time, Schmitz's system had already been severely tested, by the investigations of the newly founded American Securities and Exchange Commission, and by the nationalistic policies of the Nazi government in Germany. The image (and reality) of I. G. Farben is that it was the single most essential industrial cog in Germany's growing war machine, so closely linked to the Nazis that its offices abroad were largely staffed by officials working for the German government. Yet Bosch and Schmitz faced considerable problems with German authorities in the 1930s. They were forced to confess that they had sold the non-German rights of the crucial hydrogenation process and had to pay tax on the profit made from the arrangement with Standard Oil – though Greutert firmly stood up to the German tax officials who had demanded to see their books.

The problems in the United States speedily turned into farce when the SEC investigators tried to uncover the real owners of so much of the GAF stock hidden behind the nominal owners, Chemo and Voorindu in Holland and Mithras in Zurich. A steady stream of GAF directors, headed by Schmitz's brother (who had lived in the United

States since 1909 and had replaced his brother as chairman of GAF in 1936) and including Teagle, had to admit in public that they did not have the faintest idea who actually owned their group. American pressure encouraged Schmitz to dismantle the single most obvious link between Farben and GAF – the dividend guarantee provided to I. G. Chemie by its parent. This simple step had to be approved by the German authorities, and came up against a fundamental element in Nazi dogma, the simple belief that Germans should show themselves openly abroad and that cloaking of foreign interests in industrial groups smacked of the sin of 'internationalism'.

Farben was not alone in running for cover in anticipation of war. In 1939 Schmitz's old group, Metallgesellschaft, transferred control of its American subsidiaries to a Swiss holding company, itself controlled by a Dutch paper company, and virtually every other major German industrial group constructed similar edifices, in Sweden, Switzerland and Holland. Only Krupp's was so arrogantly confident of a German victory that it turned down the chance to effect the same sort of nominal changes in ownership of its US subsidiaries as Farben had carried out.

But Farben's problem had not been solved when war broke out on 1 September 1939, and was compounded a week later when Eduard Greutert, the key link in the chain, inopportunely died. According to Borkin, 'I.G. officials were so preoccupied with the camouflage problem that they could hardly talk of anything else at his funeral.' Worse was to come when the Nazis invaded Holland in May 1940, and Dutch assets in the United States were blocked by the US Treasury Department. GAF was included because two Dutch holding companies apparently owned so much of its stock. In the few days between the announcement of the blockage and its legal implementation, I. G. Farben executives managed to persuade the German government to allow it to loosen its links, in theory anyway, with I. G. Chemie and thus with GAF. Nevertheless, in private discussions (which were to prove highly damaging when they came to light after the war) they assured the government that 'the ties between I. G. Farben and I. G. Chemie would not be completely severed but would continue to exert its influence on General Aniline and Film.' In fact 'it had taken all necessary measures to ensure that end'.

The legal connections between Farben and I. G. Chemie were formally severed at the latter's Annual General Meeting at the end of June 1940. The real links remained as strong as ever: the parent may have relinquished formal *ownership* of its Swiss subsidiary, but it had certainly not surrendered *control* – although this distinction was to prove of crucial value after the war in two respects: the split made it much more difficult for the Americans to prove the connection; and it ensured that the proceeds from any subsequent sales of I. G. Chemie's assets would very largely go to the predominantly Swiss share-holders of the ordinary shares. Nevertheless the bonds which remained were both personal and institutional.

Although Schmitz retired from the board in 1940 to increase the apparent degree of 'neutralisation' and boost visible Swiss influence within the company, yet the board remained packed with his 'trusties' (the German word *Vertrauensmann* conveys the correct impression of sturdy loyalty). It included two brothers-in-law, Schmitz's: Albert Gadow and Greutert's: August Germann (Germann's son Walter was to run I. G. Chemie for ten years after the war).

Greutert's bank had been reconstituted, and his place was taken by his protégé, Hans Sturzenegger, who had been trained in Farben's finance department and, according to a British report during the war, was 'closely identified with the Nazi Party and the German government'.

Chemie's chairman was none other than Felix Iselin, who by 1940 had emerged as one of Switzerland's leading lawyers, chairman of the auditing committee of the CIBA chemical group, a colonel and a very senior intelligence officer. One of his colleagues told the British during the war that he was 'a prominent representative of absolutely German interests ... he goes to Berlin to take orders from Hermann Schmitz and then telephones them to New York from Basle, thus pretending to protect Swiss interests where he is really protecting the interests of I. G. Farben.'

The Germans also retained control through the usual tangle of interlocking shareholdings. Sixty thousand of the crucial preference shares in I. G. Chemie were held by the Industrie Bank, which also controlled the Sturzenegger Bank. Industrie Bank was nominally owned by 'friends' of a certain Theodor Wolfensberger but was generally assumed to be controlled by Farben interests. The owner of the other forty thousand preference shares, a Lausanne company, the Société de Participations et de Dépôts, was itself controlled by Perpetua, another company within the Farben orbit.

The Deutsche Landesbank of Berlin, which controlled 16 million francs' worth of I. G. Chemie shares, or approximately nine per cent of the votes, was another important intermediary. After the war Farben officials admitted to American investigators that the bank 'was controlled by Farben, not through stock ownership but by reason of its dependency upon Farben for business'. In an effort to insist on the bank's neutrality, its manager went out of his way to insist to the investigators that nearly three-quarters of the bank's shares were in fact owned by ... I. G. Chemie. And so on, down to an annual payment of $150,000 to Farben by I. G. Chemie, agreed in May 1939 and never cancelled ('this contract is of particular importance', noted the American official, 'in view of the statements made by representatives of Chemie to the effect that all contractual relationships with Farben have been terminated').

None of these manoeuvrings helped protect GAF once war had actually broken out. In a typical inter-departmental fight in Washington, the Secretary for the Treasury, Henry Morgenthau, insisted that his department control GAF – as the symbol of German industrial penetration in the country (one of his weapons was the use made of GAF for patronage purposes by his rival, the Alien Property Custodian, Leo Crowley). The British had already warned the Americans, repeatedly and loudly, that I. G. Farben's American subsidiaries would be used for espionage on a large scale. In the Ozalid copying division, which had been brought under GAF's control only just before the outbreak of war in 1939, technicians, many of them German, had infiltrated the design offices of 3,500 American industrial plants, including defence installations and experimental laboratories. The film activities of Agfa-Ansco were also obviously of considerable strategic importance and even the dyes produced by the old Bayer plants were required for khaki uniforms. In early January 1941 Morgenthau removed many key executives and placed two dozen others under close supervision, and the next month ninety-seven per cent of its shares were taken over by the Treasury. Once Morgenthau had installed his own men to run GAF, he allowed his rival the Alien Property Custodian to take it over, but by then American officialdom had got the message: GAF was the very symbol of Nazi penetration of American industry. The Nazis contemplated some form of retaliation by liquidating American-owned assets in Germany, but this was opposed by the German Foreign office which warned that 'we would thereby furnish the Americans with a frank admission of what we have been so far trying to conceal by cloaking – i.e. that these actually exert German interests in the companies involved, and on a considerable scale'.

By that time Farben's American interests had been taken under the official protection of the Swiss government. In 1941 the Swiss minister in Washington, Walter Bruggemann (whose influence with the American government was enhanced by the fact that he and Henry Wallace, then Vice-President, had married sisters), and a young Jew, Werner Gabler, who had good government connections, were both active in supporting what the Swiss clearly perceived as their country's interests. They tried to retain Washington's leading law firm, Covington and Burling, but the firm pleaded conflict of interests because they were acting for the Dutch government; they went instead to a young but brilliant lawyer named John J. Wilson and thus forged what eventually and improbably proved to be an invincible alliance.

2 / Unravelling

The three and a half years between 1941 and 1945 during which the United States was at war with Germany provided the only period of truce in the long battle between the United States authorities and the owners (whoever they were) of I. G. Farben's American businesses. In Washington Wilson held only a watching brief ('my retainer was so small I won't tell you', he declares, in contrast to the very considerable fees he earned later from the same client). But, under wartime regulations, he was not even allowed to talk to Hans Sturzenegger. He had good reasons for keeping quiet, since 'under the Alien Property Act they [the U.S. authorities] had pure legal title which enabled them to sell ... by the grace of God they did not sell during the war ... my idea was to learn what I could and not rock the boat to precipitate a sale'.

It never occurred to anyone else in Washington that these were not enemy-held assets, belonging to a group that became a synonym for the whole Nazi military-industrial war machine, mass employers of slave labour, crucial conspirators in the Nazi attempt at world conquest. In Switzerland, everything looked rather different. The Swiss obviously hoped that, given a few cosmetic changes, all would be well. The danger was spelled out at a reparations conference held in Paris in November 1945, which allowed the Allies to use the proceeds from the confiscation of German assets in neutral countries as reparations including those 'which are, in reality, German assets despite the fact that the nominal owner of such assets is not a German enemy'. The next month a special meeting of I. G. Chemie shareholders girded themselves for battle against the possible consequences of the decision. They changed the name, to eliminate the fatal taint of being an 'I.G.'. The new name would be the bland Interhandel.*

* Internationale Industrie und Handelsbeteilingungen.

Schmitz's brother-in-law stepped down as managing director, to be replaced by Greutert's nephew, Walter Germann.
As a final flourish the bearer shares were eliminated. The
directors felt able to declare that 'undeniably all the available
documentary evidence of the ownership is legally unimpeachable'. And already the Swiss establishment had taken its
stand. The *New York Times* reported that 'Financial circles in
Switzerland say that if I. G. Chemie is really a camouflaged
German asset the Swiss directors are gravely culpable at law'.

After the Washington Agreement was signed in May 1946
Wilson was at last able to get a passport to visit his clients.
'They were so cautious they didn't trust me for a long time',
he says, but after he had spoken at length at a board meeting
they devised a joint plan of action. The Swiss embassy in
Washington was to declare 'at least an avuncular interest',
while Wilson would keep an eye on the Justice Department.

During 1946 hopes of a settlement rose, as did the shares
in Interhandel, the first of many such false boomlets. By
December they had risen 300 francs to 745 even before the
board put forward its arguments. These sounded impressive:
'documents furnished in connection with implementation of
the Washington Agreements' apparently showed that not
more than one quarter of the shares had been in enemy hands
since the middle of 1941, and the board had proved, to the
satisfaction of the Swiss Compensation Office, that its own
shares had been acquired with its members' own money,
again before the middle of 1941. The board even proposed the
basis for a settlement. If the Custodian of Enemy Property
were to sell the fifteen to twenty per cent of the shares which
the directors were prepared to admit had been enemy held,
then the directors would lend their support to a sale to an
American group. This did not seem at all improbable. James
H. Rand of Remington Rand was anxious to buy GAF to fit in
with his group's expansion plans in chemicals and photographic equipment. But he soon retired from the scene, baffled
by legal complexities he never properly understood. The
board of Interhandel was, however, sure of its ground:
members of the board of directors, it declared, 'who have
already suffered acutely under suspicion of acting as German
agents, are willing to sell provided an acceptable price is

offered. All that is needed is recognition by the U.S. Treasury as non-enemy assets of the shares not then German-owned.'

The gulf between them and the Americans was enormous. Malcolm Mason expressed the burning sense of indignation against the Swiss claims which possessed all those in successive administrations dealing with the case in the next fifteen years. 'When we look at a bear in sheep's clothing', he told the members of the American Society of International Law in 1958, 'we recognise it for what it is because we have been bitten before and because it is our livestock that is threatened. When the Swiss look at a bear in sheep's clothing, to them it looks just like any respectable Swiss gentleman. Swiss financial circles have made a good thing over many years of supplying sheep's clothing. I think in this instance they have cried sheep once too often. Here we have a transaction – a purported purgation of German control of Chemie which every Alien Property Custodian in the world knows was a classic example of cloaking. Farben said in advance it would be a cloaking transaction. The Swiss, however, are now officially convinced that the bank clerks had pulled themselves up by their own bootstraps and had bought out the Farben empire.'

In such an explosive atmosphere the formal outbreak of legal hostilities could not be long delayed. As so often, the actual declaration of war was provoked by a fear which turned out to be groundless. Wilson, like virtually everyone else in the country, assumed that Thomas Dewey would win the 1948 presidential election, and he was scared that the Justice Department would sell GAF before the arrival of Dewey's men (who would, presumably, have been less hostile to the Swiss). So in October 1948 he sued the government for the $103 million at which his clients valued the GAF stock, thus blocking any sale until the litigation was settled.

In March 1949 President Truman's Attorney-General, Tom Clark, returned fire, saying that I. G. Chemie was merely a 'cloak or dummy' for I. G. Farben and claiming $9 million in back taxes on profits resulting from the 1929 agreement between Standard Oil and the Germans. Thus began nearly ten years of intermittent legal hostilities, effectively between the Swiss and U.S. governments.

The war was not fought only in the American courts. In Switzerland dissident shareholders put considerable pressure on the directors of Interhandel (who controlled the company because they controlled all the preference shares). In the United States minority shareholders – and potential buyers of GAF – also intervened; and the Interhandel board, still headed by Iselin, tried to copy the tactics used so successfully by Richard Merton in the 1920s, to obtain by political clout what they could not achieve in the courts – the point was made bluntly in the *Neue Zürcher Zeitung* in 1954: 'the time seems to have arrived when an official démarche by the Swiss Federal authorities to high American authorities might prove opportune and effectual'.

The order of battle had been established even before Wilson sued the government. The ruling that I. G. Chemie had, indeed, been controlled by genuinely Swiss interests at the relevant times had passed right up through the Swiss legal machinery, and the American authorities had already flatly disagreed with the successive judgments. Some preliminary skirmishes followed. Initially, the Swiss tried to prevent Hans Sturzenegger, one of the plaintiffs, from testifying in the United States. The Americans were told that such a step would be a breach of basic Swiss constitutional principle. But, Wilson pointed out, 'he was a primary party to the case, so they could require his appearance without subpoena ... they had already picked him out as our Achilles heel'.

The Swiss soon climbed down, and Sturzenegger had to testify for five gruelling months ('his English got better', says Wilson grimly, 'I warned him to be literally truthful, other-wise he would face indictment for perjury'). But if the banker was co-operative, his archives could never be. Swiss officials had already enjoyed a chance to see the mass of documents placed in court by the American authorities 'under the rules of legal discovery', and they produced a large number of their own. But they could not and would not allow any of the files of the bank to be brought into evidence. The importance the Swiss attached to the case was demonstrated most dramati-cally when their authorities seized the relevant files to prevent Sturzenegger from complying with any instructions issued by an American court. They did not rely exclusively on Clause 47(b): they also stated firmly that the American request fell within the scope of 'economic espionage' as defined in 1935 and subsequently enshrined in Article 273 of their penal code. The 'phoney' war was now over.

The Americans promptly accused the Swiss of conspiring to prevent the records' being produced, claiming that Interhandel had induced the Swiss authorities to act on their behalf, not, on the face of it, an unreasonable claim. Nor were the Swiss protestations of good faith supported by the quality of some of the documents that were produced. To be sure, the numbers were impressive: by November 1953 the Swiss had obtained consent to release over 63,000 of them. But these included one particular set of Interhandel accounts which the Department of Justice proved were contained in account books with a stationer's mark which showed they were printed eighteen months later than the entries in them. They were thus clearly a retrospective reconstruction of events. (The board later admitted that the books of the company 'were kept in a preliminary version' which was available to the Swiss government; the Department of Justice had been shown only a 'final version which omitted certain items', even though the American courts had ordered the Swiss to produce the same documents and books which had been examined by the Swiss government.)

Yet, despite the inconsistencies, the general Swiss view was that the interests of Interhandel and Switzerland (not to mention capitalism itself) were synonymous. As the *Neue Zürcher Zeitung* put it in a 1954 editorial: 'Switzerland is directly concerned not only because of the effects on the sequestration conflict, as for example Interhandel, but also because of the vindication of the principle of inviolability even in wartime of the rights of private property on which the capitalist system rests. Suspension of these rights during the war by several European countries, including even neutral Sweden, only serves to strengthen communist principles'. The only break in the ranks came the following year in the newspaper owned by the Migros co-operative movement: 'It is known far and wide,' wrote the paper, or rather Gottlieb Duttweiler, Migros' undisputed boss, 'that Interhandel undertook to camouflage the interests of I. G. Farben. ... the Swiss authorities are not empowered to give protection to obscure frauds and, as it were, by using the good name of Switzerland, to sanction them'. He went on to point out that no qualified Swiss industrialists ever sat on the I. G. Chemie board, thus reinforcing his argument that the members were mere dummies, 'lawyers who knew nothing of the chemical industry and did not possess enough technical knowledge to justify the investment of such a vast amount of capital'.

Duttweiler's outburst could safely be ignored; he was a maverick, and was about to set up his own bank, a good enough reason to attack the banking community. But there were other distractions to the main battle. In 1950, when the deadlock seemed complete a settlement was nearly reached. The Swiss asked for $14 million, Attorney-General Clark offered $12 million, not an unbridgeable gap – but then a firm of Zurich stockbrokers organised a campaign against the directors and accused them openly (even in newspaper advertisements) of selling the genuine Swiss shareholders short. To defend themselves the directors promptly raised their demand to an unrealistic $35 million which naturally scuppered the deal.

With so much money at stake the Interhandel shares were a favourite counter on the Zurich stock market. In early 1952 they soared to over 1,350 on confidential New York reports – less unfounded than many such rumours – that there would be a lump sum payment to Interhandel. In May they were up to 1,800 because of a ruling that companies should be regarded as neutral if less than a quarter of their shares were enemy held; and had not the Interhandel board said that only fourteen per cent of the company's shares had been in enemy hands? But late the following year the stock led the market in the opposite direction. 'Not since the end of World War II has the Zurich stock exchange been so disturbed as last week when the Interhandel stock slumped heavily', noted the *New York Times*. (The stock had been 1,675 and then went down to 1,250.)

This particular perturbation, like so many others, was caused by developments within the United States. The legal situation had been complicated because two Jewish refugees, the Kaufmans, who owned a mere eighty-six shares in Inter-handel, asked the court for their rights, as genuinely non-enemy shareholders, to be recognised (in their statement they went along with the American view as to the real ownership of the vast majority of the shares). Eventually they were allowed into the case, which seemed to be going against Wilson until the District Court in Washington which was hearing the case appointed a Special Master, an independent lawyer, to explore the nature of the Swiss laws involved. The Master, William Hughes, was chosen as the only name common to the lists presented by both sides, and his findings did not help the government case ('he didn't have the judicial temperament', says one of the U.S. lawyers, 'he was terribly long-winded'). He found that the Swiss government 'had acted in accordance with its own established doctrines in exercising preventative police power by constructive seizure of the Sturzenegger records'. Even more crucially, he came to the conclusion, which may have been legally impeccable but ignored the realities of Swiss life, that there was 'no proof, or any evidence at all, of collusion between the plaintiff and the Swiss government in the seizure of the papers herein ... the plaintiff has sustained the burden of proof placed upon it and has shown good faith in its efforts [to comply with the production order]'. He thus effectively cleared the Swiss of the charge of conspiracy to prevent the documents being produced and, for the first time in an American court, allowed the legitimacy of Swiss banking secrecy.

Nevertheless, in February 1953 the District Court in Washington ruled that, apart from Swiss law, the petitioner had control over the bank's records, which could be crucial for the litigation, and that Swiss law did not furnish an adequate excuse for the petitioner's failure to comply with the order to produce the documents. To make matters worse, the decision was confirmed that November and the case was kept alive over the following years only on a series of niggling technicalities.* But Wilson kept plugging away, even getting individual waivers from Sturzenegger's clients to

---

* When the case was finally settled, Wilson reckoned that he had been before the Supreme Court four times and the Appeals Court eight times.

allow the bank's books to be produced.

In the mid-1950s the action was elsewhere, mostly in Congress, where repeated attempts were made by the powerful lobby which the Swiss had assembled to prevent the sale of remaining 'enemy' assets but, equally, to encourage attempts to allow their return.* In 1954 Senator Everett Dirksen introduced such a bill. This was vigorously opposed by the Attorney-General, Herbert Brownell. Proceedings were confused by an elephantine interruption by none other than Merton's discarded lawyer, now Secretary of State, John Foster Dulles. He airily argued that Congress had the power to deal with alien property as it saw fit, and that its powers were totally unaffected by the 1946 reparations agreement. His arguments sent shock waves through European countries, whose governments had assumed that the agreement was as binding as a Treaty. Fortunately for the good name of the United States, the Justice Department view prevailed. One argument which first appeared at the time was that American investments abroad would be at risk if the government did not accept the bill. 'There are dangerous implications for our own citizens in America,' warned Senator Homer Capehart, 'by giving even an indirect sanction to the idea that a confiscation of corporate property is somehow justified'. (The Swiss were immensely cheered by this evidence that someone in the United States understood their position, and the Interhandel shares soared.) The arguments were sometimes extreme: Senator William Langer claimed in a number of speeches that the current 'confiscation' was the result of a Soviet plot (engineered by the ubiquitous Harry Dexter White), and indeed both sides could play the 'Commie plot' card. A Senate sub-committee considering one of the bills was told by a retired GAF executive, Harry L. Derby, that secrets could be passed behind the Iron Curtain if foreign control were restored, even on a temporary basis.

The issue of sovereignty came openly to the fore when the Swiss, despairing of getting anywhere in the American courts,

* The Interhandel supporters were powerful and well funded. But the congressmen who agreed with them were in a minority, despite the use of well paid lobbyists, including 'Wild Bill' Donovan, the former head of the OSS, who had returned to private practice.

appealed to the World Court at The Hague, after the Americans had turned down an earlier offer to submit the case to arbitration. The Swiss case was based on the assumption that the assets involved were Swiss owned and therefore the Swiss had jurisdiction over their disposal. The Americans retorted that the assets were located in the United States and therefore not covered by the Washington Agreements, which concerned only German owned assets in Switzerland.

The Swiss minister, Max Petitpierre, said that nothing less was at stake than 'the importance of international agreements that provide for arbitration of disputes which cannot be settled in a friendly manner ... it was completely incomprehensible that the United States could oppose the court's jurisdiction'. The Swiss were so alarmed at the prospect that the Americans would sell off the GAF stock before any ruling by the World Court that they asked for 'interim measures of protection' (the court acted with exemplary and unusual speed in ruling that they were not entitled to such an injunction), the Americans continuing to argue that the matter was purely of domestic importance. The whole affair had now reached its maximum apparent point of stalemate, yet within a few weeks two revolutionary developments had broken the deadlock. During October 1957 the Supreme Court agreed to consider the case, to decide whether Interhandel had indeed broken the law by 'refusing to obey' the court instruction to produce the bank files, or whether it was simply 'unable' to carry out the court's instructions.

At the same time Interhandel itself was totally reorganised. Already in 1955 Walter Germann had been forced to explain the investments in which he had placed the twenty per cent of Interhandel's money which was not tied up in GAF. None of these were very inspiring: a half share in the Bank Hoffmann, a small chemical company, an equally insignificant bank in Panama, some film ventures. They were all made without the shareholders' knowledge, and none had justified themselves. He had been commuting across the Atlantic before the habit became fashionable in financial circles ('he only went home to get his laundry done') and, although the trips were fully justified by the need to guide the progress of the GAF case, he had become suspect to the Swiss establishment ('they thought he had been living high on the hog: that he was just visiting his girlfriend') whose reputation had become so involved with that of Interhandel.

The clean-up started the month after the Supreme Court agreed to hear the case, with the elimination of the famous six per cent preference shares, now all owned by the Industrie Bank, which were repaid at par. In February 1958 the deal was completed, and Sturzenegger retired from Interhandel's board. That same month the Zurich stock-market – which by then was used to the gyrations in the stock – was startled by news that the Union Bank of Switzerland had been buying control of Interhandel in the market. In June UBS, acting on behalf of the whole Swiss establishment, took charge of Interhandel with the prospect of making an enormous profit from any settlement. To emphasise the seriousness of the commitment, the heads of all three major banks went onto the board, together with the chairman of the Swiss Bankers' Association, but it was Dr. Alfred Schaefer who became general manager and vice-chairman, soon taking over from the figure-head banker who had been initially placed there to replace Felix Iselin. (As early as 1946, Schaefer had been involved in syndicates set up to buy enterprises which even the Swiss admitted were controlled by the Germans.)

The excitement in Zurich over the reorganisation of Interhandel was rather obscured at the time by Wilson's success before the Supreme Court*, which heard the case in May 1958 and handed down its ruling the next month by eight votes to none.** Both the decision – and its unanimity – surprised observers. The court accepted the findings of the Special Master and ruled that the Interhandel representatives were unable to produce the relevant documents because of Swiss banking law, that they were therefore not in contempt of court in not producing them, and so had not refused to obey the court's rulings.

* The case was nominally the then Attorney-General, William Rogers, v. 'Société Internationale pour Participations' – the French equivalent of Interhandel.
** One justice, Tom Clark, absented himself because of his previous involvement as Attorney General.

From a Swiss point of view, the Supreme Court ruling constituted a magnificent vindication of Clause 47(b), with its unique provision that breach of banking secrecy was a criminal offence. This obviously weighed heavily with the justices: 'It is hardly debatable', they chorussed, 'that fear of criminal prosecution constitutes a weighty excuse for non-production, and this excuse is not weakened because the laws preventing compliance are those of a foreign sovereign ... the very fact of compliance by disclosure of banking records will itself constitute the initial violation of Swiss laws.' The success owed a great deal to Wilson's insistence that Interhandel be seen to try to comply with the court's instructions. The Petitioner, said the justices, 'explicitly recognises that it is subject to procedural rules of United States courts in this litigation and has made full efforts to follow these rules. It asserts no immunity from them. It asserts only its *inability* [a word italicised in the judgment] to comply because of the foreign law'. It would have saved the Swiss a great many problems over the next fifteen years if they had noted the conditions under which the Court accepted the validity of Clause 47(b), but for the moment all was joy. 'This was the greatest day in any lawyer's life', said Wilson. 'From then on there was an atmosphere of settlement ... the judgment ensured that the case would come to court or be settled'. The log-jam had indeed been broken, but not necessarily to Interhandel's advantage. Wilson's joy derived partly from looking forward to arguing the case again on its merits, without having to face the production of the Sturzenegger files. He was by no means sure that he could win; his opponents, the lawyers within the Justice Department, were much more confident than he was. Nevertheless sheer Swiss stubbornness had paid dividends. After the Supreme Court's decision, the arrival of Alfred Schaefer on the scene, and as the memories of I. G. Farben's atrocities faded (though not in the minds of U.S. government officials, many of them former refugees), a deal seemed more and more likely. The curious part of the affair was that Wilson, a leading Republican (who went on to defend John Ehrlichman for his part in the Watergate affair), failed to find common ground with his own party, and the peace treaty had to await the arrival

of a – theoretically much less sympathetic – Democrat administration.

3 / Settlement

The Supreme Court opened the way to a settlement – or a
legal judgment on the case itself. Within a year, the World
Court, suddenly seemingly irrelevant to the case, had thrown
out the Swiss application to hear the case on the grounds that
'the Swiss had not exhausted all the remedies available in the
U.S. courts' (the previous week a rumour had swept through
Zurich that the Court had come to precisely the opposite
conclusion).

In the United States a sell-off seemed likely. The previous
year the Attorney-General had gone through the necessary
formalities with the Securities and Exchange Commission to
prepare the GAF stock for sale. After the decision, the
brokerage house of Bache offered $84 million for the govern-
ment's stake in GAF, planning to divide the business into
three and sell each part off to a reputable buyer it had already
lined up (dyestuffs to W. R. Grace, the film business to
Paramount Pictures, and Ozalid to Daystrom). A Swiss
spokesman was reported as 'happily blurting out' that 'we're
on the very eve of settlement', and, in the Senate, Kenneth
Keating tried to tack onto a bill to provide up to $500 million
to compensate Americans for damage caused by Nazis, a
clause that would have allowed the Alien Property Custodian
to sell off GAF.

But the imminence of sale lured the vultures back to the
prospective feast. In Germany the trustees in liquidation for
I. G. Farben suddenly woke up to the possibility that they
might share in the proceeds, and Robert Schmitz, nephew

of Hermann,* saw the possibility of realising a life-long ambition and sharing in the proceeds of the business with which his family had been so involved.

The Farben intervention appeared to be the more serious: the trustees claimed that for two years they had tried to get clarification of its relationship with GAF, and how far it was to be compensated for what it described as 'an indirect investment of $100 million', a sum which, it added, 'appeared to be held in trust by Sturzenegger'. The trustees sued in the United States, where, they reckoned, they stood a better chance than in Switzerland. Fortunately for the other parties, the court threw out their application and they decided not to appeal, though not before they had given everyone else involved a nasty shock.

Schmitz's intervention had longer term consequences. In late 1958 he talked to Hans Sturzenegger in Basle. According to Joseph Borkin, Schmitz told Sturzenegger that 'Interhandel had failed in its efforts so far because it had never been able "to command the interest of those who counted in the highest echelons of the American government".' Schmitz advised a new approach. Interhandel should convey full and irrevocable powers of negotiation and final settlement to an outstanding American who 'would be above politics and yet would have entrée to every door of the administration'. Schmitz's recommendation was 'Electric Charlie', Charles Wilson, former chairman of General Electric, who had also served the Roosevelt administration during the war. He was agreeable, and was given what appeared to be an irrevocable power of attorney with absolute powers. The Interhandel stock jumped for joy on his appointment, but in Washington William Rogers, the Attorney-General, flatly refused to see him.

Matters did not apparently improve with the arrival of the Kennedy administration in early 1961. Charles Spofford, Charles Wilson's lawyer, arranged for Dr. Schaefer himself to see William Orrick, the new Assistant Attorney-General in charge of Alien Property – not by any means the 'highest echelons' which Schmitz had aimed at. But the meeting was

---

* Robert's father was Hermann's 'American' brother, D.A., who had taken over as chairman of GAF in the 1930s.

counter-productive, indeed stormy, with Orrick ordering Schaefer to leave the room after the banker had attacked the American government's handling of the case. (Schaefer's timing was terrible: he had hoped to see the Secretary of State, Dean Rusk, and the Secretary of the Treasury, Douglas Dillon. But his visit coincided with the Bay of Pigs crisis.)

At this point Dr. Schaefer obviously became disenchanted with the lack of progress made through Charles Wilson. Fortunately for him, another avenue opened up. A certain Dr. Gutstein, a lawyer and friend of Schaefer, introduced him to another of his clients, Prince Stanislas Radziwill, who had married Jacqueline Kennedy's sister, Lee Bouvier. No echelon could have been higher. Moreover, the Kennedy family – possibly inspired by a meeting between Wilson and Joseph Kennedy at the latter's Palm Beach house – was obviously taking an interest in GAF.

Although Radziwill himself claimed never to have been retained by the Swiss or to have accepted money from them, other confidants of the Kennedys were put on the GAF payroll. (This was not a novel form of patronage, although a Senate Committee had concluded in 1953 that the GAF board was not used for such purposes.) Among the new appointees were Joseph Kennedy's lawyer, William Payton Marin, who became vice-chairman and the driving force in the company, and several other family friends.

Radziwill's first idea, with which the Swiss apparently agreed, was far-fetched. The Department of Justice would return the GAF stock to Interhandel, which would sell it and use the proceeds to establish a development bank to supply credit to underdeveloped countries. The idea was presented to Robert Kennedy, the Attorney-General, who insisted on dealing only with Schaefer, man to man with no witnesses present. In Borkin's words: 'According to the Justice lawyer who was present when the letter [to Kennedy from Radziwill] arrived, it looked like a royal wedding invitation, enclosed in two richly appointed envelopes and embossed with the Radziwill crest'. Kennedy naturally dismissed the idea of a development bank, which may well have been merely a means of lending respectability to the transaction, but agreed that Schaefer and Orrick could work out a deal. He clearly recognised the political danger; indeed, he may have exaggerated its effect on the Jewish vote as a bargaining counter in his dealings with Schaefer. But the moral dimension in the case seems entirely to have escaped him. It was simply a problem to be solved.

The next step was to ease out Charles Wilson, who quite naturally felt betrayed by Radziwill's involvement, and to fill in the details of a settlement which Kennedy had proposed: that the United States would keep eleven per cent of the proceeds of any sale to cover the shares that even Interhandel admitted had been in German ownership twenty years previously; the remainder would be divided fifty-fifty.

An outline agreement was reached in April 1962 between Orrick and Schaefer, but a few months later Orrick switched to the Department of State and a new Deputy Attorney-General, Nicholas Katzenbach, took over the negotiations, a change which helped explain the delay of over a year between the first and second meetings between the two principals. In the meantime Katzenbach had decided to help defuse the political row which he knew would result from the settlement by arranging for the shares to be sold by competitive auction. Moreover, he struck a bargain with John Wilson, who had fought off the competition and had re-emerged as Interhandel's lawyer. Katzenbach agreed – albeit reluctantly – that the original outline agreement would be adhered to. In return Wilson agreed to withdraw his client's objection to the Keating amendment permitting the sale of the stock (by now, both the amendment and Interhandel's objections had become hardy congressional perennials).

The signature of the bill in October 1962 removed the major legal obstacle to the sale. But Katzenbach then interpreted the terms in a way which greatly increased the American share of the proceeds. A number of items were due to 'come off the top' from the proceeds – the back tax claim for $17.5 million, and $6.5 million to repay GAF for the Interhandel shares it held as a result of Schmitz's financial manoeuvres in the 1930s. It had been assumed that these would be deducted equally from the money due to the American government and to Interhandel. Katzenbach wanted the full amount – $24 million – to be deducted from

Interhandel's shares. John Wilson says that the tax claim – which dated back to 1929 – 'wasn't worth a damn ... nevertheless at Christmas [1962] it looked as if negotiations were off'. They weren't. Six weeks later, Schaefer, Wilson and Katzenbach settled the deal on the basis proposed by Katzenbach – and the Americans were also going to get $5.277 million in cash and dividends held by GAF in 1942 and seized with the company's other assets.

This looked like a victory for the Americans. But it was also a major source of additional profit for the Union Bank of Switzerland as the biggest shareholder in Interhandel. For GAF had owned 60,000 out of Interhandel's 166,000 shares, and it was going to pay only $6.5 million for them, representing their market value when they were seized. But by 1963 their market value was $50 million – 3,500 francs a share. The profit went entirely to the Interhandel shareholders, who saw their share of the money they got from the settlement leap by nearly fifty per cent with the cancellation of the 60,000 shares previously held by GAF.

Nevertheless Schaefer remained dissatisfied, according to Victor Navasky, who gives John Wilson's account of the final meeting in his book, *Kennedy Justice*.

> Being a hell of a good Swiss banker, he [Schaefer] naturally expressed his unhappiness with the deal. Nick said if you want to take an appeal to the Attorney-General you can see him tomorrow. Schaefer said yes – he'd see him. At dinner Schaefer expressed the classical Swiss point of view – that he had been short-changed.
>
> The next day we went to the Attorney-General's office in the forenoon. Bobby, two Swiss, Nick and I were there. Schaefer started off by complaining that they were being short-changed. He remarked he had two million people watching this transaction, the most important international event in Switzerland. The Attorney-General said, 'I have one hundred and ninety million people watching me.'
>
> RFK: 'My boys tell me we could lick you.'
>
> Wilson: 'General, why don't we leave the merits out of this. I have been in this case for many years, and I can't tell you to a moral certainty that I can beat you but you can't

tell me to a moral certainty that you can beat me. So let's get on with the negotiation.'

They were in the big room for twenty minutes with Katzenbach at one corner of the Attorney-General's huge desk, Wilson at another and the two Swiss facing Kennedy. 'Here was a confrontation between cold-bloodedness and stiff-neckedness,' says Wilson. 'Throughout the conversation there were "whams" on the door. The Swiss would nervously look at it, and Nick would wink at me. Finally I said, 'General, why don't you let him out?' The Attorney-General said, 'I believe I will,' at which point his dog Brumus leaped in and lay down beside me, probably smelling my terriers.

President Kennedy went out of his way to defend the settlement, again on purely practical grounds, when asked a loaded question at a press conference about the apparent change in the government's attitude to GAF's real owners:

'No, I would say that the agreement is an equitable agreement. It could have gone on ten years more in the courts, and it has been now fifteen or twenty years and lawyers have enjoyed it, but I don't think that there is anything else. I don't think we would get a better arrangement if we continued the litigation for another ten years. We feel that the arrangement which has been worked out will return the assets to those who have a claim to them, and I think the division of resources is fair.'

Kennedy's staff were most unhappy at the settlement, and there was despair among the lawyers engaged in preparing the case, which they were convinced they could win. There was also grumbling in Congress, but the most damaging revelations emerged much later in a number of columns by Drew Pearson. He drew attention to the directors with Kennedy connections appointed to the board of GAF. And, even more damagingly, a source in the Justice Department leaked the one and only letter in which Schaefer had been unwise enough to commit Radziwill's name to paper. In his other correspondence on the subject, notably to Charles Wilson's lawyer, Charles Spofford, Radziwill was referred to only obliquely as 'the party in question' or 'our friend in London'.

The revelations appeared within a few months of President Kennedy's assassination so the connection* was not politically exploited (nor has anyone ever enquired whether the involvement of that old stock market operator Joseph Kennedy resulted from any investment he might have made in Interhandel. After all the board members appointed by his children were his friends, rather than theirs.)

The Kennedys' judgement that the political fall-out would not be fatal was vindicated in 1964 when Robert Kennedy was running for Senator against Kenneth Keating. In a despairing gesture – and with both eyes on New York's crucial Jewish vote – Keating attacked the Interhandel settlement, but the attack fizzled out partly because he had been involved in the settlement himself.

Nevertheless there were still numbers of formalities to be gone through before the stock could be sold. It took six months for a legal settlement to be reached satisfying to 1,100 parties who had somehow become involved in the case.

It took a year more for the company to be prepared for sale. The share structure had to be changed, with the two classes created in 1929 to preserve German ownership merged into one. A committee of 'wise men' had to decide how the stock should be offered, and bids invited.

By early 1965 the interest surrounding the offering was intense. One of the hottest stocks around at the time was that of another government offering, the communications satellite company, Comsat (issued at $20 in June 1964, the stock had soared to $70 within six months). But the major factor in fuelling the excitement was the assumption that GAF, crippled because of its ownership by the government, would flourish as never before once restored to private ownership.

The idea did not, at the time, seem unreasonable. In the twenty years after it was taken over by the government, five other chemical companies (Hercules, Celanese, Cyanamid, Dow and Monsanto), all of which had been smaller than the German group, had overtaken it. GAF had increased its sales

---

* More details about the Radziwill involvement emerged four years later when Robert Schmitz sued, unsuccessfully, for a $7.5 million 'finders fee'.

by 284 per cent (to $179 million) and its earnings by 153 per cent (to $8.1 million in 1963: they were $10.7 million in 1964). But Kodak and du Pont, its nearest pre-war equivalents, had moved far faster. For the first twelve years under government ownership, GAF suffered from what officials called 'the dead hand of "conserving the asset"'. Precluded from raising equity or loan financing it could not exploit its new products – its Ansco division, for example, developed the first really practical negative-positive system for motion picture film, but the company did not have the capital to put it into production. In addition GAF had to buy a lot of raw materials – like sulphuric acid – from its own competitors, to its own obvious disadvantage. Things changed in the mid-1950s when GAF absorbed General Dyestuffs, the former I. G. Farben sales company, and as the then chairman, John Hilldring, put it, 'we started acting like a chemical company instead of like a government ward'. Nevertheless, lack of finance and uncertainty about future ownership ('Who owns you this week?' customers would ask the company's naturally dispirited salesmen) resulted in the virtual absence of long-term planning and a steady drain of key personnel. Nevertheless, the company retained its technical and manufacturing assets as one of the leading makers of dyestuffs and film products in the country, and its Ozalid division was still the country's largest producer of dry-process reproduction equipment.

As a result the sale was a success, far greater than anyone expected, even though the conditions were strict: to prevent anyone getting control, for instance, personal investors were limited to a thousand shares each and institutional investors to fifty thousand apiece. On 9 March 1965, a Wall Street syndicate headed by Blyth and First Boston acquired the stock for $329 million – $15 million more than the only other bidder. Yet only two months earlier the government's budget estimates had allowed for receipts of only $100 million from the sale, less than one third the actual sum. Interhandel received $122 million (5,000 Swiss francs per share) net, nearly ten times the $14 million for which the board had been prepared to settle ten years previously. Their only concession was their promise to retain the money for the time being in the United States, in deference to fears that too sudden removal of so large a sum would 'adversely affect' the American balance of payments position.

The story since then has been of almost uninterrupted anticlimax. The shares were snapped up at the offer price of $30.65. This valuation provided the winning syndicate with a gross profit of over $12 million, but seemed by no means excessive, for the price of the few thousand shares which had previously been available had tripled in the year before the auction to reach nearly $50. All looked set fair. There was a new president, Jesse Werner, who had been with the group since 1938, and was the first career executive to head GAF. And he appeared at first to make all the right moves: heavy investments combined with apparently sensible purchases of specialist companies in areas close to GAF's own activities. He even changed the name, as was fashionable in the 1960s (officially, General Aniline & Film turned into GAF only in 1968).

But it was too late to catch up on the twenty wasted years. As *Forbes* magazine wrote in 1971, when Werner was fighting off a former director, Seymour Milstein, who charged him with incompetence – and worse – in running the company's affairs: 'GAF would appear to be in some of the sexiest businesses in the U.S. economy – chemicals, film, copying machines. But in virtually every field in which it operates GAF competes with IBM-like giants – du Pont in chemicals, Eastman Kodak in film, Xerox in copying machines. Even high-powered companies like 3M and Sperry Rand have blanched before competition like that.'

In the 1970s things got worse, and the wheel of Farben came full circle. In 1974 GAF, together with eight other companies (including Bayer and BASF, two of the groups into which I. G. Farben had been divided at the end of the war) pleaded guilty to conspiracy to fix the price of dyestuffs. Four years later, GAF sold the old dyestuff plant that had been the heart of its former empire to none other than – BASF. At the same time it admitted defeat in its losing battle with Eastman Kodak in the consumer photographic business. But its struggles were not over – and three years later it was forced to sell a third of its remaining businesses.

None of this, of course, worried the Swiss. Within eighteen

months of the receipt of the money, Dr. Schaefer had put before the shareholders of Interhandel two possible scenarios as to their future. Neither seemed very promising: to 'look for lucrative investments after years of unprofitable existence ... or to give up its tax privileges as a holding company to become a financing institute' working with leading European banks. The welcome alternative: a takeover by Dr. Schaefer's bank, which already controlled nearly half the capital. It could thus take into its balance sheet the considerable surplusses accumulated because it had bought its Interhandel shares at well below their final valuation (not to mention the boost provided by the cancellation of GAF's shares in Interhandel). Nothing could have been more appropriate or satisfactory – a boost for UBS's capital base to nearly a billion Swiss francs, putting it well ahead of the competition, for the first time in its history.

PART FIVE

Peace and its Problems

1 / Strength through tranquillity

The deal hammered out between Dr. Schaefer and Robert Kennedy confirmed what had already become apparent with the Washington Agreements – that Swiss stubbornness and the national backing provided for the bankers could prevail even over the banks' most implacable enemies in the American government. And although the Swiss banks have expanded with unprecedented speed in the years since 1963, and although their influence in the world's financial markets has become greater (or at least more public), yet their image has suffered from an almost continual series of setbacks since then. To adopt the words of the British poet Robert Browning, after 1963 it was 'never glad confident morning again' for the Swiss banks.

Fortunately for the big banks, their progress for the first fifteen years after the war was steady rather than spectacular. Indeed it took them some time even to return to the size – and more especially the level of profits – they had enjoyed in the 1920s. In 1945 even the biggest Swiss banks were not enormous in international terms, nor were they very large repositories of foreign owned funds. That year the country's 500 or so banks could muster assets of a mere $5 billion, of which only seven per cent were owned by foreigners, figures which had multiplied astonishingly to $139 billion and a quarter by 1976. Only in 1951 did the SBC report profits higher than the level recorded in 1929; after a leap at the end of the war, profits had been becalmed at around 15 million francs (their 1928 level) for three years, before taking off in the early 1950s, and more than doubling in the decade. For progress has not been regular. After the horrendous experiences of the pre-war era the bankers were not going to be hurried. Rudolf Speich set the tone as early as 1944, when on taking over as chairman of the SBC he laid down that 'in the

181

banking business only supreme caution can be the basic thought behind every action and constitute its guiding principle'. For the first decade progress was steady but not remarkable, though it was greatly helped by the London Conference of 1953 which settled Germany's debts. As so often the sheer stubbornness of the Swiss paid dividends: they were Germany's fourth largest creditors – or the second largest taking into account the 'clearing debt', the residue of the imbalance of Swiss-German trade before and during the war; and they would not even take part until the 'clearing milliard' was included in the discussions. The debts were written down by a half: but Swiss private creditors (as opposed to foreigners whose money had been invested by Swiss bankers in Germany) retrieved a surprisingly high proportion of the money owed by German public bodies and private companies.

For the years between 1946 and 1963 were the only period in the modern history of Swiss banking in which there were no real problems (only twenty-four banks were liquidated in eighteen years, none of any great importance). By contrast the process of centralisation accelerated as smaller, local banks found the going too competitive and sought the shelter of larger groups – which generally meant the welcoming arms of Dr. Alfred Schaefer. In the two decades after the takeover of the Federal Bank – which had put it on a par with the other two big banks in the country – UBS took over five local banks and three private ones. In the same period the country's cantonal banks together absorbed only six, and the UBS opened only six branches, relying mainly on its takeovers of local banks to increase its geographical coverage.

The process was not always painless, especially when UBS was competing with the Swiss Bank Corporation, which also absorbed three other banks. The nastiest battle occurred over the Volksbank of Interlaken, an important town in which neither of the bigger banks had a branch. The SBC had been represented on the board since 1946, when the bank had got into trouble and the larger institution had subscribed additional capital in the form of preference shares. Five years later the manager was back asking for a further injection of capital. 'The request was turned down because of the unsatisfactory trend of business', says the official history of SBC.

The manager, whose term of office even at that time ran only on a provisional basis, subsequently announced he had found a prospective purchaser for the preference shares. On his assurance that there was no large bank behind the purchase, the Swiss Bank Corporation handed back its block of shares and its credits were returned to it. Thereupon, in 1952, the Union Bank of Switzerland took over the current assets and liabilities of the Volksbank Interlaken, and the manager, when called to account, admitted that he had practised deceit ostensibly out of antipathy for the representative of the Swiss Bank Corporation on the Board of Directors.

It took the SBC another twelve years before it opened a branch in the town to compete with the bank which had been so rudely snatched from its grasp.

But the astonishing growth of the Union Bank was not achieved only, or mainly, through sharp-elbowed takeovers. Schaefer almost single-handed created an unprecedented phenomenon in Swiss financial history: a centrally controlled major bank with a proper management structure and clear policy guidelines. By contrast the SBC has always been a Federal institution: although its head office is in Basle, the powerful barons in the Zurich head office have never really acknowledged Basle's authority. UBS is different: 'General Schaefer's army' it was called, answerable to one remarkable man. With his ramrod bearing and the pince-nez perched firmly on his nose, Schaefer, according to his associates, 'looked the prototype of the heartless banker ... it was Schaefer's way to say one thing and then do the opposite ... I've seen Schaefer give a speech about the need for prudence in banking and then turn around and agree to some of the most speculative deals imaginable' – though because of his unequalled flair for understanding a company's true financial position these seemingly risky deals were usually sound enough. ('The balance sheet of a good Swiss company', he once said, 'is like a girl in a bikini: the delicious is visible, but the essential is always hidden.')

Robert Holzach, one of his protégés, who became chairman in April 1980, described how Schaefer built up the bank's corporate clientele: 'The old established insurance companies, the machine manufacturers, and the chemical industry were bound by tradition to one of our competitors. So we had to go to the newcomers – to the smaller insurance companies, to the car importers who brought in all the Volkswagens after the war. They were looking for a bank that was more dynamic than you normally are if you are bound by tradition.' Schaefer was never a two-dimensional figure: apart from a quarter of a century as spokesman for the whole banking industry he was also highly knowledgeable about oriental history; and it was as a friend of Marc Chagall that he came to fund the stained-glass windows in Zurich's Frauminster.

Even the Union Bank grew spectacularly only after 1958, when a number of countries simultaneously allowed their citizens the freedom to convert local money at will and to export it to their favoured haven. Even though the exchange rates of major currencies were fixed, a very large number of investors gravitated, naturally and inevitably, to the safety of Swiss banks. So the 1960s was a decade of incredible growth. It had taken the Crédit Suisse, for instance, the whole of the 1950s to double the size of its balance sheet (the same growth rate as it had enjoyed in the previous decade), but in the 1960s its balance sheet multiplied over five and a half times, from just under 5 billion francs to 28 billion – more than all the country's banks together had shown a quarter of a century earlier.

This growth in the 1960s was not accompanied by a parallel increase in profitability which had leapt in the previous decade but slowed down as the bank – like its brethren – tried to cope with the onrush. This brought with it a number of problems. The most basic was simply matching the new money, which consisted mostly of short-term deposits, with the requirements of the bank's customers, who were mostly looking for long-term loans. The result was that prudent bankers vastly increased their liquidity, the money they had readily available to guard against sudden withdrawals: in the first three years of the 1960s the Big Three almost doubled their liquid resources. At the same time, foreign and domestic borrowers flocked to Switzerland for the first time since the 1920s. The demand for loans jumped four-fold in the years after the dramatic lifting of foreign exchange restrictions in a number of countries, especially Germany, in 1958.

Unfortunately for the banks their favourite customers, the major Swiss industrial companies, were not interested even in maintaining their previous level of borrowings. They had always been frugal, and had not fallen into the hands of the banks to nearly the same extent as their German counterparts. There were exceptions: one of Geneva's best hotels, the Hotel des Bergues, was long owned by the SBC as a result of an historic default; and all the major banks, especially the Crédit Suisse, have a number of industrial shareholdings. But as a matter of deliberate policy the SBC sold off most of its investments in the years immediately after World War II. Moreover, as Professor Sayers noted in 1962: since the War 'the trend to self-financing [by industry] has become more pronounced and some branches of industry have become completely, or at least partly, independent of bank credits'. The 1971 loan portfolio of the SBC, historically the bank most involved with the country's most capital-intensive businesses, its major chemical companies, shows that less than five per cent of the bank's loans went to the chemical sector, by contrast nearly nineteen per cent went to finance property transactions (and nearly five per cent more to the construction industry).

These figures provide a key to understanding how the major banks coped with the onrush of funds after 1958. After they had satisfied the horde of foreign borrowers and retained an ample proportion of liquid funds, they increased their historic commitment to property and, for the first time in Swiss history, actively solicited the personal savings and credit business of the average Swiss citizen (they needed his long-term savings deposits as a counterbalance for the mass of short-term foreign money they were absorbing).

The pioneer in this was, as usual, the Union Bank, which in 1967 finally took the plunge directly into the most important sector of the personal financial business, mortgages. In one year, it completely absorbed three mortgage banks in which it already owned a substantial proportion of the capital. And during the decade all three major banks started up savings schemes and went out of their way to woo the ordinary private clients they had scorned for so long.

The Big Three could cope with the inflow of money. But the Swiss economy couldn't, and neither could another type of banking institution: the many small, generally foreign owned institutions which had sprung up in the fifteen years after the war. The government started to struggle against the inflow in 1962, when for the first time in the history of Swiss banking legal limitations were imposed on the domestic loan portfolios of any Swiss bank with assets of more than 10 million francs. This attempt to reduce the domestic effects of the ever growing inflow was markedly unsuccessful, as were repeated appeals to more orderly progress. In January 1964 the government reacted sternly. Confronted by the way prices had leapt – a scandalous ten per cent in less than four years (more than they had risen in the whole of the previous decade), it clamped down on foreign investors. No interest could be paid on new money they deposited, nor could it be invested in any sector of the Swiss economy. A statutory limit was placed on increases in bank loans (like many of the other measures, this reinforced a previous 'gentlemen's agreement' with legal sanctions), and activity in the construction industry, where the boom had had the greatest impact, was severely curtailed for a year. No office blocks were to be built, nor any luxury homes (which in the Swiss context at the time, meant a freeze on houses costing more than $48,000 to build). The whole package provided a classic example of how swiftly the Swiss people can act if they feel that their banking industry is harming their interests.

These restrictions enabled the bigger banks to draw breath, as it were, after the headlong expansion of the previous few years. But it was very different for the many small banks that had, mostly, been founded since the war. These were counted in the statistics as 'other' banks since they could not be categorised as institutions that served a specific purpose so far as the natives were concerned, mortgage, cantonal, local or savings banks. These outsiders were, basically, tolerated only because they had no contact with Swiss economic life. They were not allowed to look for deposits within the country, and because they were of no concern to the Swiss, they were virtually uncontrolled. And there were a lot of them. By 1970, the 'other' banks (including a number of branches of

American and British banks) had grown spectacularly: over a hundred institutions, with assets of over 12 billion Swiss francs, were under foreign control. Between 1945 and 1966, 145 banks had been established, of which 109 were 'other' banks, more than had been founded in the previous two and a half centuries. Of these, 44 were based in Zurich, 21 in Geneva, and another 20 scattered through the Ticino. There were only 20 in the rest of the country, including such hitherto important centres as Basle. The same split applied to the – much smaller – number of private banks and 'other financial institutions' founded in the same years.

The concentration found in Italian Switzerland was no accident. The Swiss did phenomenally well out of the Italian economic miracle of the 1950s and 1960s. They employed large numbers of Italian workers and enjoyed the profits from vast amounts of Italian savings placed in Swiss banks, without having to take any of the responsibilities usually associated with either employment or money management. The wave started in Lugano, in the tip of Switzerland that extends south to within a hundred miles of Milan, the centre of Italy's economic recovery. By the late 1960s Lugano, a town of under 25,000 inhabitants, had thirty banks. Then the boom moved south, to the hitherto inconsequential border town of Chiasso, marking a new stage in what was becoming a sophisticated business. Whereas in the early days masses of banknotes were moved across the frontier, by the 1960s the banks were matching the funds they received with loans granted through banks in Italy.

In the Ticino, most of the business was conducted through branches of major banks, or the crowds of foreign financial institutions attracted there. Not only banks but even two major New York brokerage houses, Bache and Hutton, established branches in Lugano, together with their banking colleagues.

But in Zurich and Geneva the business went increasingly to what can most easily be described as 'ethnic' banks. Whereas the Italians – and most of the Latin Americans with Swiss bank accounts – were merely placing a portion of their assets out of harm's way, a new class of client emerged in the 1950s who called for a new type of institution. They were mostly the victims of the little-publicised movement that swept long established Jewish communities out of North Africa and the Middle East, where they had lived their lives in peace and prosperity, some for up to a thousand years, until the continuing turmoils associated with Arab independence movements and the creation and survival of Israel turned them into refugees. Lebanon provided a temporary haven, but trouble broke out there as early as 1958, and Switzerland seemed safer. So, just as refugee Chinese built up their banking businesses in Hong Kong and Singapore in the 1960s and 1970s, so the Jewish refugees decamped to Geneva and Zurich. There, in their clannish way, they stuck together. They would not entrust their money to foreigners. They relied on their own kind. In this, of course, they were merely copying the habits of the French Protestants who had done so much to establish Geneva as a banking centre three centuries earlier. Like the Huguenots, these newcomers were traders even more than bankers, and they greatly reinforced Switzerland's role as the natural centre for the complicated byways and intricacies of international trade (a function symbolised by the name of the most successful 'new' bank of Middle Eastern provenance, the Trade Development Bank).

Sometimes, of course, Switzerland housed, not the brains behind international financial transactions, merely their legal headquarters. The most obvious example was the little canton of Zug, which specialised in providing a virtual tax shelter for expatriate companies. By 1963 there were 300 such concerns in the canton's capital, a town of a mere 20,000 inhabitants. Many other banks and trusts were set up by specific groups or individuals to help their financial affairs. This industry traces its origins back to Hermann Schmitz and his manoeuvrings on behalf of Metallgesellschaft before World War I. It depended, then and subsequently, on the willingness of considerable numbers of Swiss professional people to be enlisted as financial mercenaries. And there never seems to have been any shortage of apparently highly respectable Swiss willing to act as front men.

In his book on tax havens, *Les Paradis Fiscaux*, the French journalist Alain Vernay provides a marvellous snapshot of the attitude of 'real' Swiss bankers to these upstarts and those who worked for them. The phrases used formed a kind of code, which, however, was not too difficult to decipher.

'I have never heard of the bank you mention' is the most absolute of condemnations. Slightly diluted forms of condemnation include phrases like 'That particular bank is much favoured in certain Arab/Argentine circles.' From that you can understand that the bank in question operates in Switzerland but for foreign borrowers and equally foreign depositors and that it is highly risky to become involved in such affairs. They will say, 'I know very little about this bank, but Mr. X, who is a leading figure in political circles, and Mr. Y, who is a leading lawyer, are on their board of directors. They are both very busy men, but you could ask them about the bank'. Deciphered, that means that the aforementioned leading citizens have been prepared to lend their good name to the establishment but have nothing to do with running it, and that the guarantee provided by their presence is therefore rather limited.

The situation echoed the use of front men by local entrepreneurs pin-pointed by the cantonal Bank of Berne fifty years previously. The results were the same: disaster on a multiplying scale at the first hint of pressure, creating problems which the existing Swiss machinery could neither prevent nor control. By the end of the 1960s twenty-three of the ninety-one banks founded in the first seven years of the decade had been forced to shut up shop. The basic problem was the sudden collapse of a grossly overheated property market, which left the banks with their funds tied up in virtually unsaleable assets while their depositors (most of whom had entrusted their money to the bank for limited periods of well under a year) were clamouring for their money back. The problems were sometimes compounded by overlending to a single client. One 'industrious clerk', Felix Wyler, had worked his way up the Aituna Bank over a quarter of a century, 'never leaving any doubt as to his integrity or honesty', according to one contemporary newspaper report. 'Then suddenly he exceeded his competence: authorised by the board to allow foreign customers credit up to 20,000 francs (which was later increased to 80,000, then 200,000), he went in one case to

900,000 francs. Once liquidity difficulties began, Wyler obviously tried frantically to improve the situation with some daring manoeuvres. It seems that he had no accomplices, and not the slightest intention to enrich himself.'

This sad story could be repeated in a number of cases, though there were only few where it could be said that the guilty party 'had no intention to enrich himself'. The rush of bankruptcies was embarrassing enough for the Swiss authorities, but in two cases the ripples spread further than the tiny financial establishment along the Bahnhofstrasse in Zurich and the Rue de la Corraterie in Geneva. It was all very well for the financial editor of the *Neue Zürcher Zeitung* to say that 'four-fifths of the irregularities which the Federal Banking Commission has had to deal with in recent years concerned foreign banks'. But the case of Julio Muñoz and the quarrel over the money deposited in a Swiss bank by Algerian revolutionaries could not be dismissed merely as squalid domestic scandals among foreign immigrants of no concern to 'real' bankers, let alone the Swiss government or the Swiss people.

2 / The one unwanted client

The groups of refugees, or rich foreigners, who felt their money was safer out of their own country and who founded the 'ethnic' banks in the 1950s and 1960s would, in most cases, have been welcome customers to the existing Swiss banks. They founded their own institutions partly out of an inherent clannishness, parallel to that of the Swiss, but also because the Swiss banks did not, traditionally, have any real contacts in the Middle East.

In Central and Latin America the situation was very different. In the nineteenth century hundreds of thousands of

Swiss had emigrated to the New World. Like the Italians, a great many had settled in Argentina and Brazil. As we have already seen from the banks' wartime activities, their links with their 'colonies', particularly in Argentina, were close. Inevitably, therefore, the dictators, their families, and the limited number of oligarchs who traditionally ran the hemisphere thought of Switzerland when they wanted to remove their money from the grasp of opponents or successors.

The pace of deposits accelerated in the 1950s with the Populist threat to the rich personified by President Perón in Argentina, and by the rise of the left throughout Latin America symbolised most obviously in the abortive revolution in Guatemala in 1954. Oil-rich Venezuela provided Swiss bankers with a steady source of clients despite its (relative) political stability and its low tax rates. In other countries American aid was diverted wholesale to Switzerland, as were the profits from the temporary rise in commodity prices resulting from the Korean War. Wherever the rich chose to settle, their money was almost invariably entrusted to the Swiss. Perón, for instance, fled to Madrid when he was deposed – but his money (like that of the rich families he had opposed) was safely deposited in Swiss banks.

Virtually all of them were welcome customers. The solitary exception was President Trujillo of the Dominican Republic. Whenever you ask any Swiss bankers about their general lack of inquisitiveness about their customers, they invariably point to the late President as an example of the way they screen out undesirables. His is the only case trotted out; and the practice is universal. It really is most peculiar. Granted that Trujillo was a pretty extreme example of the bloody tyrants who proliferated around the Caribbean at the time, he was not *that* exceptional. Even President Somoza of Nicaragua, an almost equally bloodstained ruler, was welcome. 'Well I really don't know about him. It's difficult to interfere in the affairs of another country' was the lame explanation for his acceptance given me by one official.

Trujillo was chosen as the one exception to the rule that anyone's money was welcome. The decision was even institutionalised: the private banks of Geneva actually passed a resolution barring their members from dealing with him.

The bankers' instincts were right. Their biggest asset was their image of discretion so they were anxious, above all, to avoid the notoriety attached to any public association between them and undesirable characters of any description. In their eyes Trujillo had committed the ultimate sin: he had allowed himself to be murdered while much of his money was still at home and had not yet been discreetly transferred to their custody. Even before his death his notoriety was too much to stomach. His murder, and the subsequent fate of the money – allegedly $180 million – which his legitimate family removed with them to exile in Madrid attracted enough inches in the world's press to confirm their suspicions.

Trujillo's legitimate family – the Trujillo Martinez – entrusted their money to an apparently respectable Spanish financier, Julio Muñoz, son-in-law of the Marqués de Villalonga, chairman of Spain's biggest bank, the Banco Central. Muñoz used the money to build up a world-wide financial empire. The ultimate holding company, Cotran, registered in Panama, controlled a Luxembourg group, the Société Holding Bancaire et Financière Européenne. This in turn controlled banks in Italy, in the tiny Pyrenean tax haven of Andorra – and in Switzerland. But Muñoz was not content with a mere 'ethnic' banking institution. First he acquired the Banque Genèvoise de Commerce et de Crédit. This was a relatively modest 'local' bank with five branches, founded, like so many others, in the 1860s. Muñoz, seemingly, had little difficulty in acquiring eighty-three per cent of its capital. He then started buying shares in a much more important institution, the Spar und Kredit (Savings and Credit) Bank of the lovely little town of St. Gall, the first time since the 1890s that a foreigner had acquired a major stake in a bank catering for a Swiss clientele. The Spar und Kredit Bank was not one of the country's most distinguished financial institutions, it had been twice reorganised in the 1930s, and in 1955 had been forced to apply to the Swiss Bank Corporation for a loan of 10 million francs. For St. Gall had never been a financial centre after the ignominious collapse of a bank founded with German backing in the 1850s, designed to make the town the major financial centre of Eastern Switzerland (and indeed Southern Germany as well). After the collapse of the 'Deutsch-Schweizerische Credit-

Bank', the Toggenburg Bank, one of the two which combined in 1912 to form the Union Bank, had catered for the textile and embroidery companies which had provided the district with its livelihood. The Spar und Kredit bank looked after the Roman Catholic bourgeoisie of the town, and was therefore in a completely different category from an 'ethnic' bank. Nevertheless it was clearly vulnerable to external pressures, and Muñoz's presence was soon felt. In December 1962 rumours of increasing Spanish influence were so widespread that the board was forced to affirm that the Swiss character of the bank was 'guaranteed in every respect', that the majority of the shares were in Swiss hands, and that the bank's business was exclusively domestic.

This may have been true at the time, but was soon to change. In early 1963 the St. Gall bank made a share issue, ostensibly to raise more capital. In fact only a third of the new shares were issued to the public – for 12 million francs in cash. The remaining shares were used to buy control of the Muñoz owned Geneva bank – at an excessive price. The Spar und Kredit Bank paid 300 francs for every share in the Banque de Commerce, triple the rate at which it had raised new capital two years before. Muñoz further weighted the rate of exchange between 'his' shares and those in the St. Gall bank by agreeing to forego dividends on the shares allotted in exchange for those of the Geneva bank. As a result of these manoeuvres, his group ended up with forty-seven per cent of the St. Gall bank, more than enough to give him control. He then legitimised the bank's existing foreign loans by getting the constitution changed to allow the bank to lend abroad.

All these changes were approved by the board, which included a Federal Councillor, Adelrich Schuler, and a well-known local industrialist, Herr Job. Muñoz himself did not go onto the board, being described merely as its 'financial adviser'. His advice was disastrous: an ever-increasing proportion of the bank's funds were poured into the tourist developments he was funding in Italy, Spain, and Andorra. These were hard hit by the property slump of 1963–5 – and even if they had done well would have been entirely unsuitable investments for a savings bank.

Within eighteen months, the whole edifice collapsed. The

first problem came to light when Trujillo's five illegitimate children, the Trujillo Levaton family, as they were known, clamoured for their rights. They had taken refuge in Florida, and their case was presented by that well-known New York lawyer Richard Nixon (chosen, presumably, through his long-standing friendship with another Caribbean exile in Miami, Bebe Rebozo). The legal tactic employed was to attack the President's youngest legitimate son, Ramades (also called Ramfis). He had married a French actress, Danielle Gaubert, and spent his time training race-horses in Normandy. So it was in the unlikely setting of a court house in Rouen that, in late July 1964, Ramfis was accused of fraud and theft, allegations brought in a Swiss court by the 'Miami five', on the grounds that he had helped himself to $150 million from the family's Swiss bank accounts. He was released on $2 million bail. In November he was duly extradited to Geneva to face the charges, which were speedily dismissed.

The ripples from the case spread to St. Gall the following April, when the Spar und Kredit Bank was forced to close its doors because of rumours that it was shaky. Within a few weeks the directors applied for, and were granted, a twelve month moratorium, under court supervision – with even small savers allowed to withdraw only 500 francs each. Worse was soon to come. Muñoz and the general manager of the St. Gall bank, Hermann Hug, were both arrested in early June in an atmosphere of mounting crisis – the authorities even attempted a press blackout. The bank's board, which had dismissed earlier reports of problems as 'mere rumours and newspaper reports', went on the attack. In the *Neue Zürcher Nachtrichten* and other papers under the same ownership, Councillor Schuler (who was also the *Nachtrichten*'s home affairs editor) blamed the wretched Hug for the whole affair. The Trujillos then tried to salvage some of their money by placing a sequester order on the assets. But Muñoz's father-in-law personally guaranteed whatever funds Muñoz had withdrawn from the general portfolio of his Luxembourg holding company to cover the loans he had been granted by his various banks.

Muñoz was soon allowed out on bail to embark on a

fruitless fund-raising mission to Belgium, Italy, and Spain, but attention was then diverted to much the most serious aspect of the whole affair. The SBC soon stepped in and took over the St. Gall bank's assets and liabilities – thus preserving the savings of the town's bourgeoisie (much to the fury of the citizens of Geneva, no such rescue effort was mounted on their behalf). So although the Swiss authorities could no longer pretend that the problems of foreign bankers did not affect them, the SBC's action saved the structure of domestic deposit banking.

The heart of the problem emerged only slowly during June. It concerned no less a person than the chairman of the Federal Banking Commission, Max Hommel. He had been the Commission's permanent secretary during the war years and had then gone into private practice as a trust manager. He was soon brought back as a member of the Commission, was appointed vice-President in 1954 and President a year later. In the words of one senior official who had the painful task of interviewing him after the Muñoz crash, he was 'a simple clerk, quite inadequate for the job of chairman'; a fair commentary on the limitations of the body he headed.

Muñoz had persuaded him to become financial adviser, not of his banks, but of a couple of textile businesses in his group. Technically, Hommel was not acting against the rules, which allowed someone in his position to take on private directorships and consultancies – for the Commission was not part of the government, merely an independent body that reported direct to the Federal Council. But Muñoz then lured Hommel into supporting him actively in his dealings with the board of the St. Gall bank. Hommel appeared as a friend of Muñoz with him at board meetings, supporting Muñoz's case for the bank to grant even larger loans to his tourist schemes. In the indignant words of the *Neue Zürcher Zeitung*: 'although Hommel must have known as early as the middle of 1963 that the loans of the Spar und Kredit Bank both were based on fraudulent security and exceeded the limits acceptable for a Savings Bank rooted in the Swiss middle-class, in October 1963 he accepted an invitation from Muñoz to go to Spain at the Spaniard's expense. The President of the Banking Commission does not seem to have severed his connection with

Muñoz even when the Banking Commission felt it necessary in February 1965 to summon a delegation from the bank because of its outstanding loans to the Muñoz group, a step which in the president's own words, is "an alarm signal of considerable volume".' When the scandal broke, Hommel shocked the banking establishment by concentrating his efforts on trying to arrange a takeover of the St. Gall Bank, rather than on his official role.

For months he compounded his sins by denying his involvement to the government officials who interviewed him. The blindness of Hommel – and the majority of the board of the bank – was the more inexcusable because the warning signs had built up so unmistakably in the previous couple of years. The 1962 accounts – which were finally agreed only in the following June and which had been signed by the whole board – criticised the bank's lending policy. The Banking Commission, which was never informed by Hommel of his involvement, summoned the board and criticised not only the loans to the Muñoz group but also the purchase of the Geneva bank's shares at an inflated price. In November 1963 the auditors had warned of over-exposure to foreign clients, especially to Muñoz's Italian bank, the Credito Commerciale e Industriale, where the loans were only just matched by the borrower's own assets. A few months later, the Banking Commission had repeated the warning. Nevertheless, the loans from both the Geneva and the St. Gall banks had subsequently been increased.

The Commission again had to summon the board following the 1963 report from the auditors, in which they refused to confirm that the assets were intact and the share capital safe. Even these alarm signals do not seem to have aroused any great degree of urgency: the report was submitted only in June 1964 and the Commission took another six months to get together with the offenders. In December 1964 the board finally promised to cut off further credits to the Muñoz companies and to require additional security from the borrowers.

The auditors' objections – which prevented the board from publishing an annual report, or summoning an annual general meeting – finally confirmed the public's worries about the bank's stability. But by then it was too late, and once Muñoz's shares had been officially sequestrated following the bank's collapse, he lost interest in saving the bank or its depositors.

The crisis was threefold. The SBC's action averted the threat to bank stability, but the way that a truly 'Swiss' bank had fallen under undesirable foreign control was alarming, as was the role of the directors. 'The fact that neither a National Councillor educated in national economy like Adelrich Schuler, nor a director of an important Swiss enterprise like A. Job ... thought fit to resign their directorships ... seems odd', thundered the *Neue Zürcher Zeitung*, and prevented blame being placed solely on the shoulders of Muñoz and Hug. That old nightmare, first described so vividly by the cantonal Bank of Berne half a century earlier, of non-executive directors unwilling to take adequate responsibility in the face of strong-minded executives, became a blatant reality.

But far more serious was Hommel's involvement. At a superficial personal level, confidence in the Banking Commission was restored by appointing as Hommel's successor Hans Streuli, a septuagenarian former finance minister. But the wound ran deep: in a speech before the Swiss Senate, the Conseil des Etats, the country's senior auditor wondered aloud whether 'the system by which the Banking Commission is a semi-official organisation can be maintained'. The Federal Finance Minister, Roger Bonvin, recalled that the Federal Council had investigated the desirability of revising the banking law a couple of years before, and that it would 'once more investigate whether a change in banking law is necessary, once the Federal Prosecutor's report was completed'.

Since 1965 nothing in Swiss banking has been the same. Although the process of change has been gradual, it has been continuous since the Muñoz affair. Not that the first steps were dramatic. In the words of the *Financial Times*, the Banking Commission 'which until then had been a largely part-time and devoutly *laisser-faire* institution, pulled up its socks and started going through such regulations as there were in the 1934 law with a toothcomb', only to discover enormous gaps in them. But the structure of the Commission was not changed, and nothing was done to alter the practice by which public figures were forced to rely for most of their income on private directorships and consultancies – posts that inevitably brought the risk of the conflict of interests which had led Hommel astray. The only statutory gesture was to subject members and officials of the Banking Commission, not, as previously, to the relatively mild provisions of Clause 47(b) but to the sterner provisions set out in Article 320 of the Federal Penal Code.

A couple of years after the St. Gall crisis the rules covering loans on property were tightened. And in 1969 a new Bill on banks controlled by foreigners was finally introduced – after ferocious and not entirely unsuccessful opposition from a consortium of banks in Zurich which claimed that it was discriminatory and restricted commercial liberty. The Bill was largely confined to ensuring that banks with over fifty per cent foreign ownership made it clear in their advertising that they were not truly Swiss – 'to prevent the exploitation of a Swiss base as a guarantee of honest dealings', in the words of the *Financial Times* (the original proposal was that they should make their non-Swiss origins evident in their actual names, but this was watered down). New banks would have to abide by the credit and monetary policies of the Swiss National Bank, and in granting permission for new foreign banks the authorities were to pay some regard to 'reciprocity', the ability of Swiss banks to open in the applicant's home country.* But this Bill was merely a stop-gap affair. In 1969 the Federal Council started the long process of submitting a first draft of a new banking Act to the cantons for consideration. For the St. Gall affair, however dramatic or shocking, had simply not been on a large enough scale to shake the Swiss establishment from its leisurely habits.

* The immediate object of this clause was to prevent the Chinese from following the recent Russian example in setting up their own bank in Zurich.

3 / Troublesome Jews –
and homicidal Algerians

The Muñoz affair was by no means as devastating internationally as it was internally. Far more serious – because they involved the country's international image – were the consequences of the Israelis' efforts to wrest from the Swiss banks the funds supposedly deposited in the 1930s by Jewish refugees who had subsequently disappeared into death camps, together with the next of kin to whom they would have bequeathed their funds.

The alleged inability of heirs and successors to prize open the accounts in which they were sure their deceased relatives had placed the family loot forms a regular thread running through banking history. In 1958, when Swiss-Israeli tension was at its height, there was a great deal of publicity about the fate of the fortune allegedly deposited in Switzerland by King Feisal of Iraq before his assassination that year. The legal position was compounded by the devious reputation of the institutions involved, and the belief that a great many Jews had deposited money in Swiss banks (the figure of $500 million was freely bandied around). Not that the legal position was simple. In most cases, if the (supposedly thorough) efforts made by the banks to trace the next of kin proved unsuccessful, then the money reverted to the client's country of origin or his last known domicile. But the legal position was little understood. It has always been assumed that unclaimed money reverts to the banks, as it probably does in many cases. It is difficult to imagine anyone handing back to the German government in the 1950s funds deposited by German Jews twenty years earlier.

Indeed, the considerable increase in the capital and reserves of Swiss banks in the late 1950s was (and still is) attributed by many outsiders to the absorption of untraced

Jewish funds. This is totally untrue – there were all sorts of reasons behind the growth, notably the retrieval of German loans dating back to the 1920s and 1930s and subsequently written off in the banks' books. Yet the rumour shows the lasting damage done by the characteristic bland stubbornness with which the Swiss faced Jewish insistence that their case was different.

The first demand dated back to 1954, when the Israeli government presented an official diplomatic note, based on Article 8 of the Final Act of the Paris Reparations Conference of January 1946, in which neutral governments were 'asked to make available whatever assets they had of Nazi victims who had died and left no heirs'. It was only in 1961, after years of inconclusive negotiations with the individual banks, that the Swiss got around to breaching the sacred wall of bank secrecy to implement the Paris resolution. Even then the proposed legislation was vague. It talked of 'assets of any kind in Switzerland, the last known owners of which are foreign nationals or stateless persons of whom reliable news has been lacking since May 9th 1945 and who are known or supposed to have been victims of racial or religious persecution'. The Israeli objections to this proposed law were natural: the law was merely advisory, not mandatory; it was up to the banks to decide whether the law applied to any particular accounts, and there was no reason for an uncooperative bank to 'suppose' that the holder of any particular account was a victim of persecution if it meant surrendering a deposit. The officials of international Jewish organisations acting for the Israeli government insisted that the only reliable solution was a law 'compelling' banks (and other financial institutions, like insurance companies) to declare assets that had not been claimed since 1945. The next year the Israelis gained their point – but only 10 million francs were finally recovered.

The figure was, indeed small, but the bankers themselves believe that it was reasonably honestly calculated and that the largest drain of such funds occurred through trust funds administered by Swiss lawyers.* This position is accepted by

* The SBC's Zurich office, possibly the biggest single repository of Jewish funds, contained only 1.5 million francs in 'lost' deposits. At a guess, therefore, the 10 million figure was an underestimate, but not [continued]

Jewish officials, who point out that the Swiss attitude has been much misunderstood. Following the initial resistance the Federal authorities carried out the final agreement punctiliously, despite the precedent it set in breaking bank secrecy. The Swiss, say the officials, were far more co-operative than the government of Sweden – the natural depository for the fortunes of Baltic Jews. Sweden's then – Socialist – government resolutely refused to put through any special legislation to help trace the money, and the eventual offer made by the Swedes was so derisory that the Jewish agencies indignantly rejected the money. Yet it is the Swiss who have attracted all the subsequent criticism for their alleged insensitivity.

Much more complicated were the international implications of the fate of the funds deposited in an ethnic bank by those most implacable enemies of the state of Israel, the Algerian revolutionaries. The money involved, though considerable (42 million francs) was not the heart of the matter. The laxity of Swiss banking practice and the welcome accorded to all and sundry (President Trujillo apart) could and did involve the Swiss government and courts in an appalling diplomatic dilemma. The courts had to decide whether, if an official deposited money in a bank, the money was his or the organisation's in whose name he held it in trust. And who was to decide on the legitimacy of the government which developed from the organisation on whose behalf the funds had been deposited? Was the official entrusted with the money? The Swiss courts? The government which the official came to oppose so vehemently? The terrible embarrassment caused over more than a decade to the Swiss courts in having to act almost as an international tribunal derived directly from the way Swiss bankers conducted themselves.

The case was unusual in that neither side accused the other of being interested in making away with the money. Both

a wild one. If one accepts a figure of 25 million – my personal guess – then two conclusions follow. To the banks' own credit the smallness of the sum supports their much-derided willingness to trace the heirs of the funds left in their charge. Second the figure is another nail in the coffin of the idea that their vaults were a major refuge for the assets of German Jews, and represent a tiny percentage of the sums entrusted to the banks by non-Jewish Germans.

could claim historic stature. The official entrusted with the 42 million francs, Mohammed Khider, was one of the fathers of the Algerian revolution. He had been elected as a deputy for Algiers in the French National Assembly immediately after World War II. Three years later, in 1949, he joined Ahmed Ben Bella as one of the founders of the Organisation Secrète set up to fight the French. He was one of the *'neuf historiques'*, the group of nine who met on neutral Swiss soil in 1954 to set up the Comité Révolutionnaire d'Unité et d'Action.* He was one of the three emissaries sent to seek help from Colonel Nasser; and he was one of the group round Ben Bella hijacked by the French and held captive for five years during the height of the war against the French waged by the CRUA and its successor, the FLN.

When Ben Bella and his associates were released, Khider, as the FLN's treasurer, had to find a secure refuge for the tribute levied by the FLN from Algerian workers in France. He naturally went to the ethnic Banque Commerciale Arabe in Geneva. This had been founded four years previously by François Genoud, a sinister figure much trusted by both Khider and Ben Bella. During the war Genoud had been associated with the Grand Mufti of Jerusalem, an extreme Arab nationalist whose anti-Zionist fervour led him to support the Nazi cause. Genoud stationed himself in Algiers, running the Banque Populaire Arabe, which held forty-five per cent of the shares in the Geneva institution, whose director was a Syrian, Zouhair Mardam Bey.

Khider had always been a 'hard-liner' even amongst the hard men of the FLN, even denouncing the Evian agreements of 1962 between the FLN and President Charles de Gaulle as a sell-out, although they led to Algerian independence. And it did not take long for relations between him and Ben Bella to deteriorate. In April 1963 Khider gave up his post as secretary-general of the FLN to Ben Bella, who was also already President of the fledgling Algerian republic. Khider was removed from the FLN's Politburo, which ran the country, at a Party Congress only a year later. He was

---

* This meeting was held under cover of the excitement of the World Cup final football match between Germany and Hungary being played at the time in Switzerland.

replaced by Ait El Hochine, and at first Khider was co-operative, proposing that the funds in his account in the BCA be frozen pending the resolution of his disagreement with Ben Bella. This was fundamental and political. Khider declared that his government was 'slipping dangerously towards fascism and totalitarianism'. He then fled to Switzerland, proposing to use the funds to finance the opposition to Ben Bella, on the grounds that it represented the 'true' revolution which Ben Bella had betrayed.

El Hochine arrived in Geneva on the 12 June 1964 to take responsibility for the funds, but Mardam and Khider immediately took steps to spirit them away.

Already in March Khider had transferred the funds to a numbered account. Genoud, who was in Geneva, managed to stall El Hochine for nearly a month, so it was not until the beginning of the second week in July that the Algerian government officially opened its case against Khider and the bank to try and recover the money. All the while, Khider was actively supporting the rebellion against Ben Bella led by Ait Ahmed, his brother-in-law (and another of the *neuf historiques*).

By the time the writ was issued it was too late. All the examining magistrate could do was to work out just how money had been spirited away. The first step had been taken three days after El Hochine's arrival, when the money had been transferred from deposit accounts into current accounts, so that it could be withdrawn more easily. Without any notice to help the bank prepare for the eventual loss of the 42 million francs – over half its total assets of only 80 million – the money was split into units of 2 or 3 million and transferred to four numbered accounts held by a friend and associate of Khider. By the time the specialist accountant employed by the magistrate came to examine the books, all trace of these accounts – including the names of their owners – had disappeared, and Mardam categorically refused to provide any information about the money or anything else. The accountant could establish only that between the 4th and the 20th August, after the enquiry had been opened, the money had been withdrawn in the form of fifteen cheques, each for a million marks. These had been drawn by Khider's bodyguard, acting under the assumed name of a Moroccan called Houdhoud, and the money salted away safely in Germany. The trail then went cold. In November Mardam and Khider were arrested and accused of resisting lawful authority and misleading the magistrate, but they were later released.

Within a few months, Ben Bella had been overthrown by Colonel Boumédienne, who evidently had more important matters on his mind, for his government let the matter drop. Then in January 1967, Khider was mysteriously gunned down in the streets of Madrid, and although the Genevan authorities had not pursued their criminal charges, the Algerians then sued the bank and Mardam for the return of the 42 million francs. The Swiss government, acutely embarrassed, nevertheless co-operated to the extent of asking all the banks in Geneva if they had received any of the money. Nevertheless the Algerians could not understand that the courts would not necessarily do what was diplomatically convenient, and took the leisurely progress of the case as an affront. To them nothing less than the legitimacy, not only of their government, but of its revolutionary predecessor, the FLN, was at stake.

The legal battle lasted a further seven years: it took the Geneva court until 1971 to decide in favour of the Algerian government and to order the bank and Mardam to pay the money (plus the interest which had accrued since the case was brought in 1967). This judgment was upheld in 1973 by the Cantonal Appeal Court, only to be upset the next year by the Federation's highest judicial body, the Tribunal Fédéral. By that time, Ait El Hochine, the man in whose name the action had originally been brought on behalf of the Algerian government, had followed Khider into exile, which did not simplify the legal situation.

The courts first had to decide whether the Algerian government was the legal successor to the FLN which had originally deposited the money. This was not effectively in dispute, since Khider himself had always claimed that the money belonged to the Algerian people and that he was merely acting as trustee. But the next question – who actually deposited the money? – was the subject of two dramatically different legal interpretations. Much to the relief of the Swiss government the Geneva courts ruled that the relationship between Khider and the FLN should be judged under French law, because that was the system prevailing in Algeria when the money was deposited (this was pretty rich, since at the time both Khider and Ben Bella had been battling to expel the French, bag, baggage and legal system, from Algeria). Under Swiss law, it could be said (and eventually the Tribunal Fédéral did say) that Khider had a 'trustee' relationship with the FLN, a *contrat de fiducie*. This gave him unlimited power to dispose of the assets involved in the contract, even though the contract also stated that they belonged to someone else. The effective owners simply gave up control to the fiduciary. But French law did not provide for such a relationship, so common sense could prevail. And common sense told the Genevan courts that there were numerous signs that the money belonged to the FLN.

The depositor's address, for a start, was the FLN's office. More damningly, in 1963, after Khider had resigned from his position as secretary-general of the FLN, the Banque Commerciale Arabe had credited to his personal account a cheque for £2 million drawn on the Arab Bank of Beirut apparently made out to the FLN itself. When the Arab Bank queried the transaction, the BCA had blandly stated that the money 'had been credited to the account you requested' a clear assumption that Khider's personal account was being treated as one opened by the FLN. It was also clear to the Geneva court that Mardam and Khider had conspired to remove the money in the summer of 1964 by their manoeuvrings with the four 'ghost' accounts.

Had this doctrine prevailed, it would have blown a major gap in the defences of the Swiss banks against foreign interference. Swiss bankers had been horrified at the behaviour of the examining magistrate in trampling all over the bank's accounts and holding them up to the public gaze – they were equally astounded at the irresponsibility of the FLN in confiding the funds to Khider without taking the precaution of drawing up any contract with him. Had other parties been able to go to court to claim funds deposited by someone else on their behalf, then every government in Latin America and many in Asia and Africa would immediately have sued in the Swiss courts to reclaim money deposited by former rulers.

Fortunately for the banks, the Tribunal Fédéral ensured that the *status quo* remained undisturbed. The court briskly dismissed any idea that French law was involved in any way. The bank was in Switzerland, and moreover, when the account was opened, the client had agreed to abide by the bank's conditions of business. So Swiss law was applicable both generally (because of the bank's location) and specifically (because the client had agreed to abide by rules drawn up under Swiss law).

The court could then return to well-trodden ground in ruling that the opening of an account was simply a contract between the two parties involved, and had nothing to do with anyone else. It then dismissed the notion that the Algerian government's ownership of the money gave it any rights: 'the fact that the FLN owned the funds in no way implied its willingness to appear as such before third parties. In the absence of such willingness, it could not enjoy direct representation ... it is clear from the plaintiffs' own words that they thought it important to exclude any reference to the FLN in their dealings in Geneva, to ensure that the secret was not winkled out by the agents of a hostile government.'

The argument did not end there, nor did the embarrassment for the Swiss government. Not content with the judgment, Mardam went on to claim from the Algerian government the legal expenses he had been awarded by the Tribunal Fédéral. The Algerian ambassador in Berne refused to pay, stating that by diplomatic usage the matter should be handled through the Swiss ambassador in Algiers. Obviously unwilling to rub salt in the Algerian government's wounds, the Swiss foreign office refused to go through the 'normal diplomatic channels'. Undeterred, Mardam then went to the court to sequester the forty-five per cent of the shares in his bank owned by the Algerian bank and, thus, by the government. The Tribunal Fédéral duly agreed. Then, later in 1977, in a quite separate court case, François Genoud obtained a ruling that the shares did not in fact belong to the Algerian government but were held by Mardam on behalf of a third party whose name he was, naturally, unwilling to divulge. Finally, in July 1978, fourteen years almost to the day that Mardam and Khider had spirited the 42 million francs out of the way, the Tribunal, relying again on the 'fiduciary' argument, allowed Mardam to claim the shares – which, the Tribunal agreed, he held anyway. As for the money itself, everyone simply assumes that it had been spent over the years in financing the opposition to the Algerian government. In that sense, Khider's ghost had succeeded, with the help of the Swiss banking law, in continuing the fight for what he had seen as the 'true interests' of the Algerian revolution.

PART SIX

Oh Switzerland, what crimes are committed in thy name

1 / The bane of Bernie

The 1960s were a unique period for the three major Swiss banks. During the decade they increased their dominance of their local market; historically they had controlled about thirty per cent of the total assets of the country's banks; in the 1960s the percentage leapt by nearly twenty per cent, at the expense of the cantonal banks and, above all, of the regional and local savings banks. The increase was due partly to their – equally unprecedented – rate of opening new branches and aggressively pursuing the business of ordinary private clients. But their growth was mostly due to their sudden rise in the international banking league. By 1970 all three, for the first time in their history, were among the fifty biggest in the world, as a result of the expansion rate which they had never seen before, and are exceedingly unlikely to match in any future period. For even the stodgiest of the big banks, the Crédit Suisse and the Swiss Bank Corporation, increased their balance sheet totals over five times in ten years, well over double the steady and by no means negligible rate they have generally managed in peacetime. They also launched out onto the newly burgeoning international financial markets, and stood out in their ability to attract the increasing tides of 'Euro-dollars' floating free of American domestic financial markets.

The corollary to their exposure to the international limelight was a corresponding fall in their image among the general public outside Switzerland. By 1970 they had been indelibly besmirched as the receptacle for all the world's ill-gotten gains. The collective title 'Gnomes of Zurich' was coined only in 1965, but it seemed so appropriate that it was immediately and universally adopted by newspapers the world over. By 1970 it was natural for 'Adam Smith' to ask Paul Erdman, in whose bank he had just invested, 'I bet we must have one Mafioso. What's a Swiss bank without at least one Mafia account?'* It was a decade epitomised by the publication in 1967 in *Life* magazine of a single, rather blurred, photograph of a Mafia courier, weighed down by two worn leather Gladstone bags full of money, plodding flat-footedly towards a Europe-bound jet. This image stuck in the memory of all who saw it; for millions of Americans it symbolised an automatic mental connection between the Gnomes of Zurich and criminals of every description, from fraudsters and stock market manipulators down to, and most glamorously including, the Mafia.

The most successful opponent of these criminals and, by extension, of the banks which sheltered them, was Robert Morgenthau, then a senior official of the U.S. Department of Justice, and son of the Secretary of the Treasury who had proved such an implacable enemy in the 1940s (the father's book advocating the elimination of Germany's industrial potential is dedicated to the son, then serving in the U.S. Navy). The investigations he conducted against the bankers can be traced back to the activities of Bernie Cornfeld, showy, flash, an aggressive seeker after publicity, a being totally alien to their image of immaculate discretion and probity. Yet it was precisely because of the permissive financial atmosphere prevailing in the country that Cornfeld's ill-fated financial empire, Investors' Overseas Services, was based in Geneva. As Morgenthau remarked in 1970, when tens of thousands of IOS's clients were facing the total loss of their money: 'If IOS had been subject to our [American] disclosure laws perhaps the financial difficulty it has found itself in since the beginning of the year would have been avoided. Similarly, if foreign financial transactions were subject to disclosure requirements the comparable deterrent effect might have been felt.' Had it not been for Cornfeld's activities, and the freedom which he was allowed in Switzerland, American investigators would not have been so keen – or so politically free – to pursue other Swiss-based malefactors.

But Geneva offered Cornfeld far more than a convenient

---

* To which Erdman snapped, 'Don't be silly, we're trying to go public.' But then he was always an exception.

no-questions-asked headquarters. It provided him with a seal of financial respectability. His salesmen could stress that they were working for an outfit based in a country which had proved itself a rock of financial responsibility and discretion. They used the brand name of Switzerland frequently and forcefully and introduced its attractions to a new public, considerably more widespread geographically and demographically than any reached by previous sales efforts: in marketing terms they dragged the name of Switzerland down-market. Inevitably, when the combined forces of virtually every financial law-enforcement agency in the United States set off in hot – and well-publicised – pursuit of IOS, they were also publicly impugning the good name of Switzerland. IOS was, of course, only nominally a Swiss organisation, but its employees made every possible effort to identify themselves with their adopted country. 'In many "hot money" markets', wrote the authors of the standard work on Cornfeld, 'one of the chief appeals of IOS to the clients was the idea that their money would be going to a Swiss Bank.' This claim did not escape the Swiss diplomatic representatives in Central and Latin America. At one point the commercial attaché in Panama circulated an unprecedented memorandum bluntly declaring that IOS was merely a Panamanian impostor, not a proper Swiss corporation at all. To defend himself Cornfeld entwined himself with the Swiss financial establishment in several ways. Like so many other outsiders he hired respectable 'front men' as more or less active directors and executives (these included the nephew of the chairman of the Federal Banking Commission). He also took care to appoint the Crédit Suisse as the bank legally responsible for IOS's cash, and a Dutch affiliate of theirs acted as the custodian of IOS's securities. This association, although merely a formal one, was highly convenient – and much exploited by Cornfeld as a mark of respectability. In addition, however, some Crédit Suisse employees, attracted by the generous commissions payable to IOS salesmen, sold them actively to the bank's clients – although this was never the policy of the bank itself. The rival Swiss Bank Corporation tested the water first. A young executive bought a few units, then tried to sell them back to IOS, relying on the clause in the contract which provided for a complete refund if the units were returned within the fortnight after transaction. Finding the clause inoperative, the bank stayed clear of IOS.

So did the Swiss regulatory authorities until the jittery aftermath of the Muñoz affair. Even then it was only when IOS finally floundered that the Geneva prosecuting attorney started an investigation. (This was pretty leisurely: although Cornfeld was arrested and kept in jail for a few days, it was only ten years later, in 1980, that his case came to trial. He was acquitted on all counts.)

But much earlier – in February 1967 – a parliamentary question from a – conservative – Genevan representative embraced both the aspects of the Cornfeld operation which worried the Swiss and avoided those which manifestly did not. It was Cornfeld's success in selling his units to Swiss citizens which lay behind the question, that and the number of young foreigners, mostly Americans, Cornfeld was employing. Soon afterwards, the cantonal authorities started to clamp down on them, claiming that they were registered as 'students' and were therefore not entitled to work.

But the more substantial issue was that in 1964 Cornfeld had taken over the Overseas Development Bank (for the first few years it was merely a 'finance company of a banking character'). As a result of the Parliamentary question, the Banking Commission sent Cornfeld a splendidly feline epistle, ostensibly objecting to the fact that the ODB was overly involved with a single client – IOS. In fact the letter was designed to prevent the IOS group from expanding its Swiss operations – after the Muñoz scandal, the Swiss were certainly not going to allow another foreign financial adventurer to compete for the savings of the Swiss people themselves.

Before the foundation of the ODB, Cornfeld had relied on another Geneva based institution, the International Credit Bank – which initially held a twenty per cent stake in the ODB. The ICB had been founded in 1958 by one Tibor Rosenbaum; two years later Gladis Solomon, one of IOS's founding group, sold Rosenbaum a mutual fund programme in Liberia, where he was visiting his friend President Tubman. Rosenbaum's bank was invaluable for Cornfeld's salesmen, particularly in Latin America, in the first few years of

the 1960s. They could do a 'switch-sale', offering potential
clients the opportunity to smuggle their money out of the
country and deposit it (at pretty unattractive rates) in a real
live Swiss bank. Only then did they gently steer their clients
towards the theoretically more appetising menu of funds being
peddled by IOS. This role became less important once IOS
had its own bank, but it was entirely appropriate for Rosenbaum to continue to be involved with IOS. For just as
Cornfeld symbolised the greedy, irresponsible happy-go-lucky
international investment world of the 1960s, so Rosenbaum
(who died in 1980) summed up in his rather short and
unhealthy frame all the picaresque mystery associated with
the post-war mushroom growth of ethnic banks in Geneva.

Rosenbaum's life story was, almost literally, incredible.
Born the son of a rabbi in the small Hungarian town of
Kisvarda in 1923, he was studying for the rabbinate (under
his original name of Pinchas Rosenbaum) when, in 1944, the
Nazis occupied Hungary and started a belated drive to round
up the Hungarian Jewish community and deport its members
to concentration camps. By this late date, the Nazi extermina-
tion machine was highly developed, and Adolph Eichmann
brought his key subordinates with him to Budapest to guarantee the thoroughness of the operation. Rosenbaum was one of
a small group of young Jews, mostly, like him, rabbinical
students, who displayed unbelievable bravado in what was
called 'Operation Hazalah', an attempt to evacuate as many
Hungarian Jews as possible to Israel (or Switzerland) by
every means from bluff to bribery. Rosenbaum travelled
seemingly unscathed for months, armed only with a season
ticket for Budapest's tramway system – the only identification
document in Hungary that did not mention the holder's
religion. Rosenbaum frequently dressed as an SS man,
bluffing his way into prison and using his status to release
Jewish prisoners – at one point he even shot two real SS men,
pinning notes to the bodies warning that death would be the
inevitable fate of any Jew who posed in Nazi uniform. Other
disguises included that of a Nazi dignitary, and the uniform of
a crack Hungarian regiment, complete with green feathered
hat. It is not surprising that he emerged from the war a
legendary figure, although, inevitably, there are cynics who

claim that Rosenbaum simply escaped on the so-called 'Kastner' train which brought 14,000 Jews out of Budapest in
exchange for 5 million Swiss francs (held, naturally, in a Swiss
bank). On the Kastner train was another theological student,
William Stern, whose sister married Rosenbaum. Stern later
became famous as a property dealer in Britain, and afterwards
notorious when he was declared bankrupt, owing more to his
creditors – over £100 million – than anyone in British financial
history. (Because of their experiences, a whole generation of
European Jews, like Stern and Rosenbaum – and many of the
founders of Israel – seem to have acquired an outer moral
skin which made them impervious to ordinary considerations
of commercial morality.)

When Rosenbaum emerged in 1946 as the Hungarian
delegate to the first post-war World Jewish Congress he could
have had his pick of official positions in the Jewish establishment. He became the intimate – and implicitly trusted –
friend of most of the first rulers of Israel, especially Pinhas
Sapir, the famous Israeli Finance Minister. But he preferred
to set up as an independent businessman, asking only that his
friends should deal through him. His first company, Helvis,
based in Geneva, specialised in trade between Europe and
Israel (one of his first contracts was to buy arms in Czechoslovakia in time to defend Israel after the declaration of
independence in 1948.) 'A small, nervous, irascible man who
goes from peaks of euphoria to depths of depression', according to one account, he was a dealer and deeply convincing
salesman rather than a banker, anxious to display himself as
the friend of the great and good, but, like many men with a
salesman's impulsive temperament, gullible and over-ready to
welcome clients – and the business they brought – which he
should have avoided.

He soon became well-known – and not only within Switzerland – because of the apparent monopoly he enjoyed, either
through Helvis or through the bank he founded in 1958, over
the Israeli government's commercial and financial dealings –
covert as well as above-board – with the outside world. (This
monopoly was emphasised by the nickname, the Kosher
Mafia, applied to Rosenbaum, Sapir and their colleagues.)
The phenomenon worried even the Israelis. In 1975, after the

International Credit Bank had collapsed and its mass of connections with Israel was laid open for inspection, a member of the Knesset enquired in despair, 'Are there no other banks in Switzerland apart from the Mafia bank?'

Rosenbaum's fall from grace had started eight years earlier (there had been an earlier unhappy incident in the 1950s, when the director-general of the Israeli health ministry had gone to jail because of bribes paid him by Rosenbaum to ensure that Helvis got more than its fair share of the ministry's contracts, but that cloud soon passed over). In 1967 he was nearing the attainment of a life-time's dream, an open, formal relationship with the Rothschild family, still the nearest Jewish equivalent to royalty. He already had many friends in high places; for some years he had been very close to President Tubman – who had appointed him Liberian consul in Geneva – a relationship extremely useful to the Israelis, then cultivating such 'moderate' black African states to counterbalance Arab hostility. He was also close to the then British Prime Minister, Sir Harold Wilson, who was a firm Zionist, and as leader of the Labour Party, politically sympathetic to the Israeli government. This was a typical case in which Rosenbaum was taken as an 'interlocuteur valable' between the Israeli government and its friends abroad. Arieh Handler, the ICB's London manager, was also included in the chain, and received a friendly hearing from the Prime Minister's entourage – or even from Wilson himself – when he telephoned 10 Downing Street.

The Rothschild connection was a double one. After the Seven Days War in 1967, Rosenbaum assembled a group of rich Jews, headed by Baron Edmond de Rothschild, to form the Israel Corporation, an enormous closed-end trust to provide private capital for major investments in Israel. But even nearer his heart was a plan to form a joint venture with the London branch of the family. The preparations were well advanced. Raaphy Persitz, a young Israeli from an impeccably respectable banking family, and himself a former Israeli chess champion, was sent to work in the London bank for a year. But then came the fatal series of articles by Sandy Smith in *Life* magazine exposing the extent of Mafia activities. Fatal for Rosenbaum's dreams because the bank towards which the

Mafia courier in the famous photograph was flying was his. This was too much for the London Rothschilds, a branch of the family fastidious enough to refuse to deal with Cornfeld, who had formed a joint company with their French 'cousins'. But the *Life* articles also dramatised the major role played by Swiss banks in the operations of an organisation much nearer to the heart of *Life*'s readers than the International Credit Bank – the Mafia.

2 / Kosher and other Mafias

The first American criminal to employ the services of Swiss banks at all systematically was almost certainly that ever-inventive financial genius Meyer Lansky. (The slight qualification is inevitable: none of the characters in the drama was a great record-keeper, and the story is shrouded in a cloud of rumour and exaggeration even more impenetrable than usual.) Allowing for the inevitable qualifications and disclaimers ('a matter of common talk ... but I certainly would not want to be quoted on it'), the story can be traced back to the 1932 Democratic Convention in Chicago, at which Lansky went out of his way to meet Huey Long, the Kingfish, the Lord of Louisiana. Within a few months they were to do business together. Lansky paid the Kingfish $20,000 a month to allow slot machines in Louisiana, ostensibly for 'charitable purposes', although out of the first $800,000 profit made in New Orleans the widows and orphans received precisely $600. And once Fiorello La Guardia, the new mayor of New York, started to clamp down on gambling in that city, Lansky's friends were allowed to open up more sophisticated gambling at the Beverley Country Club, not in New Orleans itself, but in adjoining Jefferson Parish – by no coincidence the heartland of a late Louisiana Mafia chieftain, Carlos Marcello, always known as 'the little man'. Governor Long was afraid that the payments involved would become public knowledge, and as a result Lansky came up with the idea of depositing the money in a Swiss bank.

The plausibility of this account is reinforced by the mysterious activities of Long's 'chief fund raiser', Seymour Weiss, described as 'a shoe clerk turned innkeeper turned kingmaker, the treasurer who kept no records'. For when Long died he left a mere $115,000, far less than would seem likely given the cash he had received. It was always assumed that Weiss then rifled the famous 'deduct box', the cash box at the Roosevelt Hotel in New Orleans (which he managed) in which the Long loot was stashed, and invested it in a number of more or less legitimate businesses, but this does not account for all the money received by Long and Weiss during their partnership. Yet the secrets of Long's hiding places in Switzerland and elsewhere remained inviolate. Although his bitterest political enemy – Henry Morgenthau – sent the Internal Revenue's most famous agent, Elmer Irey ('the man who got Capone'), to pursue Long, and later his family for alleged income tax offences, the hunt was called off in the late 1930s because it was so crucial to keep Long's successors loyal to the Democratic Party. But even at the time, 'many have been the fantastic stories that the dictator had sizeable sums deposited in Canadian banks or other places outside the country for future use.'

What had started as a one-off expedient to avoid embarrassment for a particularly prominent political leader gradually became a habit with the Mafia. Bugsy Siegel's downfall came about when he cheated his Mafia partners on the furnishing and decorations of the Flamingo, Las Vegas's first gambling palace. His mistress, a southern beauty named Virginia Hill, apparently flew with the 'skim' to Zurich where she deposited it. (Siegel claimed that she was looking for choice Swiss materials for the Flamingo, but this explanation was brushed aside and his disloyalty was rewarded with several bullets in the head. Ms Hill duly returned the money.)

By the 1950s when the Mafia controlled the enormous gambling business which flourished in Batista's Cuba, regular cash shipments were organised from Havana to Switzerland, albeit using couriers less glamorous than Virginia Hill. After the arrival of Fidel Castro, the action moved to Las Vegas and the transport chain became more complicated. One courier would be used to carry the money to the coast, generally to Miami, and another either directly to Switzerland or through the Bahamas. The bank then most frequently mentioned as the recipient of Mafia funds was the Crédit Suisse; but, despite the publicity, the mafiosi were not major customers, and they were sensible enough to camouflage themselves thoroughly. No questions would be asked, no eyebrows raised, at the regular visits of a soberly dressed business man depositing large quantities of perfectly ordinary dollar bills.

Nevertheless, during the 1960s Lansky contrived two refinements: like so many other bank customers he organised his own bank; and he used a particular feature of American tax law to 'launder' the money and return it to the United States washed, as the saying went, 'in the Alpine snows'. The Mafia bank was the Exchange and Investment Bank in Geneva, founded in 1959 as the 'Standard Bank' in Zurich, which changed its name to the Wechsel und Investitionsbank three years later, and in 1965 moved its registered office to Geneva and adopted the final English version of its title. The Exchange and Investment Bank was only one among many such ethnic banks, but because of its ownership and clients it became a convenient symbol. When Nello Celio, Switzerland's jovial, well-loved Finance Minister, was introducing a Bill to control the activities of foreign banks, he was clearly thinking of the EIB when he supplied the portrait of a – supposedly mythical – American shareholder in a Swiss bank. This worthy had been arrested in New York in 1926 for car theft. 'He was arrested again in 1931 for contravening the laws on prohibition, again in 1937 for theft and again in 1940 for kidnapping, armed robbery and extortion ... ten years later the same American was sentenced and imprisoned in New Jersey for participation in an illegal gambling house. Finally in 1953, he was imprisoned again for contravening the immigration laws.'

This mythical character was only a minor shareholder in the EIB, for its major owners were in fact Garson Reiner and Benjamin Wheeler, two New York brassière manufacturers who helped start the peekaboo trend in women's fashion when their company, Exquisite Form Industries, introduced the see-through bra in 1964.

Other shareholders more nearly resembling the Celio model included Ed Levinson, a Las Vegas casino operator for the Lansky syndicate, Benjamin Sigelbaum, a Lansky associate with similar duties, and Lou Poller, a friend of the imprisoned Teamster Union leader, James R. Hoffa, and former president of the Miami National Bank. This institution was the staging post for millions of dollars, mainly skimmed off the casino tables in Las Vegas. But Lansky, 'cashier and den father of deliverymen' as *Life* described him, was the 'indispensable man'.

The mafiosi and their friends invested in their own bank partly to enable them to bring their money back to the United States. Until 1970 it was possible under American tax law to borrow – your own – money from – your own – Swiss bank and claim the interest you paid – to yourself – as a legitimate charge against your income tax. By contrast, income received from abroad was not specifically mentioned on the standard American tax return form. So criminals could – and did – build up perfectly respectable business empires using funds originally obtained by criminal means – a practice which was clearly impossible without using a complaisant foreign financial institution.

But the Mafia's cosy set-up was threatened by two unauthorised operators, Carmen Giampola and Frank Crea. Giampola worked in the wire department of the head office of the Chase Manhattan Bank. In the words of Thurston Clarke and John J. Tigue, he and Crea

devised a plan to defraud the Chase Bank of almost $12 million. Giampola transmitted a forged cable from the New York Office to Chase's correspondent bank in Switzerland, the Union Bank of Switzerland. The cable instructed the Union Bank to charge $11,870,924 to Chase's Swiss account and transfer the money to the Exchange and Investment Bank ... after the money had been transferred ... a courier in league with Crea and Giampola would have picked it up and hidden it in a numbered account in still another Swiss bank. The Exchange Bank would then have denied ever having received the money. Its denial would have carried weight, since there would have been no ostensible reason otherwise for Chase to have cabled the money ... This plan was thwarted only because an alert employee at the Union Bank became suspicious because of a technical irregularity in the cable and asked Chase Manhattan in New York for confirmation of the transfer. Chase replied that the cable was fraudulent, and Crea and Giampola were arrested and convicted.

When the Exchange and Investment Bank was named as an (unindicted) co-conspirator in the case it was time for the Mafia to move on, or rather down the road to bank with Tibor Rosenbaum. The links were provided by Lansky's supposed 'financial adviser', John Pullman, and Sylvain Ferdmann, the man immortalised in the *Life* photograph when he was carrying loot from Philadelphia to Switzerland. (This route was unusual, since it involved neither Miami nor the Bahamas.) Pullman was then in his sixties, with a classic history of involvement in all kinds of Mafia activities. He had once served a prison term for violating American liquor laws, and had exchanged American for Canadian citizenship in 1954. Together with Sigelbaum and Levinson he was a director of the Mafia's principal bank in the Bahamas, the Bank of World Commerce; and his brother-in-law was the brains behind the island's major gambling development, Resorts International (a company which brought into the Mafia's orbit President Richard Nixon, who had to be dissuaded from attending the opening of its new casino during his first year in the White House). In 1965 (under American pressure) the Bank of World Commerce was struck off the Bahamas' financial register, and this brought the Mafia and Rosenbaum even closer together, through the ICB subsidiary in the Bahamas, the Atlas Bank. This had been the idea of Sylvain Ferdmann, a young 'banker and economist' who had been a roommate at Harvard of Ed Cowett, Cornfeld's right-hand man and legal adviser.

In the early 1960s Pullman had had the job of carrying the 'skim' money from Miami, the mob's clearing-house, to the Bank of World Commerce in the Bahamas and thence to Switzerland. The sums were enormous – up to $12 million a year from Las Vegas alone. He soon handed the assignment over to Ferdmann who had spent the early years of the decade on what became known as the 'Ferdmann bicycle circuit', collecting money from IOS salesmen in the dozen or more Latin American countries where they did business. But Ferdmann let his new employers down badly. In the words of *Life* magazine:

> On March 19, 1965 as he was loading his satchels into the trunk of an auto at Miami airport he dropped a piece of paper from one of his pockets. It was found by a parking attendant who turned it over to the authorities. It was a note on the letterhead of the International Credit Bank.
>
> 'This is to acknowledge this 20th day of December 1964, the receipt of Three Hundred and Fifty Thousand ($350,000) dollars in American bank notes for deposit to the account of Maral 2812 with the International Credit Bank Geneva, the said sum being turned over to me in the presence of the named signed below.'
>
> John Pullman was listed as a witness on the note. Under his own signature the cautious Ferdmann had added this postscript:
>
> 'The above is subject to the notes being genuine American banknotes'.

Poor Ferdmann. By all accounts – especially his own – he is spending the rest of his life compensating for some youthful indiscretions: 'When you're a young man sometimes you do things you later regard as having been foolish.' And when Clyde Farnsworth from the *New York Times* ran him to earth eight years later he pleaded: 'I'm scared since 1967. I'm bloody scared. Please leave me out of your story. What I've said has always been taken out of context. I'm not a public figure. I'm just trying to make a living. From a business point of view I've had more than I can take.'

The *Life* series may have destroyed Ferdmann's peace of mind. But it was also an implicit admission of defeat for the FBI which had not been able to pin serious charges on any of the characters in the affair. So the Bureau handed over its information to *Life* and thus indirectly achieved its object. For the furore created by the series – which included detailed information on Mafia activities in many aspects of American life from sports to the Brooklyn waterfront – provided an enormous boost for Robert Morgenthau, the man who had been actively engaged in pursuing the many malefactors using Swiss banks since the early 1960s. For Rosenbaum was persuaded by his Israeli colleagues that he ought to co-operate with the American authorities, and soon he was supplying them with a tantalising stream of reports, many of which, however, required confirmation which could be obtained only from the files of other, less co-operative institutions.

3 / The protagonists

Robert Morgenthau is a man more impressed by the duties that should accompany wealth and power than by the many privileges that go with them. This Puritanism is partly a matter of heredity. His family belonged to 'Our Crowd', the upper-class Jews of German descent who formed a separate élite in New York in the late nineteenth century. In the words of Victor Navasky: 'having watched his father (a gentleman farmer who published an agricultural paper before he became Secretary of the Treasury) move among the financial titans of the world, he would not find the spectre of great wealth intimidating'. But there was more to his background than that. His grandfather, as ambassador to the Ottoman Empire, had been instrumental in preventing the Sultan's Armenian subjects from being massacred. This staunchness was long remembered by the Armenians in New York who all but worshipped their saviour's grandson when he was campaigning for election for his present job as District Attorney of New York. His father was a man whose moral fibre remained unbroken by his years as Secretary of the Treasury. From two generations of forebears, therefore, Robert inherited a lack of respect for authority, together with considerable reserves of stubbornness amounting, his detractors would say, to bloody-mindedness.

But this is not how he appeared to the team of brilliant young lawyers he assembled during his decade as U.S. Federal Attorney for the Southern District of New York. 'He had a great knack of choosing people', remembers one of them, 'he was a great body snatcher, and he had this unusual ability to generate enthusiasm ... he would nudge you into doing things ... for every question you asked he had four others to suggest.' What they admired most were his abilities as a financial detective: 'about as smart as they come ... a dazzling memory ... he doesn't look dumbly at the evidence, he uses his imagination to see what must be going on ... he thinks about how people behave in certain situations.'

Morgenthau's only weakness lay in his ambition to succeed as a politician. 'Given his obvious unsuitability for political life, he must have been ambitious to have tried at all,' says one admiring former associate. In private, Morgenthau, usually hidden behind an unsmoked, heavily-chewed black cigar, is sardonic, allusive, and immensely persuasive. 'He's very witty and clever in private, we had a very high-spirited office, but he's stiff and wooden in public and on television.' Nevertheless he managed to get more votes than any other Democrat when he ran against Nelson Rockefeller for the governorship of New York in 1962, and his popularity among the voters of Manhattan when he campaigned for the first time for his present job in 1974 almost embarrassed his supporters.

His attempt to beat Rockefeller interrupted his tenure of an office seemingly tailor-made for him, which he held from 1961, when Robert Kennedy appointed him, to late 1969, when the Nixon administration finally engineered his dismissal. His decade as Attorney in New York was epoch-making.

The Attorney-General of the United States appoints ninety-three U.S. Attorneys, chief prosecuting officers for districts varying in importance from Wyoming, where the attorney has only one assistant, to the Southern District of New York, with over seventy assistant attorneys in an office responsible for nearly one in ten of the Federal prosecutions undertaken in the entire country. For the Southern District includes Manhattan – and thus Wall Street and the greatest concentration of corporate and financial activities in the country. The variety of crimes committed in the District can be grasped from the contents page of Morgenthau's last report of his activities. From water pollution to consumer fraud (which he was the first attorney to take seriously), from pornography to the bootlegging of untaxed cigarettes, from hijacking to loansharking (only two of the nine subsections in the chapter dealing with 'organised crime'); as the British newspaper slogan put it 'all human life is there'.

One crucial chapter in this report is entitled 'The Role of Foreign Bank Secrecy'. The inclusion of this subject emphasised that Morgenthau tackled 'white-collar' fraud on a much more comprehensive basis than any of his predecessors. He was responsible for two major initiatives: he did not rely on cases referred to him by other agencies, but actively took the initiative and looked for them; and he saw no reason not to tackle white-collar crime, wherever it led him.

'When I came into office', he told Navasky, 'the general policy was not to indict and try lawyers and accountants on the grounds that they are professional people and that this would be too harsh a step' – even though the U.S. Attorney's Office in New York had been famously independent of political influence (and of its nominal masters in Washington) for some decades before Morgenthau arrived. But he and his staff felt that 'we've just got to meet this kind of crime if we're going to say that nobody's beyond the reach of the law ... I feel that the people who hold positions of power or trust and violate them are probably a more serious danger to a democratic society than organised crime or crime in the streets.'

And this was where Switzerland came in: 'although many abuses of secret foreign accounts have been by members of organised crime,' Morgenthau told a congressional committee,

it should be perfectly clear that to an even greater extent they are also used by affluent members of society, including leaders of finance and industry, to cheat the Government of taxes and to further and conceal other criminal conduct. The foreign bank with its secret accounts is where the organised underworld and the purportedly respectable businessman meet ... we have reason to believe that there are thousands of other cases of criminal conduct cloaked by secret bank accounts which have not even been touched by our investigations ... often we have had very complete information on criminal activity but have been unable to prosecute because the foreign bankers would not furnish witnesses competent to introduce their banking documents into evidence ... I estimate that deposits in secret bank accounts held for illegal purposes have a value in the hundreds of millions of dollars.

Morgenthau refused to adopt the permissive attitudes almost obligatory for liberals at the time: on censorship, drug-taking, the hated draft laws, he stood with the conservatives. At the same time his relentless pursuit of his vision of financial law enforcement made him the arch-enemy of many in the financial and political establishment, as much by his lack of political consideration as anything else. Early in his tenure he had shown a sweeping disregard for the political tact expected of a man in his position – prosecutions of the politically powerful tended to be accelerated rather than slowed down if hints were ever dropped. The atmosphere soured even further as his investigations led him from the use of Swiss banks by criminals to the protection provided to the same wrongdoers by major – and politically powerful – American financial institutions. 'To me it is shocking', he told a Senate committee, 'that a United States bank, by opening a branch abroad, can lend its facilities to citizens who are defrauding the government and violating our laws and then successfully deny its obligation to make account records available to the Department of Justice by claiming that the laws of a foreign country would be violated.' His investigations bore fruit: he successfullly indicted a variety of leading professional figures, including several partners of a major firm of Wall Street brokers.

After his abrupt departure Morgenthau left behind more than the memory of a number of successful prosecutions, because he had managed to infect other agencies with his own enthusiasm. In 1958, according to Neil Sheehan, the New York regional office of the Internal Revenue Service made a confidential investigation after $30 million in suspicious money transfers were made to Swiss accounts in one year through two Swiss banks. The report concluded that these accounts 'posed a serious threat to our tax system' and recommended a Grand Jury or congressional investigation and a tightening of American laws. But nothing was done. Then came Morgenthau. He empanelled a Grand Jury which brought in a number of prosecutions, and he also set about persuading the whole hierarchy of the IRS to work with him: 'He wouldn't take no for an answer', remembers one former associate, 'he had this quiet intensity ... we had endless numbers of meetings with layers of IRS people, endless presentations to get the initial commitment of lower level personnel ... he showed the IRS quantities of records which did not themselves show criminal conduct but showed areas where investigations would be fruitful ... he really started things rolling with the IRS'.

With the Securities and Exchange Commission, he was knocking on an open door. In the early 1960s a whole generation of officials there were reinvigorating an agency that had fallen far from the standards of relentless policing set in the pioneering years after its foundation in 1934. Soon bevies of SEC men were camping almost full-time in Morgenthau's offices. He also received a great deal of help from the U.S. Post Office. Will Wilson, an assistant Attorney-General, lifted the veil a little to a congressional committee which he told: 'there is available in the Postal Department on a very confidential basis surveys of the amount of mail banking, that is, deposits by mail in foreign banks, and there have been some surveys which are very revealing as to the volume of business being done by American citizens through the mail with foreign banks' – although a later report criticised the IRS for not making better use of the mail watch techniques in 1968–71, when its agents were monitoring airmail received in the United States from Swiss banks. The Post Office also employed a handful of inspectors abroad, who proved invaluable in acquiring speedy and reliable information through their own contacts.

Morgenthau's only institutional failures, curiously enough, were with the agencies supposed to regulate the banking community itself. 'If I ask questions about transactions with Swiss banks,' said the regional controller of one such agency bitterly, 'then they'll phone my bosses and complain.' And within New York, the state banking commission was most reluctant to clamp down on the activities of foreign banks because they were afraid of retaliation – which seemed likely because American banks were invading Europe in such numbers at the time. 'The bank regulatory authorities just looked the other way,' said a former associate in disgust; they were clearly as overawed by the power and political clout of the institutions they were supposed to be controlling as their counterparts in the Federal Banking Commission in Switzerland.

Shielding the Swiss bankers were their major New York brothers. 'I was more frustrated by the respectable people who were accomplices than by the hustlers ... the big U.S. banks were just looking the other way, that was one of the things that got me most ... their excuse was that if we put pressure on them they'd lose business', he once told a friend. But his particular wrath was directed at the Swiss bankers, because of his interpretation of the lessons of Interhandel: 'they knew they could commit perjury because of the I. G. Farben case'. The attitude boiled over when Roy Cohn, a prominent New York attorney and former associate of Senator Joe McCarthy, accused him of carrying on a vendetta against him. Morgenthau's reply was double-edged. 'Merely because a District Attorney doesn't like someone doesn't make him immune from prosecution ... actually I do have one real vendetta and that is against Swiss banks and those who use them to hide their money and avoid paying taxes'. A senior SEC official summed it up even more succinctly: 'It was a marriage made in heaven between Swiss banks and crooks ... at least part of the blame should be placed on the jet aeroplane.' But it was not just the jet aeroplane that produced the amazing boom in business in the 1960s between Wall Street and the Swiss banks. The Swiss had always been subject to waves of enthusiasm for Wall Street. But the invasion they led in the middle and late 1960s was unprecedented. Cynics who believe that the bankers invariably get the worst of deals for their clients could find support from the figures. Over two-thirds of the $2.176 billion invested by Swiss banks and their clients in American corporate stocks between 1954 and 1969 was disbursed in the three years 1966–1969 – a period when the stock market boiled over at a level it has been struggling to regain ever since – characteristically they had been net sellers in the four previous years, when average prices were much lower. But all the time they were churning their portfolios – foreigners, mainly Swiss, accounted for at least fifteen per cent of Wall Street's turnover in the late 1960s. They were also reputed to hold double that share of the market for Eurobonds, sometimes convertible into a company's ordinary shares, which flourished in the heady atmosphere of the late 1960s. For the Swiss banks were caught up in a fever which infected the whole investment community, but they seem always to have held (or bought) the short straw. Almost invariably, they were avid buyers of stocks which, more often than not, simply disappeared from view over the next few years. Names like Four Seasons Nursing Homes – a characteristically 'hot stock' which subsequently went to the wall – bring tears to the eyes of market operators reminded of former loves long gone to the bankruptcy courts. Swiss bankers today freely acknowledge that they were over-sold by the promoters. And they were the most gullible of investors. Only two months before it plunged into its dramatic bankruptcy, Penn Central Railroad managed to float a $50 million loan in Switzerland. This flotation followed some dreadful profit figures that prefigured the disaster to come, and an unusually hard winter when railway traffic was constantly interrupted.

By the end of the 1960s, the portfolio of even the biggest Swiss banks was heavily weighted towards loans destined for investment on Wall Street. An American professional speculator, a self-confessed supporter, did some calculations for the benefit of a Senate Committee on the basis of figures provided to the Swiss National Bank. He concluded, that leaving aside mortgage, nearly half the loans made by the UBS were backed by securities of all kinds (as opposed to physical assets). Three-quarters of the total, he reckoned, were quoted U.S. investments – the others being commodities or European stocks or unlisted securities. He then assumed that all the loans secured by such assets were employed to invest in securities, and came up with a total of over $1.1 billion invested in Wall Street and financed by loans from the Swiss banking community. His conclusions clearly carried some weight – he had discussed his figures with a number of bankers – and were also on the conservative side. Although he emphasised that 'only' $1.1 billion in credit had been extended, this amounted to over one-eighth of all the money lent to investors for buying on margin, and, added to the much greater weight of investments not requiring loan backing, the total represented a major – and totally uncontrolled – factor on the American markets, and an equally important element in the banks' profit and loss figures.

The enormous increase in links between Americans of all descriptions and the Swiss banks ensured that the unique advantages they offered were publicised to thousands of dubious citizens, who were far from eager to have their activities revealed to American tax or regulatory authorities. The appeal was not confined to Wall Street operators or the Mafia. In *Dirty Money*, Thurston Clarke and John J. Tigue spelled out how heroin dealers, for instance, required the 'full services' provided only by Swiss banks. They could 'store excess profits that cannot be safely spent and that are not needed to finance new shipments ... transfer money to foreign suppliers ... earn interest and pay, make investments ... launder the money'. Switzerland provided the unique combination of sophisticated 'full service banks', political stability, and secrecy. Not all nefarious customers required all these elements – when, in the early 1970s, the major American corporations went into the bribery business in a big way, either to sell their products to corrupt foreign governments, or to help President Nixon's re-election campaign in 1972, they did not always use Swiss banks. Because the deals were one-off affairs, not requiring a continuing relationship, or permanent political stability, banks in Panama were good enough for Braniff Airlines to slip their money through to CREEP, American Airlines used Lebanese banks, and other companies used any foreign agents or subsidiaries that seemed convenient at the time. This is not to say that the recipients of American bribes, especially in Iran, didn't use Swiss banks.

They did; so did all the parties to any serious permanently corrupt or criminal relationship. In the late 1960s enormous sums from dealing in arms, drugs, or just the black market in general were generated in Vietnam where none of the Swiss were represented – although many other foreign banks had opened offices in Saigon. Most of the money was then routed clandestinely to Hong Kong, which possessed a strong international banking network – and its own traditions of bank secrecy, which the American investigators could not penetrate. Yet much of the money involved eventually found its way back to Switzerland – Hong Kong was simply too unsafe politically. This lack of ultimate security spread even to the Bahamas – 'home' of many dozens of dubious banks, a fiscal paradise where it was *de rigueur* in the 1960s for 'everyone' from Bernie Cornfeld to Tibor Rosenbaum to Meyer Lansky (and including twenty-one of the biggest and most upright banks in the United States) to open a subsidiary. But the politicians there were not reliable. Morgenthau told a Congressional committee: 'It was extremely easy for anybody to form a bank in Nassau under conditions which made it impossible to get any information about the bank or its officers and directors.' Then the Bay Street Boys, the small group of whites who had ruled the islands for years to the great benefit of themselves – and the large number of crooks who hid under their capacious wings – were overthrown by a reformist black government in 1967. Inevitably 'the British and the legislature in Nassau became equally concerned and they passed a very simple bank law down there not long ago. The law merely required publication once a year of the names of officers and directors of any bank formed under their laws and the amount of resources, the gross resources of that bank, and following the enactment of that law in Nassau, I am advised that almost 100 banks went out of business rather than publish the names of their officers and their total resources.' Swiss bankers were made of sterner stuff.

4 / The perpetrators

Secrecy and subterfuge are the white-collar criminal's best friends. The surest invitation to illegal conduct that man can devise is a hidden conduit for transmission of funds safe from the eyes of law enforcement officials. That is exactly what secret foreign bank accounts do. Although such accounts may be used with perfect innocence by some depositors, they are too tempting a lure for the tax evader, the securities swindler, the corrupter of public employees, the fraud and the cheat ... The 'little tin box' of the 1930s has been replaced by the Swiss bank accounts of the 1970s.

This statement to a Senate committee by Whitney North Seymour, Jr., Robert Morgenthau's successor as U.S. Attorney in New York, is a tribute to the universal use of foreign bank accounts by white-collar criminals by the end of the 1960s. But the habit was relatively recent. Veteran officials at the SEC believe that the connection was originally made in the 1950s by an international conman who ended up calling himself Jack van Allen. They speak of him with some awe: 'He was one of the foremost conmen we have ever come across: he convinced his victims that they were his allies'. Crucially, he was also a great traveller, a frequenter of European café society and thus more internationally minded than his stay-at-home contemporaries. He had been forbidden access to the American stock markets following a conviction in the mid-1950s for distributing unregistered stock, but he was able to use Swiss banks in the early 1960s in a similar case, which became famous as the 'Gulf Coast Leaseholds'. This was an – initially successful – attempt to pass off worthless stock onto the American public at up to $16 a share – although after the promoters had banked their money the stock fell to under a dollar. The fraud introduced a new twist, the use of a

Liechtenstein trust. This handy instrument, dating back to the 1920s, was much favoured by the better-off Europeans with whom van Allen mixed and from whom he probably borrowed the idea. The advantages of backing up Swiss bank secrecy by channelling the actual transactions through a Liechtenstein trust were greater than a mere 'double banking' against intruders. The owner either of a 'fiduciary establishment' (the legal name for the trust) or an *Anstalt* (a 'financial establishment', the device usually employed by Europeans for concealing their personal wealth) gained enormous advantages. In the words of Dr. Magdalena Schoch, these include:

> tax-free profit distributions, reduced capital tax, absence of supervision and examination by the tax administration, absolute tax secret [sic] and banking secrecy, liberal formalities and low costs for setting up the entity, no licensing requirements, low minimum capital, anonymity of the provider of the capital and the beneficiaries. This somewhat abbreviated list is found in a book written by Dr. Ivo Beck, who introduced himself on the title page as an attorney and owner of a fiduciary office in Vaduz (Liechtenstein), giving the address, telephone number and cable address.

Dr. Beck and his select band of colleagues registered the legal entity required and signed the necessary papers. The name of the owner did not have to appear anywhere, and the accounts of the nominal Liechtenstein concern would generally be kept in the vaults of the Swiss bank which acted as intermediary (or 'cut-out' as they say in spy stories). Van Allen and his colleagues set up four of these invaluable devices through one of Dr. Beck's competitors to buy the stock (which cost the trust exactly $20.80) and then sell it for a tax-free profit of more than $4 million. Then, as Morgenthau described the operation: 'Part of the proceeds of the sale of the stock were passed from this trust to another trust, operating under Swiss secrecy laws, which served as the pocket-book for an investment advisory firm which plugged the stock in its market letter. The transfers between conspirators were accomplished by payments from one account in a Swiss bank to another, thus insuring maximum secrecy.' Unfortunately for the conspirators, one of them pleaded guilty and told all.

So did the Swiss lawyer who had been the titular head of two of the trusts. (He had previously filed false affidavits to the government's investigators – feeling at the time, as he explained to the court, that his duty lay with his clients rather than with the law or truth, or any of those silly old abstract concepts.)

Even before the Gulf Coast Leaseholds case came to trial, two of the fraudsters who, the SEC surmises, learnt their 'tradecraft' at van Allen's feet had been exposed. They were both specialists (jobbers) who made the market on the American Stock Exchange. Jerry Re and his son Gerard used front men to buy at a low price large quantities of stocks which they were about to launch onto the market. At first they employed friends – including a 'friendly neighbourhood bum' and schoolfriend of Jerry Re's. When he was smoked out, Gerard used an account at the Zurich head office of Crédit Suisse. The bank obediently channelled the orders through its New York subsidiary, the Swiss-American Corporation, in the name of José and Gerardo Miranda*.

The Crédit Suisse connection proved invaluable in enabling the Res to carry out their elaborate operations. As specialists in the stocks they were rigging, they habitually went short as the price rose, thus disguising their part in the operations and limiting their own profits – while simultaneously boosting those of the lucky Mirandas.

The Re case set several precedents, notably as the first major securities case for a generation initiated by the SEC – albeit only after the Amex's own authorities had failed to act. It showed the convenience of foreign bank accounts for criminals. Earlier, the even more notorious 'Salad Oil Swindle' had showed how vital information about such accounts could be to financial detectives. The prime mover in this affair, a man named Tino de Angelis, together with four of his accomplices, had deposited over $500,000 in the Geneva

---

* One minor mystery of the whole affair is whether these two Cubans actually existed; their Christian names, after all, were the hispanicised form of the Res' first names. Although one of their associates and an SEC official both met a man calling himself José Miranda in Havana – accompanied by an obvious hooker calling herself his wife – the mystery was never cleared up.

branch of the Union Bank. Initially, de Angelis claimed that he'd forgotten all about the account and then, when reminded of its existence, argued that it had been used to pay kickbacks to a Spanish oil dealer. Only when the account was opened up and compared with freight payments was it found that the money had been drained out of de Angelis's company, Allied Vegetable Oil, by overpaying the freight charges to Spain. But in most cases the Swiss bank accounts were not made available: not only was tax evasion merely a matter for 'administrative law', Switzerland's financial markets, unlike those in the United States, were effectively free from any legal restrictions. Because no crime under Swiss law had been committed by most of the operators Morgenthau was pursuing, no international judicial co-operation could be expected – though the Swiss authorities did help to indict six fraudsters, including the executive directors of VTR Inc., a corporation quoted on the American Stock Exchange. They had conspired to sell 85,000 shares of the company's stock at conspiratorially escalating prices through an elaborate network involving not only a Swiss bank and a Liechtenstein trust, but a German bank as well. In this virtually unique instance, Morgenthau was able to persuade the Swiss that a crime had been committed under local law.

Morgenthau was not the first investigator to try and breach banking secrecy. As early as 1935 the Internal Revenue Service was firmly told by its Swiss equivalent, the Federal Tax Administration, that the only legal source of information was the actual owner of the bank account involved. And in 1957 in a case where the FTA had to admit that Swiss tax law had been broken by an American with an account in a Swiss bank, the Swiss still would not breach bank secrecy; they would tell the Americans only the information they had gathered when looking at the books of the corporation owned by the American suspect.

Morgenthau's first brush with the Swiss concerned Walter Germann, the former managing director of Interhandel, who had gone into business on his own in 1960, eighteen months after the Union Bank had taken charge of his old company. As the basis for his business he had, seemingly, taken with him the ragbag of banks and other interests he had purchased on behalf of his former employers. He founded the Bank Germann in Basle, and took over the Bank Muench, another Basle private bank founded in 1938. These two in turn controlled a number of banks in other tax havens, including the Banque Commerciale de Monaco in Monte Carlo, the Swiss Antilles Investment Company in Curaçao, Incadel in Nassau, and the Banco Suizo-Panameno in Panama. Germann orchestrated his group to help a network of American clients whom he had met during his repeated visits to New York and Washington in the 1950s. During the early 1960s he continued his habit of staying at the Hotel Carlyle in New York to receive clients for whom he provided a variety of services. He laundered money, arranged to transport it through a courier service, and even engineered its disappearance. He also probably invented at least one device of his own, the 'three-cornered window-dressing loan', which enabled shaky companies to bolster their cash position by showing, quite legitimately, that they had a substantial sum in a supposedly reputable Swiss bank. But the 'deposit' was purely notional: through one of his other concerns, usually Incadel, he arranged an equally notional, matching 'long-term loan' to the company, ensuring that the money never actually left Switzerland, while still providing a boost to the company's apparent liquidity.

In all, Germann assembled a sizeable empire. His Swiss bank had assets of $7 million, and its Panamanian associate was nearly double the size of the parent, with reported assets of $13 million, although these, allegedly, were 'substantially overvalued'. Unfortunately for Germann, in 1966 he was called as a witness before a Federal grand jury. He testified vaguely, courteously, to the grand jury's questions, claiming that precise answers would not be possible until he had refreshed his memory from his files in Switzerland. ('He's the only guy I've ever seen bow and click his heels to a grand jury', one investigator told *Forbes* magazine.) At the end of May he fled; he was found guilty of contempt of court and fined $25,000 and $1,000 a day until he reappeared. But of course he never returned. The following April a real-estate scheme underwritten by one of his banks to provide German investors with week-end chalets collapsed.

This problem, on top of his other troubles, was too much for him; he committed suicide while supposedly on holiday in the fashionable resort of Klosters. Initially his family claimed that he had had a heart attack, but after his banks had been forced to close their doors it emerged that he had committed suicide. His death merely amplified an already important scandal – the Swiss Bankers' Association was even forced to issue a statement emphasising that neither of his Swiss banks had been members.

Although he had been found guilty only of 'civil contempt of court' which was not an extraditable offence, his mere appearance before the grand jury in New York set off shock waves. After his death the ever-inventive financial rumour mill claimed that he had been poisoned because of his clients' fears that he would return to the United States and provide the jury with some more specific information about them. His appearance had certainly worried his depositors and started a run on his group. 'The news that Germann had been sub-poenaed', one investigator told *Forbes* magazine, 'may have caused a run on the bank. The key to this whole deal is secrecy. Nobody is going to leave hot money with a guy who might be pressured into talking.'

One of Germann's most unfortunate clients was the Swed-ish boxer Ingemar Johansson. He unsuccessfully tried to evade payment of over $1 million in taxes on the money he had earned from his three heavy-weight title fights with Floyd Patterson in 1960–61. The IRS brought an action against him, against Feature Sports, the company that had organised the fights, and three of its directors, including Roy Cohn. Johansson claimed that he was a Swiss resident and that he was employed by a Swiss company, both grounds for exemp-tion from United States taxes under the country's 1951 Income Tax Convention with Switzerland.

In 1964 the American tax court swept aside these flimsy arguments with a blast of robust common sense. It ruled that Johansson's contract with Scanart, the Swiss company, was a farce: it had been signed two weeks before the company had been registered, and Scanart itself had no legitimate purpose but was simply a device to enable Johansson to escape taxation in the United States. And although the Swiss authorities were prepared to certify that he was a 'resident' of their country, the court again took a commonsense view in pointing out that he had spent only 79 days in Switzerland recently 'as compared with 120 days in Sweden and 218 days in the United States. Except for his activities in the United States during this period his social and economic ties remained predominantly with Sweden'. His only links with Switzerland were an apartment – and a bank account.

Johansson's great mistake had been to earn the income within the United States (and in the most public possible fashion). This error was not committed by thousands of others. 'Obviously,' Morgenthau told a Congressional committee, 'the ways in which secret foreign bank accounts are instrumental in avoiding payment of income taxes are almost as varied as the ways of earning the income in the first place.'

The easiest way was to ensure that the money was 'earned' abroad rather than in the United States. In Morgenthau's words:

> If the American businessman receives his earnings from a foreign source, he can deposit portions of it in a foreign bank and declare on his domestic income tax as much or as little of his true revenues as he chooses. There is small likelihood of detection if he keeps double books carefully. Businessmen who make purchases abroad for resale here frequently keep phony double books fraudulently inflating the foreign purchase price so as to decrease the apparent domestic profit. The seller kicks back the difference to the buyer's foreign account.

One of the biggest overseas based U.S. businesses was the PX system, the stores which supplied American military forces abroad. In 1970 two salesmen, Fritz Claudius Mintz and Morton Penn, were indicted for channelling kickbacks of about two per cent on a wide variety of goods, including toys, cameras, cosmetics and ladies clothing paid to corrupt PX purchasing agents through a number of accounts at the Zurich head office of the Bank Leu. A former PX employee, Sidney Rosenstein, and his partner, Irving Braverman, set a much more important precedent. They were evading taxes on the six per cent commission their companies, McInerney Sales and Foremost Brands, received from the contracts they obtained from PXes throughout the world. Between 1965 and 1968 over $1 million a year passed through their Zurich bank account, in the name of the Continental Trade Company, a sham corporation in Liechtenstein. According to the prosecuting attorney, Continental was 'nothing more than a dummy organisation, whose sole purpose was to secrete the money in the Swiss bank account so Rosenstein and Braverman would not have to pay the money in taxes'. The prosecution backed up this assertion with the help of a most unexpected witness, a young assistant to Dr. Herbert Batliner, the Liechtenstein lawyer who had set up Continental Trade and who was nominally responsible for its – equally nominal – activities. But the defendants had forged his name to a number of documents. Since forgery is an extremely serious offence even in Liechtenstein, Dr. Batliner immediately resigned as director of Continental. Rosenstein and Braverman quickly found a substitute, Dr. Alfred Buehler. But he was not an impressive figure. There was a splendidly farcical scene at the Waldorf Astoria in New York, whither he had been summoned by Rosenstein and Braverman to impress their American suppliers with his qualifications as a middleman in selling their products to PXes. His inability to speak English seemed, they felt, to reduce the potential effectiveness of his sales efforts! Buehler cannot have realised the dangers to which he was exposing himself in leaving Liechtenstein. Two days after the conference at the Waldorf, and following only one day's testimony in court, he fled from the United States – and was promptly found to be in contempt of court.

Dr. Batliner's sense of grievance was strong enough for an IRS agent to persuade him to send his assistant to testify. The assistant, Dr. Peter Mounani, had never been a director of Continental, but he nevertheless proved an ideal witness; he produced fake invoices, bank records and a signed agreement stating that Braverman and Rosenstein were the real owners of Continental Trade. Furthermore, he clearly knew nothing about the business – he thought that a PX was some kind of army sergeant.

Dr. Batliner was a rare exception, though there had been one other case where a Liechtenstein lawyer agreed to testify in court in New York. While he was in New York his telephone was tapped by the F.B.I., and Morgenthau's men, who became concerned when he kept phoning a certain number in Washington. Within a few hours a senior CIA official turned up in Morgenthau's office to explain that the lawyer was one of their agents and that the number he had been phoning was that of his CIA controller. Eventually Morgenthau and the CIA did a deal. The witness was whisked out of the country via a private plane from Miami to the Bahamas, and Morgenthau's men got his sworn deposition – in Paris.

But these were exceptions. Most of the cases involved purely domestic earnings. Sometimes – as with racketeers – the use of the Swiss banks enabled the money to be laundered and to serve as a basis for tax deductions on 'loans' of their own money from the banks. Sometimes, as Seymour said, they simply replaced the historic 'little tin box'. Randolph Thrower, the IRS Commissioner, put it bluntly to a Congressional Committee:

> Accounts in foreign banks are often used as repositories for money representing income not reported on U.S. tax returns, much in the same way as bank safety deposit boxes have been used in this country ... we have found taxpayers who, faced with the prospect of enforced collection of substantial amounts of additional tax, have converted assets to cash and transferred the funds to banks in countries with secrecy laws.

Thrower gave a couple of examples from the many he came across:

> At the conclusion of an investigation of his income tax, one taxpayer converted his assets to cash and fled the country. A portion of the money, $100,000, was found to have been deposited with a U.S. bank and subsequently transferred to a foreign bank. During the taxpayer's voluntary exile, his son regularly received checks from the foreign bank. In a similar example an automobile dealer was convicted of tax evasion and served a three-year prison sentence. He agreed to the substantial tax deficiencies involved but before it could be collected, he converted his assets to cash and

transmitted over $500,000 to a Swiss bank. Faced with a five-year sentence for concealing assets to evade payment of his taxes, the automobile dealer arranged with the court to go to Switzerland and retrieve the money. He returned with most of it and turned it over to the court.

The list of businessmen who sought refuge in Switzerland was seemingly endless. Two of the most notorious were Francis Rosenbaum, a wealthy and well-known Washington lawyer, and Andrew Stone, a multimillionaire maker of furniture and munitions. Their Chromcraft company was awarded a five-year $47 million contract by the U.S. Navy to supply rocket launchers. They discovered that they could make the launchers for a mere fraction of the price they were quoting, and formed a double skin of dummy companies to conceal the fact. They invented two nominal 'sub-contractors' one in Beverly Hills, the other in New York, which submitted bills to Chromcraft that were promptly paid. In their turn, five Swiss and Liechtenstein companies – equally nominal, all seven owned by the two conspirators – submitted bills, again promptly paid, to the two 'sub-contractors.' This ingenious device enabled the pair to siphon $3 million out of the country with the help of two banks, including the Union Bank's branch at Aarau (the one with the sphinxes on its facade, symbolising discretion). One of the banks proved loyal by submitting spurious letters and documents to support the two, the other simply clammed up. (Rosenbaum was a lavish user of Liechtenstein trusts. In 1976 he was convicted because of a fraud perpetrated seven years earlier in which he had conspired to embezzle $4 million from Penn Central so as to divert loans intended for repairing the poor old railroad's equipment to Finanz AG, a Liechtenstein *Anstalt*.)

But these cases represented only the tip of the criminal iceberg. Morgenthau was speaking for all his fellow investigators when he complained that: 'for every case which we have prosecuted there are roughly six where we have specific information that a crime has been committed but we are unable to prosecute, either because we lack the resources to complete the investigation or because the evidence we have is inadmissible in court.'

Only too often his team got a tantalising glimpse of a maze they could not completely untangle. An apparently impecunious Boston bookmaker, Francis A. Vitello, maintained an account (codename Unitechnic Finance Corporation, sub-account BOSTON) with the Union Bank, with a balance of well over $1 million. 'Ironically, in March 1964, one of Mr. Vitello's associates, who was then a prominent Washington attorney, stole over $700,000 of these funds by fraudulently transferring that sum to another Swiss bank under a forged authorisation letter. Vitello was able to recover the money partially through the investigative efforts of an Internal Revenue Service agent who did not report the transaction to IRS and who was later convicted of bribery in an unrelated matter.'

Other glimpses came through Tibor Rosenbaum, who co-operated actively with Morgenthau's team after 1967 – although only too often, his information was useless because there were no means of proving it in court. Occasionally they could rely on rough tactics. When Edward Gilbert, a well known stock market operator, was forced to flee to Brazil, he could rely on $1 million of investors' money tucked away in Switzerland. As a former IRS agent, Anatole Richman, told the Senate banking committee: 'the bank only co-operated after the Internal Revenue placed a lien on a substantial amount of assets which the bank alleged were assets of the bank. In an attempt to prove that the assets in question did not belong to Gilbert, the bank provided the Internal Revenue Service with Gilbert's records.' The Treasury and other federal authorities were also able to 'turn' Alfred Lerner, president of the First Hanover Corporation, a New York brokerage house, who had copied the Res' ideas in organising hidden profits on 'hot' new issues, like Weight Watchers. Lerner plea-bargained with the prosecutor, was indicted on one count, received a modest fine, and then co-operated in smoking out other criminals (although at least part of his time as a roving agent was spent investigating the Moscow Narodny Bank in Zurich, finding out whether the Russians were engaged in subverting the American way of life – as exemplified by the country's stock markets).

Morgenthau's investigations, compounded by his well

publicised frustrations at not being able to bring more of the miscreants into court, ensured that Swiss banks acquired an appalling reputation.

They were associated in the public mind even with cases in which their authorities had co-operated. The Swiss bank connection was seized on by the headline writers in the *New York Times* when the Swiss police helped foil a plot by a German calling himself Coeppicus. He and an associate tried to cash cheques adding up to over $1 million drawn on the account of the Human Resources Agency, a result of the total chaos thus prevailing in the agency's Brooklyn office. Inevitably, the first step taken by the fraudsters was to open an account (with the Swiss Volksbank in Zurich); and it was this, rather than the ready co-operation provided by the police or the bank, which the headline writer found irresistible ('American seized in Netherlands in plot on HRA – admits link to an attempt to shift $1 million to bank in Switzerland').

The Swiss banks also seemed to occupy a disproportionately large share of the limelight when a major chemical company, Olin Mathieson, was convicted of paying illicit kickbacks to its Cambodian importer of drugs supplied under an American aid programme. Olin Mathieson itself did not use a Swiss account although their – evidently well-connected – Cambodian importer, Dr. Arnaud, was a client of one of Geneva's most exclusive private banks, Ferrier Lullin. The money eventually came to rest in his Genevan accounts, but these were not central to the case. In any type of illicit stock market operation, they clearly were.

Whereas tax evaders and general criminal practitioners, not to mention the Mafia, tended to rely on the Swiss offices of Swiss banks, the deviants from Wall Street needed their bankers close at hand. Even though government authorities had automatic access to accounts in the New York branch of a Swiss bank, this little difficulty was easily overcome. The Senate Banking committee was treated to a description of the procedure by Anatole Richman who had gone to the Swiss Bank Corporation's offices in New York and stated that he wanted to open an account. In a private room he told an official of the bank:

that I had some money to hide and that I wanted to open a numbered account. The bank official insisted that I could not open such an account in the United States and that I would have to visit Switzerland and contact the bank directly. He maintained this position throughout the interview and by the time I decided to leave I was convinced that I would not be able to open the account in the United States. As I was leaving the bank, the official handed me a brochure which contained information regarding the Swiss bank. He then stated that if I corresponded with the right bank perhaps they could help me. Underlined in red was the address of the Swiss bank. I wrote to the bank in Switzerland and, shortly thereafter, via airmail, I received an application and the conditions set forth by the bank. It was interesting to note that the bank charged a fee of $1\frac{1}{2}$ per cent for handling my money. This fee was charged against withdrawals; therefore as long as I kept my money at the bank, I would not be charged a fee.

Richman's seemingly farcical evidence ended with an important point: 'it would have been very easy for me to send large sums of money out of the country each day'. The mechanism was simple: he could have bought money orders up to any amount at an American bank, making them payable to the Swiss bank of his choice, and then sending it on with instructions to credit it to his account.

Richman was the only witness to refer to the SBC, nor did its name figure in any of the numerous court cases involving its brethren. Uniquely among the big banks, it seems to have confined its activities to soliciting savings accounts such as the one it offered Richman. The names of the other members of the Big Three appear regularly enough to suggest that the contrast was no accident but a matter of policy, that the SBC was careful to confine itself to clients merely wishing to get away from American tax authorities and the lawyers representing American wives, scruples not shared by Crédit Suisse or the Union Bank (although their New York branches were not involved, since the business obviously went direct to branches at home less susceptible to U.S. pressure). Other banks frequently mentioned were mostly small, recently established, thrusting ethnic-type institutions. The lordly private banks of Geneva and Zurich – the Pictets, the Lombard Odiers, the Julius Baers and the Rahm & Bodmers – also shone, as the French say, among the absent from the congressional hearings. But enough of their brethren were mentioned to confirm the saying: each type of criminality has its own type of bank adapted to it.

The partnership between banks and brokers was immensely profitable for both sides. By the late 1960s twenty-eight American brokerage houses had offices in Switzerland, six of them opened during the decade. For, as one broker told *Forbes* magazine, Swiss bank business 'was good clean stuff. It comes in volume, payment is prompt, and we've never had any troubles with them. Once the communications got screwed up and the bank was about a week and a half late in paying; they insisted on paying interest'. They could afford to: they have always charged their clients the full retail brokerage fee on any transaction, although they paid only the finest of wholesale rates to the brokers on the same transactions.

The close and continuing contact with Wall Street could easily drift into conspiracy. When Edward Gilbert involved a Swiss bank in his schemes, it effectively became a co-conspirator in his crime. It was prepared to provide sufficient funds to enable Gilbert to complete his illicit stock-market manoeuvres, but he had to pay nine per cent (well above the market rate for bank loans in those far-off days), both Swiss and American brokerage fees, and twenty-five per cent of the profits, which the bank reckoned every quarter, adding the sum to the amount due and then charging interest.

More routine transactions were helped by two devices, both possible because the Swiss banks were 'universal' institutions, also carrying out the work done in the United States by brokers. First was the 'omnibus' account. The select group of brokers with such accounts were exempted from the strict controls over credit extended to clients ('margin' regulations) and imposed on ordinary stock transactions. To gain exemption a broker had to sign a statement that he would not use the facility to break margin requirements – a very sensitive point, since unlimited margin had done so much to cause the boom that preceded the great crash of 1929. A Swiss bank could –

and did – blithely sign such a statement, but, because of bank secrecy, the SEC had no means of knowing whether the bank was honouring its pledge. This blatant gap in the SEC's defences was closed only in 1969 when, belatedly, the Federal Reserve Board was persuaded to confine the facility to American-owned concerns, but not, seemingly, before every sharp operator in New York had exploited the opportunity.

The operator would also be able to use the anonymity provided by the bank to avoid every sort of tax or regulation. Pierre Leval, then one of Morgenthau's assistants and now a federal judge, described the arrangements to a Senate committee:

> Stock market traders often feel that with the brokerage commissions they must pay on the buy and the sell, it is hard enough to make a profit without having to pay taxes as well. An account in a foreign bank offers an ideal solution to the tax problem. It creates some administrative difficulties for day-to-day traders since communications with Europe are slow and expensive and since the foreign bank in a different time zone will be closed during a part of the US trading day.
>
> In recent years many accommodating US brokers have worked out with the Swiss bankers a device for servicing the needs of such a customer. The customer will close his brokerage house account and open an account with the Swiss bank. The Swiss bank will open a special sub-account in its name with the broker. The customer will continue to call the broker as before to place his market orders, and the broker will execute them. But the brokerage house will not retain any records showing that the transaction is executed for the customer's account. The transactions will be entered in the account of the Swiss bank. Since the American broker maintains constant contact with the Swiss banking client either by telex or by telephone, it will be easy to make the customer's order appear to have originated in Switzerland. The customer will then have to pay two commissions, one in the United States and one in Switzerland; but he will have to pay no taxes.

One thing inevitably led to several others: to the sweeping

aside of margin requirements, for a start, and the abandonment of any pretence that it was the Swiss bank, rather than the American speculator, who was placing the order. For soon the deals were being done directly, merely being booked to the Swiss bank's account. And they often involved some form of market manipulation, because secrecy ensured that the details of market rigging would be lost. As an investigator told *Forbes*, 'the big problem is to recreate the market. You put together the buy orders and the sell orders. When the buys – or more likely the sells – come through with a Swiss bank as agent, there is no way of finding out who the principals are. You can't get behind the façade of paper.'

Nevertheless the investigators did on enough occasions to demonstrate the spread of the habit. Two classic cases involved well-known American brokers and small Swiss banks in breaking margin requirements. André Bakar, a Tunisian who had been promoted to a vice-presidency at the brokerage house of Shearson Hammill because of his success in attracting Arab clients, had put them in touch with Weisscredit Bank of Chiasso. Bakar persuaded a number of clients – including Frank Stranahan, the golfer (and heir to the Champion spark plug fortune), and a well-known Florida wheeler-dealer, Victor Posner, to use Weisscredit to evade margin restrictions, borrowing up to eighty per cent of the cost of stock, four times the legal level of twenty per cent. In 1969 Bakar was summoned before a Grand Jury: he turned the full voltage of his considerable charm on the Jury when asked by the prosecutor, whether he had discussed these illegal credit restrictions with his clients: 'You are asking me the same question, Mr. Marks, three times and I am telling you and I repeat to you, dear sir, that with all due respect to you and to these lovely people [the Grand Jury] so help me God, I have never, never, went [*sic*] into details about these particular transactions or credits between the American investor and the bank. I was an order taker and I was very glad to get that business.'

Bakar, the bank, and its general manager were found guilty of contempt of court. The customers, for whose benefit the margin requirements had been broken, could not be indicted as the law stood at the time – it was changed shortly afterwards, and it was the Weisscredit case which finally persuaded the Federal Reserve Board to clamp down on the abuse of 'omnibus accounts' by foreigners.

(Weisscredit was not the most imposing or venerable of institutions. Its owner, Elvio Zoppi, started his career running a café at a crucial Swiss staging point for smugglers near the Italian frontier and drifted into providing a foreign exchange service for his Italian clients. He then diversified into the wholesaling of fruit and vegetables. But the change was more apparent than real: under the boxes of choice Italian produce, large quantities of cash could be and were stashed away, as Zoppi's vans, prominently marked *Frutta e Verdura*, – fruit and vegetables – made their regular crossings of the border.)

Another small, recently founded bank, Arzi in Zurich, also made history as the first to accept the jurisdiction of an American court as a result of a joint exercise in margin-breaking it had conducted with Coggeshall and Hicks, a previously reputable New York brokerage house. (Arzi really had no choice: the investigators discovered microfilmed copies of cancelled cheques to the bank from some of the broker's customers). After the senior partner of Coggeshall and Hicks, the (Swiss) manager of its Geneva office, and three of its salesmen had been indicted by a Grand Jury in New York, the bank joined with other defendants in pleading guilty and taking its medicine – fines totalling $100,000 to match illicit transactions totalling more than $20 million. Among a number of other margin cases was one involving one of Wall Street's more bizarre operators, William Mellon Hitchcock, both a member of the Mellon family and the friend and protector of that guru of the drug scene Timothy Leary. His illicit dealings with the Paravicini Bank came to light when the bank sent copies of some of its records to a leading Washington law firm, Arnold and Porter, as evidence to reinforce the pursuit of some of the bank's defaulting debtors. Once the records left Swiss soil, the sacred mantle of Clause 47(b) no longer protected them, and they were seized after an informer tipped off the authorities.

To ignore margin requirements was merely to break a set of essentially technical regulations – though the Swiss showed how essential they were when they de-stabilised the market by dumping stocks owned by operators whose purchases had fallen by more than ten per cent. But of course the banks were also employed for more deeply criminal purposes. 'Boiler house' operators like Jack van Allen and his colleagues used them to puff up the value of stocks. The Res – and others following them – had used their services to rig the markets in new issues. In the 1960s too, insiders often employed them to conceal their activities: Max Orovitz, a major figure in an important real-estate company in Florida, the General Development Corporation, carried out a number of exceedingly curious transactions through the Union Bank (although the SEC caught up with him, the motives behind them – and the real beneficiaries, suspected of including Mafia members – remained a mystery behind the blank facade presented by the UBS).

Towards the end of the decade, Wall Street developed take-over fever. Bids were made every day for every sort of company, for every variety of reason. In 1968 the Congress had tried to staunch the flow with the Williams Bill, which provided that any single holding of ten per cent or more in a stock had to be declared. The Bill failed in its object. In the two years after it was passed, 104 cash tender offers were filed with the SEC: no fewer than sixteen involved foreign banks from a number of financial centres; 'hundreds of millions of dollars are being furnished annually by foreign sources to assist in endeavours to gain control of American companies', the Senate committee was told by Hamar Budge, the chairman of the SEC. Many of these cases broke some, if not all, the rules of the game. Hambros, the venerable British bank, was concerned in a bid in mid 1969 for Bath Industries, whose principal activity was building destroyers for the U.S. Navy. Hambros – together with the Swiss subsidiary of the major French Paribas bank and a Swiss investment company called MAD – plotted with one of Bath's directors, one Ernest J. Blot, to seize control of Bath. This mad scheme was blotted out by the American courts. And when – also during 1969 – Kirk Kerkorian made his first attempt to seize control of MGM, he used a German bank and the London branch of a Texan bank to borrow the necessary funds – breaking the margin regulations in the most spectacular fashion to do so.

A few months earlier, when Resorts International, a highly suspect Bahamas concern running casinos on the islands, tried to seize control of Pan American Airlines, the sources of the foreign financing required were so mysterious that not even the SEC could trace them. Some of Resorts' directors were very close to the new President, Richard Nixon, but another case was politically even more explosive. Randolph H. Guthrie, the senior partner of his old New York law firm, represented Paribas and its Swiss subsidiaries and, as *Time* reported in early 1970, 'last fall was instrumental in arranging a $40 million loan for the New York-based conglomerate Liquidonics Industries to gain control of UMC Industries, a St. Louis defence contracting firm. Had the deal been arranged through an American bank, it would have violated SEC margin requirements. Guthrie asserts – and he has not been disputed – that margin requirements do not apply to foreign banks. Liquidonics was unable to repay the $40 million, so the Swiss bank took over its stock and gave it to a subsidiary. The new chairman of UMC Industries: Randolph H. Guthrie.'

But by that time the action had moved to Washington. Even President Nixon was unable to protect the Swiss – and to a lesser extent the American – banking community from a most unwelcome exposure to the light of day.

5/ Mr. Morgenthau goes to Washington

It was clear that new legal weapons were required if the fight against white-collar crime were to be made more effective. Morgenthau's fight for these weapons culminated in the Bank Records Act of 1970, even more permanent a legacy of his time as Attorney than his influence on Federal law-enforcement of white-collar crime. The Act filled an obvious gap. Some foreign banks may have been deterred by a ruling in July 1968, when a U.S. court decided that First National City Bank was obliged to produce files from its German branch, but this was clearly not going to be enough to control the Swiss banks. Nor would administrative changes suffice. New legislation was clearly required. The regulators were fully aware that a hard core of really determined and ingenious criminals would always find a way round even the most tightly drawn laws and regulations, but the wholesale violations of the previous few years could be stopped: 'making wrongdoing complicated eliminates many of the players' was an elementary truth attributed to Ira Pearce of the SEC (and known to his colleagues as 'Pearce's rule').

Morgenthau set the legislative ball rolling by briefing Wright Patman, the radical, populist chairman of the Banking Committee of the House of Representatives. Patman held a day of hearings in December 1968 to give Morgenthau, his colleagues, and the SEC team under Irving Pollack a chance to air their views on the horrors of the existing situation and the pressing need for new legislation. The hearings were largely educational – indeed, those held over the following two years both by Patman's committee and by his Senatorial brethren have provided a major source of information for many writers including the author of this book. But at the time Congressmen and newspaper readers were appropriately horrified to hear of the devices employed by malefactors of great wealth, the 'great and the bad', to evade the law or simply their tax bill. 'I recall', exclaimed one Congressman, 'when I was practising law I thought a fellow who kited a check was devious, but I am finding out now he was really a novice.'

The public had been already softened up, not only by the series in *Life*, but also by a stream of articles by serious and well briefed journalists, some of whom I have already quoted earlier in this chapter. The misdeeds of Bernie Cornfeld and his colleagues, and the steps taken by the regulatory authorities against them figured prominently in the early hearings. This was a fascinating reversal of roles: Cornfeld had used the good name of Switzerland to provide him with financial credibility in the eyes of his potential customers; now the American authorities returned the compliment by citing his activities as ammunition against indigenous financial groups.

The evidence was well orchestrated, and equally well conducted by Patman. After he had, as it were, laid down his baton, he could reasonably conclude in public (as he had already decided in private) that legislation was required as a matter of urgency. He summed up the case when he presented a bill in December the following year:

> At the conclusion of these hearings it became clear that the use of these secret foreign bank accounts and foreign financial institutions as part of illegal schemes by American citizens and others created a tremendous and grave problem of law enforcement in the United States. Secret bank accounts are the underpinning of organized crime in this country. They are a haven for the unreported income of Americans. They can be used to buy gold in violation of American law. They can be used to buy stock in our market or in the acquisition of substantial interests in American corporations by unidentified persons under sinister circumstances ... I feel there is a deep-seated resentment by the ordinary citizen who must pay his taxes and has neither the resources, ingenuity, nor criminal intent to use these secret accounts to avoid paying his legitimate taxes.

The Swiss banks struggled vainly against this hostile atmosphere. They hired lobbyists: in late 1968 the Big Three issued the first edition of their booklet *The Truth about Swiss Banking*, stating firmly that 'the purpose of banking secrecy is to protect the innocent, not to shield the guilty, and history has demonstrated its usefulness' – emphasising its role in protecting German Jews. Also prominent was the reliance on 'the individual's right to privacy' and its erosion 'through mounting government surveillance of citizens' activities and attitudes', which 'raises disturbing questions in any free society', a defence that might have found a ready response in the early 1980s, but which was completely out of tune with the atmosphere of the time. Nor did the banks make any real impression on American attitudes with a more substantial gesture.

In October 1968 the SBA had issued a strongly worded circular to its members. The practices it discouraged were revealing – the banks' enemies could have taken it as an admission of guilt – on all counts. The banks were told to moderate the tone of their publicity, for example. One particular advertisement for Crédit Suisse welcoming customers to 'our world of banking' at its new Wall Street offices had been regularly cited as evidence of Swiss aggressiveness. 'There should be no public or individual soliciting of clients which might have the effect of inducing American citizens or residents to contravene American law.' Banks were recommended to be reluctant to open numbered accounts in future, to stick to the American levels when granting loans on margin, not to vote against the sitting board during proxy fights, and not to work with 'corporate insiders' to help break the rules. No real disciplinary measures were, however, envisaged against banks that ignored the circular's recommendations, although the Association's members were asked to inform on their offending brethren, and if they did, said the SBA: 'we shall protest to the firm in question and ask them in future to adhere as closely as possible to our recommendations.'

The Swiss also hoped to divert the American legislators by making sympathetic noises: 'the difference between the two judicial systems', cooed Hans Mast of Crédit Suisse (referring, naturally, to tax offences) 'created obstacles to the prosecution of crime, a fact that naturally also gave rise to concern in Switzerland.' And leading bankers emphasised that they were prepared to compromise during the negotiations which were just starting for a treaty of mutual assistance on criminal matters, and provide greater help where offences which were crimes in both countries were concerned. But these noises seemed irrelevant when in early December 1969 the Patman committee started detailed hearings on the 'Bank Records and Foreign Transactions Bill'. This Bill, despite its innocuously technical title, filled in many of the gaps the investigators had discovered.

Domestic financial institutions were to be required to maintain records of checks and other financial transactions under Treasury Department regulations. Unusual or sizeable deposits or withdrawals of U.S. currency would have to be reported when they exceeded $5,000 on any one occasion or $10,000 in any one year; individuals who had transactions with foreign financial agencies would have to maintain records on those transactions. Finally, filling the 'Stranahan-Posner' gap, borrowers who violated margin requirements on securities loans would be as liable to penalties as the lending institutions already were.

The Nixon administration was obviously not going to like the Bill. But the first form taken by its opposition was both dramatic and counter-productive. On 17 December 1969 Morgenthau was suddenly sacked. That morning, he received a hand-delivered letter requesting his resignation from John Mitchell, the Attorney General – and a former partner of Randolph Guthrie, who was in Morgenthau's sights because of the Liquidonics takeover. Morgenthau hit back with justified hyperbole: his removal, he asserted, had had an immediate and 'dramatic impact on the willingness of individual citizens to come forward with vital evidence ... the White House, for all its statements about law and order, has failed to recognise that in law enforcement, as elsewhere, the customs and principles of "the old politics" are no longer relevant.'

In dismissing Morgenthau against the advice of the (Republican) governor and senators representing New York, Nixon and Mitchell – for the first but by no means the last time – were venturing onto legally untried territory. The Kennedy administration had taken literally the provision that 'each United States Attorney is subject to removal by the President' when John Kennedy dismissed the Republican Elliot Richardson as U.S. Attorney in Massachusetts (he was, of course, to be sacked again in the 'October Massacre' by Nixon in 1973). But Morgenthau's position was anomalous: since he had taken a year off to campaign against Nelson Rockefeller for the governorship of New York, his tenure of office extended into 1971 and did not, as was normal with U.S. Attorneys, coincide with the presidential term.

At the first meeting of his committee after Morgenthau's dismissal, Patman hinted that it had been necessary because Morgenthau's enquiries had led him too uncomfortably near to the President and his closest associates: 'Mr Morgenthau's greatest crime in my judgment is that he went after the really big law breakers – the big banks, the big stockbrokers, and the big criminals. It is hoped that the appropriate committees of the Congress will very carefully keep an eye on the crime-fighting activities of the Southern District of New York. I think there is only a faint hope that the standards set for that office by our witness this morning will be followed.' Inevitably, Morgenthau's dismissal made life difficult, not only for the opponents of Patman's Bill, but also for his successor, Whitney North Seymour. In the event, despite a certain formality in his approach, he was an effective, if not an innovative prosecutor. (His wings were rather clipped because the Justice Department, jealous of the independence Morgenthau had enjoyed, formed a specialist team to reduce the overwhelming role of the Southern District of New York in fighting financial crime.)

The administration also hoped to water down the Bill by giving the Secretary of the Treasury discretion in deciding which records banks were to retain. In mid-December a delegation of bankers discussed the Bill with Treasury officials headed by Eugene Rossides, the Assistant Secretary for Operations and Enforcement. This meeting soon became legendary. 'The administration once favored the tough Patman Bill', reported *Business Week*, 'Administration people even helped Patman draft it. Then, recalls one New York banker, we made some noise. The administration talked with bankers, decided the Patman Bill was unworkable, and promised to come up with its own substitute measure.'

The reality was less dramatic; for one thing, it was the Justice Department, not the Treasury, which had helped draft the Bill. And, as the *Washington Post* noted, 'this is a subject, of course, on which bankers ought to have their say. The strange thing is that they had not been consulted while their Bill was being drafted.' But, as so often in politics, reality mattered much less than atmosphere, and this was in favour of the Bill: 'like everybody else we are in favour of motherhood', admitted the head of one bankers' grouping, 'and our organisation has gone on record in favor of this Bill.' Any opposition was suspect: 'the biggest American banks, by opposing the Bill', snorted the *New York Times*, 'risk fostering the growth of white-collar crime out of ignorance or pure greed.' Nor did the banks help their case when Rossides was forced to admit that in recent years they had reduced the length of time for which they retained records. Randolph Thrower, the Commissioner of Internal Revenue, rubbed salt in the wound when he told the committee that 'many domestic banks follow a practice of destroying records at the earliest possible date after they have met the needs of the bank and the bank's customer.' This, to the banks' opponents, was an admission of complicity in the illegal practices the Bill was designed to curb.

Because of the hostile atmosphere generated by the dismissal of Morgenthau, the debate was heavily loaded against administration officials, like Rossides, when they pleaded for time to clarify the undoubtedly complex regulations required to identify which precise records, out of the billions generated yearly by the banking system, could conceivably be of use in fighting crime, and whether Congress, through the Bill, or the Secretary of the Treasury should prescribe the documents to be retained. The administration's witnesses showed willing. Seymour recalled how 'the conviction of Frank Costello would have been impossible without microfilmed bank records of checks to prove payment', and how, in the Olin Mathieson case, 'microfilms of American bank records were of critical importance.' No one was impressed. It was equally useless for Rossides to return in March 1970 with clarifications, which, he claimed tended to strengthen the Bill. It was equally useless when he revealed new regulations – including an unprecedented provision that if a taxpayer claimed a deduction for interest on a foreign loan, 'our assumption would be that the taxpayer is dealing with his own untaxed income', a startling break with the normal presumption of a taxpayer's innocence. It was useless for him to stress the importance of the negotiations on the tax treaty with the Swiss. It did not help when even Pierre Leval testified that some of the provisions regarding record keeping seemed to him somewhat extreme and inflexible. It did not help when Randolph Thrower revealed the new sections that were being added to personal tax forms, including key questions like: 'did you at any time during the taxable year have any interest in ... or other authority over bank securities, or other financial account in a foreign country?' Patman remained hostile and unimpressed. The Treasury, with its back to the wall, finally came up with a list of specific transactions of which records had to be kept, allowing no discretion to either the Secretary or the banks (who formed a curious alliance with Patman on this point: he didn't want the Secretary to have discretion because he was afraid that a pro-bank administration would let the provision lapse; the bankers were afraid that a Secretary hostile to the financial community – like Henry Morgenthau? – might use the provision for his own political purposes).

When the Bill went to the Senate, Rossides was prepared to admit defeat on the international side, accepting compulsory 'very detailed, substantial record-keeping,' as he told the Senate resignedly, in each of six precisely defined areas. But he stuck successfully to his demand for discretion in the domestic area (which included, in theory, every check made out by every American citizen or resident), limiting the requirements to such documents as the Secretary deemed actually or potentially useful in the fight against crime by the Justice Department, or regulatory authorities.

If Rossides thought he had had a hard time in the House, worse was to come in the Senate. William Proxmire, the Chairman of the Senate Banking Committee, was as dedicated a supporter of the Bill as Patman. Worse, he had a personal interest in violations of margin restrictions, because, as he told a witness, his father had lost the then enormous sum of $250,000 through speculating on excessive margin in 1929. Far from weakening the Bill, the Senate version brought in two new clauses to prevent the spread of anonymity in financial transactions. The first prohibited American brokers and dealers from carrying out any transactions for a foreign financial institution unless the latter was prepared to certify that it was not acting for an American citizen. This was not likely to be terribly effective, given the ability of the Swiss banking community to reconcile perjury – before foreign courts anyway – with their consciences. Second, and nearer home, any American citizen who placed a stock market order through a foreign financial institution would have to give permission to the foreigner to disclose his identity to the

American broker with whom the foreigner was dealing.

The new clauses provoked a split within the administration. The SEC was still dominated by aggressive officials appointed in the 1960s who believed that the provision would help them more than it would hurt the American balance of payments by discouraging foreign investment. Rossides believed the opposite, but his worries were largely discounted by Proxmire. When they were raised by officials from the New York Stock Exchange, he pointed to their statement which indicated that a net capital inflow of almost $1.5 billion resulted from international securities transactions. During that same year, the unexplained capital outflow, commonly called 'errors and omissions', was $3 billion or twice as great. 'Isn't it conceivable', he asked 'that some of the $1.5 billion inflow was really American money coming back from secret foreign bank accounts? ... a restriction on capital inflows on securities transactions would not necessarily impair our balance of payments if it were offset by a corresponding restriction in the outflow counted under "errors and omissions".' To which there was no answer.

In the end the administration was faced with a Bill that effectively corresponded to the original text. In a final session in which the House and Senate reconciled their differences, the stronger language usually won. The only victory for the opponents of compulsory recordkeeping in international transactions was some verbiage providing that the SEC should have due regard for the need to avoid 'burdening unreasonably persons who legitimately engage in transactions with foreign financial agencies ... and regard to the need to avoid impeding or controlling the export or import of currency or other monetary instruments'. And there was one minor change to Clause 235, which set out the size of foreign transactions which should be reported: originally this was phrased to cover annual expenditures of $10,000 or more; thanks largely to pleas that this would affect the high-living crews sent abroad by television networks, the phrasing was changed to cover only the export or import of 'monetary instruments' in individual lumps of $5,000 or more.

Because the passage of the Act coincided with a deep depression on Wall Street, a continuing state of apathy followed by a steady decline in the value of the dollar, foreign investors kept away from the American markets for much of the 1970s, so the Act seemed something of a white elephant. At the time, however, American bankers were furious. When the Treasury produced its regulations they protested vigorously. Even after they were watered down the California Bankers' Association took to the courts claiming that the regulations clashed with at least three constitutional amendments (as well as landing them with mountains of additional paperwork). In 1972 a federal district court in California supported the banks – partially at least – in ruling that the domestic reporting provisions went too far. Finally, two years later, the Supreme Court – albeit narrowly and with some powerful dissenters – put its seal of approval on the whole Act, domestic reporting requirements included.

The length of the process had allowed the contributors to the Nixon re-election campaign in 1972 to use foreign banks without fear of immediate discovery, and it was not until the second half of the decade that the new law was properly enforced. Even then the SEC had not started to discover on a regular basis the real names of foreign buyers of American stocks, and as late as 1977 a Congressional committee was accusing the Treasury of pussy-footing, of moving from the front of the standard tax form – 1040 – the basic question whether the taxpayer had a foreign bank account (it had been removed, but was later reinstated, albeit not on the front page). But by that time the clauses requiring the reporting of all foreign cash transactions were being used to some effect against drug smugglers, and the Internal Revenue had launched a number of operations designed to uncover tax dodgers who were using foreign banks. 'Tailwinds', one was called, and another was obviously named by an historically minded tax man. 'Project Haven' he called it.

6/ Tidying up

Unlike the American banking community, the Swiss authorities were not too unhappy with the Bank Records Act. Writing in 1973, Ulrich Meier of the Federal Tax Administration expressed merely relief that the Act was not aimed specifically at his country, but was a catch-all measure. The Act, he thought, was akin to the Swiss approach to these problems and represented an attitude that could usefully be followed by other countries thinking of similar legislation.

For the Swiss had been put on the defensive and were terribly anxious to show themselves co-operative with the Americans. In 1970 two important decisions by the Tribunal Fédéral indicated a shift in judicial thinking. First, the American government was allowed to plead as an injured party to try to recover some of the money of which the U.S. Navy had been defrauded by Andrew Stone and Francis Rosenbaum. What is more, the Department of Justice was allowed access to some of the records kept by the conspirators' bank, the Zurich based Bank Für Handel und Effekten. But the Swiss investigating magistrate was not going to allow the American tax authorities indirect access to banking secrets: the Department of Justice had to provide an affidavit that the records would not be used in the United States for 'fiscal purposes'.

But these were admitted for the first time in a case coyly entitled 'X v The Federal Tax Administration', decided later that year. Raymond and Helen Ryan, a wealthy couple from Evansville, Indiana, a town not previously thought of as a centre of tax evasion, were being pursued for tax fraud, in connection with deposits of several million dollars in Swiss banks, and the matter eventually landed up in the Federal Supreme Court. In a major decision the court held that, because fraud and not merely tax evasion was involved, the

American authorities should have access to the documents required to pursue their case. The argument rested on a choice of cantonal laws: in some cantons tax fraud, like tax evasion, was not a criminal offence; but the court ruled that the applicable law lay in that of the cantons – Zurich, Geneva, Basle – which housed major financial centres, and which all treated tax fraud, where forged or falsified ('substantially untrue') documents were involved, as a criminal matter.

This decision was greeted with some derision by the American investigators as an attempt to demonstrate that the Swiss legal authorities were co-operating quite nicely, thank you, and that therefore there was no need for the Treaty being painfully hammered out at the time. The gesture was not ineffective. John Lannan, an American legal academic, admitted that 'A cynic might argue that "X v The Federal Tax Administration" was decided to placate the United States which was viewing with increasing disapproval the aplomb with which Americans were using Swiss banks to neutralize American laws. Regardless of the Court's motives, its decision was an unprecedented departure from the traditional Swiss position on banking secrecy', only to swallow the bait a few pages later when he was arguing against the 1970 Act: 'The ubiquitious surveillance of the financial lives of all United States citizens is unnecessary and wasteful, particularly in the light of the more co-operative Swiss attitude' expressed in the same case. Lannan, like so many outsiders, did not understand the Swiss capacity for defence in depth of their most cherished institutions.

For by 1975, after the Tax Treaty between Switzerland and the United States had been concluded, the court effectively reversed itself. In the dry words of the American tax court handling the Ryan case:

> The Swiss Federal Supreme court held that while under the Tax Treaty information from bank records could be made available to the Internal Revenue Service under certain conditions, the treaty did not authorize the Swiss Confederation Tax Administration to furnish the Internal Revenue Service with evidence from the bank records in a form that would be admissible in evidence in a trial in the

United States Courts. Pursuant to the decision the Swiss Confederation Tax Administration refused, so we are informed, to furnish the evidence requested for use in this proceeding.

The treaty, the tortuous negotiations it required and the lengthy debates that led to its eventual acceptance by the Swiss Parliament were a textbook demonstration of the gulf which separated the two countries. The two negotiating teams were ill-matched: the burden on the Swiss side rested on one man, Dr Kurt Merkase from the Ministry of Justice ('a charming curmudgeon', said one American, 'he was supposed to be semi-retired but all that meant was that he turned up in a high-necked sweater'). The State Department tried to keep clear of the whole thing by nominating a team of experts from other departments, notably Justice and the SEC, and these thoroughly enjoyed their bouts with the Swiss. There were also some embarrassing moments after it transpired that the American ambassador to Switzerland, Shelby Cullom Davis, had clashed with the SEC while he was working on Wall Street.

This particular embarrassment was kept private: more public – and much more confusing to the poor Swiss trying to gauge the real policy of the Nixon administration – were the results of John Mitchell's friendship with Robert Vesco, who was in the process of taking over the remnants of Bernie Cornfeld's IOS empire. A former IOS sales manager, David Tucker, complained to the Genevan authorities that Vesco had illegally removed some IOS shares belonging to him from his account at the IOS controlled Overseas Development Bank. The investigating magistrate, Judge Pagan, backed up Tucker's complaint, and after a farcical interrogation at the Genevan Palais de Justice, which Vesco spent emphasising his importance as an international financier, a thoroughly disgruntled Pagan announced 'You have endangered the reputation of Swiss banking by your actions. I intend to set an example in your case to demonstrate that Swiss justice knows no double standard ... It is in your own interests, therefore, that I am issuing an arrest warrant against you', and Vesco was carried off to St. Antoine's prison for the night.

It was a troubled night for America's diplomatic representatives in Switzerland. John Mitchell was instantly contacted by Vesco's lawyers, and he immediately telephoned the American embassy in Berne. The next morning Vesco was duly released on bail. The accusations were maintained, but not for long. Tucker was paid off, and Pagan's superiors negotiated a settlement with Vesco's lawyers behind the magistrate's back. Officially 'the complaint having been withdrawn, the charges were not established'. Pagan, unaware of the diplomatic pressure, was naturally furious at the apparent slur on his professional reputation. 'You don't think I laid charges without sufficient grounds, do you?' he told reporters, 'If this sort of thing continues, pretty soon one won't be able to prosecute criminal fraud charges in Geneva.' He made matters worse when he told a 'news agency' the simple truth, that the charges had been solidly proved but that Tucker had been bought off. But the 'news agency' was in Vesco's pay, and when the allegations reached the Genevan papers Pagan was officially censured by the Magistrate's office and removed from any further investigation into the affairs of Vesco or IOS.

(The Swiss police went even further to help Vesco when they provided his men with their register of the occupants of Geneva's hotels to help trace the whereabouts of a young SEC official who was on their tracks, and whom they were hoping to compromise sexually.)

That Swiss judicial procedures could prove flexible if enough pressure (or publicity) was applied became even more obvious when Clifford and Helga Irving made their famous attempt to foist their fake autobiography of Howard Hughes onto the public. A key element in their conspiracy consisted in persuading their American publishers, McGraw-Hill, to pay the $650,000 advance to them. But what else are Swiss banks for? In early 1972 Helga Irving simply opened an account (number 320496) under the name of H. R. Hughes at the head office of the Crédit Suisse in the Paradeplatz itself. She then opened another account at the less conspicuous Winterthur branch of the Swiss Bank Corporation in the name of Hanna Rosenkranz, the family name of her former husband. McGraw-Hill then credited the advance to account number 320496; Helga Irving promptly withdrew the money and as promptly redeposited it in Winterthur.

The fun started when attorneys acting for the real Howard Hughes asked for an affidavit from the Crédit Suisse that their client did not have an account with them. Although such hypothetical leading questions were absolute anathema to the bank – indeed had been a primary weapon used in vain by Nazi investigators in the 1930s – yet the public interest in the case was so great that a way out had to be found. The bank swiftly confirmed that Howard Hughes was not one of their clients; and when the attorneys applied for a court order to have the account opened up, the cantonal judiciary duly interpreted the Ryan ruling 'constructively'. They held that there was sufficient reason to suppose that the documents relating to account number 320496 had been falsified to authorise the bank to release them.

The Americans were not alone in harassing the Swiss. In the late 1960s the arrival in power in West Germany of the Social Democratic Party after twenty years of conservative government worried the country's richer inhabitants enough for 20,000 of them to hunt for 'tax oases' through setting up their own personal *Anstalts*. The scandal soon burst into the open, and names like the film star Curt Jurgens and the playwright Rolf Hochhuth were bandied about. Action was eventually triggered off when an unnamed retailer of great wealth allegedly transferred several million dollars free of any taxes into Switzerland, and by the end of 1971 the two countries had concluded their own double taxation treaty to prevent the use of such nominal corporations for tax evasion (no 'mail box' companies were to be allowed unless they did real business – and with West Germany at that).

The Swiss argument with the British government was more spectacular. In November 1972 the brilliant British investigative journalist Michael Gillard revealed in the *Daily Express* that there had been a major diplomatic incident following investigations by Stanley Little, a former police officer who was then head of the foreign exchange investigatory squad at the British Treasury. The squad was small, 'but it was about our most cost-effective department, each one of them managed to reclaim millions of pounds' recalls one Treasury official. (Many more millions escaped their net: virtually everyone in the City of London at the time seemed to possess his own pet device for transferring funds abroad in defiance of England's strict foreign exchange controls. A favourite device employed what was known as the 'Kuwait gap' using funds deposited in London to the credit of a Kuwaiti citizen who would then place a similar sum in a Swiss bank.)

Little, apparently helped by a number of diplomats at the British embassy in Berne, had managed to persuade Juggi Wyter and Maurice Favey, who both worked for a small ethnic bank in Geneva, to provide the names of its British clients. The institutions involved included the Mirelis Bank and a much bigger associated group, the Société Bancaire de Genève. Before its takeover by Barclays Bank, the Société Bancaire, like the Mirelis banks, had been controlled by a group of Jews from Iraq and Syria, notably the Bashi family. They were greatly helped by a Genevan banker named Jean Martin (whose death in June 1972 was fondly and publicly commemorated by the Bashi family). The Syrian and Iraqi Jews were amongst the richest from the Middle East, and had the greatest problems – it was a capital offence, in Syria at least, to open a bank account abroad. Because of the likely embarrassment to the clientele, who included a major proportion of their brethren in Britain, the matter was hushed up, even though the diplomatic embarrassment was so great that Pierre Graber, Switzerland's Foreign Minister, had to go to London especially to sort it out. In the end the two employees were prosecuted under the Banking Act, and two British diplomats left the country hurriedly. Little himself was warned not to go anywhere near Switzerland – had he done so, he would presumably have been charged under Article 271 of the penal code, the one hurried through in the 1930s to stop Gestapo agents operating in the country.

This continuing spotlight on Swiss banking secrecy in fact helped the American negotiators in their tortuous negotiations: 'we kept coming up against the Swiss ability to invent retroactive traditions', complained one of the American team, but they persisted. 'The SBA expected us to give up a lot earlier than we did,' he continued, 'I reckon this was the beginning of the age of enlightenment.' On some points the Swiss were immovable: the bankers succeeded in squashing any idea that securities offences should be included among the crimes on which assistance would automatically be available. Swiss tradition held that insider trading by a banker in advance of a merger was not an indictable offence. However, the final draft ('it was a hell of a complicated document, it was written by a committee and then some', said one of the American negotiators) greatly broadened the possibilities of judicial assistance by the Swiss, albeit not the certainty of it; 'the treaty was like an apartment lease, you can't go by the letter, it was a framework under which the Swiss could provide assistance if they wanted to, or it gave them an excuse not to ... we really can't force the Swiss to help us'.

For the Swiss fought every inch of the way and were particularly sensitive over the possibility that information wrenched from them might be spread abroad too widely. They failed to keep their records confidential when they were used in American courts, but they did at least ensure that records could be obtained only for a specific purpose ('they felt that the Italians had screwed them by obtaining information on one pretext and then using it for currency accusations as well'). Moreover, their magistrates would retain control over the flow of information, for it could be released only by a Swiss court, and not by federal or other authorities on their own initiative.

The biggest – indeed unprecedented – breach in bank secrecy was made in the three articles relating to organised crime. Provided that the Swiss authorities were sure that the Americans were not using the clause to delve into other suspected crimes, then banking secrecy would be lifted even before any formal charges had been brought. In general, however, banking secrecy would be lifted only where activities deemed criminal in both countries were concerned – and then only through the Swiss authorities.

Despite its carefully hedged provisions, the treaty led to a widespread accusation – made not only by the bankers – that the Americans were again extending the jurisdiction of their legal system abroad; sophisticated commentators pointed to the parallel with the anti-trust laws, which the Americans had also tried to export. (No one made the opposite point: that the Swiss, in effect, were exporting their judicial sway in extending the advantages of their exclusion of tax evasion from the criminal law to any foreigner who happened to have the money to open an account in Switzerland). But the basic opposition was expressed by the Radical Liberal party, at the time Switzerland's biggest. It was afraid that the draft could set precedents for treaties with 'other countries outside Europe'.

Nevertheless the treaty did eventually get through both houses of the Swiss legislature in time to be ratified in the summer of 1976 and to come into effect early in 1977. But by then agencies of both governments had come to some form of – albeit implicit – understanding. In 1976, for instance, the SEC was seeking a 'disclosure' ruling in an American Court against an American citizen who had tried to conduct his illicit stock market operations through a Swiss bank. The bank promptly agreed that it would provide the court with a full list of all the transactions it had handled in the stock concerned, but in return would not have to reveal the identity of its clients. If the SEC wanted to pursue the matter further, then it could use the standard procedure of *lettres rogatoires*.

The same sort of spirit prevailed in the fascinating case of a certain Colonel Harwood who had run an investment advisory service called the American Institute Counsellors. The good colonel was obsessed with sound money and the price of gold, as were many other investment advisers who also publicised the virtues of Swiss banks at the time, like Robert Kinsman and Harry Browne. (They all illustrated the theme that the reasons for using Swiss banks were largely negative, emphasising the uncertainties brought about by inflation rates and currency fluctuation, both greater than at any time in living memory. They all stressed the element of distrust – of your country, its currency, and its economic prospects, even distrust of your wife in opening such accounts.) But Colonel Harwood went too far, and the SEC moved in with a sweeping condemnation:

> The Commission's complaint alleged a fraudulent scheme and course of business whereby the defendants [who included the grandiosely named American Institution for Economic Research, and sundry Swiss and Liechtenstein

corporations, including the Swiss Life Insurance group and Crédit Suisse] directly and indirectly offered to sell and sold to US investors various gold-related securities in near total disregard for and in violation of virtually the whole panoply of federal securities laws, including the securities registration, anti-fraud, record-keeping and broker-dealer, investment company and investment adviser registration provisions.

Faced with this comprehensive list, an American judge had no hesitation in forcing the hand of Crédit Suisse, which held the assets underlying the mutual funds and insurance policies sold by the group – a splendidly named collection including MAUSAs (Metric Accounting Unit Storage Agreements) and MSPLs (Monte Sole Participating Leases). The court ordered the bank to transfer the assets from Switzerland to the United States; the bank refused, but the judge threatened to seize on the very considerable funds held by the bank within his jurisdiction. At that point Crédit Suisse's collective heart and mind changed direction, and the bank promptly established an irrevocable letter of credit to match all the Harwood group's assets it held in Switzerland. The same realism prevailed when the SEC negotiated the case with Bernard Muller, the newly appointed Secretary of the Swiss Banking Commission, who handled the Swiss end of the case because it concerned a mutual fund, which the commission also supervised. The SEC negotiators believed that 'the Swiss were troubled by those using their national jurisdiction to violate other countries' laws ... even the banks understood ... But Muller was tough, he was only too well aware of the secrecy laws and the requirements of Swiss sovereignty ... in the end we accepted less than we asked for. Neither side was happy.' The solution seemed sensible enough. The whole structure was to be wound down and the assets distributed under the supervision of the Banking Commission and of Coopers and Lybrand, the leading accountants. As the money was refunded, so the amount held by the American court would be reduced (the Americans were not making the same mistake they had over the Washington Agreements in 1945 and were not going to give up their financial hostages until the agreement had been carried through). Bernard Muller personified this new-found spirit of tough but reasonable co-operation, but his appointment and all it signified had come only after five traumatic years.

PART SEVEN

The Road to Normality

1 / The strains of success

The 1970s should rightfully have been the decade when the Swiss banking community came into its inheritance. It was the first time since before World War II that the bankers were able to capitalise fully on their greatest inherited skill – their ability to deal more expertly than other people in gold and foreign exchange. For the first time in a generation both were freely traded – and in ever increasing volume.* With gold the advantages were multiple: the Swiss had been pressing its virtue on their clients even earlier when the price was still artificially stabilised at (or only ten per cent above) the level at which it had been pegged in 1934. Indeed it was a tribute to the Swiss belief in gold – and the resulting importance of the Swiss in the market even in the 1960s – that the South Africans moved the major part of their gold sales from London to Zurich – a move largely engineered by Dr. Alfred Schaefer, whose bank naturally handled much of the business. Then the price escalated, reaching over $830 an ounce in early 1980. Even when it finally settled back within the $400–$500 range this still represented a tenfold rise in a commodity of which the bankers and their clients were the biggest private holders in the world.

Moreover, in a decade of wild currency fluctuations, the historical solidity of the Swiss economy and a rate of inflation almost invariably below the European average was recognised

---

* It is characteristically Swiss that the country houses two compartmentalised gold markets. That in Zurich is bigger and more internationally minded, and prices are set in the international unit of dollars per ounce. In Geneva the banks think in terms of the price in Swiss francs per kilo. Because of the erratic fluctuations in the exchange rates Zurich would sometimes (especially in 1973–4) be buying gold because the price was looking healthy in dollar terms, while Geneva could be bearish because the Swiss franc was appreciating against the dollar faster than gold.

273

by a jerky but seemingly inexorable rise in the value of the Swiss franc against any other currency. This was generally measured against the dollar, which fell from over four francs to well under two in the seven years after its value was untied from that of gold in 1971 – but in the middle of the 1970s the franc started to appreciate even against the Deutschmark, the currency of Switzerland's biggest trading partner, at which point the country's exporters really did have something to grumble about.

For the same reasons Switzerland – and above all its currency – became more than ever a refuge for frightened money. Its banks did not attract the biggest share in the billions of petro-dollars accumulated in the oil-producing countries after 1973, partly because the major banks had never been interested in the Middle East and partly because the Arabs were not frightened enough to have the classic profile of a client of a Swiss bank. Nevertheless the sums managed by the banks rose astronomically. The growth was not fully reflected in the banks' balance sheets. These reverted to the much more sedate progress they had enjoyed before the 1960s – but only because the Swiss National Bank spent most of the decade fighting off the tide of funds desperate to invest in Swiss francs. Even when diverted from the country's currency, the money remained in the care of the Swiss banking fraternity, whose growth in profits came increasingly from the funds earned from managing the money. The sums and the movements were so huge and unprecedented that the Swiss National Bank and the Federal Council had repeatedly to be given more powers by Parliament. It was only in 1971, for instance, that the Federal Council managed to get the Coinage Act changed so that the government could change the parity of the franc at will and intervene effectively in the foreign exchange markets. Repeatedly the SNB had to impose restrictions on bank deposits made by non-residents, and at times the 'negative interest rate' – the cost of actually putting new money on deposit – rose to forty per cent. At times the defensive measures involved arbitrary and decidedly non-Swiss actions. In late 1974 the bank lifted the ban it had imposed three years earlier on new deposits, but the consequent rush was so massive that three weeks later it had to impose retroactive penalties (levied at a rate of three per cent every three months) on the deposits that had flooded in during the three week gap. The banks had to accept such unprecedented interference because they were faced with a nation for once united against them in its determination not to allow the flood of foreign money to boost their country's inflation rate.

This sort of stubbornness did not help successive governments to cope with the economic crisis caused by the first oil crisis of 1973–4. In December 1974 the voters overwhelmingly rejected a package of measures recommended by everyone of note in the country, including all the four political parties in the coalition which had ruled Switzerland since 1959 (when the Socialists were finally deemed strong and sober enough to be allowed into power). This would have enabled the Federal Council not to have to rely on going cap in hand to Parliament for permission to conduct virtually every item of economic policy. But the voters did not want the higher taxes that formed part of the package. The results were dramatic: federal aid to the cantons was cut, building virtually ceased for lack of finance, and in 1975 Switzerland recorded the worst single year slump recorded among industrialised countries in the whole of the anguished decade.* The country's Gross Domestic Product fell by 7.3 per cent – and the effects even spilled over into 1976, when it fell another 1.4 per cent. But by then the voters had relented, and in June 1975 they accepted the need for higher taxes.

The sheer brutality of the treatment worked; and although the international value of the franc rose nearly forty per cent in the two years after the oil shock of October 1973, yet in the years 1976–1980 the country again managed to combine some economic growth with a return to inflation rates which were the envy even of her German neighbours – in the late 1960s the balance was the other way round. Swiss inflation averaged 3.8 per cent during the five years 1966–71, against an average

* Switzerland alone could afford such shock treatment, since the major victims were not its own citizens but the immigrant workers who had flocked to find work there. In the three years 1973–6 the number of foreigners in 'gainful employment' in Switzerland slumped by over 300,000, from 897,000 (one for every seven native Swiss) to 669,000.

of 3 per cent in Germany.

But the strain had its effect. It enabled the Swiss National Bank to tighten its grip over the country's monetary system, for the banks themselves were obviously unable to act as monetary policemen. Moreover their growth in the previous decade had left them unprecedentedly vulnerable. Because they had invaded the personal financial sector with such enthusiasm, their policies affected the average Swiss citizen as never before – most noticeably in respect of his mortgage rate. Even their growth abroad came under suspicion – in the words of one moderate socialist: 'the fact that Swiss banks have shifted their centre of interest to abroad constitutes a permanent risk for the country's economy. Besides, this policy leads the banks to oppose any change in the banking system.'

Obviously their disproportionate size in terms of the Swiss economy (and above all the Swiss money supply) made them the single element most requiring control by the authorities. Moreover, because the rise in the Swiss franc could so easily be attributed to the funds the banks had sucked in so successfully, they were an easy target for Swiss workers – and even industrialists – whose livelihoods had been affected by the remorseless rise in the value of the franc. As in the 1930s the Swiss banks provided massive supplies of ammunition for their critics. In the 1970s all their controls – both within the banks themselves and the external framework covering their activities in general – proved repeatedly and spectacularly inadequate. By contrast with the 1950s and 1960s, the structure of the banking system did not change to any great extent (although, stirred by public pressure, the Big Three accepted a mutual self-denying ordinance by which they agreed not to open any more branches and to cut down on promotional activities like advertising on television), but the climate of public opinion, and the consequent stringency of the regulatory framework within which the banks operated changed beyond recognition.

The first sign of political trouble came in 1970 when the lower house of the Swiss Parliament was debating the new Banking Law, which was designed largely to help control the influx of foreign banks. Although this was the first revision of the Banking Law since 1934, the proposals were modest and clearly derived from the domestic consequences of the fall of Muñoz's bank in St. Gall. Creditors – especially depositors who had entrusted their savings to banks – were to be afforded greater protection, and it was to be a criminal offence to mislead or lie to the Banking Commission, the National Bank, or a bank's auditors. Hommel's successors in the Banking Commission were also to be subjected to rather greater discipline. But that was all.

During the debate at least one deputy tried to ensure that the mortgage rate charged by banks would be regulated, and an even more ominous sign for the bankers came from an improbable alliance of the extreme right and left wings of the Swiss political spectrum, both declaring themselves opposed to banking secrecy. From the left came a voice which was to become increasingly familiar, outside as well as inside Switzerland, Jean Ziegler, and he was supported, although only on this issue, by the right-wing deputy James Schwarzenbach, whose maverick new party had just secured a sweeping electoral success on an extreme nationalist platform, most noticeably directed at the millions of foreign workers who had been so essential in forging the country's post-war prosperity. Schwarzenbach, like Pierre Poujade in France in the 1950s, proved to be a transient phenomenon, but he loomed large on the scene at the time as representing a powerful *petit-bourgeois* backlash against recent directions in Swiss life. He opposed banking secrecy because, for him, it symbolised the shoddy ethical standards which permeated the world of high finance and big business.

Far more durable were the themes touched on by the newly-elected Ziegler. He was an improbable figure: a flamboyant, flashy sociologist of extreme left-wing views, a friend of Che Guevara who had intended to make his home in Castro's Cuba in the 1960s and was only dissuaded at the last minute by Guevara on the grounds that there was richer revolutionary soil to be tilled at home. This caricature of a radical chic academic (he was elected to a professorship at the University of Geneva in the early 1970s) later proclaimed in a widely circulated book *Une Suisse au-dessus de tout soupçon* (*Switzerland exposed*) that 'the world capitalist system is, in the

Hegelian sense of the term, absolute evil made manifest in practice'. Never was there a less likely person to stir up the conscience of the average Swiss. He came from that radical hot-bed Geneva, and has consistently been elected since 1970 to the Federal Parliament by the Germans; yet his reasoning was superficial; where a historian can rely on his predecessor, Léon Nicole, for a trenchantly expressed analysis of events based on the facts, Ziegler is less reliable.

But his approach was sufficiently broadly spread, and expressed in lively enough language, to worry the bankers. ('Too many little old ladies on parish councils listen to him', one banker muttered to the author). His 1970 attack was based on the unimpeachable grounds that banking secrecy allowed government officials from developing countries to hide their ill-gotten gains with impunity. But he went further: he believed that Switzerland was governed by an intricately interlocked oligarchy of bankers and industrialists whose companies were hell-bent on exploiting the poor of the Third World (the fact that most Swiss multinational companies – with the obvious exception of Nestlé – had confined their activities almost entirely to the developed, rather than the developing, world did not deter him).

Ziegler's researches may have been sketchy and his reasoning superficial, but his flair for publicity, and the grievances accumulated against the banks by many sections of the Swiss people over the years turned him into a seminal figure. The first effect of his work was academic: his 'school' included researchers far more thorough and intellectually respectable than him; but his views also found their echo in those of more moderate socialists, some of whom occupied important positions in the federal and cantonal administrations. The banks' increasing involvement in the financial lives of the average Swiss citizen, and the way they were used by the rich – and by prosperous self-employed professional Swiss people – reinforced the increasingly radical atmosphere in which the banks had to operate at home. Pressure also came from the press. Previously subservient, its tone, especially in Geneva, changed markedly in the 1970s. Swiss journalists began to ask awkward questions, and to print penetrating analyses of current financial problems.

The suspicions of the left fell naturally on the 'fiduciary deposit', an increasingly fashionable financial instrument which provided considerable advantages for the banks, and for their clients, both domestic and international. A 'fiduciary deposit' is one arranged by a bank, but which is not deposited with it, but, in the bank's name, with other banks, supposedly 'first class names', the handful of banks in any country whose financial standing was beyond reproach (although the freedom enjoyed by the bank placing the deposit led inevitably to abuses within a few years). In the 1970s these deposits were far and away the fastest growing element in the Swiss banking system – they rose from virtually nothing in 1970 to over 50 billion francs in 1976 and 165 billion by mid-1981* – although the later growth came largely from a handful of rich clients, mostly Arabs. Fiduciary deposits were typically Swiss: the banker acted purely as intermediary and risked neither his money nor, normally, his guarantee on the funds he handled. They were especially convenient in the 1970s as the banks were subjected to steadily increasing pressure not to increase their deposits in any currency too fast, and not to accept Swiss francs at all; and for domestic depositors they carried the advantage of an enhanced anonymity. Of course not all the new funds were in fiduciary deposits. In 1976 it was reckoned that Swiss banks and their clients owned 21 billions' worth of Eurobonds denominated in Swiss francs, 70 billion in other currencies, and 32 billion in 'private placements' – issues to international borrowers which did not go through the international markets.

Of these just under a quarter were in the hands of Swiss citizens or residents, and the consequent loss of tax was around 700 hundred million francs (counting only Swiss residents) or somewhere around 3 billion (if the non-residents had been obliged to pay the withholding tax levied during the decade on income received directly from deposits in Swiss banks, which furnished another good reason for the increasing use of fiduciary deposits). An even bigger drain came as a direct result of banking secrecy because of widespread under-declaration of their incomes by the professional classes.

* Two-fifths of these deposits were placed through the Swiss branches of foreign banks and thus were only nominally Swiss.

The *Déclaration de Berne* group of Socialist academics, which gathered the figures, pointed out the enormous gulf – averaging 50,000 francs a year or more per head – between the incomes declared by doctors in Switzerland's major cities, and the estimates provided by a major insurance group (which was in a good position to know because Swiss health insurance was privately financed).

The conclusions arrived at by the *Déclaration de Berne* group were confirmed by the experience in government of many more moderate socialists. After eleven years in charge of the finances of the rich canton of Vaud – which included Lausanne – André Gavillet declared that Switzerland had taken on many of the attributes of a mere off-shore tax haven. 'With time,' he told an interviewer in 1980,

> my beliefs on this subject have become increasingly settled. By enshrining bank secrecy in the law and providing it with a degree of legal protection greater and more rigorous than that available in almost any other country, the Swiss state has built up a sort of extra-territorial banking territory which has its shocking aspects in the facilities it offers. My experience over the past ten years has made me increasingly firm on this point, for I have been able to notice how banking secrecy has created a shocking degree of inequality in the way our taxpayers are treated. Too much wealth, too many big incomes escape the laws which should be applied to everyone. It is simply not equitable.

(However, the Socialists were not that successful in persuading the majority of their fellow-citizens to change the law: their ideas for increasing direct taxes, embodied in what was known as the 'Wealth Tax' proposal, were twice voted down in the mid-1970s.)

Experience also made many important public figures jaundiced over the effectiveness of the growing number of 'Gentlemen's Agreements' used to govern the relationships between the banks and government bodies. Another moderate Socialist, Jean Pierre Ghelfi, reinforced Gavillet's point of view:

> It is not right that something which involves the whole

country should be left to the judgment of the organisation concerned. May I give you an example: in 1968 a convention was agreed with the National Bank under which the banks limited their total credits. Two years later, during the debate on changes in the law governing the National Bank, M. Chevallaz – who was not yet a Federal Councillor – proposed that the whole idea should be rejected. Conventions, he said, are more flexible. You can adapt them to fit changing situations. He won his point. A few months later this convention expired. That was in July 1972. In the following weeks the banks handed out billions of francs in credits without taking any account of the general economic situation. The result: inflation, which one could see on the horizon, was greatly accelerated and ordinary Swiss citizens were its first victims. For a number of years, we have all suffered from the consequences of this decision by the major banks, who granted all the credits they could without taking any notice of the public interest. When, several months later, the two houses of Parliament adopted 'emergency decrees' to prevent the economy overheating, it was too late. That just shows the limitation of the use of conventions. In fact you just can't solve problems of that scale of importance on the basis of conventions where the application is left to the parties involved and the sanctions (when there are any) are not revealed to the general public.

During the decade, Socialist impatience with the bankers came to be shared by a growing number of officials including, and especially, Fritz Leutwiler, then president of the National Bank, and one of his vice-presidents, Leo Schürmann. Both provided a complete contrast to the tradition of discretion (and unwillingness to offend the banking community) which had prevailed at the Swiss National Bank since 1907. Both were articulate, both critical, especially of bankers and their ways. Leutwiler was the better known outside Switzerland, and within the country he soon became famous for his crisp *bons mots* ('It is the main duty of neither the bankers nor of the head of the Central Bank to be a gentleman, although this quality is doubtless fully compatible with our professions', was probably his best known). But his remark in October

1977 to a Basle newspaper that, 'During the twenty-five years I've been working at the National Bank, the bankers' predictions would have meant that a dozen times Switzerland's place in the banking world would have been taken over by a foreign centre', expressed even better his dismissal of banking fears. (It is not too fanciful to compare Leutwiler with the great General Guisan, both embodying the real Swiss virtues of sturdy, peasant common sense, courage, and unwillingness to be over impressed by the great of this world.) In 1981 Leutwiler's qualities were recognised by the international banking community when he was chosen to head the Bank for International Settlements.

But to the Swiss Schürmann was an even more significant figure. A well-known Christian Democrat, he had become widely popular in the late 1960s during a spell as '*Monsieur Prix*', charged with the task of restraining Swiss retail prices. But he was too much of a maverick to achieve his life's ambition of election to the Federal Council and took the job at the National Bank after his second defeat in December 1973. Because of his background, his outgoing, populist temperament – and the political weight he carried among people who would have never listened to Jean Ziegler – he was to become one of the banks' most dangerous opponents.

Nevertheless, such was their entrenched position, that it took a series of serious scandals in their own ranks to enable the country's increasingly hostile political and economic establishment actually to gain some control over the banking system. The first troubles dated from 1974, the year in which the German Herstatt Bank failed and the German authorities refused to help. This created a major crisis of confidence in the international financial system, whose depth has never been appreciated by the general public and which could have been as shattering as the crash of the Credit Anstalt forty years earlier.

In April 1974, three months before the Herstatt crash, the Union Bank's rising star, Robert Strebel, resigned only a few months after his appointment as one of the bank's four deputy directors general. His departure was explained as the result of the bank's losses on foreign exchange, but the bank's executives furiously denied rumours that the losses added up to nearly a 100 million francs. Six months later the bank admitted that the final figure was nearer 150 million, and attributed them to orders executed on behalf of a foreign client (who was acting for a group of associates). Allegedly the client died with his foreign exchange activities showing an enormous loss, and the positions could not be covered in time. The bank also had to admit that its foreign exchange activities had not been properly controlled. This was a very damaging admission. If it were true at the Union Bank, which was famously tightly-run, then it would obviously also apply to other banks. One of these was the British Lloyds Bank group: and in August, a few months after the Union Bank's troubles, Lloyds had to admit that the manager and chief foreign exchange dealer of its Lugano branch had lost the bank over 100 million francs.

But there were two much more spectacular victims of the troubled times which followed the collapse of Herstatt. The first to go was the hapless Tibor Rosenbaum, whose International Credit Bank had to close its doors in October 1974 – it never reopened after a two-day break for the Jewish High Holy Days. Earlier in the year the property empire belonging to his brother-in-law, William Stern, had collapsed in an enormous heap of financial rubble, as did the Israel British Bank. The shock waves from these disasters were strong enough to alert Michael Tsur, then managing director of the Israel Corporation. This giant investment trust, set up in the euphoria which followed the Six Days War of 1967, had proved something of a disappointment. Since not enough multi-millionaires had subscribed the minimum investment had been slashed – albeit only to $100,000; the board of directors had grown so large and ineffectual that in the early 1970s Baron Edmond de Rothschild had to move in and reorganise it; and its investment policy had been attacked as far too conservative. In early 1974 Michael Tsur had on his own initiative moved over $20 million in cash from two of the companies in which the Israel Corporation had invested to Rosenbaum's bank*. The money had been channelled to the

* Afterwards he claimed that this was a prudent move. Israel was expected to devalue its currency and domestic interest rates were not high enough to compensate for the probable loss in the value of the money.

International Credit Trust in Liechtenstein. Now, after the alarms of the summer, Tsur wanted it back. After some prevarications, Rosenbaum had to tell him on September 12 that the funds were lost. The subsequent bankruptcy of the ICB led to Tsur's resignation and prosecution and set in train a major political scandal within Israel – for the ICB was merely the latest of a number of unfortunate financial events involving people and institutions close to Pinhas Sapir, then Finance Minister. (It also led to widespread mourning in the Jewish community in France, 8,000 of whose members had combined Zionism with tax evasion by depositing their savings with the ICB.)

Rosenbaum, ever a victim of his own gullibility and showmanship, had twice been badly let down. For the funds of the two Israeli companies, as well as those of many other clients, were locked up in several thousand acres of Italian woodland, ideally situated between Rome and the sea, which formerly belonged to the Italian royal family. Rosenbaum had invested $30 million in the land, having been persuaded that planning permission could be obtained for it to be developed provided the right politicians were properly approached. But the money was paid to the wrong politicians, and the Rome city council promptly declared the whole area a national park, with absolutely no possibility of deriving any income from it.

Rosenbaum could also feel himself let down by German politicians. In 1972, the Hessische Landesbank, owned by the provincial government, had taken a thirty-six per cent stake in the ICB. This deal, as always with Rosenbaum, was based on personal friendships – in this case with a director of the Landesbank, Professor William Hankel (who became vice-chairman of the ICB) and with the Social Democrat President of Hesse, Albert Osswald. Rosenbaum reinforced these links by donations of DM 100,000 to SDP party funds, and to Osswald himself. In the summer of 1974 Rosenbaum asked the Germans for a credit line of DM 150 million to satisfy the Swiss Banking Commission. On October 5 the board of the Hessiche bank – itself seriously depleted through its own internal political and financial problems – refused to provide any further help to the ICB, a refusal which led directly to the bank's demise four days later. By the end of the year all was lost – although Rosenbaum managed to repay many of his creditors in the five years before his death in 1980.

The fourth major scandal of that terrible year 1974 was in many ways the most serious. In October the famous Italian financier Michele Sindona, vanished after warrants had been issued by the Italian police for his arrest. The whole of Sindona's intricate empire had seemingly revolved round the Finabank, a modest ethnic institution in Geneva he had purchased from some of his fellow countrymen early in his career – taking in the Vatican as a twenty per cent partner (he even lived at times in an apartment over the bank). Finabank served as a clearing house for the money generated by his other concerns, which would transfer it to Finabank with orders to relend it in the form of fiduciary deposits to obscure concerns in a number of tax havens, notably Fasco, in Liechtenstein. These, of course, belonged to Sindona, and the funds could then be recycled back to Italy – in order, for instance, to purchase more shares in the companies or banks which had deposited the funds with Finabank in the first place. Effectively, Sindona was stealing the companies' money. By the early 1970s, the funds were being lent on to a dubious concern in Nassau controlled in turn by Sindona's property group, Società Generale Immobiliare, which involved Finabank in losses on foreign exchange deals of almost double the bank's entire capital and reserves. But it took a further two months after the issue of the arrest warrants for the Federal Banking Commission even to warn Finabank about the apparent imbalance between its liabilities and its capital and reserves, and it was only in early January 1975 that it was forced to close its doors.

The control mechanisms then in force could do little to prevent scandals such as these. The National Bank managed to ensure that the banks at least provided them with regular monthly figures of their foreign exchange exposure, but even the modest suggestion that foreign exchange dealers should require a licence fell on stony ground. But by this time the whole Swiss establishment was rattled – the Director of Banking Studies at the University of Zurich went so far as to declare that new laws were required to limit what he described as the enormous power of the banks. Chevallaz, by now Finance Minister, had clearly had enough of conventions and was calling for tighter accounting procedures. He even suggested, after what must have been a particularly good dinner with some leading bankers, that the abolition of banking secrecy might be a good thing. Chevallaz's remarks came after vague – but public – hints by the Federal president, Pierre Graber, that banking secrecy ought at least to be curbed. 'Its abuses do us a great deal of harm', he had declared, 'they lead to implications for Swiss foreign policy which one must not underestimate', and Leutwiler had told the press that he would be happier of the banks could get along without numbered accounts.

After all the fuss, the results seemed innocuous enough. A committee was set up within Chevallaz's department, headed by the head of its legal division, Bernard Muller. Like other federal officials, he had hoped that the reform of the Banking Law would have solved the problem. Quite clearly it had not, and the committee decided that the key weakness lay in the Banking Commission. This was still very much what it was in 1934. It had a staff of only five people, and although its secretary, the late Daniel Bodmer, a member of a distinguished banking family, knew his subject inside out (his thesis on the relationship between banks and the government in the 1930s remains the standard work on the subject) yet, because of the depth of his knowledge, he ran a one-man show. His powers were, in any case, limited to clearing up and reporting after disaster had struck. He could not initiate prosecutions, only recommend them to the cantonal judicial authorities. Even more seriously, the Commission had to act through the banks' auditors, who were obliged to report only after things had gone wrong. Chevallaz accepted the report, and asked Muller to take Bodmer's job. He did, and for the first time the Commission had at its head someone for whom bankers were not objects of awe. Like Leutwiler and Schürmann, Muller symbolised the determination of the Swiss people to curb the banks, to ensure that they no longer led the country into defending their indefensible actions – and clients – abroad, to limit their economic and financial power, to bring some order into their activities, in other words to cut these 'overmighty subjects' down to a size appropriate for a democratic country like Switzerland. But they needed an opportunity, and in one week in May 1977 the long-standing weakness at both ends of the banking system, in the country's most exclusive group of private bankers, and in its most respectable big bank, gave them their chance.

2 / The revealing fall of Bobby Leclerc

In the mid 1970s a number of small banks in Switzerland disappeared without attracting the attention devoted to the bankruptcy of institutions controlled by well-known personalities like Tibor Rosenbaum or Michele Sindona. At first sight the name of Robert Leclerc, whose private bank in Geneva shut its doors in May 1977, should have belonged with that of Serge and Theodore Hervel, whose family's bank was declared bankrupt later that year, or with others, like the Robinson Bank, Metrobank, Cosmar or Atlas, whose fate also went relatively unmourned. Yet because Leclerc's bank belonged to the most exclusive grouping in the Swiss financial system, the Association of Geneva Private Bankers – the *Groupement* – his disgrace struck at the very heart of the Genevan banking system – the model for the whole country.

Since the French Revolution, the original nucleus of Genevan private banks had solidified, forming its first formal grouping in 1840 and remaining exceptionally choosy about admitting newcomers. It still includes names respected since the eighteenth century or before, the Oltramares, the Barbeys, who had joined the Lombards and the Odiers in Lombard Odier, the Pictets, the Ferriers, the Lullins and, possibly most aristocratic of all, the Hentsches. During the nineteenth century they had been joined by families like the Dariers and the Bordiers, but they remained a tiny minority élite. For at last count, Geneva contained over 12,000 'bankers' working for nearly 400 establishments. The biggest were the powerful Geneva branches of the Big Three – for there were no Geneva based banks of any consequence. There were dozens of ethnic banks, and even more branches of major foreign banks; there were even banks whose names proclaimed them to be 'private' – of which the most famous was the Banque Privée belonging to Baron Edmond de Rothschild. And these were surrounded by a penumbra of portfolio managers and real-estate advisers, whose brass plates encrusted the entrance halls of the anonymous office buildings which line the Rue de la Corraterie – supposedly the most respectable financial address in Geneva. (It is characteristic of the scorn displayed by the true Genevan private bankers for such affectations that in recent years both Darier and Pictet – the biggest of them all – have moved up the hill, away from the Rhone and their lesser brethren huddled round the Place Bel Air and the Corraterie.)

The Banking Act of 1934 made a sharp distinction between the private banks and all other kinds. The private banks did not have to publish their balance sheets, nor conform to the same ratios between capital, reserves and assets as lesser institutions. In return they were not allowed to advertise to attract deposits. This restriction did not worry the true private bankers of Basle, Zurich, Lausanne – or Geneva. In essence they were not bankers at all – as can be seen from their premises, in which retail banking operations occupy the corner of the entrance hall, or a cubby-hole tucked away down a corridor. In that sense they are not really 'bankers' at all but virtually pure portfolio managers, like the *gérants de fortune* on the Rue de la Corraterie. Some of these, like Kramer et Cie, manage portfolios of a billion francs or more, are bigger than – and just as reputable as – the smaller 'private bankers'. But the crucial difference is in their legal responsibility. Clients of portfolio managers have no legal redress, however incompetently their funds are handled – according to legend, a French client once lost 50 million francs, only to discover that portfolio managers were not covered by the Banking Act. The private bankers, of course, are covered by the Act. They are also partnerships: the 'general partners' – usually those

members of the family (for they are all family businesses) who
are actively involved in management – assume unlimited
responsibility for its liabilities; and most of them now also
have 'limited partners', mere shareholders and thus liable
only for the capital they have subscribed. These in turn divide
into non-executive members of the family and, in the larger
banks, a corporate 'limited partner' which has invested a
great deal of capital* and serves as a useful reservoir for the
profits which the partners do not wish to distribute.

Given the need for each generation to find the reserves and
the managerial talent to maintain the family tradition, it is not
surprising that a steady stream of private banks have disappeared or changed their status by takeover or absorption
into larger institutions. In the past thirty years their numbers
have halved, leaving fewer than twenty-five independent
private banks in the whole of Switzerland. Roughly the same
number perform the same functions as their independent
brethren but are, legally, subsidiaries of larger groups – the
Swiss Bank Corporation has proved a particularly tactful
bidder for these banks, enabling their former directors to
retain their freedom of action even when transformed into
mere employees. At the other extreme, a few of the bigger
private banks, like Dreyfus in Basle and above all Julius Baer
in Zurich, have converted themselves into ordinary commercial banks, partly to be able to advertise their services, mostly
because they were too big for comfort. This step, however,
creates considerable problems with the tax authorities and the
Banking Commission, which in principle does not permit a
bank's directors to be voting members of its management
board. (Conversely, in 1975, after the Herstatt crisis, one
immensely respectable bank, Tardy Baezner, actually 'privat-
ised' itself, complete with two Tardys, a Baezner, and a
corporate limited partner.)

But not even Tardy Baezner is a member of the Association.
Before the Leclerc crash this had a mere eight members,
Pictet, Lombard Odier, Darier, Bordier, Hentsch, Ferrier-
Lullin, and, staidest of all, Mirabaud. They were all Prot-

* The figures seem large only in relation to the nominal capital invested by
the partners; even the largest 'Pictet Capital' has subscribed only 20 million
francs to the firm's capital base.

estant. (Religion remains an exceptionally touchy subject in private banking circles in Switzerland; if an outsider suggests that Catholic banks or such eminently respectable Jewish banks as Dreyfus have suffered from discrimination, the temperature of the discussion shoots up alarmingly.) Nevertheless the *Groupement* is still a force to be reckoned with. For its members manage between 20 and 25 billion francs' worth of assets, about a half of all the funds managed by all the country's private bankers. Moreover at least three-quarters of their funds are managed on a discretionary basis – three times the percentage of the bigger banks – so they enjoy far greater freedom to invest their funds. Their financial power has been recognised by their membership of one of the two consortia which have been issuing bonds for Swiss official bodies since the end of the last century. (The *Groupement* on its own also underwrites the bonds issued by the City of Geneva itself, a business which, they claim, actually loses them money. For nowadays the terms are always the very finest – they weren't in Léon Nicole's day in the 1930s – and they are consequently obliged to place the bonds in the bank's portfolios, rather than saddling their clients with so unappealing an investment. To their slight surprise, outsiders do not seem as impressed as the bankers expect at this display of public spirit.)

Above all, they represent an attitude, for they have set the tone of Swiss banking since it began. 'We are not only private banks,' said Thierry Barbey of Lombard Odier, 'we are private bankers.' Tardy Baezner claims that it does not really have clients but 'friends who will stay with us', and one of the Hentsch family, when asked whether Hentsch et Cie had branches abroad, replied, 'We do not have branches; we just have friends' – although they also now have brochures in Arabic describing their services. (When I pointed this out to another banker, he replied, 'We assume that the Arab customers *we* want will already know English.' Bernard Hofstetter of the Lausanne bank of Hofstetter, Landolt capped that by saying 'we publish nothing in any language'.) Hentsch, traditionally the financial advisers to the very cream of French society, are reputed not to touch accounts of less than a million francs – a reputation they strongly refute. But in October 1972 young Jacques Hentsch, who was married to a Norwegian wife, was arrested in Gothenburg just after he had boarded a plane for Copenhagen. On him was found over $100,000 in Swedish currency, far greater than the maximum permitted in that heavily regulated (and even more heavily taxed) country. It transpired that most of the money had been entrusted to him by a local industrialist, Arne Lundberg. Rumour added that he was also carrying a little black book giving the names of many of the bank's other local clients. But he simply retired from the bank, and the scandal passed over.

The true private banker is an adviser, a friend, rather than a mere corporate machine geared to performance. In the words of Jacques de Chollet, another Lausanne banker: 'The business of a private banker is not to make a fortune for the client. The client has made a fortune for himself before he comes to you. The main task is to keep the capital – to *try* to keep the capital – in real terms, in hard currencies. That is quite difficult enough.'

For one of the many problems faced by these bankers (and their larger brethren) recently has been the extraordinary strength of the Swiss franc. Of course it was very easy to prove your competence if the client was thinking in terms of the dollar or some other lesser currency – not only North Americans but Latin Americans as well think in dollar terms – but others may reckon their worth in quite arbitrary ways. Peter Baer, who claims that he asks his clients what currency figures in their dreams to get at their fundamental scale of values, once found a Hungarian living in Switzerland who dreamt in marks – the currency in the Hungary of his youth. Moreover all the clients want to see one of the family – 'The solution', says Hans Baer, 'is to call a lot more people Baer'. A rival confidently asserts that a few minutes of his time suffices, provided that his notes are up to date on the health of the client and his nearest and dearest. 'Remember', one private banker told me, 'we are not investment advisers, we are psychologists. When our clients visit us they want above all to talk about themselves; at the end of an hour they've often forgotten completely about their portfolios.' Moreover, the bankers enjoy the inestimable advantage of being on the same wave-length as their clients when it comes to the basic question of tax: 'You are a writer', they told me soothingly, 'there is a great difference between sins of omission and sins of commission, a nuance which we in Switzerland understand very well. Simply failing to report all your earnings to the tax authorities is not a crime here. Surely you as a writer would not report what you earned in another country?'

The talents of Bobby Leclerc were perfectly attuned to an atmosphere in which success depended far more on the confidence you generated than on your abilities as an invest-ment manager. Of course success brings hordes of clients' dependants, often with portfolios far smaller than you would prefer, but they also recommend their friends, for the great trick of the Genevan bankers is to make the client feel that he is honoured merely to be accepted, that he is joining an exclusive club, in whose bosom he may find tact, under-standing, discretion – the double entrances, the coy name-plates merely proclaiming 'P. et Cie', or 'H. et Cie', the elegant but intimate miniature drawing-rooms where the interviews take place, the urbanity and linguistic facility of the partner handling your portfolio, all these attributes are essen-tial.

Not surprisingly, the private bankers of Geneva carry the attitudes which serve them so well during business hours into their private lives. Socially they are still extremely cohesive. Where in Zurich the upper banking classes live on the Berg, the wooded mountain overlooking the city, so Genevan society congregates in the old town, behind dis-creetly impressive stone walls looking down on the city. They congregate also at the local golf club (whose entrance fee, supposedly over $20,000, is probably the biggest in the world). They not only meet at the *Groupement* but they see each other constantly at 'their' club, the Club des Terrasses. 'It's just a pleasant place to be', said George Urban of Lombard Odier; 'yes, of course the press is excluded – just as it is from a London club.' And, like many other aristocracies, they are interrelated. Although arranged marriages are a thing of the past, Jean-Claude Hentsch, for example, has a brother-in-law working at Lombard Odier next door on the more respectable side of the Rue de la Corraterie, and the bankers' private life is 'very much a French family life' according to Urban. 'I have an English wife so I know what the difference is. Far more time is devoted to visiting cousins, aunts and so forth; that leaves less time for social contacts outside the family. As for giving cocktail parties it is not the usual way of entertaining.'

It was a tribute to the overwhelming charm of Bobby Leclerc – 'the most delightful man you could hope to meet', sighed one of his banking brethren – that he managed to insinuate his bank into the *Groupement*. The bank had been founded in 1856 under the name of Dumaray. When the two Leclerc brothers Jean-Pierre and Robert ('but we all called him Bobby') went to work there at the end of World War II it was owned by the L'Harpe family. And it was under their name that it was admitted to the Geneva Stock Exchange in 1964 (the only other candidate at the time was Juan Muñoz's bank, the Banque Genèvoise de Commerce et de Crédit). After Madame L'Harpe's death, the brothers changed the bank's name to their own and in 1970 it was admitted to the *Groupement* – albeit not without some hesitation. At that time the Leclercs were managing portfolios of only 700 million francs, but by 1977, thanks largely to Bobby's charm the figure was over 1,500 million, putting the new boy within striking distance of much better known institutions like Darier or Hentsch.

Apologists for him – and it is a tribute to the spell he cast that they can still be found in Geneva – claim that things started to go wrong only after the death of his brother in 1974. But this is not an adequate explanation. In the words of a fellow banker:

> It was a question of personality. Leclerc had a strong personality. He surrounded himself with young people who were totally devoted to him – no give and take. He could not concede that he had made a mistake. When things started to go wrong – and they do go wrong sometimes for all of us; retrospectively we see how the dollar has fallen, and that we did not a hundred per cent protect our clients – he was not capable of accepting the loss of face. That was why he resorted to falsifying. If a client's account showed a loss, he would quickly move money into it from another client's

account, and with his own hands type out a new statement to give it to the client. 'There you are, you've made a profit.' Sometimes we have to show a loss to our clients.

For Leclerc was nothing if not adventurous, even trying to recover the copper he believed was contained in some old German 88mm guns left stranded by the tides of war in a cave in Crete (the Greek authorities forbade the salvage operation on environmental grounds, and the old 88mm, probably the single most effective weapon deployed in World War II, did not contain much, if any, copper in the first place). But in the end Leclerc's downfall – like Tibor Rosenbaum's – was traceable to a combination of a fatal property development and his diversion of clients' deposits to obscure companies in dubious tax havens.

In the 1960s the private bankers faced a dilemma. Their clients were often extremely keen on investing in property, but they weren't; it was too speculative, too long-term, too illiquid. So numbers of them compromised – often fatally – by acting as middle men between their clients and the developers or by going onto the boards of management companies. This sort of half-hearted involvement, sometimes with developers with foreign projects, was emphatically not a recipe for successful investment. Leonard Hentsch became chairman of Finatourinvest, a Luxemburg company whose Spanish investments were not all successful, the partners of Ferrier-Lullin became deeply involved on behalf of their clients in a development called 'Buckingham Palace' in Monte Carlo, which did not live up to the promise of its name, and the problems of another development in Spain backed by a former partner of a Basle bank were compounded by losses on foreign exchange.

Leclerc, however, looked nearer home, to the Valais, where Lombard Odier were associated with a number of winter sports projects at Anzère near Sion. ('The resort is not a huge success,' said Thierry Barbey of Lombard Odier, 'but it is not a disaster.') So Leclerc was in good company, although, inevitably, given his temperament he led rather than followed his clients. In partnership with two architects he started an ambitious scheme to develop a new ski resort at Aminona, near Crans-sur-Sierre. He hoped to recoup the cost of the infrastructure – including the ski lifts and swimming pools required for such a project – by selling individual apartments in the resort's three towering apartment blocks. Outside financing came from the Union Bank, which invested 16 million francs in Aminona, but in return pocketed sixty per cent of the proceeds whenever an apartment was sold. This did not happen very often. 'Leclerc was fatally lured into becoming a real estate tycoon,' said a fellow banker. 'He invited many people – indeed he once invited all the private bankers of Geneva – for a sports week-end. He proudly showed us his ski centre. It was bad luck, in a way, that the real estate business in Switzerland became difficult. Three things happened: a law was passed* that no foreigner could buy land in Switzerland; the oil crisis meant that in any case few foreigners could afford to; and the tax laws affecting real estate development were tightened up.' To make matters worse Leclerc had underestimated the capital required.

He also had tax problems. In 1972 the inspectors dis-covered that a client of Leclerc's had not paid withholding tax, and a former director pointed out to Leclerc that the same problem could apply to investors in Aminona. It was then, apparently, that he started using Lanco, a Panamanian company set up in 1956 by his brother-in-law, Maurice Gouy, to hold his own personal investments. Lanco's account (number 3501) was transformed into the vehicle for diverting clients' funds into Aminona with, or later, without their knowledge or consent. The procedure was obviously pretty informal, to say the least. (When the accounts were inspected after the crash it was found that figures had been inked and typed in after the event, and when Lanco's account was finally closed, Gouy obligingly signed 247 blank payment orders 'merely', he claimed 'to help my brother-in-law' – a statement naturally contested by Leclerc.) In theory, the manoeuvre saved Leclerc's clients nearly 3 million francs in withholding tax on the 41 millions apparently channelled through account number 3501. Lanco was not the only Panamanian company used by the bank: Bertrand de Muralt, one of Leclerc's

---

* Called the Lex Fugler.

partners, became secretary of Biga (of which Leclerc was chairman), a 'bank within a bank' used by de Muralt to lend to some of his own clients' funds borrowed from others.

Although the bank's auditors had been complaining for some years about the inadequacies of the bank's capital base, it was only at the end of 1976 that the Federal Banking Commission turned nasty; by that time Leclerc's personal finances had become inextricably enmeshed with those of the bank (a year after the bankruptcy the examiners still could not disentangle the muddle). The Commission pointed out that Leclerc's personal account was in debit to the tune of 6.4 million francs, and only thirty-eight per cent of this figure was covered by securities. This was illegal, said the Commission, and the position had to be rectified immediately. Within a few weeks the bank was able to report that the debt had been reduced to a mere 300,000 francs.

Worse was to follow: that same month came the most notorious assassination in modern French political history, that of the Prince de Broglie, a member of one of France's most distinguished families, and himself one of the founders of the political party created round the then French President, Valéry Giscard d'Estaing. The Interior Minister, Prince Poniatowski, in a panicky outburst immediately accused some petty criminals of the murder, but the scandal grew, and attention soon switched to de Broglie's involvement with a Luxembourg company, Sodetex, allegedly connected with the arms trade and also with the Matesa scandal, which had rocked the Spanish government of General Franco several years earlier. Leclerc was named as a director of Sodetex, a position he claimed he had accepted light-heartedly enough after meeting de Broglie at a shooting party. When Leclerc went to Luxembourg he found that his name had been attached to all sorts of decisions taken at board meetings he swore he had never attended. French clients began to worry, to check on their position with the bank and to discover that they had lost money.

But the collapse came only on Thursday, 5 May 1977, when the bank's auditors discovered that Leclerc and his partners had committed the ultimate sin for private bankers: they had used clients' funds (channelled through yet a third Panamanian company, Cobie) to balance Leclerc's own account with the bank. By the next day, the Banking Commission had decided that closure was inevitable and convened a meeting for the Saturday morning, to include all the other members of the *Groupement*, together with representatives from the Union Bank. It was a frightening time. One leading private banker told me, 'I didn't sleep for the eighty hours following the discovery ... it was terrible. I'd given up smoking eighteen months before, but I chain-smoked right through that week-end. On Saturday we sat down at seven in the morning to try and untangle the situation and didn't finish until 3 a.m. on Sunday', when the bank applied for *sursis bancaire* – the type of moratorium prescribed in the 1934 Banking Act to provide some breathing space for an afflicted institution.

Naturally every private banker in Geneva feared the worst – a run on his bank which could so easily lead to his personal financial ruin. 'The Monday morning was the worst,' the banker continued. 'My partners and I arrived at the bank at 7 a.m., expecting a rush of clients come to claim their money. We'd scraped together all the liquid funds we could lay our hands on to try to stem the tide. We waited and waited ... 7.30 ... 8 o'clock ... and still as the morning wore on no one arrived. Then, late in the afternoon, we felt the first repercussions – a trickle of Leclerc's former clients, transferring to us.'

For the rest all was anticlimax; by the end of the week, the news from Geneva – which concerned, after all, a bank that had hitherto been unknown to the general public – was completely overshadowed by the press conference given by the Crédit Suisse at which the spectacular losses from its Chiasso branch were announced. But the results lingered on: tragically Bertrand de Muralt shot himself with his army revolver and the body of another executive, Charles Bouchard, was found at the bottom of a lake. It was soon apparent that Leclerc's bank was hopelessly bankrupt: a credit of 10 million francs had been suggested at the week-end meeting, but the eventual deficit amounted to nearer 400 million. After bankruptcy (*sursis concordataire*) was declared in January 1978 Leclerc appeared in front of the president of the local commercial court, that same Judge Pagan whose zeal had led him into

such problems when he had arrested Robert Vesco. Pagan
sent Leclerc to prison as well: but Leclerc had to have open
heart surgery and in November 1978 his lawyer pleaded that
'justice can at least recognise an accused man's right to die at
home'. By April 1979 Leclerc was allowed out of prison, and
his health seemingly improved enough for him to renew his
interest in racing (one of his former clients remarked that 'he
is living better than us' on seeing Leclerc at a restaurant in
Gstaad during some particularly interesting show jumping
trials). The bank's creditors were able to get back only nine
per cent of the amount the bank owed them; while Leclerc's
3,000 odd clients were taken on by a subsidiary of Barclays
Bank for a small consideration.

Since the Leclerc crash – and the wheels of Genevan justice
have not yet ground their way to completing the case against
him – the other bankers have all agonisingly reappraised their
position. Some have simply stayed put, but the three biggest
have all taken the opportunity to carry through long thought
out plans to diversify into managing corporate pension funds
as well as the personal fortunes of private clients. Lombard
Odier has gone it alone, Pictet joined up with the Mellon
Bank from Pittsburgh ('Why? because they're the best', said
the man from Pittsburgh), and in July 1979, after a long
struggle, Hentsch was finally allowed by the Banking Commission to take three Arab billionaires into partnership in a
new joint venture, in which, naturally, Hentsch and the other
Swiss partners have a sixty per cent controlling interest. In
Zurich Julius Baer broke with the most fundamental traditions of private banking by openly launching – nay advertising
– their investment management services in Britain. But after
the Leclerc affair nothing was the same – even in Geneva.

In July 1978 the partners in Ferrier-Lullin, the oldest
established private bank of them all, sold sixty per cent of
their bank to that most seductive of wooers, the Swiss Bank
Corporation, for 60 million francs. To them the step seemed
logical: M. Lullin had no heirs, the other partners were able to
retain their positions – and banking secrecy ensured that the
parent would not know what the newly acquired subsidiary
was up to. In any other financial centre – even Zurich, even
Basle – the sale would have been seen as a sensible (and

highly profitable) step; in Geneva it ranked with the Leclerc crash as a betrayal of the private banking ethos. Not that it has affected the bank. It still looks and feels the same, does the same job as it has since Revolutionary times. There is still a Ferrier around – and the only sign of a revolution is that a woman is managing some of the clients' portfolios.

3 / The resistible rise of Ernst Kuhrmeier

Chiasso is a dreary little frontier town, almost totally dependent on its rôle as a major repository for capital fleeing from Italy, one symbolised by the presence of fourteen banks in a town of only 10,000 inhabitants. It lacks the historical *raison d'être* of the better known towns of Italian-speaking Switzerland, like Lugano and Locarno, holiday resorts on sparkling lakes, names evoking the conferences held there in the 1920s to solve all Europe's problems. Chiasso has prospered since World War II simply because it is the first stop in Switzerland on the road from Milan north to Como and the frontier. And in the generation after 1945 it vied with Lugano, fifteen miles to the north, as a banking centre, serving not merely the Ticino, Switzerland's only Italian-speaking canton, but, far more, the financial needs of northern Italy. Milan is less than an hour away, and within a hundred miles live 12 million of Italy's most prosperous inhabitants, including precisely those classes most likely to require a Swiss bank. The traffic was not new; nor were the bankers.

The SBC had taken over a bank in Chiasso in 1908. Five years later Crédit Suisse opened its first ever branch in Lugano (previous expansion outside Zurich had been through the takeover of local institutions). In 1917 the Banco di Roma opened a branch there, and three years later the Union Bank, characteristically, established itself in the Ticino by taking over a local bank with branches in both Lugano and Locarno (opening another branch in Chiasso early in World War II). As the first profits from the Italian economic miracle of the 1950s began to trickle over the Swiss frontier, the SBC finally opened a branch in Lugano, which by the mid 1960s had overtaken Basle to become Switzerland's third most important banking centre, housing not only branches of the big Swiss and Italian banks, but a dozen newly founded ethnic institutions as well. As an ever increasing number of Italians prospered and wanted to export their surplus capital, so the market became less sophisticated, and it became even more important to have a presence at Chiasso. In 1955 Crédit Suisse took the plunge, and opened the branch that was later to become famous as the scene of the 'Chiasso scandal'.

When this exploded, twenty-two years later, it represented the biggest loss – at least a billion francs, around half a billion dollars – ever suffered by a single bank that continued in business; other disasters have invariably resulted in bankruptcy or, at the very least, loss of the stricken institution's independence. The explosion and its aftermath – including the trial of the branch's principal officers two years later – laid open the interior of the Swiss financial house as brutally and as revealingly as a bomb can expose the intimate domestic arrangements behind a previously discreet suburban façade. The squalor, moral and physical, lurking behind long drawn lace curtains has provided the material for many famous plays and novels. The gradual – and inevitably only partial – unveiling of the reality behind the affairs of the Crédit Suisse branch in the Piazza Indipendenza provided an unprecedented opportunity to explore the hidden face of Swiss banking.

Over a period of over fifteen years, the branch's manager, the late Ernst Kuhrmeier, built up an enormous 'bank within a bank' based on Texon, a holding company in Liechtenstein. By the time of the final reckoning Texon had grown to include Italy's largest wine and food business (responsible for forty per cent of Italy's wine exports), a number of luxury hotels, a major tourist resort near Venice, a considerable international transport business, and dozens of other businesses in toys, plastics and other industries. It even embraced a well-

TheThe resistible rise of Ernst Kuhrmeier 301

respected engineering company in Switzerland which Crédit Suisse was proud to have as a client, unaware that by then the bank actually owned the company. By 1977 Crédit Suisse had, without realising it, guaranteed the investment of nearly 2 billion francs in what it now calls its 'Italian empire' and had to write off half that enormous amount as soon as it had taken a close look at the conglomerate Kuhrmeier had built up on its behalf.

Chiasso was a 'frontier' town in which immense success was apparently available to the bold and fearless. Crédit Suisse badly needed to seize this opportunity. For it had stagnated, it had dropped from its former pre-eminence, passed in size by the thrusting Union Bank and also trailing its equally staid and respectable rival, the SBC. Crédit Suisse remained the bank for the Protestant *haute bourgeoisie* of Zurich, whose money it managed, and it remained close to many of the major industrial concerns of German-speaking Switzerland. But it was terribly slow to expand its network, either through opening branches or taking over smaller banks. The Chiasso branch was only the second it had opened since 1945, established before the bank was represented in such important centres as Winterthur or Locarno.

The branch's first manager, running a modest establishment with a mere dozen employees, was one Rino Pessina, seconded from the Lugano branch. With him came Ernst Kuhrmeier, son of a former Crédit Suisse employee, himself sufficiently well considered to have spent a year at the Swiss National Bank. Within two years Kuhrmeier had manoeuvred so cleverly that Pessina returned to Lugano and he took over the management himself. The profits Kuhrmeier reported apparently justified his appointment: he built up the branch so that each of its 280 employees generated profits three times those created by the average Crédit Suisse employee. Kuhrmeier's dynamism was vital to the bank's head office, which used him as a spur to lesser managers, frequently citing his profit record, as his branch's results outstripped those of all the bank's other branches outside Geneva – even those of Basle and Lausanne, cities of far greater significance than Chiasso on any normal scale of business values.

In a country where the Italian minority is rather despised,

it was not unusual for a German speaker to take the top post in an Italian-speaking branch, although it did not help that Kuhrmeier never really hit it off personally with his Italian clientele. Very often they were industrialists of consequence, used to treating the usually rather junior Swiss bank employees with whom they dealt with some disdain.

This attitude was not appreciated by Kuhrmeier. He was a large, Teutonic-looking bull of a man, choleric, dominating, autocratic: 'he had this German thoroughness combined with an Italian imagination and temperament – a fatal combination', said one observer. And he had an ideal field to operate in. For the two decades of his managerial reign coincided with the maximum outflow of capital from Italy, which grew steadily with the political uncertainties of the 1960s and 1970s. Sometimes the Italian authorities turned a blind eye, and Italian banks often collaborated in the flow. Sometimes the arrangements were sophisticated. (Bernie Cornfeld's salesmen used an elaborate system of bankers' drafts to transfer their clients' funds from a bank in Como to the Finter Bank in Chiasso.) But mostly they were crude enough: every Wednesday for years on end Kuhrmeier's right-hand man, Claudio Laffranchi, would drive to Milan and spend an afternoon in a private room at the Banco di Roma or the state-owned Banca Commerciale Italiana, receiving currency from wealthy Italians. They had to trust him as a representative of Switzerland's most respectable bank, for he did not provide them with anything as damning as a receipt.

It was Kuhrmeier's impatience which provided the initial impetus for the creation of Texon. In the early 1960s the Italian textile industry was going through one of its periodic crises and Kuhrmeier's superiors were unwilling to provide loans for anyone in the sector. Kuhrmeier was, rightly, confident that the Italian flair for design and promotion (combined with Italy's then low wage rates) would enable at least a select band of entrepreneurs to buck the trend, and was looking for ways to help them. Then, confronted in his office one day by an Italian industrialist eager to leave his funds with Crédit Suisse, he came up with the solution: a bank-within-a-bank, fuelled by some at least of the funds entrusted to him, but not subject to the – to him – idiotic restrictions imposed by head office.

The technique he used was not unusual: he founded Texon as a *Finanzanstalt* in Liechtenstein with the help of his friends and neighbours, the law firm of Franco Maspoli (who died in 1974) and Alfred Noseda. In his day, Noseda's father, John, had been one of the most highly respected lawyers in the Ticino, regarded as such even by Nello Celio, another lawyer of Ticinese origins, who was a friend of his. Shortly after the war John Noseda was murdered by a local tradesman who accused him of being responsible for his ruin. Thanks to his father's unimpeachable reputation, Alfredo was able to attract reputable associates, including Dr. Elbio Gada, a former director of the cantonal tax office, and Dr. Alessandro Villa, who had previously been in charge of the cantonal company registry.

Texon was duly registered at the largest and most reputable '*Anstalt* manufacturer' in Vaduz, that of Dr. Peter Ritter*. The intimacy of the connection between the bank and its legal advisers was symbolised by the fact that the two offices, in neighbouring buildings, possessed an interconnecting door. This gave access from the corridor just outside Dr. Villa's office to the next stretch of corridor in the building, just outside the office of Sergio Catenazzi, Kuhrmeier's confidential assistant, who was in charge of administering the bank's thousands of investment accounts.

To get Italians to invest their funds in Texon required some ingenuity. Swiss banks were in the habit of establishing *Anstalts* to conduct their private affairs: and they also guided their clients into fiduciary deposits, supposedly in banks with impeccable reputations. This was crucial: although such deposits avoided the thirty-five per cent Swiss withholding tax on dividend and interest payments, they were not guaranteed by the client's bank (under Swiss tax law, if the bank provided such a guarantee, the money was treated as though it had been deposited in a Swiss bank and was thus liable both to tax, and to the increasing restrictions placed on such

* In 1975 – only eighteen months before Texon's collapse – it was transferred to the office of Franz Gstohl. His son and John Noseda – Alfredo's son – had been friends at the University of Geneva.

deposits.) Kuhrmeier combined the two ideas. He persuaded his clients to place the funds as fiduciary deposits with Texon: but to get them to do so, he had – on his own initiative – to provide Crédit Suisse's guarantee to all the sums deposited in the tiny *Anstalt*.

With the profits he started a portfolio of investments, which he could use as security to persuade his head office to provide Texon – allegedly merely a client of the law office next door – with official Crédit Suisse guarantees, albeit of only up to £3.5 million, and to cover, in part anyway, the commitment he had already undertaken in the bank's name.

The Texon empire grew as Kuhrmeier and his lieutenants expanded their investment portfolio and as they were forced to take equity interests in client companies whose affairs had gone sour. The crucial dividing line between merely supplying funds and actually controlling a company was probably passed for the first time with Salumificio Milano, one of Italy's largest sausage and salami companies. This had been a normal commercial client, not of Texon, but of the branch itself, but in the mid 1960s it got into difficulties and defaulted on a bill of exchange. Rather than admit the potential loss to Zurich, Kuhrmeier transformed the amount due into a loan from Texon. Later Salumificio Milano became probably the first company in which Texon became a major equity shareholder, albeit under duress.

As the bloom faded on the Italian miracle, the same pattern was followed in three major investment areas: wine and food, plastics, and a tourist development on the island of Albarella, fifty miles south of Venice. By the early 1970s Texon was technically insolvent, but Kuhrmeier doubled and redoubled the stakes, largely, it seems, to provide backing for the individual ambitions of impetuous entrepreneurs. The biggest investment was in the conglomerate known as Winefood. Here the involvement started, innocuously enough, with a loan to the widow of Luigi Calissano, a Piedmontese winemaker; Texon went on to make further loans to the owners of Chianti Melini (producers of two well-known chiantis, Granaio and Selvanella) and equally reputable brand-leaders in Frascati and Valpolicella. By the end of the 1960s enough of the loans had gone sour for a rescue operation to be required. Dr. Villa came up with the idea of consolidating the wine companies now under Texon's wing with Salumificio, under the overall management of an Italian wine salesman, Alberto di Marchi. Described by friends as 'charming, though scatter-brained', di Marchi proceeded to use Texon's money to turn Winefood into the biggest conglomerate of its kind in Italy. He invested heavily in vast wineries – which proved invaluable during the 1970s in boosting the reputation, and thus the sales, of Italian wines throughout the world – especially in the United States, and extended its interests to include the leading hotel in the smart spa town of Albano, and Milan's smartest (and most expensive) restaurant. At home he endowed Chiasso with a smart new hotel, the Corso, designed for executives on expense accounts.

Di Marchi's major rival within Texon was Giancarlo Rizzi, one of Kuhrmeier's closest associates, who was put in charge of Texon's rapidly expanding interests in plastics and toys. Here again the first involvement was seemingly harmless: Texon's purchase of a Milanese plastics and toy manufacturer called Ampaglas from one of Kuhrmeier's closest friends, an Italian businesswoman called Nelly Cacciami. Rizzi, as confirmed an empire-builder as di Marchi, bought up dozens of other companies in toys, packaging, furnishings and baby nurseryware, including a major subsidiary in France, Ampa-France, and names well-known in Italy like Furga, Grazioli Giocattoli, and Perego Pines. In the ten years to the end of 1976 Texon spent well over $100 million on Rizzi's purchases alone.

In a spending spree that owed much to Kuhrmeier's growing reputation as a soft touch (combined with his persistent unfamiliarity with Italian business ways) Texon bought up dozens more companies. At least one – Norditalia, an insurance company which had been technically in liquidation for several years at the time of the purchase – was acquired under pressure tantamount to blackmail, that the truth about Texon would be brought into the open if the companies were not bought. Nevertheless some of the purchases were relatively sound: the thirty or more small transport companies specialising in the carriage of fruit and vegetables in the Gottardo Ruffoni group eventually proved very viable, and there were a number of Swiss companies within the group, including some property interests, a couple of hotels and two companies, Duap and Nencki, both successful manufacturers of specialist components for auto engines.

But the third major investment created even bigger problems. An ambitious scheme to develop the island of Albarella, it was originally brought to Kuhrmeier by Armando Pedrazzini, a former partner of the Maspoli-Noseda law firm. He subsequently became the Swiss lawyer for Michele Sindona – whose dealings with Kuhrmeier remain obscure. Under the original scheme, the project was due to be virtually self-financing. Investors in this exclusive new resort (on an island which was, at the time, a mosquito-infested mess) would, supposedly, buy their own building plots and houses through Chiasso-based companies which would actually own the property. Nevertheless, Crédit Suisse's head office back in Zurich rejected Pedrazzini's original request for a substantial development loan.

So Kuhrmeier used Texon to finance the scheme. In the end the idea was squashed by the Guardia di Finanza, the Italian financial police, probably tipped off by one of the many enemies Pedrazzini had accumulated during his wheeling and dealing career. Deprived of their tax attractions a sudden flood of 'Albarella Club Holding' shares soon appeared on the market. The scheme had virtually collapsed, leaving Texon to take it over as by far its largest creditor. But the project was incomplete: like so many similarly ambitious holiday projects designed to appeal to a wealthy clientele, it had depended on an enormous initial investment in infrastructure – starting with an eight mile causeway from the mainland.

By the mid-1970s, then, Crédit Suisse was guaranteeing deposits made to finance an enormous and equally ramshackle empire. Kuhrmeier's ambition appeared limitless: through Pedrazzini, he even toyed with the idea of rescuing Sindona's doomed American bank, Franklin National, at a time when, even if the Texon empire had been profitable in lire terms (which it manifestly wasn't), it would still have been a major loser on capital account. For the early 1970s, the period when its investments reached their peak, coincided with the biggest currency upheavals since the 1930s: and the lire rested at the bottom of a league headed by the Swiss franc. In the eight years before 1977, the lire dropped in value by seventy per cent against the Swiss franc. At the same time the number of people who knew about the links in the Kuhrmeier chain – from the branch to the law office to Texon to its numerous subsidiaries – grew. Everyone in Chiasso knew of the connection, and neither of the other two major banks would have anything to do with any individual or company connected with the empire.

As early as 1967 the other bankers in the town complained that the high interest rates being offered by Texon – through Kuhrmeier – constituted unfair competition. Following a noisy meeting of the Chiasso Bankers' Association, Kuhrmeier promised to mend his ways, but ignored his obligations.

Given the known close association between Texon and Crédit Suisse, not to mention the amount of money, the growing size of the empire, and the numbers of people involved, the central mystery of the Chiasso affair is how it lasted for fifteen years.

For Kuhrmeier made no attempt to keep a low profile. He bought a luxury villa at Castagnola, a smart residential suburb of Chiasso, and he was lavish in his gifts to his fellow bank employees. Hampers were routinely sent every Christmas to Zurich, and he would slip a couple of hundred dollars' worth of lire to the wives of fellow executives when they went shopping with the Kuhrmeiers in Milan.

Kuhrmeier was so confident of promotion to a major position at head office that in the mid-1970s he even bought a plot of land near Zurich in anticipation of his future housing needs. The explanations start with the seduction of the bank's internal auditors on their annual tour of inspection. According to Max Mabillard and Roger de Weck in their book on the scandal: 'Before the auditors were allowed to poke their noses into the loan department, Kuhrmeier invited them on a courtesy visit to an important client ... by this tactic the morning was lost in polite chatter. At midday everyone was taken to a grotto, Ticino's colloquial name for a typical country eating place. Good fare was washed down with liberal amounts of merlot, the local red wine, which helped to make the atmosphere congenial ... by afternoon the auditors were in a mellow mood. However, since Kuhrmeier had invited them out for an evening of "fireworks", the temptation was to spend the after-lunch work hours recuperating for that night's festivities.' These generally included a dinner at Texon's own Hôtel Corso, after which 'it was not rare after a night of festivities that an auditor found upon returning to his room at the Corso an appetising young woman in his bed.'

The orthodox, less romantic version of the bank's astonishing and continuing ignorance of what was going on attributes the blame to the increasing laxity of banks' control systems as they expanded at an unprecedented rate during the 1960s. In an era when profit and expansion were the keywords, the auditing department became a refuge for the bank's failures, and even without the treats described so graphically by Mabillard and de Weck, the auditors would be extremely reluctant to question the policies of the bank's rising star. Moreover, they lacked imagination. They announced their arrival in advance, thus enabling guilty dossiers to be trundled through to the next door offices to the tender care of Messrs. Maspoli and Noseda. And if they did sound the alarm signals, they were heard but faintly in Zurich, where head office saw Texon as mortals view the moon: they never saw its hidden face.

This is getting nearer the truth, but it conceals an absolutely crucial psychological point: that in the back of their minds a number of senior executives must have been aware, at quite an early stage, of the incestuously close connections between Texon, the Maspoli-Noseda law office, and Kuhrmeier. The likeliest interpretation (and one stressed by Mabillard and de Weck) is that they thought of Texon as Kuhrmeier's 'little bit on the side', the instrument he was using to salt away a nest-egg to provide for his future financial needs. To them this was not an ideal arrangement, since it involved the bank's credit, or at least its guarantee, but it was not unprecedented, and it couldn't easily be rectified, given Kuhrmeier's unique position within the bank. 'I was the branch manager above all suspicion,' he told the court at his trial. (Revealingly he blamed the bank's head office for losing its nerve: Texon, to him, fell into the category of internal problems which could have been solved without any public fuss. One shudders to think what other scandals may have been hushed up if other banks have adopted this cavalier attitude.)

But the mandarins at head office had misread the situation. Kuhrmeier was not building up a comfortable nest egg for his old age: he took only minimal sums out of Texon. To impress the rest of the world – and serve his personal ambitions – he was building up an empire, and one that got out of hand well before the final crash. The blame, therefore, lies not with the control systems or with the people who operated them, but with the assumptions underlying the lack of curiosity shown by his superiors, the toleration of the extra-marital financial affairs above a certain level in the bank. They carefully did not try to find out what was happening on the dark side of the Texon moon because they wanted to keep Kuhrmeier, however much of a cowboy they suspected him to be.

The central figure within the bank in the Chiasso affair was its chief inspector, Joseph Müller. Grim, taciturn, renowned and feared as a hard man given to fearsome inquisitions of suspect employees, he doubled as head of the bank's security systems (he also lectured to the local business school on bank security). It was he, for instance, who handed over the ransom money when a Fiat executive was kidnapped in 1977. In 1966 he descended on Chiasso with a team of senior inspectors and for several months they went through the branch's accounts with a fine-tooth comb. They could not have escaped examining the connection with Texon, for the *Anstalt* was already the branch's largest customer and, moreover, was drawing its money largely from other client accounts. This inspection was by far the most thorough to which the branch was subjected during Kuhrmeier's tenure of office, yet obviously the Müller team did not find the Texon relationship sufficient of an anomaly to warrant any restraining action.

Müller became a friend of Kuhrmeier, and, three years after the inspection, was able to benefit from the friendship. Müller was building a house for himself; costs had got out of hand and he was unwilling to go to his own bank manager for additional funds. But Alfredo Noseda obliged, presumably with money supplied by Texon (the loan was for eight years, and the repayment was made on schedule in March 1977, while Müller was back in Chiasso adding up the damage caused by Texon to Crédit Suisse).

Müller's inspectors may have overlooked the significance of the Texon connection, but the Swiss tax inspectors didn't when they embarked on an unannounced audit three years later. They were looking for breaches of the withholding tax regulations, and, because the branch had guaranteed the Texon loans, it was indeed breaking the law. Tax should have been paid, and the inspectors deemed the matter urgent enough to report it to Zurich. Head office paid 500,000 francs in back taxes, warned Kuhrmeier to submit to the bank's legal department any future propositions submitted by the next door legal neighbours, and finished by emphasising the importance the bank attached to avoiding further difficulties with the tax authorities. In reply, Kuhrmeier sent one of his rare letters (for obvious reasons he preferred the telephone) to Hans Escher, the executive responsible for the branch.

Escher's problem was that he was himself impeccably honest and could not conceive of any fellow employee indulging in any illicit business. So when he visited Chiasso the next year and heard from disgruntled competitors about the elevated interest rates being offered by Texon he contented himself with a general warning forbidding the bank's branches from guaranteeing fiduciary deposits. Thus form was satisfied, even if the reality remained as it had been before.

But knowledge of the Texon connection was not confined to the tax inspectors and head office. The outside executive with the most detailed knowledge of what was going on in Chiasso was undoubtedly Robert Jeker, now one of the seven members of the bank's executive board (albeit the one in charge of the least significant rag-bag of departments.) Jeker is the very image of a Crédit Suisse man: reserved, polished, a freemason, a major in the army. Early in his high-flying career with Crédit Suisse, Jeker worked for two years, from 1964 to 1966, in the loan department of the Chiasso branch. He claimed later that he had assumed that Texon was merely a financial group belonging to the law office next door. However, it is difficult to see how he avoided knowing the truth. He handled the mail addressed to Texon as a matter of course, and was responsible for the branch's most sensitive client, known as the Travelling Turk, a member of one of Turkey's richest families who had no less than 100 million francs deposited with Texon, as well as money on deposit with the branch itself. (It was Jeker who ensured that only the Travelling Turk had the power to sign for his Texon deposits, whereas other members of the family could be trusted as signatories where the deposits with the bank itself were concerned.)

Jeker's involvement grew more complex when Kuhrmeier had to take a direct interest in the Salumificio Milano business, and Jeker was an early member of the Texon-appointed board. By 1969 the fast rising Jeker was Crédit Suisse's manager at Basle and, like Müller, found himself asking Kuhrmeier for a loan – in this instance to buy the land on which to build a house. Jeker later explained that he asked Kuhrmeier for the 250,000 francs from Texon because he was looking for discretion. Moreover the loan was for a mere three years, was properly secured on Jeker's insurance policies and, he claimed, he did not want to become entangled in the complications which would have ensued had he borrowed the money directly from the bank. It was only in 1974 that Crédit Suisse's internal regulations were tightened to prevent any further loans from – supposedly – outside sources.

(At the trial ten years later, Jeker claimed that he had asked Kuhrmeier whether Texon could oblige one of his industrial clients with a loan, for the same reasons which had led Kuhrmeier to set up Texon in the first place – he believed the loan would be good business, but it contravened the bank's lending policies. According to Jeker, Kuhrmeier claimed that Texon was in liquidation and Jeker believed him, even though he himself was simultaneously borrowing money from the same source.)

The third internal beneficiary of Texon's lax lending policy was a potentially dangerous critic within the Chiasso branch itself, Meinrad Perler, a headstrong young securities analyst from French-speaking Fribourg, enticed away from the UBS by Kuhrmeier in 1963 to run the branch's securities department. Although Perler became a director of Ampa-France, the

French subsidiary of Texon's toys and plastics empire, he was always suspicious of the connection between Texon and the bank, and in 1972 he had a flaming row with Kuhrmeier about Texon in front of the branch's senior management. Kuhrmeier silenced Perler by telling him that Texon was simply a client and that head office was fully aware of the connection. Like Müller and Jeker, Perler benefited from Texon's generosity, in this case to cover up losses on unfortunate stock market speculations – and Kuhrmeier used his influence with Müller to prevent a hostile report on Perler's personal finances from reaching his superiors.

Nevertheless Perler could not be completely silenced. In 1976 Sergio Marzano, a young electronics specialist in the branch, decamped with 2.5 million francs entrusted to him in connection with the computerisation of the branch's business. Perler went to the police, and Kuhrmeier was naturally furious at the possibility that they might probe too deeply. Perler then plucked up his courage: he was due for promotion to the rank of director, but before accepting the promotion he warned Bernard Henggeler, Müller's successor as the bank's chief inspector, about the growing menace presented by Texon, both when Henggeler visited Chiasso to investigate the Marzano affair and at a bank dinner where they found themselves seated together. Getting no response, he gave up hope that his superiors would curb Kuhrmeier's activities and accepted the promotion, though in a separate letter he warned Kuhrmeier's boss, Serge Demiéville, about the Texon business.

By this time Texon was becoming something of an all-purpose slush fund, with political overtones. According to Kuhrmeier he was even forced to pay off outraged German clients of the local political hero Nello Celio, who had been the lawyer to a property company, Immobiliare Letizia, before his election as Federal Councillor in 1968. Celio's German clients had allegedly blackmailed him, demanding their money back to prevent them complaining about their investment. Even if these accusations were unfounded, the connections between Texon and the cantonal Christian Democrat party were genuinely close. Fabio Vassalli, the head of the cantonal administration, had deposited 130,000 francs with Texon. In return, he received 7,800 francs annually in interest and 30,000 francs each from Texon and from Crédit Suisse directly. But this was as nothing compared with the cost of extricating the bank, as well as Vassalli, from an audacious piece of blackmail practised by a well-known local smuggler, Luigi Croci Torti. (His route, known locally as the Ho Chi Minh trail, was by a side road leading through the little village of Stabio). Croci Torti became a major client of the branch, couldn't repay his loans, and in 1975 stood accused of fraud. He promptly warned Vassalli (and the president of the local Christian Democratic party, Alfredo Stefani) that 'if he was a smuggler so were the bankers' and that he would reveal the whole Texon story at his trial. His loans were repaid, and he was bought off. The cost, over 20 million francs, was borne by Texon and, in theory, was to enable him to settle his family comfortably in Brazil – unfortunately for all concerned, he didn't go and was still around when the whole story came to light.

By 1976 these scandals were public enough for Philippe de Weck, the director-general of UBS, to send to Hans Wuffli, Escher's successor as general manager responsible for the Ticino branches, a copy of a note which provided the bank's guarantee on monies destined to be placed as fiduciary deposits with Texon. This unusual warning was reinforced a few months later when the great Alfred Schaefer found himself sharing a car with the then chairman of Crédit Suisse, Felix Schulthess, on their way to a board meeting. Schaefer warned Schulthess to keep an eye on 'that fellow Kuhrmeier of yours'. But somehow the warnings got lost in the overstretched bank's internal machinery and no action was taken.

4 / The astonishing resilience of Crédit Suisse

Kuhrmeier's downfall was triggered not by any of the numerous warnings conveyed over the years to Crédit Suisse's top management, but by the troubles of that disreputable establishment, the Weisscredit of Lugano – which had already figured in the Congressional hearings in 1968–70. In December 1976 its management found that its own *Anstalt*, Finanz-und-Vertrauenshandelsanstalt, which held most of the bank's assets, was in difficulties. The general manager, looking for a potential buyer for Weisscredit, naturally approached Serge Demiéville, who had taken over responsibility for the Crédit Suisse's Ticinese branches from Wuffli the previous spring. For Demiéville himself had worked for Weisscredit until 1968. During the subsequent discussions, the Weisscredit directors brushed aside ideas that their *Anstalt* would be a problem to Crédit Suisse, since the latter possessed such an important *Anstalt* of its own in the shape of Texon. At the end of January 1977 Demiéville included this remark in his report to the bank's executive committee, at which point Oswald Aeppli, one of the Crédit Suisse's five general managers, blew his top and angrily demanded that the full truth about Texon be discovered. (He may also have been anxious to inherit a clean slate when he took over the chairmanship from Schulthess at the end of March.) At the beginning of March Henggeler was sent to Chiasso – armed by Wuffli with a copy of the guarantee given him the year before by de Weck. A series of interviews, notably with Perler, confirmed his suspicions. On the 18 March Kuhrmeier was summoned to Zurich, and from that point on, despite his assurances that Texon's problems were purely temporary, a mere matter of liquidity, discovery was inevitable. Müller was sent off to Chiasso – where he startled the bank's employees by interviewing them with a pistol prominently displayed on the desk.

It took him less than a month to winkle out the full story which had evaded his whole team over a decade earlier, and by the 12 April he was back in Zurich, having submitted his report to the central management.

By that time the Ticinese rumour mill was racing away, set off by a local panic which worried the locals far more than the troubles of Crédit Suisse. For on the 2 March the Federal Banking Commission ordered the Weisscredit to close its door. In the words of the *Financial Times*: 'Most of the Weisscredit's small depositors, including local shopkeepers and Italian immigrants who feared for their savings, held public protest meetings in an area where public protests are as rare as princesses and Ferraris are common.' Crédit Suisse's first reaction to the report was cool enough: Kuhrmeier and his trusted associate Claudio Laffranchi, together with the wretched Perler, were suspended, and on the 14 April the bank put out a laconic and utterly misleading press announcement. This stated blandly that enquiries carried out by the bank's internal auditors had revealed problems concerning the profitability and liquidity of an 'important foreign client of the bank's Chiasso branch (a financial holding company with investments in Europe and overseas)'. The statement went on to admit that the branch's management had concealed the situation, had gone beyond its mandate and had consequently been suspended while investigations were completed. The bank finished by assuring the public that it would be kept fully in touch with developments, little realising how literally, explosively, true this soothing formula would turn out to be.

The announcement did little to stem the rumours – although the immediate journalistic estimate that the bank's losses would amount to 250 million francs proved conservative (as so many apparently wild journalistic guesses have proved to be in the long history of Swiss banking).

In the next ten days the head of the bank's legal service, Hugo von der Crone, was despatched to Liechtenstein to take formal, legal control of Texon on the bank's behalf, but it was not until Sunday 23 April that the lid blew off the Chiasso kettle. The bank issued a statement far more honest and complete than its previous explanation, spelling out the extent of the Texon empire, and ending up with the remark that the bank 'remained in close touch with the authorities conducting the legal enquiries'. The contact was not close enough. That day the local prosecuting attorney at Lugano (whose assistant, ironically enough, was the young John Noseda) interrogated the three senior managers of the Chiasso branch and then placed them under arrest. By the next morning the story had reached Zurich. The moment could not have been worse chosen. Hans Wuffli had taken over as chief general manager only at the end of March. He had been a leading light in the attempts made in the previous few years to provide the bank with a greater sense of urgency and dynamism. His ideas had largely been blocked by long entrenched habits and personalities on the board and in the top management, but his attempts had also made him numerous enemies within the bank, enmities reinforced by his arrogance and aloofness. In the words of Oswald Aeppli, 'he was not always very fortunate in dealing with people and many ... were vexed by his self-confidence and, at times, intolerance ... This trait may have contributed to the fact that he did not take sufficient notice of the warning signals.' The same bland indifference had been displayed in early March by Felix Schulthess when, in his last annual statement as chairman, he had rejoiced in the record results achieved by the bank in 1976.

On Black Monday Schulthess and Wuffli clearly panicked at a meeting convened by the Swiss National Bank and attended by directors of both the other big banks. Late that evening the SNB telephoned round a brief, laconic statement, which for the first time indicated the sheer size of the problem. In the course of the discussions, it revealed, the National Bank, the UBS and the SBC had spontaneously offered a credit of 3 billion francs to the Crédit Suisse should this prove necessary. This was presumably designed to show the underlying soundness of Switzerland's banking structure, but, like so many such statements, merely confirmed the worst of people's fears.

At 7.30 the next morning the general management of Crédit Suisse convened and effectively disowned Wuffli and Schulthess by denying that the bank needed any support. That morning the bank's traders managed to prevent a slump in its shares by using a convenient technical device. When the stock opened, they put in an offer to sell stock at a price more than ten per cent below the level at which the shares had closed the previous day. This automatically led to a suspension of the market for a quarter of an hour cooling-off period, enough for the bank to rally its forces. But it did not help in the currency markets, on which the franc slipped noticeably, not only against the dollar, but even against the Italian lire.

Yet the bank itself did not suffer. The directors did not even have to activate the plan they had devised in the aftermath of the Herstatt affair three years before, designed for precisely such emergencies. The general management had then spent two full days devising means of mobilising the maximum liquid cash in the shortest possible time. They did not have to use the plan – or indeed any of their reserves – that week. More money than usual was withdrawn from the Chiasso branch itself, but by June even the initially nervous small investors had come flooding back.

Internally, however, the next three weeks saw the most profound upheaval in the bank's history. The key step was the establishment of a commission of enquiry, with its members drawn from the board of directors (some of whom declined the honour). But the group included, crucially, the precise, commanding figure of Eberhard Reinhardt, who had headed the general management until his retirement in 1973.

The first results of the enquiry were announced at the press conference on 12 May which so completely overshadowed the Leclerc scandal. Three key scapegoats had been found: Schulthess, who had been chairman until the end of March, relinquished his honorary chairmanship; Wuffli had resigned, after the shortest period in office of any leader in financial history, a mere five weeks. With these two there were no recriminations, in public anyway, for the board of directors went out of its way to emphasise that they in no way impugned the 'personal integrity and honesty' of the dear departed. The situation of Serge Demiéville was rather different. The press statement carefully separated his departure from the others: 'The special commission,' it read, 'has no reason to suspect him of having behaved dishonourably in the Chiasso affair.' The distinction was crucial. Demiéville had to go because of another, unconnected, problem which had also surfaced in the first months of 1977. He had failed to control the bank's involvement with Melina Certosa, a troubled Italian flour-milling group, ending up lending it 50 million francs, treble the authorised level.

By contrast, two of the figures who might have been expected to suffer, Jeker and Müller, escaped unscathed. 'The enquiry revealed nothing special as far as they were concerned,' it stated categorically (during the internal enquiry, Jeker had intimated that 'it cannot be excluded that Müller knew more than us'), and on May 18 they were both promoted to the rank of director general. But the accusations went higher. At the trial two years later a naturally bitter Wuffli pointed out that Aeppli had been head of the bank's legal services since 1969 and therefore, in theory, responsible for monitoring Kuhrmeier's agreement not to extend the bank's guarantees to further fiduciary deposits. 'But he was untouchable: he was classed as a sort of national monument', Wuffli grumbled to the court. The same rough justice applied at branch level. Although Meinrad Perler had at least tried to warn his superiors of the problem, he was also dismissed from the bank's service, as of course were Kuhrmeier and Laffranchi.

Generally, the immediate reaction within the bank was a sort of dislocation, as apparently solid verities and long established executives were overturned, together with some bitterness. ('They're laying turf outside the offices on the Paradeplatz' went one inside story. 'Why?' ... 'So that the money we're throwing out of the windows won't make any noise.') The statement on May 12 revealed that the bank had provided Texon with guarantees for 2.17 billion francs, plus another 350 million to cover guarantees provided to Italian banks for the loans they had made to the numerous companies in Texon's sprawling empire. But the exact position became clear only six weeks later at an event unprecedented in Swiss banking history, an extraordinary general meeting to explain virtually the whole truth behind a major scandal. A venerable tradition of total discretion had been abandoned. But the revolution was not confined to Crédit Suisse's public accountability; never had a managerial revolution been so complete. For on the face of it Wuffli's successor as chief general manager, Rainer Gut, lacked all the qualifications which had been required of the post's occupants since the bank's foundation. Where all his predecessors had been Protestant, usually from the select handful of Zurich families which had dominated Crédit Suisse for a century, Gut is a Catholic, and although his father did indeed run a bank, it was the cantonal bank in Zug (his grandfather worked in a soap factory). His career had been equally unorthodox, for he had served a decade on Wall Street, working first as the New York representative of the Union Bank and then working for the legendary André Mayer at the ruthlessly competitive investment bank of Lazard Frères. He was first hired by Crédit Suisse to run their investment banking subsidiary in New York, which he shook up with arrogant thoroughness. The job done, he had returned to Switzerland only in 1973, and his responsibilities – the bank's Far Eastern interests and a great deal of its stock market activities, including domestic underwriting and the Eurobond business – were far enough removed from Chiasso for him to be 'whiter than white.'

The shareholders' meeting on the 24 June was elaborately prepared. Zurich's best public relations outfit had been hired, and Aeppli was rehearsed for days in advance, with his staff throwing at him questions far harder than those he received at the meeting itself. (The preparations rather backfired. The day of the meeting coincided with the first publication of a new daily paper, owned by the maverick Migros co-operative chain. Its very first headline contained the accusation that the bank's shareholders were being elaborately bamboozled by a well-prepared board.)

Over 3,000 shareholders crammed into an enormous exhibition hall (so big that the faces of Aeppli and the other speakers were projected onto enormous television screens hung behind the platform and half way towards the back of the hall), and for five and a half hours sweltered in an atmosphere overheated by arc lights. The lengthy main speeches came from Aeppli and from Peter Schmidheiny, chairman of the venerable Zurich engineering group of Escher Wyss, speaking for the commission of enquiry. The facts were

set out, and blame placed firmly on Kuhrmeier, his dominance of the branch, his personality. Texon was to be put in
the books at a value of 1.7 billion francs – 100 million had
already been written off and the remaining difference between
the 1.7 billion figure and the 2.17 billion mentioned six weeks
earlier was accounted for by assets which had already been
recuperated or sold off.

Aeppli emphasised just how big Texon was. 'Our Italian
empire', as Crédit Suisse executives referred to it, included
hundreds of companies, many of them extremely important.
'Texon is not a ghost village,' he said. And the empire was
already being evaluated: a 'Texon General Staff' had been
mobilised, involving twenty executives from head office, and
in all a hundred lawyers, management consultants, accountants and tax experts had been seconded to help them. Within
the bank itself, the stable doors were being shut, and its whole
operational structure reorganised.

The length of the speeches, and their honesty and
thoroughness satisfied most of the shareholders. There were
natural complaints about how slow head office in Zurich had
been to respond to events in Chiasso where, one shareholder
told Aeppli, 'the birds in the street were singing about it.'
Aeppli's reply was prompt: 'Well, why didn't you bring it to
my attention? How am I supposed to know in Zurich what the
birds are singing about in Chiasso?' A more serious criticism
came from a Zurich lawyer, Jurg Meister, a regular defender
of small shareholders, one of whom had been the victim of the
bank's deviousness. Early in the scandal he had tried to sell
his Crédit Suisse shares but was dissuaded because, he was
assured, the bank would support its own share price. In the
event it couldn't, and the client lost money. But Meister was
the exception and overall the meeting proved a triumph. Only
a few shareholders noticed the tune playing on the public
address system as they wended their weary way out of the
hall: it was 'Auld Lang Syne'.

The astonishing ability of Crédit Suisse to absorb the
Chiasso shock was finally proved with the publication of the
1977 accounts in early 1978. By that time the bank had been
forced to write off the enormous sum of 973 million francs,
nearly half what Texon owed it (it had also, of course, taken

over directly the credits previously granted to Texon's subsidiaries by Italian banks, which added 350 million francs to
the bank's total 'Texon exposure'). But it had not blinked an
eyelid in doing so, merely taking the whole sum out of its inner
reserves (partially refilling them by revaluing its properties,
notably the bank's headquarters on the Paradeplatz). It did
not even find it necessary to reduce its dividend although it
did dispose of its controlling interest in the country's leading
chain of department stores. Finally it was preventing any
trouble with the Swiss tax authorities by repaying the
depositors in Texon only three quarters of their money, retaining the other quarter to account for their liabilities for
withholding tax (and the negative tax on deposits introduced
during Texon's later years).

Institutionally the ability to absorb such a shock without
flinching was a tremendous tribute to Crédit Suisse's financial
soundness. But the shock waves spread wide. The angriest
reaction came from the UBS (which had already tried to
capitalise on Crédit Suisse's troubles in a splendid series of
advertisements, explaining its own rigid and uncompromising
internal controls). Alfred Schaefer complained to the Swiss
National Bank, and his successor, Philippe de Weck, told a
journalist, 'I completely disagree with the way Crédit Suisse
settled this business. The bank should never have covered the
loss solely by relying on its inner reserves. It did not do it for
prestige reasons but in doing so it has rendered an extremely
bad service to the banking world and to the whole principle of
internal reserves.' De Weck went on to say that the policy
simply provided ammunition to critics of the banks who point
specifically to their lack of transparency. He was right. The
size of their hidden reserves had always been amongst the
banks' most closely guarded secrets. They had always claimed
that they were merely adequate to provide for ordinary
contingencies. So the fact that those of Crédit Suisse were so
huge that it could brush aside the massive Chiasso loss was a
severe political embarrassment. Beat Kappeler, the economic
adviser to the Swiss Trades Union movement, put his finger
on the same spot: 'We are not against the principle of reserves.
But we feel that the bank's customers, its employees, the
banking authorities and the public in general have the right to

know the real worth of a bank's assets. It is in the public interest.'

But otherwise the bank has scarcely put a foot wrong since Chiasso. Within the organisation, the shock has enabled Wuffli's successors to carry through the reforms he projected. Previously the board would not agree to shift under-performing executives or the need for a separate marketing department. All has now changed, and since 1977 the bank's new department has been responsible for such diverse initiatives as a financial package aimed at small businesses, new types of mortgage credits, and a special advisory service for financial institutions like pension funds and insurance companies. For the first time, Crédit Suisse has led the field.

Following the success of the famous meeting, the bank has maintained its unprecedentedly high profile. It has sponsored the high spot of the country's cycling year, Tour de Suisse, it distributed ski caps which became seemingly ubiquitous on the slopes, and it has actively looked out for promotional opportunities (when, for instance, the Swiss Youth Orchestra needed money, it took only a single phone call to Rainer Gut to put it on a sound financial basis).

More fundamentally the whole management structure of the bank has completely changed. The – much-reinforced – auditing department now reports directly to the chairman, and not, as before, merely to one of the general managers. Board members are expected to circulate round the branches to see the bank's activities for themselves. And where previously the bank's general managers had seemingly taken an interest in the tiniest administrative details (one observer remembers Reinhardt worrying over the exact details of one minor change in the lower management), a new structure has been introduced to give them time actually to think about the bank's business. The most obvious change was that, whereas previously every branch manager – and dozens of others – reported direct to a general manager – a perfectly practicable system until the 1960s, but unworkable when the number of branches tripled within a few years – under the new dispensation most of them were placed under the wing of a 'branch department'.

The reorganisation of 'our Italian empire' has proved a

longer and as yet unrewarding business. By 1980 Crédit Suisse could claim that, although it is not actually taking any dividends out of its southern dominion, it is at least showing a marginal profit, and is probably worth more than the 750 million francs to which its value had been reduced in the books. Since 1977 the empire has absorbed the energies of some of the parent's ablest executives. Initially the Texon team was headed by von der Crone (who had had no connection with it before the crash) and included Jeker and Müller. The bank has been brutal: even though some of the managers employed by Texon were able enough, they were all replaced within a couple of years, generally by other Italians. The bank was lucky in being able to rely for advice on Fides, a subsidiary which is Switzerland's largest management consultancy – so the Swiss influence remains strong; 'We have exported our management style', said von der Crone, even though Crédit Suisse has been careful to keep a low profile and run each business separately, to minimise both the size of the empire and its Swiss parentage.

(Very few Italians realise that the Winefood group remains Italy's largest wine exporter. As a result the bank was able to provide all its Swiss-based employees with a Christmas treat soon after the crash – the chance to import their regular annual allowance of 200 litres of wine at highly advantageous prices. The experiment was not repeated, however. The bank had several wine importers among its clients. Their complaints were loud and successful.)

A number of businesses have been sold – including the luxury hotels. Factories have had to be closed down (another good reason for keeping quiet about the Swiss connection), and today only Albarella remains a cash drain. The bank simply had to invest further sums to complete the island's development. No hotelier or property developer was going to put in his own cash with such an owner. But now the bank talks of a 'profitable future from this unique site'.

Not even the trial, which occupied six well-publicised weeks in the summer of 1979, upset the even tenor of Crédit Suisse's ways. It should have done: when the prosecuting attorney opened the case he went out of his way to emphasise that the penalties he was demanding – five years in prison for Kuhrmeier and Laffranchi and eighteen months with remission for the three lawyers – had been lessened by the gross negligence of the bank in operating its controls. He had also watered down the charges. Whereas at an earlier trial he had accused the directors of Weisscredit (two of whom had fled the country) of fraud, the principal charge against Kuhrmeier and his colleagues was simply *gestion déloyale*.* 'The lacunae in the bank's organisation were such,' he went on, 'that the prosecution very nearly gave the benefit of the doubt to the accused according to Article 63 of the Penal Code, which allows the plea of extenuating circumstances when the temptation to wrong-doing is sufficiently strong.'

The bank's only bad time thereafter came, predictably, from Wuffli and Perler, the two men who had been treated most harshly. Wuffli defended his relative inaction in face of de Weck's warnings (he claimed that Department N – responsible for branches like Chiasso – had assured him they had revised the credit limits applicable to the branch). He alleged that Aeppli was at least partially responsible for Chiasso, bitterly criticised the style employed by the internal commission (whose work was singled out even by the prosecuting attorney as being implacably thorough) and even intimated that he had been driven to resign by its inquisitorial tactics.

Perler was even blunter. He gave a press conference the day before he was due to testify – on the grounds that the prosecutor would be careful not to ask him any questions to which he might give uncomfortable answers – at which he spelled out just how much (quite a lot) he believed head office had known about Texon. But the theme was not pursued. For once the prosecutor had made his opening stand against the bank, his main target seemed to be Ticino's Christian Democratic establishment, especially Vassalli, who had been forced to resign as a Conseiller d'Etat in 1977 when it was revealed that he had not fully declared his earnings from Texon to the

* Literally this means 'disloyal management'. Legally it is similar to 'misappropriation of funds'. But it also carries with it overtones similar to the old British military notion of 'conduct unbecoming an officer and a gentleman' for it was a favourite Swiss pretence that their bankers were gentlemen.

tax authorities, and Alfredo Stefani who, as head of the party in the canton, had acted as middle man in the dealings with Luigi Croci Torti.

As expected, the verdict largely followed the prosecutor's demands. The two principal accused were to serve four and a half years, while the three lawyers received only sixteen-month suspended sentences. The President of the Court agreed with the prosecutor as to the negligence of Crédit Suisse's head office and added some harsh words ·of his own about its 'tolerance'. But he and the prosecutor were both unfair to the principal accused (one of whom, Kuhrmeier, died shortly afterwards) in claiming that they had acted with the aim of profiting from their misdeeds, a thoroughly Swiss notion, but miles adrift from the ungraspable truth, that Kuhrmeier was building an empire, not providing for his old age.

But by that time the general public had long forgotten the case. In 1980, when the new style Crédit Suisse conducted one of its regular public opinion surveys it found that a majority of those polled believed that the UBS was the institution involved in that unfortunate affair at Chiasso. For was not the UBS famously the most aggressive of the Big Three and therefore the most likely to lose money because of its thrusting policies? Even the loss of a mere billion francs, in other words, had not been sufficient to shake the image of the Crédit Suisse as the most Swiss of banks. And perhaps the image is not too far from reality.

5 / Towards the Twentieth Century

'We'll get over the international repercussions of Chiasso', said Hans Baer after the full extent of the scandal had been revealed; 'its domestic implications could be much more important.' He was right. Chiasso did permanently alter the political atmosphere in which the banks operated at the time, it led even Leo Schürmann, the Christian Democrat vice-president of the Swiss National Bank, to demand an end to banking secrecy. But for all its efforts, since then, the Socialist Party has not succeeded in mobilising the Swiss people to accept any very fundamental change in the relationships between the government and the banks.

This has not been for want of trying. 'It is not illegal,' cried Helmut Hubacher, the party's president, 'to choose "le bon timing" for a political initiative.' Claiming that bank national-isation had been a – rather neglected – element in the party's programme since 1952, Hubacher immediately launched a sweeping new proposal that the government should take a stake in the major banks and should be represented on the banks' boards. But there was moral force as well as political expediency behind the idea: 'money has a smell' said Jean-Pierre Ghelfi, in defiant contradiction of centuries of Swiss tradition.

Within eighteen months of the uproar of May 1977 more moderate voices had prevailed. But the issue remained an important one. In the words of the *Financial Times*: 'Con-fronted with the unpromising task of unearthing a genuine left-wing cause in the wealthiest and most politically stable country of the western world, it [the Socialist Party] focussed on the banking secrecy issue for positive popular support.' When the party launched an initiative in late 1978 its contents were relatively modest (even though they were drawn up under Rudolf Strahm, one of the stalwarts of the *Déclaration de Berne* group, which had done the most detailed and damning work on abuses of banking secrecy). The initiative was basically concerned to prevent the abuse of banking secrecy to facilitate domestic tax evasion. It also called for more informa-tion from the banks, more co-operation in cases of financial crime, flexibility in banking secrecy, a greater degree of international aid, limiting the power of the banks in industrial companies, and an insurance scheme to prevent depositors losing their money when banks went under.

The proposition will be voted on in the early 1980s, but the omens look bad even for this moderate package. As is only to be expected, polls conducted by the banks show a low level of support for the initiative (and continuing popular support for banking secrecy), and these figures were confirmed by the set-back suffered by the Socialists in the general election held in late 1979.

But the Swiss love of consensus, of enveloping radical proposals in a covering of cotton wool, will mean that although the Socialist initiative will be defeated, the government is likely to meet it half way. (Already the government has imposed a 5.6 per cent tax on retail sales of gold – without even consulting the banks.) More radical is the proposed closure of a major tax loophole, the failure to tax fiduciary deposits arranged through Swiss banks. The idea of levying a five per cent withholding tax on them is gradually working its way through the Swiss legislative system. And within two years the country will have a new banking law. This is unlikely to be dramatic, but it will represent a further step in the tightening of the control system initiated in the mid-1970s. These changes, both by the National Bank, 'responsible for the soundness of our country as a financial centre', in the words of one official, and the Banking Commission, 'responsible for the soundness of individual banks', were more profound than any others in the history of Swiss banking.

These changes had already started before the Chiasso scandal with the arrival at the Banking Commission of Bernard Muller, backed by a notably independent board headed by Dr. Hermann Bodenmann, a well-known lawyer and politician. Both appointments were constitutionally significant, representing a shift from the strict separation between the government and the Commission which had been the previous practice. The personal shift was equally significant. As one banker put it: 'Before 1976 the Banking Commission was staffed by people who were, basically, afraid of the bankers. But Muller was a senior civil servant; to him banks are like any other organisation; he is simply not impressed by them.' The same change of attitude is reflected in Leutwiler's classic remark: 'We are no longer assuming that every banker is a gentleman, and that if he is a gentleman, he obeys the rules.'

In a few short years Muller has stood on its head the historic relationship between banks, their auditors and the

Commission, which is now at the head rather than the bottom of the pile. Like the good public servant he is, Muller claims that neither the legislative nor regulatory frameworks have changed, merely the Commission's methods and organisation. But he is obviously relishing the quiet revolution he has initiated. The staff has risen from a derisory five when he arrived to only thirty today, although he has followed the practice of American regulatory agencies in hiring keen young lawyers and accountants eager for a few years' government experience as the best training ground before launching into private practice. He has seized on a key lever: the duty of the banks' external auditors to banks' clients and shareholders as well as the Banking Commission (and thus the public interest). For the 1934 Act intended that the auditors should be the Commission's eyes and ears, that control should be exercised indirectly through them rather than directly by the Commission's own staff.

To make this more than a pious hope the major banks had, first, to divest themselves of their auditing subsidiaries – a step which was well under way before Muller's arrival. He then had to reinforce the figures which they extracted from the banks and passed on to the Commission. Above all Muller had to alter the balance of fear, to ensure that the auditors were more scared of misleading the Commission than of their clients. For auditors' inhibitions had been at the root of most Swiss banking scandals – even Chiasso might have been prevented if the external auditors had not concentrated their efforts on Head Office and instead gone to individual branches.

Muller's style was set early in his incumbency when – at the suggestion of one of his staff – he sent an innocent-sounding enquiry to the banks' auditors asking for the costs of the audits they conducted. The figures varied so wildly, and some were so unbelievably low, that the superficiality of the auditing procedures became glaringly apparent. They were soon sharply revised – upwards – and the auditors were issued with guidelines as to what constituted an acceptable audit in future. Equally inadequate were the figures provided to the Commission. Until Muller's time it had to rely on publicly reported figures which, the Commission cheerfully admits, were pretty meaningless; even today, even the biggest banks publish figures for – say – the interest they receive which are not entirely accurate. Auditors had provided fuller reports only when they found discrepancies. Now they provide the commission with raw data, before anything has been deducted for the hidden reserves so beloved of Swiss bankers.

The growing independence of the auditors may have removed the need for the truly independent public auditing service for the banks suggested by Leutwiler in the aftermath of Chiasso, for the Commission has not only laid down new criteria, but has now established a track record as a credible disciplinarian. Ironically one of the first cases led indirectly to the uncovering of the Chiasso scandal. For in line with the new guidelines, the auditors of the Weisscredit had reported to the Commission that although the accounts of the bank itself seemed in order, those of the *Anstalt* towards which the bank's directors were guiding their customers manifestly were not. (An additional factor was a tax amnesty declared by the Italian authorities which was leading to a spate of withdrawals from banks in the Ticino.) At the first report Muller telephoned his chairman and, armed with his consent, closed the bank at lunchtime – and it was of course the downfall of Weisscredit which brought matters to a head at Chiasso.

But the major landmark was the case of the Solothurner Hypothekbank, which had been granting mortgages based on the cost of building a new house, not on the property's much lower value in a depressed market. The bank's regular auditors had recommended a provision of a mere 7 million francs to cover the gap. The Commission ordered a special audit which recommended that the provision be increased to 30 million. Largely as a result of the losses the bank was taken over (by the ever-eager Union Bank), and the regular auditors brought suit against the Commission for daring to question their figures (and thus their professional competence). They lost. Indeed the Commission has won a number of similar cases, forcing higher professional standards onto the auditors; in one case the creditors of a failed bank sued the auditors for professional negligence and came away with 6 million francs in damages.

In other cases licences have been withdrawn without much

hesitation. For example, the Migros bank had to report losses which it had been hoping to hide, the Commission has found bank directors showing as assets shares in fact bought with clients' funds – and one major bank was disciplined when it poached a branch manager, complete with his list of clients, from a rival. The manager was sacked, the bank reprimanded.

The Commission has gone on to start investigating the relationship between the banks as portfolio managers and their clients – and in one case even called for working papers used by auditors when examining the clients' relationship with the bank. It is also speeding up the work of the auditors – at the moment they have to provide the Commission with figures only within the year following the end of each given accounting period; and the Commission is even contemplating the day when the general public (not to mention the banks' shareholders) will receive the same, real, undiluted figures as it does.

But probably the subtlest step in Muller's reforms has been to enforce the directives issued by the Swiss Bankers' Association. In the past, these have often been unenforceable gestures designed to appease public opinion. But the Commission is now using a seemingly innocuous clause in the 1971 Banking Law which provides that a bank's directors must behave 'irreproachably'. The Commission now judges the banks' behaviour by whether they have scrupulously and 'irreproachably' followed the directives issued by the Association, the sort of indirect policing beloved of the Swiss, with their mutually exclusive loves for law and order and for lack of government interference.

For the Swiss Bankers' Association, eager to drag its more recalcitrant members towards the twentieth century, this firmness has been most helpful – and so, of course, was the banks' defensiveness after Chiasso and Leclerc. During the two years after Bobby Leclerc went under, the SBA came out with a series of strict directives regulating the routine to be observed with clients' funds – directives the Pictets and the other major private bankers were even keener to enforce than the Association itself. A standard formula was provided for portfolio managers, and the 'Leclerc gap' was filled with the provision that any non-routine investment – in commodities or real estate, for instance – could be undertaken only with the client's specific written consent. Options and forward foreign exchange transactions were frowned on; and securities issued by the bank itself, or by companies associated with it or the directors, were forbidden territory. Another directive prevented banks from ignoring their clients' wishes when they used their votes at company meetings.

But the greatest publicity was given to the Convention signed by the SBA and the Swiss National Bank a few months after Chiasso exploded (the Banking Commission would not participate because of the provision for an independent Arbitration Commission, as it did not want to be bound by anyone else's decisions). In theory at least the Convention required banks to know the actual identity of clients, not to take funds entrusted to them 'for improper purposes' and to avoid aiding or abetting tax evasion or illegal capital flight. In theory, this severely limited the age-old practice of sending employees abroad to attract new customers. But there was one major loophole: lawyers could still open accounts in their own name for an anonymous client provided that they attested that they knew the owner's name and that 'no improper transactions within the meaning of the agreement are involved'. The Association itself claimed that it was merely codifying the practice already followed by the majority of Swiss banks, but no one believed them, nor did anyone really expect the Convention to have many teeth. It did.

In October 1979 a banker apparently connected with Barclays Bank's Swiss subsidiary was arrested in France while arranging for the illegal export of capital to Switzerland. He was sacked, but Barclays explained that they were not contravening the Convention because the bank itself was acting only in a passive role, it was not actively soliciting clients who were evading foreign taxes – although middle-men did so.

A year later the Arbitration Commission reported on its first three years' work. It was by no means negligible. Fifteen cases had been brought to its attention of which ten had been dismissed because they related to acts undertaken before the Convention had come into force. But in the remaining five cases bankers were fined a total of 732,000 francs (duly

forwarded to the Red Cross). The worst offender (believed to
be a cantonal bank which paid 500,000 francs) had continued
to follow the age-old practice of sending its employees abroad
to pick up clients' funds.

In a society as passionately devoted to free enterprise as the
Swiss, the changes loom large: 'People exaggerated twenty
years ago,' said one banker, 'when they said we weren't
controlled at all, and today they go the other way in claiming
that we are over-controlled.' For Parliament continued to
grudge even the National Bank additional powers. Only after
1978 could the SNB conduct a proper monetary policy –
during the height of the crisis it had had to rely on a series of
emergency decrees; and even that long awaited revision of its
charter provided it with by no means all the powers it
requested.

The adequacy of the banks' capital has provided a classic
case of the new machinery in action. The BIS Club of central
bankers told Leutwiler in no uncertain terms that the major
banks were financing speculative activities through their
subsidiaries in countries like Panama and Luxembourg where
the regulations concerning banks' capital were either minimal
or non-existent. In the event it was the Federal Banking
Commission which was the first authority in the world to
apply ratios to consolidated balance sheets – in other words to
force the banks to show that all their business, wherever it was
conducted, had enough capital behind it. In 1979 five banks
were told to increase their capitalisation – a long way from the
pre-Muller days, when, as one banker said: 'If one of the big
banks was undercapitalised, it would merely state that it
would make the necessary rights issue at its own convenience,
and the Commission would not dare question its proposals.'

The next step was to tailor the Commission's requirements
to the general public interest, not so much by raising the levels
of capital required (the present eight per cent ratio of capital
to a bank's assets is high by international standards) but by
concentrating on specific problems. The new and elaborate
scale bears most heavily on the big banks – the ones which
obviously have the greatest proportion of international business and will therefore require the most new capital; they have
to provide twenty per cent capital cover for their banking

premises (a warning to other banks not to copy Crédit Suisse, which covered so much of the 'Chiasso gap' by revaluing its offices); and – a result of politically inspired worries about the banks' powers over Swiss industry – they have to provide forty per cent cover for their industrial holdings. This will bear particularly hard on Crédit Suisse, which had by far the biggest industrial portfolio even before it absorbed its 'Italian empire' – which, however, will probably be treated as a special case.

The banks – claiming that the change is merely part of their general policy – are certainly bending with the wind. In 1979 Philippe de Weck of the Union Bank told a journalist that his bank had established the value of money deposited by citizens of forty-six African countries. 'It was insignificant', he said, 'a few millions from each country' – a mere fraction of the estimates made by the *Déclaration de Berne* Group (he had not, however, done the same for Latin America, the source of most of the Third World funds deposited in Switzerland). But de Weck has gone further: 'I've established an internal rule by which the executive board has to be told if any foreign political figure comes to open an account ... I believe the Swiss banks should establish a general rule in such cases'. He even wanted the 1977 convention extended to ensure that foreign political leaders would not be allowed to deposit money privately in Switzerland.

More generally both UBS and the Swiss Bank Corporation have gone out of their way to emphasise that there are limits to their expansion, especially abroad. Nikolaus Senn, the chairman of the UBS executive board, said: 'Twelve years ago our international business was a tenth of what it is now. We need time to consolidate, to see if we are in the best position organisation-wise.' The UBS also made a little-publicised about-turn from its previous efforts to carve itself a dominant position in the international bond markets. During the second half of the 1970s the bank's portfolio managers were under strong and consistent pressure to stuff their clients' portfolios with the bonds being managed by the bank's underwriting department; they also had to report the volume of their stock market transactions every month, another form of pressure to increase the bank's profits at the clients' expense. The bonds were not unsound – they were simply not very good value. It was all very well for a client to contemplate a portfolio issued by the likes of Mobil and Shell, but the cannier one would know that UBS had secured these issues by granting exceptional terms to the borrowers. All this has now changed following a revolt by the bank's powerful Geneva branch. 'In the end the portfolio managers have to win,' said a UBS man. Moreover, all the banks are under pressure to improve the service they provide: the growth over the past twenty years has simply overwhelmed the managers – some of whom look after up to 800 accounts. (The major banks are not alone: Bobby Leclerc was, in theory, responsible for 750 of his bank's 3,000 accounts.) And as the bank grows larger, so an increasing number of clients desert. Helmut Saurer of Julius Baer remarked to the author that when his bank wins clients from one of the major banks: 'It need not be bad management which makes them change. It's the other, personal element. They often complain that there is no continuity. They dislike constant changes of management.'

Even the Swiss Bank Corporation – by common consent a bank where the client always did come first – has changed. Its chairman, Hans Strasser,* told me: 'We have set a target ratio between growth abroad compared with growth at home and this balance has to be observed by our branches. The proportion is checked every three months, and if one of the sectors grows too fast, they have to slow down. Although we are an international bank, we want to remain Swiss-based.'

The screws are also being tightened within the country. Early in 1980 the big banks unilaterally increased the mortgage rate without consulting anyone. (These days, if the banks act together they are accused of forming a cartel. If they break ranks and, for instance, expand their branch network, they are accused of anti-social aggressiveness.) There was a monumental political row – for the banks had increased their percentage share of the mortgage business from twenty-seven in 1973 to thirty-eight five years later. Leo Schürmann and the National Bank put pressure on them, and a few weeks later they had to

* The first bank chairman of working-class origin, a demonstration of class stratification in what is commonly held to be a democratic society.

withdraw the increase. But, a few months later it was found that even though the major banks could afford the losses caused by keeping the rate down, many local and cantonal banks manifestly couldn't, and from 1 April 1981 the rates were raised.

The incident was used by Jean Ziegler and others as an example of the unbridled power of the big banks – even though they had been forced to rescind their decision. Rather it showed their inadequate appreciation of the consequences of their close, if recent, involvement in the personal finances of the average Swiss citizen. In the words of André Gavillet: 'It was a revealing case. The banks had perfectly sound arguments to justify such an increase, even though I thought that this increase could have been deferred, as it finally was. So it wasn't the action itself which I would find blameworthy, but the offhanded way it was announced. While mortgages form only a minor part of the big banks' business, it was shocking to see them impose such a change on the country.'

'Salami tactics' Hans Baer called American efforts to slice away at banking secrecy, and recently the regulatory authorities, backed by the courts, have managed to advance yet further against Swiss banking secrecy. In early 1981 a flurry of speculation by clients of the Banca della Svizzera Italiana – the largest independent bank in the Ticino – in the shares of St. Joe Minerals was followed immediately by a takeover bid by the giant Canadian drinks company, Seagram's. When the SEC tried to penetrate banking secrecy, it was politely rebuffed, for insider trading is neither illegal nor immoral in Swiss eyes.

The American courts could not act directly against the bank, because (unlike Crédit Suisse in the Harwood affair) it did not have any assets in the United States. Nevertheless a federal judge backed the SEC (which had frozen the $2 million profits made by the bank's clients), giving the bank a mere week to name the investors involved, and taking a robustly common-sense view of the case: 'It would be a travesty of justice', said Judge Milton Pollack, 'to permit a foreign institution to invade the American markets, violate the law, withdraw its profits and then claim anonymity'. In the event the bank persuaded its clients to allow their names to be revealed. And another judge encouraged the SEC to 'hold on to your dream of ultimate disclosure' when ruling on the results of similar speculative buying before Kuwait's government-owned oil company launched a bid for another American company, Santa Fe International. In this instance the judge even allowed the SEC to advertise to warn the unknown speculators that it was pursuing them in the courts and could oblige them to give up their profits even if their identities remained unknown. The Santa Fe case established yet another precedent: the SEC investigators were unable even to serve legal papers on Lombard Odier, one of the Swiss banks involved, because of the peculiarities of Swiss law, and had to serve them on Lombard Odier's subsidiary in London.

The Americans are not alone in applying pressure. In an extremely discreet out-of-court settlement at the end of 1979, the Swiss finally gave way in the long-running battle over the monies deposited nearly twenty years earlier by Mohamad Khider; and since the fall of the Shah, and the consequent immediate nationalisation of all his possessions, the Iranian government has been applying continuous pressure to get at the fortunes they believe he and his family had tucked away in Switzerland. In 1979 the Federal Council ducked the question, telling the Iranians to act through the courts, and the canton of Geneva, at least, allowed them to inspect its land registers to define the properties involved (although the neighbouring canton of Vaud, where the Shah had a villa, was not so helpful). Yet the pressure did have one effect: the banks were obliged to produce figures for the deposits they held belonging to Iranian nationals at the end of 1978. Net of borrowings, they amounted to a billion francs, together with just under a billion in fiduciary deposits – a favourite refuge for Iranians. This was far from the 4 billion francs which Jean Ziegler had alleged had been transferred in the eight months before the fall of the Shah, let alone other estimates of a total of over 20 billion francs in all.

The majority of the deposits held by the Big Three came from the Central Bank, rather than private clients. But the overall figures were suspect, because they did not include securities, and the Genevan private banks were excluded from the survey. So queries remain. We know, from American

Congressional enquiries, of the scale of the sums paid to the Iranian Royal family in bribes, and how a high proportion of these were channelled through Swiss banks. Yet the relative openness and frankness shown by the Swiss was unprecedented, for they knew that the tide had turned against them. Finally, their historically reiterated warning that government restrictions would lead to loss of business is coming true – although they had cried wolf too often in the past for their plaints to be heeded in time.

During 1981 the Swiss even started to lose some of the gold business they had gained from London in the late 1960s and early 1970s. At that time the Russians were frightened that lax security at Heathrow Airport would lead to leaks as to the quantities they were selling; and the South Africans had taken offence at the arms embargo imposed by Britain's Labour government. But at the end of 1980 the Swiss customs started to reveal the figures for the import and export of gold, following the government's imposition of a 5.6 per cent tax on gold trading. The Russians in particular took fright and both they and the South Africans took offence at the apparent habit of Swiss gold traders of liquidating their own positions in the metal as it fell out of international investment favour during 1980 and 1981, so that they were unwilling to sell gold brought in direct from the mines.

The attractions of the London gold market were greatly boosted by the help provided by the Bank of England, in providing secure and discreet storage space – as well as helping to ensure that the British government did not impinge on the market's freedom from interference – or taxes. For the competition is mounting; as Nicholas Deak, chairman of the foreign exchange dealers Deak Perera, noted after the Austrian government had allowed holders of savings deposits to be identified only through a pass book: 'Austria's new banking regulations are even more effective in protecting foreign money from prying eyes than those of Switzerland, where secrecy laws have been eroded over the years under pressure of foreign tax collectors and anti-crime forces ... many people do not realise that Swiss banking procedures have undergone important changes over the years.'

But the erosion of secrecy has a long way to go, and the

banks know it. A few years ago, in an unprecedented exercise, the Swiss Bank Corporation asked its branch managers what would happen if banking secrecy were lifted. The replies were reassuring: 'It wouldn't be good for the bank,' Strasser told me 'but it wouldn't be the end of the world, it wouldn't seriously damage our bank.'

So, for once, the banks seem prepared for the worst. But even if it happens, even if there is a serious dilution of Clause 47(b), would anything really change? Indeed has anything fundamental changed over the past few traumatic years?

6 / The melody lingers on

On 20 June 1980 two French customs officers pleaded guilty *in absentia* to industrial espionage under Section 273 of the Swiss Penal Code. Two months earlier they had been lured into a trap by the Swiss police when engaged in trying to suborn a bank clerk to buy lists of French citizens with Swiss bank accounts.

No peace treaty has ever been signed in the eternal cold war between the French authorities and the Swiss guardians of so much of their citizens' wealth. Although the outbreak of hostilities in the 1930s ended in apparent victory for the Swiss, this was never really accepted by the French, for the smuggling of currency and securities never ended even in wartime. At the end of World War II the American authorities heard all about it from 'two well-placed observers'. The diplomatic pouch was used, so were French army officers with legitimate business in Switzerland, and 'many French inhabitants of the region are accomplices in the handling of this traffic'. But most of it was possible through the bribery of ill-paid French customs officials.

After the war they recovered their morale and succeeded in

infiltrating the banks of which their countrymen were still the most important customers. In 1954, following French espionage, eleven Swiss were arrested on the grounds of 'grave misuse of office in favour of a foreign power'. In December 1967 the French finance minister, Michel Debré, abolished exchange controls so that, for the first time in generations, the French were legally entitled to open accounts in Switzerland. They still were when near-revolution broke out in France in May 1968, resulting, naturally, in an enormous flood of funds out of the country – a flow which led to the reimposition of controls in November that year. But even during the short period when capital export was legal the French preferred to keep their transactions strictly private. Michel Jobert, the head of the private office of the Prime Minister, Georges Pompidou, later recalled how, during the upheavals, he received daily police reports. 'That was how I noticed that many influential people had been involved in accidents on roads leading to Switzerland where they had no business to be. It was obvious that they had taken to the Swiss banking road and that they were involved in this rush which filled Swiss coffers with thousands of millions of francs' – a flood which some estimates put as high as a billion dollars.

The French again took the initiative in the mid-1970s when their customs officials managed to buy a list of French clients of the Swiss Bank Corporation from an informant called Jean Pierre Wagner. The deal was profitable for both sides: the French got several thousand names (estimates vary from three to seventeen thousand) and reclaimed millions of francs in back taxes. For his part Wagner was well rewarded and now, prudently, lives in France.

The war heated up in 1978 when two Swiss bank employees tried to extort up to 2 million (French) francs from some of their French clientele. They were caught by the French authorities, but the Swiss refused to help with prosecuting them, alleging that the treaty of mutual co-operation did not cover customs matters, and in 1980 the Swiss got their revenge on the French customs officials. Their instrument was Hermann Stroehlin, a young computer specialist who had access to clients' lists in the course of his work for the Union Bank. Stroehlin was married to a French girl and bought a ruined mill in the Burgundian countryside as a holiday home. The French tried an ingenious form of blackmail, parking stolen cars round the mill and accusing Stroehlin of receiving them. According to a senior French customs official: 'Yes, it's true that after the stolen car business we did ask Stroehlin to work for us, which was accepted tactics in this game. But he refused, and it was only after having sold his house – for 95,000 francs to a Spanish chef – that he came to us, of his own accord, with his propositions. From that moment on he was preparing a trap for us.'

Stroehlin then clearly started to work with his superiors to trap the French in their turn, for his next step was to introduce two French customs officers, Pierre Schultz and Bernard Rui (who had been deeply involved in the Wagner business) to a supposed informant, M. Ralf, in reality Ralf Elsener, the head of UBS's security services. The customs officers were introduced to him in Zurich on 10 April, the offer was made, and a new meeting arranged five days later in the buffet of the station restaurant at Basle, on the very frontier with France. As soon as Rui and Schultz had sat down, a ring of thirty policemen closed in and put them under arrest charging them with economic espionage, and, significantly, using a warrant signed the previous day.

The row was immediate and loud. French customs officers came out in a short sharp strike to show solidarity with their colleagues, and the French Foreign Office delivered two protest notes to the Swiss. But they closed ranks. As so often, Leo Schürmann summed up the general Swiss attitude in this case towards the French authorities. 'They have', he said, 'a passion for centralisation and regulation. They have installed a whole system of laws and decrees which seem to me both excessive and pernickety. That's their right. But it is not up to us to enforce them, especially as they do not correspond to our idea of collective life and public order. As much as I feel that we ought to help to prevent criminal money from taking refuge in Switzerland, because it is tantamount to contributing to violation of the peace and tranquillity of Switzerland, so I feel just as strongly that we ought not to hinder foreigners who have not committed any criminal act in our eyes from protecting themselves against their local tax authorities.'

He was supported by Jobert, who argued that the 'anti-social' act of smuggling money into Switzerland was merely the result of policies which he found 'unbalanced or irresponsible'. This sort of attitude prevailed over Rui and Schultz. According to French press accounts, they were 'literally forced' to plead guilty *in absentia*, and were duly sentenced (Rui to twelve months in jail and a fine of 7,000 Swiss francs, while Schultz was given three months and fined 2,000 francs). The French concluded that the Government of Valéry Giscard d'Estaing was anxious above all to avoid a public trial which would have sparked off an outbreak of speculation about fiscal transgressions in general, capital flight and other subjects which the President and the government would have found awkward, if not downright embarrassing. But the French authorities were not deterred. On 28 November, six months later, police investigating the head office of the Banque de Paris et des Pays-Bas (generally known as 'Paribas') discovered a list of 450 French citizens with numbered accounts held in the bank's Swiss subsidiary. Before the police had finally decoded the names, the government of President Giscard d'Estaing had fallen, to be replaced by a Socialist administration under Francois Mitterrand. This immediately triggered off a further flight of French capital and yet another round of newspaper articles pointing out how easy it was to export money illicitly to Switzerland (reporters from one enterprising paper, the iconoclastic left-wing daily *Liberation*, succeeded in smuggling over a million francs in – chocolate – coins to Switzerland).

Paribas was at the centre of the storm: 55 of its clients – selected because their Swiss assets were more than a million French francs – were prosecuted in what, by the end of 1981 had become a major political scandal. For the board of Paribas, threatened with nationalisation by the new government, had used to the full the facilities offered by Swiss law (and Swiss lawyers) to transfer control of their group's Swiss subsidiary out of the hands of the parent, a manoeuvre which naturally infuriated the new government.

Although Paribas's clients had relied on Swiss secrecy, a significant sign of the times came late in 1981 when one of them, Pierre Latecoère, son of one of France's aviation pioneers and himself a wealthy industrialist, was found to have transferred 35,000 gold pieces, worth several million dollars, from the custody of Paribas in Switzerland to Canada, which he clearly thought was a safer haven. It wasn't: in the event he lost virtually the whole of his family's fortune.

*

Early in the morning of Tuesday, 10 June 1980, a well-known Lausanne industrialist and financier, Eli Pinkas, committed suicide at his luxury villa. That same morning, his ex-wife Florence (whom he had divorced in 1964 but whom he still visited most weekends) also swallowed cyanide and died at her luxurious penthouse in Cannes.

Eli Pinkas, the son of a Jewish merchant, had arrived in Lausanne from Bulgaria in 1941 to study chemistry. Two years later he married Florence, a former barmaid two years older than himself, a woman who, having been pretty, if rather blowsy, in her youth, had matured into a genuine beauty by the time of her death thirty-seven years later.

After the war Pinkas prospered modestly. His company, Socsil, developed highly specialised machines for producing the anaesthetic nitrous oxide (laughing gas). But his major success came when he developed portable gas generators, essential for the mobile hospitals used by the world's armed forces. At the end of the 1950s, in order to get the capital he needed for development and expansion, he forged new Socsil share certificates and used them as security to borrow money to pay for the development and production of his new product. Unfortunately, he could not, as he had evidently hoped, recall the certificates by repaying the loans, as Socsil's profits were not adequate.

So, over the next twenty years, he developed a wide range of techniques to raise the ever increasing amounts of capital he required to cover his original forgery. He employed to the full his position as a well-known figure in Lausanne society, although his wife's origins debarred them from the most 'correct' homes. Other businessmen entrusted money to him, and he paid over-generous interest rates. A succession of banks were glad to lend him more money on the basis of carefully forged balance sheets, backed by equally fraudulent documents 'proving' that the world's armies were eager to purchase his equipment – it was altogether natural for banks to agree not to check on orders placed by the Bundeswehr, or by the totally fictitious 'Sanitary Corps' he invented for the US Army. Bankers or friends who asked for their money back were swiftly disarmed when he offered to repay the debt the next morning. Indeed they came to feel quite ashamed of themselves for having doubted the word of a man of such prominence, whose public face was smooth, quietly confident, coolly charming, giving nothing away.

His requirement grew as he speculated unsuccessfully in gold and precious stones – of which he was very fond. He also developed a side-line in helping rich Americans (whom he and 'Flo' had met while on holiday at Newport, Rhode Island, in the 1950s), either to invest their money in Switzerland or, in at least one case, to buy a house in Lausanne in contravention of the regulations forbidding sales to foreigners.

His downfall was sudden, if belated. After a number of false alarms, it was only in the first week of June 1980 that an alert clerk in the Geneva branch of the Banque de Paris et des Pays-Bas spotted a forged document among the securities produced by Pinkas as backing for a loan. Within a few days other forgeries had been pinned down. The police were called in, and Pinkas committed suicide only a few hours before they were due to question him. After his death it was found that he owed 43 million francs to private creditors and a further 161 million to no fewer than eighteen banks – all of whom believed that they alone had the privilege of being Socsil's bankers. The two largest creditors were the Crédit Suisse and the Swiss subsidiary of Banque Occidentale pour l'Industrie et le Commerce (a French bank controlled by Sir James Goldsmith), which were owed 20 million francs apiece. But they were in good company: the sixteen other creditor banks included three Americans, two other French institutions, the Banque Cantonale de Zurich, the largest in the country, and two local banks. One of them, the Banque Vaudoise de Crédit, was owed only 7 million francs, even though Pinkas had been a director and member of its loan-approval committee.

After the crash, Hermann Bodenmann of the Banking

Commission revived the idea of a central office to monitor credits granted to companies, parallel to those operating in other countries. The bankers politely disagreed. They felt most strongly that any such body would dilute and infringe banking secrecy.

*

The Swiss Volksbank is the archetypal Swiss financial institution. It even refuses to allow its name to be fully translated into English, since the equivalents to 'Volks' – People's or Popular – carry with them connotations altogether too radical and anti-capitalist for the directors' taste. With a few insignificant local institutions, the Volksbank is now the country's only co-operative bank. It had been founded by fifty-three craftsmen and small businessmen in Berne in 1869 and had grown rapidly – too rapidly for its comfort. In the 1930s, like the majority of its fellows, the Volksbank had to be drastically reorganised and the Federal government was forced to take a major stake in it to prevent its complete collapse. The shareholding was sold after the war, but the bank – now the fourth largest in the country – retained a complicated voting system through which control remained permanently in the hands of thousands of small shareholders – together with delegates elected from twenty-two regions.

At the beginning of November 1981 this paragon of Swiss respectability was revealed to have feet of clay. The chairman, Dr. Ernst Brugger, a former Federal Finance minister, was forced to admit that the bank had been caught very badly when the market in silver collapsed at the beginning of 1980. Nearly $80 million had been written off because the bank's Geneva office had allowed (or even encouraged) some of its clients to speculate on a very large scale. Even when head office had caught up with the affair and ordered the Geneva branch and its manager, Alain Brussard (who was also a vice-president), to wind up its speculative positions these instructions had been 'ignored or wrongly interpreted', and the bank had to back up purchases made by some clients who could not meet their commitments.

The most immediate result of the revelation (apart from a fall in the price of the bank's shares from SF1825 earlier in the year to a mere SF940 immediately after the crash) was the removal of the whole of the bank's top management. But the delay in revealing the losses also led the Federal Banking Commission to tighten its regulations concerning the use of hidden reserves. Under a circular dating from 1975 – before Bernard Muller's arrival – the banks did not have to reveal if they had used these reserves to cover unusual losses, a provision employed by the Swiss Volksbank to avoid embarrassing publicity. In the first week of 1982 the Commission abruptly withdrew the circular, and circulated the draft of a new regulation to prevent any repetition of the Volksbank's attempted cover-up.

But the affair continues to drag on. The bank is suing one of its former clients, a Saudi businessman named Mahmoud Fustok, for $50 million in the Geneva courts, and had obtained a sequestration order for enough of Fustok's assets to cover the claim. But Fustok was not taking the case lying down. In June 1981, a firm of Wall Street lawyers filed suit on his behalf against the bank, three senior officials from the Geneva branch including Brussard, a recently established investment advisory business called Advicorp and four of its shareholders (all former employees of the Geneva branch of Chase Manhattan who had left the bank in 1978 after Brussard had agreed that the Volksbank would take shares in Advicorp, of which he became a director). The indictment was a lengthy one, but basically stated that the alleged conspirators had cheated Fustok out of money he had entrusted to them after inducing him to invest through their newly-formed management company.

The allegations centred on the hectic trading in silver on the New York Commodities Exchange (Comex), which had surrounded the attempt by the Hunt brothers to corner the world silver market in 1978–9. The transactions involved were mainly 'futures' contracts, promises to deliver (or accept delivery of) silver at a specified date, generally in three months time. According to the complaint the conspirators were entrusted with a series of ever increasing deposits in order to speculate on Fustok's behalf, but instead 'BPS and the other defendants utilized such actual and fictitious Comex silver futures transactions, executed and purported to have been executed through the New York brokers, as part of a scheme to cheat and defraud the plaintiff and other BPS customers out of hundreds of millions of dollars.'

Fustok was led to believe by the defendants that the futures contracts being bought for him 'were for the purpose of obtaining deliveries of physical silver'. Instead, he claimed, the BPS allegedly used the 'omnibus account' it maintained with two major New York brokers to confuse the situation. 'The names of the customers of BPS were not disclosed to its New York brokers ... a BPS customer usually had no way of knowing which commodity transactions were executed for his account other than from the information that he received from BPS.' Apparently they didn't tell him much, and what they did was misleading. When BPS bought forward contracts 'it did not immediately enter such transactions on its books and records as transactions for the account of specific BPS customers'. Instead it waited, and saddled the customers with the contracts likely to prove unprofitable, retaining the profitable contracts for itself. Other transactions were purely notional: they never went through Comex but were foisted on the customers at prices favourable to the conspirators – then using the customers' funds to meet margin calls or settle the contracts BPS had actually bought.

The allegations are numerous and detailed, covering mainly the hectic first three months of 1979, but the basic claim is simplicity itself:

> The defendants' fraudulent activities have caused the plaintiff to lose, at a minimum, the entire amount of funds and property that he deposited with defendant BPS, an amount exceeding $80 million. But since the defendants' fraudulent activities commenced in earnest at a time when plaintiff's assets with BPS had increased substantially in value, plaintiff's losses were significantly in excess of the money and property that he had deposited with BPS. On information and belief, plaintiff's losses by reason of the fraud of the defendants were in excess of $250 million.

*

On 23 June 1980, Sanjay Gandhi, the younger son and

political heir of the Indian Prime Minister, Mrs. Indira Gandhi, was killed in a flying accident. When the rescuers came to collect the remains, they found that his watch was one of the few objects which had survived the crash intact. Later that day Mrs. Gandhi sent for some of the items that had been recovered, including the watch. This request, however natural under the circumstances, was not perceived by local observers as the natural gesture of a doting mother clinging to any memento of the dear departed. Not at all. On the back of the watch, they explained, was the number of the Gandhi family's bank account in Switzerland.

Even if the banks of Switzerland were ever to change, the myth would remain, the melody linger on.

Notes and Sources

There is no single work covering the whole history of Swiss banking.

F. Ritzmann's *Der Schweizer Banker: Geschichte, Theorie, Statistik* (Bern/ Stuttgart, 1973) contains an invaluable guide as to the foundation and subsequent fate of individual Swiss banks.

The book by Hans Bauer published by the Swiss Bank Corporation in 1972 on the occasion of the bank's centenary is another invaluable source; the in-house histories published by the Crédit Suisse and the Union Bank of Switzerland were also useful. Where no sources are mentioned I have relied on the files of the *New York Times*, the *Neue Zürcher Zeitung*, the *Tribune de Genève* and the *Financial Times*, and on the many people I interviewed who preferred to remain anonymous.

Part I: The Most Swiss Community
Page 4: Ray Vicker: *Those Swiss Money Men* (London, 1974).
Page 8: For Morgenthau see Part VI. *Those Different Swiss*: this short historical sketch is largely based on *A Concise History of Switzerland* by Bonjour, Offler and Potter (Oxford 1952), *Why Switzerland?* by Jonathan Steinberg (Cambridge 1976) and *L'Empire Occulte* by Lorenz Stucki (Paris 1970).
Page 15: The story of the German minister in Berne comes from *The Eye of the Hurricane* by Urs Schwarz (Boulder, Colorado, 1980).
Page 28: The 'contemporary radical' is Francois Hopflinger in *L'Empire Suisse* (Geneva 1978): R.S. Sayers, *Banking in Western Europe* (London 1962).
Page 33: Foex was interviewed by the *Tribune de Genève*.
Page 35: The 'senior tax official' was Ulrich Meier of the International Division of the Federal Tax Administration. He was writing in the *International Lawyer* (1973).
Page 37: Paul Erdman's thesis was published as *Swiss-American economic relations 1936–54* (Tübingen 1959).
Pages 38–40: See *La Grande Crise des Compagnies Ferroviares Suisses* by Claude Bouvier (Annales 1956).
Pages 43–46: Largely taken from *Projet d'une loi Fédérale concernant l'exploitation et la surveillance des banques* by Dr Jules Landmann (Berne 1916).

Part II: The Swiss and the Nazis
The crucial source is Daniel Bodmer's *L'intervention de la Confédération dans l'economie Suisse bancaire* (Thesis: University of Geneva 1948). See also 'La question des banques commerciales Suisses sous l'influence de la crise' by Claudius Terrier (*Revue mensuelle de science et de pratique comptable*), *La Suisse de l'entre deux guerres* by Roland Ruffieux (Lausanne 1974) and *Le 3ème Reich et la Suisse* by Daniel Bourgeois (Geneva 1974); M. Bourgeois discovered and

349

told me about the first draft of the Banking Act mentioned on page 56. For Geneva's problems see *L'aventure Socialiste Genevoise* by Alex Spielmann (Lausanne 1981).

Page 59: Léon Nicole wrote in *Le Droit du Peuple et Le Travail*.

Page 62: For Dr Magdalena Schoch see Part VI. 'The Little List of Fabien Albertin' see the *Journal des Débats*.

Page 74: John J. Lannan was writing in the *Californian Western International Law Journal* (1972).

Page 75: Carl Mueller was writing on 'The Swiss Banking Secret' (*International and Comparative Law Quarterly* Vol. 18, 1969). See also page 79.

Page 75: *The Banking System of Switzerland* by Hans Baer (Zurich 1973).

Page 77: *La question des secrets des banques en droit Suisse* by Georges Capitaine (Geneva 1933).

Part III: A Profitable Neutrality

The backbone of this chapter was provided by documents from the Federal Archives – those for the Organisation for Strategic Services in Washington, and the diplomatic files at the Suitlands depository – and British Foreign Office documents from the Public Records Office at Kew.

Page 91: *The Economic Blockade* by W.N. Medlicott (London 1952).

Page 92: 'Buttressed by bitter experience' see *Foreign Relations of the United States* 1944 Vol. IV p. 713.

Page 93: *Present at the Creation* by Dean Acheson (London 1970). For Urs Schwarz see supra p. 15.

Page 95: *Histoire de la Neutralité Suisse* by Henri Bonjour (Neuchatel 1970).

Page 95: 'Only by a sick Swiss people' see 'L'image Allemande de Pilet-Golaz 1940–44' (*Etudes et Sources*, 4, 1978).

Page 96: *Diplomatic Smuggler* by Sir John Lomax (London 1965).

Page 97: The 'well-informed journalist' is quoted in OSS 17505. For press censorship in wartime see: *The Swiss Press and Foreign Affairs in World War II* by Frederick H. Hartmann (Gainsville, Florida, 1960).

Page 98: *Die Fluchtlings Politik der Schweiz in den Jahren 1933 bis 1945* by Professor Dr Karl Ludwig (Berne 1957). For the Winkler case see OSS XL 18294.

Page 101: For the Société Générale de Surveillance see OSS XL 12551. The 'unpublished American official history' is the *Monograph concerning Safehaven* by Margaret Clarke, written in 1948 for the Foreign Economic Administration, now at Suitlands, and a major source for the remainder of the chapter.

Page 102: 'American diplomatic document' Group 169/Entry 170 Box 931 (all documents listed in this fashion are at Suitlands).

Page 103ff: For Woods' correspondance see Record Group 84, ref 851.6. Under the appropriate sub-heads ('Swiss Bank Corporation', 'Royal Dutch Shell' etc.) this section also contains the relevant correspondence from the American legation in Berne and the Consulate-general at Basle, and forms the source for any other quotations in this chapter for which no specific reference is given.

Page 108–9: For von der Heydt see *Die Schweizer Hitler-Attentater* by Klaus Urner (Frauenfeld 1980), kindly translated for me by Ms Andrea von Stumm.

Page 109: 'German gold exports' see Record Group 169 FEA: Pl 29 entry 170.

Page 110: 'Recent Swiss research', see 'Les Relations Économiques Germano-Suisse 1939–45' by Daniel Bourgeois in the *Revue d'Histoire de la Guerre Mondiale* January 1981 and especially *Die Deutsch-Schweizerischen Goldgeschäfte in zweiten Weltkrieg* by Peter Utz (Berne 1978–79).

Page 110: 'A number of Swiss banks' OSS 93105.

Page 111: 'A substantial number of gold pieces' OSS L 54875.

Page 112: 'Germany has systematically collected' OSS 21746.

Page 112: 'message from the US ambassador' RG 854,516/10-744 – these numbers refer to documents in Washington rather than Suitlands.

Page 113: For Istanbul see OSS 101570 and OSS XL 15218. For Swiss National Bank see OSS 21746.

Page 114: For the SBC's holding companies see FEA Rg 169 as above page 109.

Page 115: For Vereinigte Stahlwerke case see OSS XL19019.

Page 116: For the 'S' companies see OSS XL 12759 and FEA as for page 98.

Pages 118–119: for the V. Ernst/Ruegg story see OSS XL 23136 and OSS XL 26588.

Page 119: 'the Berne manager' see State Department 854.516.179. The nest eggs attributed to the Italian leaders are mentioned in a number of documents, notably OSS 6099.

Page 119: For Vieli see OSS L 53675. *Germany is our Problem* by Henry Morgenthau (New York 1945); *Flucht von Nurnberg* by Werner Brockdorff (Munich 1969).

Page 120: 'C's note is in Foreign Office 371/49710/XCB6025. The 'reliable French source' is quoted in OSS L 49541.

III/3 How safe a haven and III/4 A lesson in stubbornness. See Margaret Clarke's unpublished monograph and two published works: *The Hidden Weapon* by David Gordon and Royden Dangerfield (New York 1947) and *Friendship under Stress* by Heinz Meier (London 1970).

Pages 121–2: 'almost the only European state' see Bonjour, Offler and Potter op. cit.

Page 125: 'as late as the end of May 1944' see FEA 169 PI 29 Entry 170.

Page 127: *Present at the Creation* op. cit.

Page 128: *Economics, Peace and Laughter* by John Kenneth Galbraith (London 1971). 'He arrived here' see *P.C. du Général* by Bernard Barbey (Neuchatel 1947).

Page 131: 'a person leaving Switzerland for Italy' OSS L 54875.

Pages 131–2: For the cover-up see OSS XL 21827.

Page 132: The Rossiez memorandum is in OSS XL 34509.

Page 133: The letter from the British commercial counsellor (and that from W.A. Brandt on Page 134) are both from Foreign Office 371/49676.

Page 134: The reactions of the US Treasury and of the State Department are both in *Foreign Relations of the United States*, 1945 vol. II pp. 899–900.

Page 135: The British diplomat is noted in FO 371/49710 XC/B6025.

Page 135: The Basler Handelsbank's debts are detailed in OSS XL 27198.

Page 136: The Hoffmann la Roche and Bosch transactions are detailed in State Department 854.516.193.

Part IV: The Greatest Conspiracy
Joseph Borkin's book was very useful, so were newspaper reports, especially
in the *New York Times*.
Page 147: The Keppelman story comes from *Treason's Peace, German Dyes and
American Dupes* (New York 1947) by Howard Watson Ambruster, a U.S.
chemical industry executive who spent forty years investigating the
American intrigues of the German chemical companies.
Page 155: The wartime arrangements are detailed in OSS XL 13255 and XL
97542.
Page 158: The 1945 meeting of I.G. Chemie was reported in OSS XL 11632.
Page 167: Schaefer's attempted post-war purchases are detailed in OSS XL
43080.
IV/3 Settlement. The later stages of the GAF saga were comprehensively
reported in the American press: the library at the American Chemical
Association kindly helped me find the most relevant material.

Part V: Peace and its Problems
Strength through tranquillity. This section is based largely on newspaper
reports, the banks' own histories and the work of F. Ritzmann.
Pages 201–7: For the Algerians see *A Savage War of Peace* by Alistair Horne
(London 1977).

Part VI: Oh Switzerland, what crimes are committed in thy name
The basic source is the evidence heard by US congressional committees in
the late 1960s: more precisely the session of the House of Representatives
Banking Committee on 9 December 1968, the hearings of the same
committee on the Bank Records Bill between December 1969 and March
1970 and the hearings before the Senate Banking Committee relating to the
same Bill in June 1970. These proceedings include not only the statements
of the protagonists but also newspaper articles and other evidence.
Pages 211–2: 'Adam Smith' (alias Gerry Goodman) tells the story in
Supermoney (London 1973).
Page 212ff: For Cornfeld see *Do You Sincerely Want to be Rich?* by Charles Raw,
Godfrey Hodgson and Bruce Page (London 1971) and *Vesco* by Robert
Hutchison (New York 1971).
Page 215: For Rosenbaum's own account of his wartime activities see
Operation Hazalah (Sauvetage) by Gilles Lambert (Paris 1972).
Page 217: The two articles in *Life* were on 1 and 8 September 1967.
Pages 218–20: For Long, Lansky et al see *Louisiana Hayride* by Harnett T.
Kane (New York 1941), *Huey Long* by T. Harry Williams (London 1970),
Lansky by Hans Messick (London 1973) and *Meyer Lansky* by Dennis
Eisenberg, Uri Dan and Eli Landau (London 1979).
Page 221: *Dirty Money* by Thurston Clarke and John J. Tigue (London 1976).
Page 224: Victor Navasky wrote two excellent articles on Morgenthau in the
New York Times Magazine 8 December 1968 and 15 February 1970.
Page 235: For the Res, see *Wall Street's Shady Side* by Frank Cormier (New
York 1962).
Pages 235–6: For De Angelis see *The Great Salad Oil Swindle* by Norman C.
Miller (London 1966).
Pages 238–9: For Ingemar Johansson see *Standard Federal Tax Reports* 1964,
pp. 93907 ff.

Pages 239–40: For Foremost Brands see *Dirty Money* op.cit., pp. 120–124, and for Bakar (Page 248) see pp. 163–5

Page 252: See especially Neil Sheehan's articles in the *New York Times*.

Page 261: For Ulrich Meier see note to page 35.

Pages 261–2: For the Ryans see US Tax cases 1970 86567ff, 58 US Tax Court Reports 1972 pp. 107 ff and 67 US Tax Reports 1976, pp. 212 ff.

Page 262: For Lannan see note to page 74.

Page 263ff: See *Vesco* by Robert Hutchison op.cit.

Pages 264–5: For the Irvings and Howard Hughes see Ray Vicker op.cit.

Part VII: The Road to Normality

Page 277: *Switzerland Exposed* by Jean Ziegler (London 1978).

Page 280: Andre Gavillet is quoted from *Les Banques Suisses en question* by Claude Torracinta (Lausanne 1981), an invaluable collection of interviews. The 'Declaration du Berne' group published its findings in *Les Secrets du secret bancaire* by Pier Luigi Giovannini and Rudolf H. Strahm (Berne 1978).

Pages 280–1: Ghelfi, like Gavillet, was interviewed by Torracinta.

Pages 283–5: For Tibor Rosenbaum's downfall see the *Jerusalem Post* (whose files were culled for me by Ruth Cale), Clyde Farnsworth in the *New York Times* (9 April 1975), and 'The Agony of the German Landesbanks' by Ernest A. Ostro (*Euromoney* January 1982)

Page 285: For Sindona see the articles by Tana de Zulueta in the *Sunday Times* of London (6-27 January 1980).

VII/2: The revealing fall of Bobby Leclerc. *X, X & Cie, The Private Bankers of Switzerland* by Gunther Woernle (Geneva 1978) is an admirable guide to the private bankers. See also 'The Mysterious Private Banks of Geneva' by the author and Alison Macleod in *Euromoney* November 1979.

VII/3 The resistible rise of Ernst Kuhrmeier and VII/4 The astonishing resilience of Crédit Suisse. See *Scandale au Crédit Suisse* by Max Mabillard and Roger de Weck (Geneva 1977) and the reports on the trial by the same authors in the *Tribune de Genève*. See also the articles by Robert Hutchison in the *Sunday Telegraph* (3–17 September 1978).

VII/6 Towards the Twentieth Century. See the two articles by the author in *The Times* (5 and 6 May 1981), numerous articles by John Wicks in the *Financial Times* and 'Swiss Banking Secrecy after Chiasso' by David Egli (*Institutional Investor* August 1977), also Torracinta' interviews. On Portfolio Management see the author's article in *Euromoney* in December 1980 and for Hans Strasser see *Euromoney*, June 1981.

Page 338: The wartime story is in OSS XL 53132. Jobert was interviewed by Torracinta.

Pages 342–344: See *Pinkas* by Jean-Paul Bruttin (Lausanne 1981).

Pages 345–346: Stephen Fay kindly drew my attention to the Fustok story.

Page 347: The Gandhi story comes from *The New Yorker*, 10 December 1980.

Index